ONE
OVER MANY

SUNY series in Ancient Greek Philosophy

———

Anthony Preus, editor

ONE
OVER MANY

The Unitary Pluralism of Plato's World

NECİP FİKRİ ALİCAN

Published by State University of New York Press, Albany

© 2021 State University of New York

All rights reserved

Printed in the United States of America

No part of this book may be used or reproduced in any manner whatsoever without written permission. No part of this book may be stored in a retrieval system or transmitted in any form or by any means including electronic, electrostatic, magnetic tape, mechanical, photocopying, recording, or otherwise without the prior permission in writing of the publisher.

For information, contact State University of New York Press, Albany, NY
www.sunypress.edu

Library of Congress Cataloging-in-Publication Data

Name: Alican, Necip Fikri, author.
Title: One over many : the unitary pluralism of Plato's world / Necip Fikri Alican.
Description: Albany : State University of New York Press, [2021] | Series: SUNY series in ancient Greek philosophy | Includes bibliographical references and index.
Identifiers: LCCN 2021024205 | ISBN 9781438485638 (hardcover : alk. paper) | ISBN 9781438485645 (pbk. : alk. paper) | ISBN 9781438485652 (ebook)
Subjects: LCSH: Plato.
Classification: LCC B395 .A5258 2021 | DDC 184—dc23
LC record available at https://lccn.loc.gov/2021024205

10 9 8 7 6 5 4 3 2 1

To my wife
Banu Beste Başol Alican

Contents

Foreword: Exploring Plato's Forms *Nicholas D. Smith*		xi
Preface		xxv
Introduction		1

Chapter 1
Plato's World: The Standard Model   15
   1.1   Introduction   15
   1.2   Why Two Worlds?   17
   1.3   What Are the Forms?   34
   1.4   How Does It All Work?   53
   1.5   Conclusion   67

Chapter 2
Rethinking Plato's Forms   73
   2.1   Introduction   74
   2.2   Stratification of Reality   77
   2.3   A Two-Level Model   80
   2.4   Classification of Forms   82
   2.5   Terminological Clues and Methodological Observations   86
   2.6   Ideal Forms   91
   2.7   Conceptual Forms   93
   2.8   Relational Forms   99
   2.9   First Principles   104
   2.10   Negative Forms?   106
   2.11   Conclusion   109

Chapter 3
Rethought Forms: How Do They Work? 113
- 3.1 Introduction 114
- 3.2 The General Enterprise 114
- 3.3 The Stratification of Reality 118
- 3.4 The Classification of Forms 124
- 3.5 The Continuum of Abstraction 135
- 3.6 Conclusion 142

Chapter 4
A Horse Is a Horse, of Course, of Course, but What about Horseness? 145
- 4.1 Bunny in the Clouds 145
- 4.2 Horses and Horseness 150
- 4.3 Modes of Existence 155
- 4.4 Second Sailing 163

Chapter 5
Ontological Symmetry in Plato: Formless Things and Empty Forms 169
- 5.1 Introduction 169
- 5.2 The Evidence 173
- 5.3 Formless Things 182
- 5.4 Empty Forms 192
- 5.5 Conclusion 218

Chapter 6
The Good, the Bad, and the Ugly: Does Plato Make Room for Negative Forms in His Ontology? 225
- 6.1 The Question of Negative Forms in Plato 226
- 6.2 Embracing Negative Forms with Debra Nails 236
- 6.3 Rejecting Negative Forms with Holger Thesleff 246
- 6.4 The Semblance and Structure of Negativity in Plato 254
- 6.5 The Relevance and Supremacy of the Good in Plato 261

Chapter 7
Between a Form and a Hard Place: The Problem of Intermediates in Plato 265
- 7.1 Introduction 266
- 7.2 Plato through Aristotle 270
- 7.3 Aristotle as Historian 293

7.4	Discrepancies and Contradictions	304
7.5	Implications for Reliability	326
7.6	Plato through Plato	335
7.7	Conclusion	355

WORKS CITED 359

INDEX 387

Foreword

Exploring Plato's Forms

NICHOLAS D. SMITH

Introduction

It would be difficult to overestimate the degree to which the works of Necip Fikri Alican have impacted our understanding of Plato's most famous and most controversial theory, according to which the highest and best realities are the Forms. As he notes in the introduction to this book, one does not have to look very far or very hard to find evidence that Plato had a two-world ontology (also called a "two worlds ontology"). His own best student, Aristotle, attributes such a view to him, and Plato himself sometimes seems to make such a commitment explicit, even as he says other things that would seem to undermine such an assessment. In this book, Alican takes us through various perplexing issues that arise when we try to understand the many ways in which Plato tries to describe his Forms and their relationship with the other kinds of entities that he recognizes.

Disclosure of My Own Bias

I should begin my discussion with a frank disclosure of my own biases in favor of the approach taken by Alican. My main philosophical interest in Plato's Forms has to do with their role in epistemology and is thus not so much focused on metaphysical and ontological questions. Some scholars, convinced that Plato has a two-world ontology, have applied that conception to what Plato has to say about the difference between knowledge (*epistēmē* or *gnōsis*) and belief (or opinion: *doxa*)[1] in *Republic* Book 5. Plato tells us that knowledge is in some relation to "what is," which he goes on to make clear is a generic description for the Forms, whereas belief or opinion is in relation to "what both is and is not at the same time," which he subsequently makes clear is a generic way to refer to sensible particulars. In brief, this already sets out the disputed territory: Should we conceive of the objects to which knowledge is related as existing in a different *world* than sensible particulars, or should we conceive of them as existing at different *levels* of a single world? Traditional accounts of Platonic metaphysics have argued for the former assessment; Alican and others (including C. J. de Vogel and Holger Thesleff) have argued for the latter view. My own special interest in such questions, as I said, has really focused on fitting whatever we say about Plato's metaphysical position to what he tells us about knowledge and belief/opinion, so let us take a closer look at where this fit occurs.

I said above that Plato puts knowledge and belief/opinion into special—actually what look like *defining* relationships[2]—with different groups of objects. Different scholars have offered very different depictions of how we should understand these relationships. Plato tells us that whereas knowledge is *epi* the Forms, belief/opinion is *epi* sensible particulars.[3] The

---

1. "Opinion" is probably more often given as the translation for *doxa* in Book 5, but "belief" is also sometimes used. Rather than choose between these alternatives, I will just use "belief/opinion" herein. Some scholars have also argued that "knowledge" does not do justice to Plato's *epistēmē*, and I am sympathetic to their complaints. I think, in fact, that it is not so much which translation we use that creates problems here but ignoring the fact that the kinds of things Plato says he is talking about are already very different from what we usually have in mind when we use epistemic language, as I will try to show.

2. Plato says (*Republic* 477d) that he distinguishes such things by the objects to which they are related (*epi*) and by what they accomplish (*ho apergazetai*).

3. I should acknowledge that not all scholars ultimately understand Plato in this way. Some think that the distinction that Plato makes is more like the one familiar from contemporary epistemology. What one *knows* is always true, whereas what one *believes* may include both truth and falsehood. The problem with this (very anachronistic, I contend) assessment of what Plato is saying appears when we find that the things to which Plato says belief/opinion is *epi* both are and are not *at the same time* (*Republic* 478d5). I have complained elsewhere that Plato's claim here makes no sense if we take

problems begin, I think, when scholars translate Plato's little *epi* here in terms very familiar to contemporary epistemology: We read that Plato is telling us that knowledge is "of" or "about" Forms, whereas belief/opinion is "of" or "about" sensible particulars. In short order, then, we have taken the putative "two worlds" of Plato's ontology and made their connection to epistemology such that the different worlds must be accessed by different cognitions, which has aptly come to be known in the literature as a two-world epistemology. Perhaps the most embarrassing result of this series of inferences is that it actually manages to defeat the very claim that Plato is trying to defend by making these distinctions in the first place, which is that philosophers, and not nonphilosophers, should rule, on precisely the ground that philosophers would use knowledge, whereas nonphilosophers would use belief/opinion in ruling. The problem is that even if this reading gives greater value to knowledge than to belief/opinion, it also makes knowledge of whatever would be going on in the state (or its law courts, for which see *Republic* 433e) impossible: If there can be no knowledge of sensible particulars, then Plato's rulers will also have nothing better than belief/opinion to bring to bear on political decision-making.

The way out of this very awkward result, I contend, is to backtrack to where it originates. First, translating Plato's *epi* as "of" or "about" creates an intentional relation between the cognition and the object the cognition is related to, and so as soon as we are thinking in those terms, we naturally fall into thinking that the cognition that Plato has in mind here is a cognitive state, like the textbook cases, "S knows that p," which is supposed to be a special case of "S believes that p." But then we immediately confront another puzzle: Since knowledge (in this way of thinking) is a species of belief, why does Plato make it a different thing altogether and not just a special kind of belief? The answer given in the text to this already confused question is plain enough but continues to be underappreciated by the scholars interpreting the text: Plato has told us that he thinks of knowledge and belief/opinion as examples of *powers* (*dunameis*), the kinds of things, he says, that "enable us—or anything else for that matter—to do what we are capable of doing. Sight, for example, and hearing are among the powers, if you understand the kind of thing I'm referring to" (*Republic* 477c; Grube and Reeve translation).

---

him to be talking either about existence or about being true or false: Nothing both exists and fails to exist at the same time, and so, too, do truth and falsehood seem to be mutually exclusive.

Now, it is obvious enough that sight is a power that puts us into contact with certain sorts of things and not others. For example, we see colors and shapes but do not (leaving the phenomenon of synesthesia aside) see sweetness or the sound of middle C. But we do not think of this relation as an intentional one. It may be that what sight produces in a given instance (a seeing) would be of or about some visible thing, but what is true of a perceptual state is not true of the power that produces that state. The power of vision applies to certain kinds of things but is not of or about those things. Vision gives us access to its objects but a power and its relations to objects are different from those that obtain to the states the power produces. If we take Plato's knowledge and belief/opinion to be cognitive states, then we have already set aside and misinterpreted the fact that he is talking about cognitive powers and not cognitive states.

Failure to recognize this difference—between a power and the states it might produce—will also result in the bizarre and implausible result that no one can have beliefs/opinions about Forms. But Plato himself seems to have his characters express such opinions (especially when he has Socrates's interlocutors speak on the subject). So here, too, we have abundant reason to be very skeptical that Plato has an "of" or "about" relation in mind when he assigns different groups of objects to the different cognitive powers. In Plato's account, *doxa* is not and cannot be *epi* the Forms, but it plainly does not follow that there can be no beliefs or opinions about Forms. So, too, *epistēmē* is not and cannot be *epi* sensible particulars, but that does not show that there can be no knowledge (states) that are of or about sensible particulars—for example, that such-and-such particular thing is a fairly good image of some Form. Plato's argument seems to be that in virtue of knowing the Form, philosophers will be maximally able to judge, of particular things, which is a good image, and which is not a good image of, for example, the just itself (the Form). That is why they will be the best rulers, and why their political judgments will be so much more reliable than those whose cognitive powers never engage the just itself, and instead conceive of justice in terms of things that both are and are not just at the same time.

Judging What Belongs to This World

From the fact that different powers take different objects, nothing follows about how many worlds will be needed to contain all such objects. No one would think, for example, that, because vision and hearing take different objects, the objects of each perceptual power must occupy different worlds from those taken by the other power. Rather, our perceptual and cognitive powers may simply reveal to us what exists in *this world*. Rejecting the two-world epistemology thus already inclines me to think that we should also be at least wary of the idea that Plato accepts a two-world ontology. But here the arguments get trickier, and here is where Alican's work really begins. The implausibility of a two-world epistemology, unfortunately, seems to me to leave entirely open whether Plato had a two-world ontology. Modern realists about numbers, for example, might contend that the role of numbers in explanation is sufficient to count numbers as real. But whether they are parts of *this world* or not will depend entirely on what we take to be the essential characteristics of *this world* to be.

So let us consider briefly how we might characterize what it means to be a part of *this world*. Someone of a twenty-first-century scientific mind might contend that *this world* is essentially the world as it is described in the physical and biological sciences. If so, it seems implausible to suppose that numbers are part of *this world*—but not at all impossible for those of us who are sophisticated cognitive beings to know some things about numbers. So not being a part of *this world*, as it would be conceived by scientism, does not seem to have any important epistemic effect on cognitive access. On the other hand, if we follow Wittgenstein and characterize *this world* as simply consisting in "all that is the case," then numbers (or at least true statements about them) will be a part of *this world*. If we are going to count how many worlds might be recognized in a given philosopher's view, then we will need to be very clear on just how the counting is to be done.

So this really gets to the heart of Alican's project: How should we count how many worlds Plato recognizes, and what difference does it make whether we accept the traditional dualism or Alican's and others' revisionist monism? One way or another, there will be Forms and also non-Forms (including at least sensible particulars). Forms in most dialogues will be described in significantly different ways and will have significantly different characteristics than non-Forms. Gregory Vlastos, however, makes the case that Plato's descriptions of Forms as existing "themselves by themselves" and also as existing "separately" is sufficient for us to accept the traditional dualist picture. Vlastos's (1991) argument is readily available to readers in his *Socrates: Ironist and Moral Philosopher* (see his additional note 2.5, 256–264: "'Separation' in Plato"), so I will not report it in detail here. Briefly, his argument relies on the fact that

Plato does seem to think that souls and bodies (at least sometimes) exist in separate realms, and in the *Phaedo* (and elsewhere) the separated soul is able to make a kind of direct contact with Forms, which indicates that Forms are a part of the distinct world in which separated souls sometimes exist. If there are different kinds of things that exist, and some of the things exist "themselves by themselves" and "separately" (which Vlastos takes to express simply different ways of making the same metaphysical claim), whereas others do not exist "themselves by themselves" or "separately," then Plato will have committed himself to a two-world ontology. I will leave it to Alican to reply to this argument in more detail, but for now, we may note that Vlastos's argument seems to risk begging the question here. Surely no one who has ever lived alone (and thus "themselves by themselves") and separately from others has thereby been shown in any sense to have exited *this world* to another during their time alone. Plato's peculiar descriptions of Forms as "themselves by themselves" and as "separate" from the things that instantiate their characters requires interpretation. What follows, then, is just that: an interpretation of what Plato has to say about his Forms and why we should not take the ways in which he describes the Forms as entailing more than a single world, albeit one in which there is a hierarchy of beings.

Different Kinds of Forms?

One of the most important aspects of Alican's work on Plato's Forms may be seen in the ways in which he categorizes different kinds of Forms into three groups: Ideal Forms, Conceptual Forms, and Relational Forms. He explains the distinctions he finds between these different types of Forms in chapter 2. It is not my role here to examine his arguments or to debate them. I think most intelligent readers will agree that Alican's classification of different kinds of Forms is sensible. The question is whether this sensible classification was something that Plato himself intended, or would have assented to, or is instead an interpretation of Plato's theory that goes beyond what we can securely find in the dialogues.

As I said above, my own primary interest lies in the intersection of Plato's ontology with his epistemology. In my recent work in this area,[4] I

---

4. See especially my *Summoning Knowledge in Plato's Republic* (Oxford: Clarendon Press, 2019).

have emphasized that the epistemology of Book 5 of the *Republic* should really be understood in terms of a process of conceptualization quite like what epistemologist Keith Lehrer has termed "exemplarization."[5] As Lehrer has recently pointed out,[6] an especially good example of this is provided at *Republic* 472b–c:

> It was in order to have an exemplar [*paradeigma*] that we were trying to discover what justice itself was like and what the completely just man would be like, if he came into being, and what kind of man he'd be like if he did, and likewise with regard to injustice and the most unjust man. (Plato: *Republic* 472b–c; Grube and Reeve translation, slightly modified)

Cognitive contact with the Form allows the one who achieves it to perceive justice in things that are like the Form in the relevant sense, but which are not the same as the Form. But in order for this to be true, the Form itself must be like something, to allow other things to be compared to what the Form is like. In the case of the Form of justice, that means that the just itself is just. That is what it is like, but unlike other things that are only more or less just (or, as Plato puts it somewhat awkwardly at 478d, such things as both are and are not—presumably, for example, both are and are not just—"at the same time"), the just itself is perfectly just. To borrow from Alican's description of Ideal Forms, the just itself is "transcendent, intelligible, paradigmatic, perfect, immutable, simple, and unique" (pp. 43–44, 91, 124, n. 16, this volume) with respect to being what it is, namely just. Nothing else qualifies as just unless it is like the just itself. By knowing what the just itself is, we are put into a position of being able to tell what other things (for example, political arrangements) are just, and also to what degree. And that is why Plato makes the claim that he recognizes would be treated with scoffing contempt by most people

---

5. See Lehrer's *Art, Self and Knowledge* (New York: Oxford University Press, 2011) and his *Exemplars of Truth* (New York: Oxford University Press, 2019). In my *Summoning Knowledge in Plato's Republic* (2019), I acknowledge that this is a version of an older view about Plato's Forms, called "paradeigmatism," according to which the Forms serve as paradigms of the properties associated with their names.

6. See Lehrer's "Forms, Exemplars, and Plato," chapter 4 of *What the Ancients Offer to Contemporary Epistemology*, edited by Stephen Hetherington and Nicholas D. Smith (London: Routledge, 2019).

(see 473c–d), which is that philosophers would be the best rulers. Only philosophers, in Plato's account, really know the Forms.

Now if this is the crucial epistemic role played by Plato's Forms, we might ask how it works in the kinds of Forms that Alican puts into categories other than the Ideal class. Do Conceptual Forms serve as exemplars in this way? If so, it must follow that they, too, are perfect exemplars of the qualities for which they are perfection standards. Can we make ontological sense of this? If not, what different epistemological role is played by Conceptual Forms, in Plato's mind? And we can ask the same question of Relational Forms. What is their role in Plato's epistemology?

The Special Problem of Negative Forms

If, as my epistemological focus has seemed to indicate to me, the primary role Plato gives to Forms is to provide exemplars, then it certainly does seem that some kinds of predicate-terms would be handled by single (positive) Forms for Plato's explanatory purposes. After all, we do not seem to require any specific conception of inequality in order to comprehend and be able to assess the relative equality and inequality. Plato's famous example of the relative equality of sticks and stones in the *Phaedo* (74b–75a) makes this point well enough, though one might wish that certain aspects of his presentation had been clearer. Plato's main point in this passage is the familiar one: Since specific sensible examples of a certain characteristic (the equality of sticks or stones) are only matters of more or less, it must be that we have a conception of a perfection standard (in this case, the equal itself) in order to judge that the specific sensible examples fall short of perfection as examples. There is obviously no need for a negative Form here (such as the unequal itself), since we can judge the degree to which something is equal or unequal simply by considering how closely or imperfectly it resembles the equal itself. Privation of equality is all that is needed to comprehend inequality.

Now, that is not to say there are no problems even in Plato's exposition of this point, for example, in his mystifying reference at 74c1–2 to equality and inequality. Were it not for his mention of inequality, the natural way to understand what he says about equality here would be to suppose that he was referring to the Form. But then why does he refer to inequality, too, and claim that inequality never appears to be equality? Is he talking about the unequal itself, or . . . ? To make matters even more obscure,

Plato also manages to refer to "the equals themselves" before making this other puzzling reference. But what on earth are "the equals themselves"? Is this a reference to some paradigmatic pair of equals allowing them to serve as an exemplar of equality? Or does he use the neuter plural as a substantive, intending only to refer to the singular, noncomposite Form of equality—as one might do by talking about tigers having stripes, where the sense seems to be that having stripes is an essential feature of being a tiger. Or perhaps this is a reference to the so-called "immanent Forms" (or "immanent characters") or perhaps the characteristic of equality that happens to be present in the more or less equal things? Each of these theories has received scholarly endorsement, but none of them has generated consensus.

I mention the problems with this example to underscore Alican's very appropriate assessment at the beginning of section 2.5 of the book: "The Platonic corpus is beset with ambiguity, inconsistency, and undeveloped lines of thought. This is nowhere more apparent and relevant than where the discussion turns to Forms, regarding which Plato is especially vague, laconic, and mercurial" (p. 86, this volume).

To return to my main point, however, it does seem that the more-or-less-ness to which individual sensible things display their characteristics can at least sometimes be conceived in terms of a single positive property and various degrees of privation. It seems that this was the general strategy of later Platonists, which made the one (*to hen*) the ultimate reality and all layers below this characterized by degrees of privation. We can see the influence of this view of negativity in the Augustinian response to the problem of evil. There is no evil in his system—just various degrees of privation of goodness.

Plato sometimes, however, at least seems to refer to negative Forms, and from a conceptual point of view, we may need to distinguish cases in which Forms at both ends of some continuum (as opposed to privations) are needed in cases where both of a pair of opposites appear to be real. If we cannot comprehend what tallness is except by comparison to its opposite (say), then this would seem to indicate a need in Plato's metaphysics for both opposites to stand as exemplars for conceptualization. The question is: Did Plato think there were cases like this and thus embrace negative Forms? Did he ever think that comparisons of justice and injustice (say) were like comparisons of tallness and shortness? Some evidence that he did comes from less puzzling texts than the one I have already mentioned in the *Phaedo*, for example, in the pairs of opposites at the end of *Republic* Book 5 (479a–b), which include beautiful and ugly, just and unjust, pious and impious, doubles and halves, bigs and smalls, lights and heavies, where his point in each case seems to be that sensible particulars display the characteristics of both opposites. If privation were his general rule, there would only be one of each pair to display, in varying degrees. Alican tackles this problem head-on in chapter 6, offering arguments as to why these apparent Platonic flirtations with negative Forms are not to be taken as Plato's actual view.

Degrees of Reality

Different readers will find different parts of this book especially interesting, but having read Alican's works for many years now, I was especially interested to see him weighing in on the curious question of intermediates in Plato. I call it a "curious question" for two reasons that Alican forthrightly recognizes: (1) Aristotle is unequivocal in attributing to Plato a view about an ontological category of things that are intermediate between Forms and sensible particulars. (2) To quote Alican directly now: "The problem is not that what Aristotle says about intermediates in Plato contradicts what Plato himself says about intermediates. This cannot be a problem, because Plato says nothing at all about intermediates, at least not in a way that makes it clear that he is talking about intermediates. The problem is that what Aristotle says about intermediates in Plato contradicts other things Aristotle says about Plato, as well as undermining some things Plato says about those other things Aristotle says about Plato" (chapter 7, n. 1).

This leaves Plato's purported belief in the intermediates Aristotle refers to a matter for speculation about "Plato's unwritten doctrines," though as Alican also notes, scholars have made great attempts to find passages within the dialogues that might be taken as references to these elusive entities. In various works of my own, I have mainly emphasized the second part of this problem and mostly simply shrugged at the first: I have argued in various places that the so-called "mathematical intermediates" are simply not to be found in several of the texts where scholars have claimed to find them.[7] Alican's own take on these objects is more balanced and less

---

[7]. My arguments can be found in "The Various Equals at Plato's *Phaedo* 74b–c" (Smith 1980) and in chapters 5 and 7 of *Summoning Knowledge in Plato's Republic* (Smith 2019).

dismissive than mine. He takes the layering of Plato's ontology to allow room for such entities, even if Plato never explicitly mentions them.

It is not my place here to debate with any of Alican's arguments, but I hope it is fair at least to express the main ground for my skepticism about including such things in Plato's ontology (quite apart from the textual silence, which, as Alican rightly insists, is no proof that Plato rejected the idea of these intermediates). I have understood the kinds of things that Aristotle had in mind in attributing this view to Plato in the way Aristotle describes them in *Metaphysics* A6:

> He says that besides the sensible things and the Forms, and between these, there exist the Mathematical Objects, differing from the sensible things in being eternal and immovable, and from the Forms in that there are many alike whereas the Form itself corresponding to these is only one. (Aristotle: *Metaphysics* 987b14–18; Apostle and Gerson translation)

My question about such objects has always been how they should be scaled in Plato's famous (or notorious) "degrees of reality." It might be that we should conceive of them as equal in reality (or truth: *alētheia*) to the Forms, not only in virtue of being eternal and immovable but also in terms of being perfect examples of their properties. A perfect square of 2' x 2', for example, is not more or less square but perfectly square, and so in that way differs in squareness not at all from the square itself. Its exemplary squareness qua square is neither more nor less than that of the square itself and its specific dimensions are beside the point. Or we might see them as being less real (or true) than the Forms because there are indefinitely many token intermediates but only one Form for each such property. It seems that Alican prefers the latter conception, but as much as numerability is sometimes given as an indicator of inferiority, relative to the Forms, such an approach confronts us with a serious problem for understanding just how Plato conceives of (and thus measures) his distinct degrees of reality. And here is where the putative intermediates do and also do not seem to fit. They do insofar as they might well be conceived as having their characters in virtue of imaging the Form (and Plato always characterizes images as less real than what they image). But whenever Plato explains why images are inferior, it seems he always does it in terms of the equivocal nature of images. They always both are and are not F (at the same time), with respect to imaging F-ness itself. But this is precisely what the intermediates do not do. They do not display or exhibit their characteristics equivocally. So the way in which Plato seems to measure the diminishment of reality in images simply does not apply to the putative intermediates.

Might Plato at some point have imagined that the intermediates, while not having this flaw, were still somehow less than Forms? Of course, he might have thought that. He might have even said it out loud and in front of Aristotle. But if so, it is really a shame that Aristotle did not explain just a bit more how and why Plato adapted his conception of the degrees of reality to accommodate a different way to measure its gradability. Even Aristotle, I note, manages to avoid claiming that the numerability of such things makes them less real, in Plato's view, than Forms. If he did, he would have had to explain how and why exemplary perfection was not all that was required for something to count as fully real. Such an amendment to what he explicitly provides in his texts amounts to a different theory of reality (or truth) than what he does offer in his writings.

Leaving intermediates aside, however, Alican rightly notes that Plato quite explicitly layers his full ontology, and the most obvious and explicit (if not the *only*, as I have been contending) way in which he does this is with his layering of images and their originals. When I teach the *Republic*, I often challenge my students to tell me just how many layers of reality Plato presents in that work. My little game is not merely intended to flummox my students (though it inevitably does do that); it is also intended to make the kind of point that Alican wants to emphasize: Plato's ontology is a great deal more complex—even if it presents only one world to us—than just one or two levels.

The first move my students make in this game is to go to the divided line. "Four levels," they tell me. "Well," I respond, "there are obviously four distinct levels on the divided line, but what is it that makes each level a different level of reality?" My students quickly realize that a difference of level of reality follows from a relation of image to original between levels. "Great," I say, "So is it your view that the second lowest level of the divided line (the one identified with *pistis* at 511e1) is associated with images of whatever belongs to the second highest level of the line (associated with *dianoia* at 511d8)?" Here my best students frown, but someone in the class usually takes the bait, in which case I challenge that student to tell me what things he or she finds at the level associated with *dianoia* that qualify as the originals of the things belonging to *pistis* while also managing to be images of what belongs to the highest level (associated with *noēsis* at 511d8). My better students' frowns now deepen while the embarrassed student who took my bait flounders and falls silent. So now I suspend my little game for a while and take them through all of the objects that scholars have imagined belonging to *dianoia* that would have the requisite property of being both image and original (including the problematic intermediates) and then ask them to look again at the text and tell me where such things are actually mentioned. Now all of the students nod as one of them admits, "They are not." "So what objects does Plato mention in association with *dianoia*?" I ask. Eventually all agree that he mentions Forms and sensible particular images of them—that is, the objects that belong to each of the levels proximate to the one in question. By now, all the students are frowning.

"But wait, it gets better," I say, by which I mean that it gets worse for students who are already finding this frustrating. "Doesn't Plato say that the cave image is supposed to be an image of the divided line?" Since they're in my class and my students are too polite simply to walk out, I mostly start getting shrugs now. "But if it is an image, then how many layers of images are added in the cave story?" And now we get to talk about how the cave story should be related to the divided line—at least for those few students who are not by now paying most of their attention to the clock, agonizingly slow, as it is, about reaching the time they can escape.

Even sophisticated scholars who know the text extremely well will find they quickly start disagreeing when it comes to playing this game that I inflict on my students. My only defense, I suppose, is that it is Plato who has inflicted this game on all of us. I expect that Plato employed the confusion his many images tended to create to make a point that was critical for him: Once we start dealing in images, we are engaging in distortion. I do not know the right answer to my little challenge, to be frank, and I am also very uncertain as to whether there even *is* a right answer to it. Several scholarly studies have focused on the uses of imagery in the *Republic*. Readers could (if they were so inclined) try to map out how many layers of images Plato does not merely mention but also puts to his own use as a writer. Does Plato think that words and statements are images of what they represent? If so, Plato, as a writer, cannot do philosophy without creating images. At any rate, he certainly makes no obvious attempt to avoid the use of imagery. What he does do, repeatedly, is caution that all images both are and are not what they appear to be. How many times could we hold a mirror up to something, and then a mirror to this mirror, and again, each time creating a new layer of reality? We do well, as Alican does in this book, to pay close attention to the layers of Plato's reality—and also not to think of each layer as constituting an entirely different world. With this advice, I now welcome the reader to Alican's sophisticated and thoughtful analyses of what are surely the most challenging interpretive problems presented by Plato's works.

Nicholas D. Smith
James F. Miller Professor of Humanities
Lewis & Clark College

Preface

This book brings together my previously published work on Plato's metaphysics and newly drafted material on the same subject. The individual essays, presented here as chapters, revolve around the theme of a unitary pluralism where a single reality hosts all ontological diversity, including Forms, sensible phenomena, and everything in between. Their transformation into an organic whole represents the culmination of an ongoing effort to challenge the traditional interpretation of Plato in terms of a dualism of worlds corresponding to a dualism of things, placing transcendent Forms in one world as against sensible phenomena in the other.

The inception of the project dates back to an email I sent Holger Thesleff in the summer of 2012. The gist of my message was a request for his conventional mailing address so that I could send him a copy of my then newly published book, *Rethinking Plato: A Cartesian Quest for the Real Plato*. I had just received a batch of complimentary copies from the publisher, and I had, in my mind, reserved one of them for Thesleff, whose work I had been admiring for a long time.

Thesleff wrote back immediately, acknowledging my admiration and congratulating me on the publication, but declining my offer to send him a copy. He was, as it turns out, in the process of downsizing his personal library. Adding my book to the existing collection would have been a move in the opposite direction. His response was both sincere and supportive, making his rejection and explanation even easier to understand than did the characteristically impeccable clarity of his prose.

Exactly one month after his initial response, Thesleff sent me a second message, this time commenting favorably on various points in the book, which to my delight, he had read in the meantime. But that second message took me by surprise because I had honored his earlier request not to send him anything and I did not think that he would have gone out of his way to purchase the book himself after declining a complimentary copy from me.

Indeed, he had not. What had happened, rather, was that the publisher, unaware of my communication with Thesleff, and every bit as impressed with him as I was, also decided, without any input from me, that Thesleff should be one of the first to get a promotional copy. Having thus received a copy from my publisher, Thesleff then resolved to thumb through the book, fully intending to dispose of it afterward through a donation to the local library but electing instead to make room for it in his own collection after all.

Thesleff's third message, composed within a couple of days of his second, was a proposal to collaborate on a paper on points of mutual interest in connection with the metaphysical outlook of Plato. Within the space of a few weeks, my fortune had improved from being unable to get my foot in the door, or in this case, my book on the shelf, to joining forces with the maverick hero of Plato scholarship, which is how I had been referring to him in print even before we met in person (see Alican 2012, 185–188).

I responded on the very same day, eagerly accepting Thesleff's proposal and boldly sharing my ideas on how to proceed. That marked the beginning of a rewarding professional relationship, which steadily developed into a close personal friendship, unfolding through regular correspondence on the intricacies of Plato scholarship and through casual conversation over coffee and meals in Helsinki.

One of the scholarly manifestations of our interaction is the present collection of essays, which begins with the original product of our collaboration: "Rethinking Plato's Forms" (2013). While that article is the only piece we ever wrote together, it is also the vital spark animating the extended project that became this book. It was Thesleff who suggested that I be the lead author of the article, and Thesleff again who named it in allusion to the title of my then recent book, thus establishing continuity while emphasizing the "rethinking" process we had undertaken together.

As for content, our joint production originated largely in Thesleff's personal insights. The methodological foundation of our approach was his distinctive interpretation of Plato's world as a single reality with "two levels" where Forms reside in the upper level and sensible phenomena in the lower level. An integral part of his interpretation, which also became, with some modification, an indispensable component of ours, was a differentiation and classification of Forms into three distinct classes: Ideal Forms, Conceptual Forms, and Relational Forms. Even though I had already developed a comparable understanding of Plato on my own, especially with respect to the unitary pluralism of a gradation of reality within a single world, Thesleff's work not only predated mine but also informed ours.

That is the story behind the original article. The rest of the present volume represents independent development. All of it was drafted, and most of it published, without Thesleff's prior knowledge, eventually being shared with him piecemeal, upon the publication of each constituent essay. The project is a personal initiative in exploration of the implications of our mutual understanding of how Plato sees the world, namely as a gradation of reality supporting two main levels and countless subdivisions, with the Forms in the upper level, sensible phenomena in the lower level, and various things of an intermediate nature in between. Despite the common starting point, my own adventures in Platonica come with many points of departure. Yet these do not add up to a divergence in essentials.

The motivation for further development dates back to a query by Christopher J. Rowe, who was kind enough to read and respond to a prepublication draft of the original article. Independently of the viability of the basic model, which he neither accepted nor rejected, Rowe raised a nagging question: What if Thesleff and I were right? What difference would that make? What he was looking for was evidence of contributions our alternative would be making to the study of Plato in comparison to competing models and conceptions. What would it accomplish other than getting Plato right, while and where the traditional model got him wrong? What specific problems would it solve, or at least clarify, in the interpretation of Plato that continue to frustrate collective progress toward a scholarly consensus?

Rowe's question was eminently appropriate in any of its formulations, but a serious attempt to answer it in the original article would have been a distraction even if it had been possible to make room for it. As things stood, however, the space available had to be devoted to setting up the model, grounding it in the Platonic corpus, locating it in the Platonic tradition, and establishing its validity as an interpretive paradigm. Those were the minimum scholarly obligations we felt in connection with the novelty of our thesis and the controversial nature of our claims. And they left hardly any room for the pursuit of additional goals.

Moreover, we were already convinced that there could be no proof, in the strictest sense of the term, that our model was "correct," so to speak, as against any other model as "incorrect." We were simply proposing a thought experiment that would help make better sense of Plato. That was the extent of the proof we were prepared to offer, in addition, of course, to meticulous documentation in the canonical corpus, with copious citations from various dialogues, which we did not consider proof in the strictest sense, since no interpreter of Plato had ever failed to find support for his or her pet theory in the words of Plato. Any sober hope of persuasion required demonstration and illustration beyond the vague promise of greater insight.

That is why I approached substantive development as a separate phase of comprehensive coverage, subsequently implemented through a series of essays, some published as journal articles and anthology contributions, some drafted specifically for the present volume. The complete project consists of seven chapters, the first and the last having had no prior publication history, and the ones in between having appeared in print as articles in peer-reviewed journals, with one exception (chapter 4), which was published as a contribution to a collection of essays. A synopsis of each chapter is available in the introduction following this preface and preceding the main body of the book.

The only disagreement Thesleff and I ever had, a major conflict by his standards, came a year after the appearance of our collaboration in print, when a follow-up I wrote in secret was accepted and published by the same journal as the original: "Rethought Forms: How Do They Work?" (2014). The follow-up was not a personal reconsideration of questionable conclusions but further elaboration on mutual convictions. I had, in fact, drafted the essay in the form of a "critical evaluation of Holger Thesleff's thinking on Plato's Forms" out of respect for the elements of our mutual position anticipated in his prior work. The reason for the secrecy was the prospect of a pleasant surprise. Yet with as much displeasure as a gentleman of northern European descent would ever care to reveal, Thesleff wrote to me in serious protest of my "excessive inclination" to credit him with our joint conclusions as if they were "his views" on Plato rather than "our views" on Plato. That was his sole objection to a journal article he had never seen in person except in the final version in print.

All subsequent work reflects my best efforts to accommodate Thesleff's call for me to assert my position as a creative partner in the original production. I believe I have generally succeeded in doing so. The penultimate chapter on negative Forms—"The Good, the Bad, and the Ugly: Does Plato Make Room for Negative Forms in His Ontology?" (2017b)—is something of an exception. This is because it was conceived as a case study comparing two opposing viewpoints, pitting Debra Nails against Thesleff and me, while thereby requiring both narration and arbitration, which naturally worked better with my remaining in the background as a reporter and referee, instead of claiming one of the viewpoints as an originator and advocate. Thesleff did not like being left alone in the limelight with Nails, but he nevertheless appreciated my formal assertion of creative partnership somewhere within the first handful of notes. His only complaint was, once again, what he described as an exaggerated sense of intellectual humility and scholarly deference on my part.

This is not to say that Thesleff and I agree on everything about Plato, or on everything in this book, or even on everything in the collaborative impulse motivating this book. But where we differ is almost always in emphasis rather than in essence. One visible difference may be his steadfast focus on the two main levels of reality constituting Plato's world in contrast to my adventurous exploration of the gradation of reality between those levels. That difference comes out more and more with each successive essay, becoming particularly pronounced in the final chapter, where ontological intermediates between Forms and sensible phenomena emerge as the ultimate mark of gradation, differentiation, and diversification.

The corresponding progression exhibits a subtle and gradual shift in emphasis from the monism of a single world with levels, which we jointly nominated in place of the metaphysical dualism traditionally attributed to Plato, to a unitary pluralism, which I developed in elaboration of the original monism, still of a single world with levels, but with remarkable diversity in between. The difference, however, remains one of emphasis, with each of us endorsing without reservation what the other emphasizes the most. Thesleff and I may not see eye to eye on everything, but we disagree on nothing of importance. What we still see in common, at any rate, includes the horseness eluding Antisthenes and the cupness and tableness eluding Diogenes.

Several other friends and colleagues have also been instrumental, either in inspiring me or in assisting me, during the production process. Those who have done at least one or the other, though typically both, include Rafael Ferber, Lloyd P. Gerson, Verity Harte, Mika Kajava, Debra Nails, Gerald Alan Press, C. D. C. Reeve, Pauliina Remes, Christopher J. Rowe, Nicholas D. Smith, Sophia A. Stone, Harold Tarrant, Ellen Wagner, and William A. Welton. I am grateful for productive dialogue with each and every one of them.

An earlier debt of gratitude, one I can only hope to pay forward, is to teachers and mentors. Any list coming close to capturing my fortune and privilege in that regard would have to include Feridun Baydar, Robert E. Bergmark, Roger F. Gibson Jr., Michael H. Mitias, and Carl P. Wellman. Yet one does not learn from teachers alone. Dialectical partners are just as important. The most memorable of mine, each a source of enlightenment, have been Timothy L. Anderson, Michael Howard Brunson, Ned Mims French II, Philip Walter Gaines, Paul Owen Martin, William Whitfield McKinley Jr., and Tara Lyn McPherson.

From a more personal perspective, I owe the inspiration for this project, as is true of everything that is worthwhile in my life, to my wonderful wife, Banu Beste Başol Alican. Like the magical heroine commanding the sun to illuminate the world in the poetic metaphor of the penultimate chapter, Banu lights up my life with the brilliance of an eternal flame of wisdom sustained by the noetic inferno of her mystical spirit. She is the reason why the sun shines. She is the reason why I can see the horseness beyond the horses. She is the reason why I cherish the story of Aristophanes above all others in the *Symposium*. And she is the reason why I believe every word Plato ever said about Diotima. She is indeed the One-over-Many.

Introduction

Aristotle famously describes Plato's Forms in terms of a "One-over-Many" formula where a separate Form corresponds to each multitude of things bearing characteristics common and peculiar to them as a group (*Metaphysics* 990a33–991a8, 1079a7–b3; *Peri Ideōn* [= Alexander of Aphrodisias: *In Aristotelis Metaphysica Commentaria*] 80.8–81.10; cf. *Republic* 596a; *Parmenides* 130d–e, 135a–d; *Timaeus* 51c). He then goes on to exaggerate their separation, placing the Forms in a different world from the sensible phenomena instantiating them, and thereby multiplying the number of worlds required to account for Plato's conception of reality (*Metaphysics* 990b34–991a3, 1079a32–34). Plato, of course, hardly needs Aristotle's help to be misunderstood in that regard, as he himself tends, on occasion, to speak of the Forms either as existing in heaven (*Republic* 509d), which sounds distant enough as it is, or as existing outside or beyond heaven (*Phaedrus* 247c), which sounds even further removed from familiar territory in ontological discourse. There is, in short, sufficient if superficial evidence in and around Plato for a thoroughgoing metaphysical dualism, both of things and of the worlds in which they exist.

Underneath all the metaphorical expressions and hyperbolical testimonia, however, lies the real One-over-Many pattern shaping Plato's metaphysics: the world itself as a single reality with various different parts, levels, dimensions, and characteristics. The aim of this book is to present and promote this unitary pluralism, essentially a monism of worlds with a pluralism of things, as an alternative to the metaphysical dualism commonly attributed to Plato as the received view of his conception of reality. That is the One-over-Many in the title. The opposition intended is not to the distinction between Forms and sensible phenomena, but to the reservation of a separate world for each, and to the restriction of reality to just those two kinds of things. There are still Forms and sensible phenomena, to say nothing of other things, but they are all in the same world as opposed to two different worlds. They also continue to differ in all the same ways, but not in separate worlds or universes. Everything is here with us, Forms and all, in the only world there is.

Unitary pluralism takes Plato to be working with degrees of reality in a single universe whose ontological constitution is best understood in terms of two main levels and countless subdivisions blending into each other through a gradation of reality where the Forms occupy the upper level while sensible phenomena reside in the lower level. This is not a strictly binary division where the universe consists of nothing but Forms and sensible phenomena, neatly separated into two distinct ontological levels in polar opposition to each other. That would be a contrived monism, a kind of dualism in disguise, replacing the traditional dualism in name only, while embracing the same distinction as before. The point is not to call the traditional dualism something else but to replace it with something else.

The alternative here may be considered monism with respect to the number of worlds acknowledged to exist, pluralism with respect to the variety of things recognized as content, the latter being indexed to significant ontological differences. The traditional dualism, in contrast, has exactly two of each, clearly and strictly so in terms of the number of worlds, and at least by emphasis and implication in terms of the kinds of things in existence, with the Forms residing in the ideal world, sensible phenomena in the material world. The alternative in this book is more conservative with respect to the number of worlds and more liberal with respect to the corresponding population of things. It restricts the number of worlds to one, and only one, that can accommodate infinite diversity in its ontological structure. This makes the model both monistic and pluralistic, depending on the perspective. It is a monism of worlds in consolidation of a plurality of things. It is, therefore, the pluralism in and of a unitary reality. Hence, a unitary pluralism.

The two main levels, together with all their subdivisions, constitute relative positions along a continuum of ontological stratification, extending from the highest reality at the top to the lowest at the bottom, without a fixed line of demarcation separating the two with any precision. Just as the oceans of the earth are different in meaningful ways from the land masses separating them, though they are both part of the same planet, so too are the Forms different and distinct from the sensible phenomena instantiating them, though they are both part of the same universe. The upper level houses the Forms, but not to the exclusion of other possibilities, while the lower level houses sensible phenomena, again with room to spare for other things. What this means is that the upper level is open to things besides Forms, perhaps intermediates and possibly also concepts and abstractions that are not fully reified, certainly not at the level of Forms, while the lower level contains not just sensible phenomena but also an assortment of things of lower ontological rank or significance, including everything confined to the lower segment of the line in the celebrated analogy of the *Republic* (509d–511e). Intermediates may alternatively, and just as reasonably, be construed as occupying a central region between the two levels instead of the lower portion of the upper level, either alternative being the same as the other, given the fluidity of the border between the two main levels.

The Forms themselves represent three distinct kinds of intelligible phenomena in the upper level of reality. They exhibit differences that make them more comprehensible in different categories than as a homogeneous collection of reified abstractions, any one of them the same as any other. Even a cursory survey supports a rough division into values, concepts, and relations. With some reflection and refinement, that skeletal breakdown can be fleshed out into a formal classification comprising Ideal Forms, Conceptual Forms, and Relational Forms.

(1) Ideal Forms are transcendent value paradigms instantiated in our phenomenal experience through their earthly manifestations in things that are deemed good in and of themselves, such as justice, piety, and temperance. Despite a predominantly moral orientation, this division is not limited to the domain of ethics. The Forms in this category are ideals, or ideal goods, broadly construed, hence not just moral values and virtues but anything of intrinsic value, including, for example, beauty, knowledge, and life itself.

(2) Conceptual Forms are reified concepts and abstractions that are ontologically significant but not intrinsically valuable. They are objectively real universals corresponding to types, properties, events, actions, experiences, and the like, all regularly invoked as part of our cognitive interaction with our perceptual field. Examples might include horseness,

redness, competition, running, and winning, to illustrate, respectively, albeit loosely, the possible subdivisions listed in the preceding sentence.

(3) Relational Forms are complementary metaphysical categories accounting for the fundamental nature and structure of the universe through pairs of contrasting relations, as illustrated, most notably, in rest versus motion, and same versus other, both pairs being familiar from the "greatest kinds" (*megista genē*) of the *Sophist* (254d–e). The relationship between the paired elements is strictly complementary and never polarized into mutually exclusive forces in diametrical opposition.

From a modern perspective, available to Plato only in approximate anticipation, these Forms are all universals with an objective reality, though they are also much more than that, as the present initiative is intended to demonstrate. To return to the skeletal scheme preceding the fuller classification, what we have here as Forms, all told, are transcendent values, reified concepts, and structural relations. Ideal Forms are the noetic sources of intrinsic value, Conceptual Forms are reified universals that are value-neutral, and Relational Forms are the ontological building blocks of reality correlated with the cognitive structure regulating our phenomenal experience.

The most distinctive characteristic of Ideal Forms is their intrinsic value, while the most distinctive characteristic of Relational Forms is their structural significance, but there is nothing inherently distinctive about Conceptual Forms. Their not being like either of the other two, however, is sufficiently informative for a provisional distinction. The defining difference between all three categories may thus be reduced to the intrinsic value that sets Ideal Forms apart from the other two, and the cosmic pairing that sets Relational Forms apart from the other two, the combined effect of which is to place everything else, hence any reified universals that are neither valuable in themselves nor paired in complementary contrasts of cosmic significance, under the rubric of Conceptual Forms. While this is not a complete picture, it is a useful distinction for a preliminary understanding of the classification scheme.

What may seem like a world of Forms versus a world of sensible phenomena is instead a monistic universe hosting various different kinds of Forms in the upper level of reality, manifested as sensible phenomena in the lower level. Strictly speaking, there is no proof, be it textual, testimonial, empirical, or logical, either of the monism or of the dualism of worlds. And the same is true of the pluralism of the things existing within. The goal here is to show that a monistic world with a pluralistic population, though no more or less open to verification than the standard dualistic reading, carries greater explanatory power and portrays Plato as a better philosopher.

Unlike the dualism typically attributed to Plato, the unitary pluralism advocated here is not just an ontological model but a philosophical vision. The traditional dualism is at best an interpretive template that is consistent with some of what Plato appears to be saying in specifically ontological terms, perhaps also extending to broadly metaphysical terms, but falling short of universal relevance. No doubt, Plato does seem at times to be referring to a world of Forms as distinct from the world of sensible phenomena. But that is only a figure of speech reinforcing the distinction, to make sure the difference is appreciated, even if it is exaggerated. With an illustrious teacher and an outstanding student, neither of whom separated universals from the particulars instantiating them, Plato must have developed an affinity for any opportunity, philosophical or rhetorical, to distinguish his Forms from sensible phenomena, with some embellishment for good measure. That is why he can consistently if erroneously be read as a metaphysical dualist, even though there is really no particular textual confirmation of that reading as opposed to a monistic alternative, unless one is inclined to take every metaphor literally for the sake of an otherwise whimsical interpretation.

The paradigm of unitary pluralism, on the other hand, provides comprehensive coverage of Plato's general worldview with greater explanatory power, including not just his ontology and cosmology but also his epistemology, ethics, and aesthetics, not to mention his social and political philosophy, which is, at bottom, a unitary pluralism of city and soul, each with its own organic structure, and the two of them together as one of the most memorable analogies in Plato, if not in the history of political thought.

The methodological cornerstone of unitary pluralism as an interpretive model is the gradation of reality in a single universe. The ontological stratification acknowledged therein introduces degrees of reality placing the Forms in the upper level and sensible phenomena in the lower level of an integrated whole, where the contrast between Forms and sensible phenomena serves as a reflection of the more fundamental division and relationship between the levels themselves, thus including both the Forms and sensible phenomena without being restricted to them. The relationship between the levels, that is, the way one level is oriented relative to the other, is not so much opposition as it is completion, much like anywhere upstairs in relation to a reciprocal downstairs. They are complements rather than opposites.

Despite a unifying focus with a central thesis and integrated strategies toward its establishment, this book is not a scholarly monograph drafted in one sitting. It is a series of five previously published essays bundled together with two new ones composed especially for this collection. The first five essays in chronological order, listed below with publication details, were originally produced in accordance with an overarching plan of development, starting with a presentation, demonstration, and illustration of the basic model, followed by various implications and applications, all focusing primarily if not exclusively on the Forms:

- "Rethinking Plato's Forms" (with Holger Thesleff), *Arctos: Acta Philologica Fennica* 47 (2013): 11–47.

- "Rethought Forms: How Do They Work?," *Arctos: Acta Philologica Fennica* 48 (2014): 25–55.

- "A Horse Is a Horse, of Course, of Course, but What about Horseness?," in *Second Sailing: Alternative Perspectives on Plato*, edited by Debra Nails and Harold Tarrant in collaboration with Mika Kajava and Eero Salmenkivi, 307–324, Commentationes Humanarum Litterarum 132 (Helsinki: Societas Scientiarum Fennica, 2015).

- "Ontological Symmetry in Plato: Formless Things and Empty Forms," *Analysis and Metaphysics* 16 (2017a): 7–51.

- "The Good, the Bad, and the Ugly: Does Plato Make Room for Negative Forms in His Ontology?," *Cosmos and History: The Journal of Natural and Social Philosophy* 13, no. 3 (2017b): 154–191.

These essays have been reproduced here, with some emendations and variations, in the order in which they were conceived, produced, and published. The revised versions, recast as chapters, use the same titles as before. They remain faithful to the main positions in the original essays, drawing on the same combination of analysis and argumentation employed there toward their establishment. Other than stylistic changes for the sake of uniformity, deviations are limited largely to refinements introduced in the process of looking for better ways of expressing the same ideas. The present publisher and I are grateful to the previous publishers for their kind permission to reprint the corresponding material with modifications.

The transition from a unitary project executed in stages to a comprehensive presentation of the results in a single volume came with a choice between preserving the autonomous nature and internal coherence of the individual essays and avoiding the accretion of redundancy in the volume as a whole. With the entire project revolving around a common platform, namely that of a unitary pluralism with a gradation of reality and a trinitarian classification of Forms, thematic redundancy was building up gradually as each essay proceeded independently to set up the same model in pursuit of its own aims and in execution of its own strategies. A tempting alternative emerging during the compilation process was to replace the mutually redundant portions with a passing reference to the basic model in its original exposition. Avoiding the cumulative redundancy, however, would have disrupted the natural flow of the individual essays, with a jarring void replacing substantive development. The most effective means of presentation, particularly in terms of perspicuity, turned out to be to retain the episodic reintroduction of the central paradigm where it became relevant in the course of each chapter.

Although this periodic reaffirmation of the unitary pluralism of Plato's world comes with a certain degree of repetition, the collective redundancy is mitigated by distributive enhancements and organizational advantages, including the continuing accessibility of each chapter as a standalone essay. This compromise of redundancy in exchange for coherence represents a match between the purpose of the project and the structure of the presentation. The point is not to advocate one reading of Plato over another, in the manner of a logical or methodological exercise in textual interpretation and philosophical reconstruction, but to establish a compelling exegetical platform that actually advances our understanding of Plato's intellectual output. The interpretation must be not just plausible but also illuminating. It must make a difference in addition to being different.

The structure best serving that aim is a succession of essays developing the central position and exploring its various implications in an effort to demonstrate not only that the alternative presented here makes sense but also that it helps solve important problems in Plato scholarship that otherwise defy a solution under the standard interpretation of Plato as a metaphysical dualist. The balance achieved between the desired form and the intended function facilitates a consistent and systematic demonstration of how the paradigm of unitary pluralism, including its inherent gradation of reality and its attendant classification of Forms, solves some of the most nagging problems in Plato's metaphysics, such as the existence of empty Forms (Forms without particulars) and Formless things (particulars without Forms), the possibility of negative Forms (injustice, impiety, ugliness, etc.), and the controversy over intermediates (ontological constructs of an intermediate nature between Forms and sensible phenomena).

These are merely the highlights of a host of issues addressed throughout this book. Each of the main issues constitutes an independent topic of discussion in Plato scholarship. The book is therefore designed to treat each problem as a separate area of concern, complete with its own background, attempted solutions, and unique complications. The key to overall success is to show how the central model, if valid and viable, contributes to a solution to each problem. That is why the respective questions were originally addressed through a series of journal articles in the first place. The goals and circumstances pertinent to each essay consequently determined the motivating impetus for the book: the consolidation of the separate subjects in a single volume where each chapter can still be consulted on its own as a self-contained solution to the specific problem it addresses.

Bringing everything together at the end was always the object of the extended exercise from the beginning, as intimated in the preface to the book. The creative process required not just the transformation of journal articles into book chapters but also the provision of a holistic and coherent reading experience from cover to cover, while retaining the independent nature and structure of the essays reorganized as chapters. The editorial aspect of the process was a matter of appraising consistency and rewriting chapters to achieve unitary integrity within a cohesive presentation. The substantive aspect was the production of entirely new material to complement the existing essays and to complete the project: the present introduction, essentially an unnumbered chapter, plus two standard chapters, one at the beginning (chapter 1), one at the end (chapter 7), with the new material adding up to half the length of the book. A brief outline of each chapter will help develop a fuller perspective of the book as a whole.

Chapter 1 ("Plato's World: The Standard Model") is an overview of Plato's metaphysics in accordance with and elucidation of the traditional

INTRODUCTION 9

interpretation, which the present volume is dedicated to replacing with a better alternative. While the very notion of a standard interpretation of Plato on any issue may be open to debate, the intention here is to set up a dialectical target for the alternative promoted throughout the book. That target is the habitual reading of a strict dualism of Forms versus sensible phenomena, including the allocation of a separate world to each, as the central metaphysical outlook of Plato.

Much of the focus is on the evidence pertaining to Forms in the dialogues, that is, on clues for what Plato takes them to be (given that he does not come right out and say what he takes them to be) as well as on what he does with them and how he conceives of their interaction with sensible phenomena. These considerations are complemented by an exegetical and critical assessment of the reasons and motivations for employing a model of metaphysical dualism in interpretation of Plato's conception and utilization of Forms. The critical dimension, however, is not a confrontational one, at least not at this point. A critique is intended only in the sense of reflective evaluation as against reception without consideration. With the remainder of the book developing and recommending an alternative model of interpretation, this chapter is dedicated to presenting the received view in the best possible light, including not just a documentation of original sources but also an examination of the associated reception.

Chapter 2 ("Rethinking Plato's Forms"), originally written in collaboration with Holger Thesleff, constitutes the inaugural presentation of the alternative model placing the Forms in the upper level and sensible phenomena in the lower level of a single world exhibiting a gradation of reality indicative of unitary pluralism. Given its chronological position in launching what later developed into a personal project executed in stages, it is focused more on explicating the basic model than on providing details or pursuing implications. It introduces the two main levels as correlative benchmarks instituting ontological differentiation in place of the polar opposition ingrained in the strict dualism of the traditional interpretation. It also proposes a classification of Forms into the aforementioned groups, consisting of Ideal Forms, Conceptual Forms, and Relational Forms, jointly forging a platform of conceptual variegation in rejection of the prevailing assumption of ontological homogeneity in Forms.

The trinitarian organization of Forms in the upper level of a single reality represents the methodological core of the recommended departure from the traditional interpretation, plotting a course away from both a dualism of worlds and a dualism of things, in favor of a monism of worlds and a pluralism of things. The diversity of Forms is not the full extent of the pluralism imagined but a revealing expression of it. The pluralism itself, grounded in the underlying gradation of reality, permeates both levels, not just the upper level of Forms. The nature and extent of the inherent pluralism is explored further in subsequent chapters, particularly in the second half of the book, where the focus is on the application of the proposed paradigm to commonly encountered problems in the metaphysics of Plato.

Chapter 3 ("Rethought Forms: How Do They Work?") elaborates on the interpretive model introduced in the preceding chapter, devoting particular attention to features requiring greater emphasis for a fuller appreciation of the comprehensive platform envisaged and for an accurate evaluation of the rationale provided. It is concerned especially with the relationship between the upper and lower levels of Plato's world as the structural pillars of a gradation of reality accommodating unity in plurality. While the two main levels are central to a proper understanding of the system, they are not the sole constituents of Plato's world, but the most conspicuous manifestations of an infinite diversity reflecting an ontological stratification pregnant with endless possibilities and implications.

The elaborative effort here is the first step toward unpacking the various dimensions and corollaries of the gradation of reality. It initiates an extended process of redirecting the focus of attention from the two levels themselves to the unitary pluralism in which they serve as guideposts to reality as Plato saw it. The purpose of this shift is not to deny the primacy of the two main levels, nor even to minimize the importance of their distinction, but to determine the differentiation and diversification they were meant to sort out in the first place. Coverage includes the notion of "ontological ascent," a conceptual process or phenomenon through which the other two types of Forms can and sometimes do come to resemble Ideal Forms, which is a sign of the fluidity of Plato's experimentation with abstraction and concept formation, which, in turn, is indicative of the pluralism of the world he envisioned. The chapter thus identifies Plato's "stratification of reality" (section 3.3) as the ontological basis for his "classification of Forms" (section 3.4) in a foundational and comprehensive "continuum of abstraction" (section 3.5).

Chapter 4 ("A Horse Is a Horse, of Course, of Course, but What about Horseness?") is the third and final chapter concerned with the presentation and promotion of the model itself rather than with the contemplation and investigation of its various implications and applications. Originally conceived as a contribution to a collection of essays commemorating Holger Thesleff's ninetieth birthday, this chapter approaches the ontology of Plato, specifically the question of his alleged dualism, from the perspective of the doxastic attitudes and perceptual predispositions implicit in competing interpretations. It thus stands apart from the rest of the contributions, both in the original collection and in this volume, as a psychological study of the reception of Plato, as opposed to a logical, philological, philosophical, or literary assessment of the ideas or works of Plato.

The main question here is not whether the traditional metaphysical dualism or the alternative unitary pluralism is a better interpretation of Plato, but why anyone would be inclined to believe one over the other, if either at all. The response unfolds accordingly as an exploration of the psychology behind the ontology imposed upon Plato by his readers. The conclusion is that what we make of Plato, especially in connection with the matter of a monism versus dualism of worlds, depends ultimately on our own preconceptions concerning the nature of reality. Focusing predominantly on the Forms and taking them as a manifestation of Plato's attempt to explain unity in plurality, among other things, this chapter exposes the conceptual groundwork for the unitary pluralism of Plato's world.

Chapter 5 ("Ontological Symmetry in Plato: Formless Things and Empty Forms") is the first installment of the second stage of the project, the practical and demonstrative phase concerned with implications and applications of the interpretive model being promoted. The center of discussion here is the ontological structure of the correspondence between Forms and sensible phenomena: Is the relationship a symmetrical one, such that there are Forms for everything and things for every Form, whereby neither Forms nor sensible phenomena ever stand alone, one without the other? Or is the relationship an asymmetrical one, allowing for the possibility of Formless things (what we might now think of as particulars without a corresponding universal) and empty Forms (what we might now think of as uninstantiated universals), perhaps one or the other, or possibly both at once?

Previous efforts to answer these questions, typically taken up separately rather than jointly, have been undermined both by a lack of evidence in the Platonic corpus and by a lack of clarity in the questions themselves. The distinctive contribution of the present approach is a fresh analysis in light of the unitary pluralism advocated here in place of the metaphysical dualism traditionally invoked to describe Plato's metaphysics.

An additional contribution facilitating a proper evaluation of the answers is the prior reassessment and clarification of the questions. The key with respect to Formless things is to agree upon the precise nature and function of Forms so that we may decide whether we are talking about exactly the same thing when we ask whether there is a Form for everything. The key with respect to empty Forms is to distinguish clearly between the question whether the Form under consideration is or is not instantiated and the question whether that particular Form exists at all. The conclusion, stated briefly, is that Formless things are not, whereas empty Forms are, consistent with a proper understanding of Plato.

Chapter 6 ("The Good, the Bad, and the Ugly: Does Plato Make Room for Negative Forms in His Ontology?") takes up the question of negative Forms, namely whether there are any in Plato's ontology. The question, to be clear, concerns negative Forms in the sense of evil, as opposed to that of logical negation, and it concerns evil in the broad or generic sense of undesirability, including, but not limited to, its particular manifestations in moral, aesthetic, and religious contexts. Hence, it asks whether Plato acknowledges a Form of the bad, the ugly, the unholy, and so on, setting aside the altogether different matter of whether he acknowledges Forms for not-good, not-beautiful, not-holy, and the like. The short answer is yes. The evidence for the short answer is that negative Forms are either mentioned or contemplated rather openly throughout the canonical corpus, in fact, with such abundance and variety that the relevant references can effectively be compiled into a representative list of passages: *Euthydemus* 301b; *Euthyphro* 5c–6e; *Hippias Major* 289c–d; *Phaedrus* 250a–b; *Republic* 475e–476a; *Theaetetus* 186a.

The long answer is that the short answer is wrong. The evidence for the long answer is that serious scholars keep trying to prove either that Plato did or that he did not accept negative Forms, as if he had said nothing at all about them and we had to deduce his position from our conception of his general philosophical outlook. This answer is pursued through a case study comparing the acknowledgment of negative Forms in Plato by Debra Nails and the rejection of negative Forms in Plato by Holger Thesleff and me. Because the format of a case study comparing two opposing viewpoints works best with a third party presenting the case and adjudicating the dispute, I do my best here to conceal my agreement, alliance, and collaboration with Thesleff, until the completion of what I take to be a dispassionate presentation of the facts and arguments on both sides. The overall conclusion is that Plato seems to have never warmed up to negative Forms, and that he would have rejected them outright if pressed on the matter, because of his unwavering association of reality with value, as evidenced most vividly, for example, in his conviction that the supreme metaphysical principle guiding the creation of the universe is goodness (*Timaeus* 29d–30c).

Chapter 7 ("Between a Form and a Hard Place: The Problem of Intermediates in Plato"), as the title makes clear, concerns the question of intermediates in Plato, both the mathematical ones in the testimony of Aristotle (*Metaphysics* 987b14–18, 1028b19–21) and any and all nonmathematical ones immediately suggested by the very possibility of mathematical ones, though not with the blessing of Aristotle himself, whose testimony actually rules out any others (*Metaphysics* 997b12–32, 1059b2–9). This is an interesting question at the intersection of the absence of textual evidence in the Platonic corpus and the availability of testimonial evidence in the Aristotelian corpus. What makes it interesting is that this evidentiary connection, indirect though it may be, should have been satisfactory in view of the close relationship between the parties concerned, but it has failed to generate a scholarly consensus with respect to the question of intermediates in Plato. This creates the perfect opportunity for probing the question further through the paradigm of a unitary pluralism grounded in a gradation of reality, the singular relevance of which makes this chapter both the culmination and the conclusion of the application phase of the extended project.

The methodological aim of the chapter is to make full use of the paradigm to illustrate, though not necessarily to demonstrate beyond any doubt, that there is room in the philosophical orientation of Plato for every conceivable kind of intermediate ontological entity, or construct, between Forms and sensible phenomena. Although this may admittedly be taken as a partial confirmation of the testimony of Aristotle, it is actually motivated by a partial yet serious dissatisfaction with the testimony of Aristotle, whose assistance is valuable but confusing. The conclusion is that Plato can reasonably be interpreted as embracing intermediates of all kinds whether or not they are in Aristotle's testimony. In the interest of full disclosure, this is not to deny that Plato can reasonably be interpreted as rejecting intermediates of any kind, nor even to deny that he can reasonably be interpreted as accepting just the ones in Aristotle while rejecting all others, but only to affirm that he can be read, with impeccable internal consistency, as accepting them all, meaning simply that this position is perfectly reasonable even though the alternatives are not unreasonable given the evidence we have to work with.

The general aim of the book, as well as that of each chapter, is friendly persuasion rather than conclusive proof, the latter of which is not a realistic option for either the monism or the dualism of worlds. The original effort, starting with the first article, was conceived as a thought experiment, and expressly presented as one, where the emphasis was on inspiration and suggestion rather than on proof in the strictest sense of the term. That conception has been a guiding principle for the comprehensive project as well.

A caveat regarding the position of the present work in relation to the oral tradition in Plato may be in order before moving on to the substantive material. The interpretive model developed here is intended as an alternative to, and hence as a replacement for, nothing more than the strict dualism of Forms versus sensible phenomena, including the duplication of worlds that comes with the radical separation commonly accompanying that perspective. The model does not, in addition, represent an alternative to, or constitute a replacement for, the Tübingen Paradigm, where the one and the-great-and-the-small emerge as fundamental metaphysical principles, prior in importance to the Forms. The Tübingen approach, whether or not it is valid, viable, or verifiable, is compatible with the model presented here, which is neither a friend nor a foe of the legendary unwritten doctrines, so long as the latter are interpreted as underlying rather than undermining Plato's explanation of the world in terms of a relationship between Forms and sensible phenomena. After all, any interpretive system assigning supreme importance to the one and the-great-and-the-small as the ultimate principles of reality is itself an exercise in unitary pluralism.

Finally, a note on documentation: References to Plato employ Stephanus numbers in correlation with the Oxford Classical Texts edition of his opera (Plato 1900–1907). Translations of specific passages, except where noted otherwise, follow the Hackett edition of his complete works (Plato 1997). The latter collection may not represent the best translation of each work, but it does represent the best compromise for convenient access, since different scholars tend to favor different translations anyway. A similar convention governs references to Aristotle, using Bekker numbers for pagination, and the revised Oxford edition of his complete works for translation (Aristotle 1984). As for terminology, the first letter of the word "Form" (or "Idea") is capitalized whenever the reference is to Plato's Forms (or Ideas), but the individual Forms themselves do not take on an initial capital unless the reference otherwise remains ambiguous between a Form and an instantiation bearing the same name.

Chapter 1

Plato's World

The Standard Model

This chapter is an overview of the metaphysical dualism commonly associated with Plato. While the overarching aim of the book is to replace the traditional dualism with a better alternative, the specific goal of this chapter is to examine the most compelling reasons for adhering instead to the prevailing dualism. The underlying motivation is to present something tangible and respectable for replacement with the unitary pluralism developed throughout the remainder of the book. Accordingly, the mode of treatment is expository rather than reactionary, making the resulting account interpretive rather than destructive.

1.1. Introduction

The purpose of the present chapter is to introduce the standard model, traditional interpretation, or received view of Plato as embracing a world of transcendent Forms opposite the world in which we ourselves exist along with everything else in our direct acquaintance. While there is hardly ever a consensus of opinion on anything meaningful concerning Plato, much less on the whole of his metaphysics, the aim here is to set up the basic template to which the interpretive paradigm promoted in this book constitutes an alternative.

The first thing to note about the standard model, so to speak, is that it requires not one but two worlds: one for the Forms and one for everything else. This binary division, whether or not it has any basis in reality, immediately raises a question: Why two worlds? That naturally leads to another question: What exactly is in one world versus the other? Since we are expected to be relatively familiar with our own world, the second question is actually an inquiry into what is in the other world: What are the Forms? And that leads to a further question: How does it all work, that is, how are all these things related, and how do they jointly account for reality? These are the questions addressed over the next three sections, together constituting the substantive bulk of the chapter.

The approach is exegetical and analytical. The aim at this point is neither to refute existing interpretations nor to offer anything in their place. This is not the place to object, for example, that a second world is not really necessary, or to suggest that two alone might not be sufficient, the latter of which is just as serious an objection as the former.[1] Such objections and questions go to the heart of the matter in the alternative developed in subsequent chapters. The point here is to specify, rather than to justify, the contents of one world versus the other, so as to understand how they are supposed to work together. This does not mean that the discussion is free of critical commentary, just that it is geared toward exposition and interpretation, combined with a dispassionate appraisal of inherent strengths and weaknesses.

The dualism of worlds, the corresponding population of each, and the associated patterns of interaction do not cover everything of importance. Yet they do constitute the greatest common denominator of issues

---

1. Note that placing the Forms in one world, and everything else in another, suggests not just that the Forms are uniform entities, but that everything else is as well. The neat and tidy division makes all Forms the same, or at least similar enough to each other that they can be placed in the same world, and different enough from everything else that they must be placed in a separate world. This we already know. And this we may well be forced to accept, because we do not know enough about the Forms to reject anything, remaining at the mercy of whatever is said about them, so long as it is not inconsistent with the principles of logic, or incompatible with how we think of sensible phenomena. But is "everything else" so uniform in its basic nature and its essential structure that its constituents can all be accommodated in the same world, that is, in just one world, opposite the Forms? And are the Forms so different from everything else that nothing else belongs in their world? If both answers are affirmative, then where do all the disincarnate souls and immortal gods belong? This is merely a sampling of the questions inspiring the opposition of this book to a dualism of worlds as the proper interpretation of Plato.

attracting scholarly interest in the secondary literature. There are, no doubt, many other topics of importance in Plato's metaphysics. The question of Formless things, for example, comes to mind, as does the matter of empty Forms.[2] The former is about whether there is or can be anything without a Form, the latter about whether there are or can be any Forms that remain uninstantiated. While these and yet other questions may be perfectly suitable for discussion in a general overview, even in one such as the present chapter, the prior aim of providing a model for contrast with the interpretation developed and defended throughout the book is best served by tightly integrated coverage of the most relevant issues as opposed to comprehensive commentary on all of them.

1.2. Why Two Worlds?

The universal motivation for postulating a second world to help account for Plato's reality is to accommodate the peculiarity of his Forms, which do not seem to go with anything we are familiar with in our everyday experience. The Forms appear, in fact, to be the opposite of conventional reality, albeit a complementary opposite rather than an antithesis, which in any event, requires an alternate reality to host these mysterious constituents. Their explicit transcendence (*Republic* 509d; *Phaedrus* 247c) confirms their reported separation (Aristotle: *Metaphysics* 990b34–991a3, 1079a32–34), thus doubling the number of worlds required to take stock of everything in existence, whether in this world or in another. Here is how Bertrand Russell (1912) describes Plato's response to the logical, ontological, and epistemological need to acknowledge a part of objective reality that is not a part of our phenomenal experience:

> Thus Plato is led to a supra-sensible world, more real than the common world of sense, the unchangeable world of ideas, which alone gives to the world of sense whatever pale reflection of reality may belong to it. The truly real world, for Plato, is

---

2. Formless things and empty Forms are discussed in chapter 5, which is dedicated exclusively to those two problems. Chapter 7 (section 7.4) includes a discussion of the "range," or "population," of Forms—basically an exploration of what Forms there are (or what things have Forms)—which is directly related to the question of the possibility of Formless things.

the world of ideas; for whatever we may attempt to say about things in the world of sense, we can only succeed in saying that they participate in such and such ideas, which, therefore, constitute all their character. (Russell 1912, 144)

The quotation is from Russell's overview of the problems of philosophy in a book aptly titled *The Problems of Philosophy* (1912). The popular nature of that work as a brief and accessible yet thematically complete introduction to philosophy makes it all the more significant that Russell singles out Plato's response as one of the best in the history of philosophy, or in his own words, as "one of the most successful attempts hitherto made" (1912, 142). His praise is specifically for Plato's solution to the problem of where to put the things that do not exist in the same way that sticks and stones do, which is what we have, for example, in justice itself versus just acts, and whiteness itself versus white things (Russell 1912, 143–145).[3]

The reasoning in Russell's evaluation is typical among scholars inferring a need for two worlds in Plato's metaphysics. Not all commentators would agree that a second world is necessary, or more to the point, that the second one can really be found in the Platonic corpus, but those who do, generally reason as Russell does.[4] The common tendency is to specify, in the same breath, both what the Forms are and why they belong in a separate world. It is difficult to do one without the other, because the perceived need for the second world is grounded in the transcendence of

---

3. Note that Russell ends up separating not just the worlds but also the kinds of reality apposite to each, and, of course, to the inhabitants of each. Despite applauding Plato's solution for attributing objective reality to things we do not encounter in our phenomenal experience, namely Forms, he explicates that reality in terms of subsistence as against existence (Russell 1912, 156). What he is saying, therefore, is not merely that Plato's Forms do not belong in the same world as everything else, but furthermore that Plato's Forms are not even real in the same sense as everything else. They subsist, while everything else exists. It is just as important to note, however, that the separation of worlds is a position Russell attributes to Plato himself, whereas the distinction between existence and subsistence is his own interpretation of how best to make sense of that separation, without suggesting that the latter likewise originates in Plato.

4. Among those who deny the dualism of worlds in Plato, Nails (2013) goes so far as to characterize the position as one of the two dogmas of Platonism (78–87), the other being the identification of the unhypothetical first principle of the all with the Form of the good (88–101).

Forms (or in their "separation" as Aristotle calls it), which is an extraordinary quality suggesting an extraordinary object. Any estimation of the number of worlds thus goes hand in hand with an explanation of the nature of Forms. The latter issue is the subject matter of the next section, but its organic relationship with the problem on hand makes references to Forms unavoidable in any account of the dualism of worlds.

While Russell's conception of Forms is not revealed in the passage quoted above, it is expressed clearly and emphatically a little later in the same work, where he unapologetically presents Plato's Forms ("Ideas") as universals:

> The word "idea" has acquired, in the course of time, many associations which are quite misleading when applied to Plato's "ideas." We shall therefore use the word "universal" instead of the word "idea," to describe what Plato meant. The essence of the sort of entity that Plato meant is that it is opposed to the particular things that are given in sensation. We speak of whatever is given in sensation, or is of the same nature as things given in sensation, as a particular; by opposition to this, a universal will be anything which may be shared by many particulars, and has those characteristics which, as we saw, distinguish justice and whiteness from just acts and white things. (Russell 1912, 145)

The identification of Plato's Forms with universals is a controversial assessment that requires, and often comes with, various provisions enumerating essential differences between Forms and universals while at the same time defending the basic identification. The details of the approach, together with the main alternatives, are discussed in the next section. The immediate task is to examine the tendency in the secondary literature to find a dualism of worlds in Plato, expounding on any ancillary positions on the nature of Forms only as they come up, and without critical appraisal, so as to focus on the prior task. The dualism of worlds is not always at the forefront of discussion, which tends to be focused more on the dualism of the kinds of things in them, but hardly anyone neglects to follow that distinction with a separation of worlds, usually explicitly, but if not, at least implicitly.

Another proponent of the duplication of worlds in Plato is David Armstrong (1978; 1989), who happens to agree with Russell (1912) that

Plato's Forms are universals (though the latter conviction is neither necessary nor sufficient to separate or duplicate the worlds):

> Once you have uninstantiated universals you need somewhere special to put them, a "Platonic heaven," as philosophers often say. They are not to be found in the ordinary world of space and time. And since it seems that any instantiated universal might have been uninstantiated—for example, there might have been nothing past, present, or future that had that property—then if uninstantiated universals are in a Platonic heaven, it will be natural to place all universals in that heaven. The result is that we get two realms: the realm of universals and the realm of particulars, the latter being ordinary things in space and time. Such universals are often spoken of as *transcendent*. (Armstrong 1989, 76)

The agreement between Russell and Armstrong is significant. They are indeed two of the most prominent philosophers of the twentieth century. But they are not Plato scholars. They are neither classicists nor philologists nor historians of ancient philosophy.[5] Russell is a polymath with inestimable contributions to logic, mathematics, history, and literature, in addition to a voluminous scholarly output covering the whole of philosophy, not to mention various speeches, debates, and publications as a notoriously outspoken social critic and commentator. Armstrong is strictly a philosopher, working mainly in metaphysics and the philosophy of mind, where he has a particular reputation for having helped restore the viability of metaphysics as a worthwhile philosophical enterprise, mistreated and misunderstood under the sweeping influence of logical positivism.

Their agreement is not coincidental. It is only natural that philosophers engaged in the analytic tradition, either in support of logical positivism or

---

5. As the author of *A History of Western Philosophy* (1945/1946), Russell is, of course, a historian of philosophy as well as a philosopher. But he is also many other things, as indicated in the main text above, which then makes it inaccurate to describe him as any one thing, or in any one way, more than any other of comparable or greater relevance. Moreover, even as a historian of philosophy, Russell is not a specialist in ancient philosophy. Note, all the same, that chapter 15 of his *History* is dedicated to Plato's Forms: "The Theory of Ideas" (Russell 1945, 119–132; 1946, 141–153).

against it, would tend to see universals everywhere, whether in affirmation of their existence or in denial of it, but in either case with an appreciation of the need to postulate a separate world in accommodation of that possibility. Such a common predisposition then raises the question whether a scholar whose specialty is Plato, or ancient philosophy in general, would see Plato in the same light. One may wonder, in other words, whether the dualism of worlds in Plato is an exclusively analytic bias.

Yet that is most assuredly not the case. Evidence suggests that there is no such bias among analytic philosophers that cannot be found among other commentators on Plato. This is not to say that analytic philosophers tend to reach precisely the same conclusions as Plato scholars but that members of either group can be quite receptive to a dualism of worlds in Plato. A prime example of the parallel tendency among Plato scholars is David Sedley (2016):[6]

> This contrast between two distinct realms is linked by Plato to two competing means of cognitive access: the intellect, and the senses. Consequently, Plato is often and I think correctly credited with a 'two world' thesis. There are two worlds: the intelligible world, populated by Forms, and the sensible world, populated by sensible particulars. Inquiry about Forms is pure intellectual inquiry, which must minimise or eliminate the use of the senses. And since knowledge is in its nature permanently true and not subject to revision, the unchanging world of Forms constitutes a suitable object for knowledge. By contrast, the familiar world of sensible particulars is suitable only for opinion: opinion, being in its very nature capable of fluctuating between true and false, is the appropriate mode of cognition for inherently unstable objects. On this basis, Plato operates not only an epistemological distinction between the

---

6. My identification of Sedley as a Plato scholar is not intended to deny or ignore his expertise, reputation, or influence in other areas of ancient philosophy, nor in other areas of philosophy in general. It is a positive assessment grounded in admiration rather than a negative one suggesting limitation. While I would have normally thought this obvious, the indignation of Szlezák in response to the identification of Krämer and Gaiser as Plato scholars (see Szlezák and Staehler 2014, 161), as if they were nothing else, has inspired me to exercise caution in such matters.

intelligible world and the sensible world, but also, and directly mapping onto this, an ontological distinction between a world of pure being and a world of pure becoming. Intellectual access to the world of being affords us an understanding of what such things as equality and beauty really and timelessly are, whereas sensory access to the world of becoming does no more than track the ebb and flow of the corresponding predicates—their becoming. (Sedley 2016, 11)

What is common to all three interpretations is not just the dualism of worlds but also the association of Forms with universals. Russell and Armstrong are both explicit in their construal of Forms as universals, while Sedley only hints at the same construal in the passage just quoted, though the hints are strong, given his repeated contrast of Forms with particulars, the latter being the standard ontological complement of universals. And what is implicit in that passage becomes explicit elsewhere in the same work: "A Form, being the *one* thing shared by many diverse but like-named particulars, is a 'one over many': not a further particular but a universal" (Sedley 2016, 13). The identification of Forms with universals, then, is a common thread running through all three conceptions of the dualism of worlds in Plato.

Although Sedley is on board with the interpretive practice of explicating Plato's Forms through the notion of universals, he is also careful to limit that association to certain dialogues rather than extending it to the whole of the Platonic corpus. He goes on, still in the same work, to repudiate a comprehensive correspondence between Forms and universals:

However, when putting this new licence into practice in those late dialogues, Plato very naturally downplayed any assumption that such objects of definition need be transcendent Forms. Hence, at least in those dialogues, the theory of transcendent forms was to give way to a general theory of universals, little concerned with the metaphysical status of its objects. (Sedley 2016, 19)

A caveat to the same effect can be found in an earlier work, where Sedley (2013) likewise warns against assuming that everything in the Platonic corpus that looks like a universal from our perspective was actually intended as a Form from Plato's perspective:

[Plato] may well be judged to have thought that wherever there is an *authentic* common property linking a group of individuals, a Form can and should be posited. To that extent, the identity of Forms with universals begins to look more plausible. However, the more widely Plato extends his conceptual analyses in his later definitional dialogues (e.g. mud in the *Theaetetus*, fishing in the *Sophist*), the less clear it becomes that he is still talking about Forms, metaphysically separated objects of pure thought, and not simply about kinds, postulated without any special metaphysical presuppositions, e.g. about their being ontologically prior to their instances. (Sedley 2013, 113–114)

Despite his support for the dualism of worlds commonly attributed to Plato, Sedley's refusal to make the association between Forms and universals a permanent fixture of Plato's philosophical career can be taken as a clue that he does not consider the dualism of worlds to be contingent upon the association with universals. He comes close to saying so himself where he recognizes a growing tension in Plato's work between the proliferation of universals and the ascription of transcendence to Forms: "One may then feel that Plato's theory of Forms did in the end metamorphose into a general theory of universals, but only at the price of leaving to one side the Forms' metaphysical transcendence" (Sedley 2013, 137).

The reason why Sedley is able to make that distinction is that the backdrop of universals is expendable in the interpretive framework of transcendent Forms and complementary worlds. As a matter of fact, their interpretation as universals might even be said to contradict the transcendence of Forms, along with the consequent duplication of worlds, given that the notion of universals originates with Aristotle, who placed them within the corresponding things (*universalia in rebus*) rather than forcing them out into the world at large (*universalia ante rem*), praising Socrates for doing the same, while criticizing Plato for his misguided innovation of separation (*Metaphysics* 1078b30–32). Whether one sides with Plato or with Aristotle, the primary consideration in the dualism of worlds is not that the Forms are universals, though they very well may be, but that they are transcendent, whatever they may happen to be.

With a separation of worlds comes the problem of their interaction, for whatever is in one remains isolated from the other, and therefore mutually irrelevant, unless we can somehow bring them together. This is the subject matter of section 1.4, but preliminary considerations at this point will help put the problem in context. If the transcendence of Forms requires a separate world for them, then their relevance to the world where we exist requires demonstration and explanation. This is a particularly difficult problem for the advocates of a dualism of worlds in Plato. They do not, by any means, ignore the problem, but they either analyze it without a solution, as Russell does, or minimize its difficulty, as Armstrong does, or leave it all up to Plato, as Sedley does.

Describing Russell as analyzing the problem without a solution may not seem fair, given his prominent role in shaping the scholarly outlook on the problem of universals. Yet that is not the problem under consideration here. The problem, rather, is how to reconcile the two worlds attributed to Plato in a way that produces a working reality out of such disparate ontological elements. That is exactly how Russell (1912) himself approaches the problem, articulating it while considering the metaphysics of the matter (142–157), but resolving it only in the context of the corresponding epistemology (158–173):

> But the truth is that both [worlds] have the same claim on our impartial attention, both are real, and both are important to the metaphysician. Indeed no sooner have we distinguished the two worlds than it becomes necessary to consider their relations. But first of all we must examine our knowledge of universals. This consideration will occupy us in the following chapter, where we shall find that it solves the problem of *a priori* knowledge, from which we were first led to consider universals. (Russell 1912, 157; paragraph break omitted)

While Russell (1912) presents the switch from metaphysics to epistemology as a temporary detour to accommodate a methodological condition requiring immediate satisfaction ("first of all we must examine our knowledge of universals," 157), the transition ends up being permanent in the absence of a correlative "second of all," as he proceeds thereafter to address the issue in entirely epistemological terms ("Returning now to the problem of *a priori* knowledge, which we left unsolved when we began the consideration of universals," 161). The fact that he considers the inception of the problem to be epistemological in nature ("the problem of *a priori* knowledge, from which we were first led to consider universals," 157) certainly justifies his return to it as an epistemological matter, but that further strengthens the critical observation that he focuses predominantly on the epistemology of the matter, leaving the metaphysics of it without a clear conclusion or obvious direction.

This is not an oversight. As early as the preface to the work in question, *The Problems of Philosophy* (1912), Russell fully admits the disproportionately epistemological focus of his approach.[7] But the admission still leaves us with a metaphysical problem that has only been addressed from an epistemological standpoint.[8] We could, and perhaps should, take Russell's preoccupation with epistemology in that particular work, together with the introductory nature of the volume itself, as our cue to look for the metaphysics elsewhere. But it is only fair to expect a solution there as well, since it is there that Russell pointedly anchors his entire presentation to Plato, particularly in a passage already quoted in part above in demonstration of his praise for Plato:

> The problem with which we are now concerned is a very old one, since it was brought into philosophy by Plato. Plato's "theory of ideas" is an attempt to solve this very problem, and in my opinion it is one of the most successful attempts hitherto made. (Russell 1912, 142)

Russell's framing interest in Plato is what leads the reader to expect a solution relevant to Plato, while his clear and insightful articulation of

---

7. Russell (1912) provides full disclosure of the epistemological orientation of his approach from the outset: "In the following pages, I have confined myself in the main to those problems of philosophy in regard to which I thought it possible to say something positive and constructive, since merely negative criticism seemed out of place. For this reason, theory of knowledge occupies a larger space than metaphysics in the present volume, and some topics much discussed by philosophers are treated very briefly, if at all" (Russell 1912, v). His justification of the epistemological focus of the book as the result ("for this reason") of his goal to say something positive and constructive suggests that he does not find metaphysics to serve that end as well as epistemology.

8. While the present volume is exclusively about the metaphysics of Forms, with particular attention to the corresponding ontology, both as it concerns the Forms themselves and as it affects the world in which they exist, the best treatment of the epistemology of a dualism of worlds in Plato will be found in the various contributions of Nicholas D. Smith (2000; 2012; 2019). The foreword to the present volume, drafted by Smith himself, may be consulted for a preliminary acquaintance with his views on the matter.

the metaphysical problem is what leads one to expect a solution relevant to metaphysics. The best candidate for an effort to make up for both voids in the original volume is a paper titled "On the Relation of Universals and Particulars," read before the Aristotelian Society and published as part of the corresponding proceedings (Russell 1911–1912). Indeed, that paper addresses the precise problem identified in the relevant part of the book (Russell 1912, 157), and left untreated in the remainder, where neither Plato nor the problem (as initially formulated) ever comes up again:

> The purpose of the following paper is to consider whether there is a fundamental division of the objects with which metaphysics is concerned in the two classes, universals and particulars, or whether there is any method of overcoming this dualism. (Russell 1911–1912, 1)

This statement of purpose is accompanied by an outright confession that no meaningful reconciliation of the two worlds is possible: "My own opinion is that the dualism is ultimate" (Russell 1911–1912, 1). Although Russell does not once mention Plato in his address before the Aristotelian Society, not even in passing, the dualism he there declares to be "ultimate," and therefore impossible to resolve, is the same dualism he attributes to Plato in his short monograph (1912, 141–157).

While Russell denies the possibility of a solution, Armstrong denies the existence of a problem. This may appear to be a matter of each overshooting the mark in the opposite direction of the other, but that is not what is going on. The reason why such a comparison may seem tempting, despite being misleading, is that Armstrong, without much argumentation, though not without justification, reduces the problem to a misunderstanding. The location of the matter outside the realm of resolution through argumentation is exactly why he favors the reduction. To be more specific, he acknowledges the need for a connection between the separate realms he had earlier placed at Plato's doorstep—"Platonic heaven" and "the ordinary world of space and time" (Armstrong 1989, 79)—but instead of seeking a solution, he submits, rightly in my opinion, that there is no problem, none, that is, with the phenomenal instantiation of transcendent Forms otherwise residing in a Platonic heaven:

> What of the need for a fundamental tie—the tie or nexus of instantiation? Many people have thought it an overwhelming

difficulty for a theory of universals. I do not think that the problem of characterizing the nature of the tie should detain us. This was Plato's concern in the first part of his *Parmenides*. There he showed conclusively that the relation of particular to form cannot be either "participation" or "imitation." But it is perfectly reasonable for an upholder of universals to claim that instantiation is a primitive that cannot be explicated by any analysis, definition, or metaphor. (Armstrong 1989, 108)

The lack of concern Armstrong displays in his denial that "the problem of characterizing the nature of the tie should detain us" (1989, 108) is entirely appropriate for the problem under consideration. Instantiation is indeed a "primitive" that neither allows nor requires further explanation. Yet it works best in a single world and not in two separate ones as Armstrong has it. This will become apparent in due course as unitary pluralism is developed as an alternative to metaphysical dualism. Demonstrating the unity of Plato's world is, after all, the impetus behind the extended project initiated as a series of essays and subsequently brought together in the present work.

In contrast to Russell's denial of a solution and Armstrong's rejection of the problem, Sedley fully acknowledges the difficulty but entrusts the solution to Plato:

In view of this causal role of Forms, the radical separation of the two worlds comes at a price. The more separate the two worlds are, the harder it becomes to understand how Forms can have any causal or indeed other impact on the world we inhabit. To his eternal credit Plato, far from shirking this problem, devoted several intricate pages of his own dialogue the *Parmenides* (127d–134c) to airing it. (Sedley 2016, 11–12)

The question whether Plato actually solved the problem, and if so, what that solution is, continues to trouble commentators, who are still nowhere near a consensus. Sedley's otherwise accurate assessment of the situation does not take us very far toward a solution. This is not a shortcoming in Sedley's appraisal. It is merely a reflection of the state of the Platonic corpus. Following the only course open to him upon leaving the matter up to Plato, Sedley (2016, 12–14) goes through the association paradigms in the *Parmenides* in an effort to elucidate the relationship between the two worlds he attributes to Plato. Like many others, though unlike Armstrong (1989, 108), Sedley settles on "resemblance" (discussed further in section 1.4 below) as Plato's solution to the problem.

Where Armstrong denies a problem, and Sedley finds a solution, they both appeal to the same set of considerations. They both use "resemblance" interchangeably with "imitation," and vice versa, in the relevant context (*Parmenides* 127d–134c), pace R. E. Allen (1960; 1965), who sees a decisive difference between the two analogies. Hence, it is true, as Armstrong (1989, 108) claims, that the resemblance analogy is rejected in the *Parmenides* as a paradigm for the relationship between Forms and particulars, and also true, as Sedley (2016, 13) claims, that the same analogy is invoked in other dialogues, at least one of which is generally acknowledged to come after the *Parmenides*, which then seems to overturn, or override, the apparent rejection. But what is really true, then, is that there is considerable uncertainty in the matter. That is how Sedley is able to credit Plato with a solution (through the resemblance paradigm) where Armstrong sees nothing more than a rejected alternative (in the resemblance paradigm).

Even if Sedley were right, and Armstrong wrong, resemblance would not settle the matter. The analogy of resemblance is not so much a solution to the problem of how two separate worlds can be connected, as it is a description of that connection, the possibility of which still requires explanation and justification. Resemblance is clearly not a conclusive answer, nor therefore a satisfactory one, to the question of how things in one world could possibly be associated with those in another if they are separated so radically as to require two different worlds to accommodate their existence. Resemblance is merely a contemplation or conceptualization of that association, not a demonstration or justification of it. A challenger granting the replacement of "association" with "resemblance" as the preferred paradigm could always resubmit the original query as a follow-up question, after the necessary modification, thus asking how things in one world could possibly resemble those in another, given that they are separated so radically as to require two different worlds to accommodate their existence.

One response Plato could offer is that we are able to grasp the resemblance in question through the recollection of our previous exposure to the world of Forms, specifically as disembodied souls prior to our incarnation in the world of space and time, where we subsequently become restricted to and by the conditions of our phenomenal experience.

But that is still an epistemological perspective rather than a metaphysical one. The ontology of the matter remains a mystery even if we accept the epistemological explanation that resemblance triggers recollection, which is grounded in and enabled by reincarnation. Recollection is neither the only conceivable response nor one that is accepted universally as Plato's considered opinion—see Thesleff (1999, 86 [= 2009, 468]), who dismisses it as a thought experiment abandoned by Plato himself—but the main point is that it is the wrong sort of answer here regardless of its plausibility in any other context.

The question here is not how we might be able to grasp the alleged resemblance but how there can be such a resemblance in the first place. The appeal to reincarnation coupled with recollection does not establish a link between the two worlds themselves. It simply assumes or presupposes such a link. It thereby puts us, as ostensibly immortal rational beings, in a position to experience both worlds, one at a time, and to compare notes afterward. The worlds themselves, together with everything in them, remain separate, while the ontology, therefore, remains a problem. This is probably why Sedley does not invoke recollection as a possible solution, though he does cover the underlying doctrine (*Meno* 81a–86c; *Phaedo* 72e–77a; *Phaedrus* 249b–250b) as part of his general overview of Plato's Forms (2016, 4–7).

My protest is anachronistic, of course, relative to Plato, who did not separate the epistemology of the matter, any matter, from the metaphysics of it. It is also irrelevant with respect to the Greek mindset in general, where truth was considered a reflection of reality and knowledge was regarded as insight into the way things are, thus making any solution from the epistemological perspective equally acceptable from the metaphysical perspective. Yet the reason that Sedley focuses exclusively on the epistemology of the problem, as does Russell before him, is not that metaphysical matters need not be addressed separately in the Platonic context so long as the epistemology is working out. The deciding reason, rather, is that there really is no solution to the metaphysical quagmire of separating, or duplicating, the worlds, and still expecting a relationship, which is exactly what Russell concludes (1911–1912, 1).

Despite their differences, all three commentators retain the dualism of worlds, which vitiates the viability of Armstrong's and Sedley's responses, while confirming Russell's position that the gap between two separate worlds precludes the possibility of a relationship between them. Armstrong may be right that instantiation is patently valid as a fundamental reality that cannot be broken down any further, and Sedley may be right that resemblance is Plato's favorite paradigm for the instantiation in question, but both answers work best without the second world, the elimination of which would naturally benefit Russell as well, since he otherwise considers the metaphysical gap insurmountable. As things stand, however, we have Russell (1911–1912; 1912) denying that there is a solution, Armstrong (1989) denying that there is a problem, and Sedley (2016) claiming that Plato solved it.

A solution to a problem that does not exist yet cannot be solved is typical of the state of scholarship in Plato, where the best minds come together on a regular basis with profound insights in mutual contradiction. The three interpretations considered here, notwithstanding their differences, illustrate one of the rare exceptions to widespread disagreement as they converge on the dualism of worlds. The next step is to specify what is in those worlds. While the interpretations here come with the worlds fully populated, the inhabitants being evident to varying degrees in some of the preceding quotations, it is best to examine the contents separately from the worlds, as they are, in fact, independent considerations.

One of the worlds is reserved for Forms. That is the whole point of the dualism. But what about the other one? What, indeed, are the Forms the Forms of? Why, things, of course. Never mind that these "things" are all in a separate world, where it remains something of a curiosity, to say the least, that they can interact at all with the Forms, which would require actual contact between the two worlds, thereby seriously undermining the presumed separation, not just the likelihood or feasibility of such a separation but the sole reason for it. Yet even if we were to ignore any and all problems concerning a relationship between the two worlds, the simple answer, "things," would still be prone to ambiguity, and therefore open to debate, given that the Forms are themselves things.

The latter difficulty can be removed by restricting the sense intended by the reference to "things," but a modified sense will not be evident in the word alone, which will continue to be ambiguous if it is ambiguous to begin with. Modifying the reference itself will be better than restricting the intension or extension. The most accurate characterization of the relationship is probably that of Forms versus the things of which they are Forms, where the contrast is no longer between Forms and things without differentiation or qualification, as if Forms were not things, but between Forms and things of the relevant kind. While this formulation cannot possibly be wrong, it is also not very informative. Even with a clear distinction between things that are Forms and things that are not Forms, where the ones that are not Forms are obviously the things of which the Forms are Forms, the reference is still to things, which is too general to be illuminating.

That is why it is more common to express the relationship in more meaningful ways, or at least in more familiar ways, since it is always easier to assign meaning to that which is familiar, or to appreciate any meaning that is already there. The most familiar way of putting it is as an opposition of Forms versus particulars. This formulation is widely used because it immediately brings out the universal nature of Forms as against the particular nature of the things instantiating them. And it is widely criticized for the same reason, that is, for making Forms out to be universals in some sense or other, while not everyone agrees that Plato's Forms are universals in any sense at all, to say nothing of the frustrating absence of consensus on what exactly universals are. As a result, those who routinely contrast Forms with particulars are typically careful to add at minimum that Forms are not just universals but universals with objective reality, lest anyone should object that universals do not really exist whereas Plato says that the Forms do. That distinction is liable to be lost on anyone holding universals themselves to have objective reality, which would then fail to distinguish Forms from universals. But those upon whom the qualification is lost in that sense would not be the ones to object that Plato's Forms are not universals. The dissenters will be those who accept the provision of objective reality but continue to reject the characterization of Forms as universals.

One alternative in such cases is to redefine or reposition the relationship between Forms and particulars as a relationship between particulars of one kind and particulars of another kind. Frank Grabowski, for example, makes the Forms perfect particulars, "combining the rigidity and unchanging nature of mathematical truths with the perceptible quality of ordinary sensible particulars" (2008, 10). M. M. McCabe, in turn, speaks of a contrast between "austere individuals" (Forms) and "generous individuals" (particulars), terms emphasizing the difference between the ontological simplicity-cum-purity of Forms and the complexity and contamination of particulars, only the former and not the latter being free of the compresence of opposites (1994, 4; cf. 3–21, 25–52, 53–94). A more conventional way out is to retain the basic terminology of Forms versus particulars while adding qualifiers. One such qualification yields intelligible Forms in contrast to sensible particulars. Another describes Forms as abstract and particulars as concrete, thus giving us abstract Forms versus concrete particulars. Yet another may emphasize the transcendent against the phenomenal, or the immaterial against the material, but the examples soon start to look alike.

The predilection for qualification is amplified by two related concerns. One is the possibility that Forms are not strictly intelligible, abstract, or transcendent, as evidenced by those that are, somehow, at least partly sensible, concrete, or immanent. The other is the possibility that particulars are not necessarily sensible, concrete, or immanent, as evidenced by those that are intelligible, abstract, or transcendent. Examples of either kind turn on the degrees of observationality attached to the distinction between the intelligible and the sensible, the abstract and the concrete, the transcendent and the immanent, and so on. Recall how beauty, for example, is portrayed in the *Phaedrus* (250b–e) as a Form that can be discerned to some extent even in our phenomenal experience.

Further examples, combined with stimulating discussion, can be found in Gail Fine (1993, 23, n. 27, 249–250), who concludes that "we should still not take the distinction between particulars and universals to be that between the perceivable and unperceivable" (1993, 250). While Fine's concern is specifically with attempts to distinguish between universals and particulars, as she is discussing Aristotle rather than Plato, her assessment that no such attempt is entirely satisfactory applies equally well to the distinction between Plato's Forms and particulars (1993, 24–25).[9] For her own part, Fine regards Plato's Forms as paradigmatic properties, or more simply, as properties that serve as paradigms (1993, 24, 63–64).

The terminology of Forms versus particulars will always remain open to objection, but hardly any commentator on Plato uses these terms in

---

9. Fine (1993) puts the difference between Plato's Forms and Aristotle's universals as follows: "But precisely how do forms and Aristotelian universals differ? Aristotle thinks they share some features. For example, he is a realist about the existence of universals, and he takes Plato to be one too—that is, he takes both Platonic forms and his own universals to be real entities distinct from such things as particulars, predicates, meanings, concepts, and classes. As attention to the *Peri Ideōn* reveals, Aristotle also takes forms to be the basic objects of knowledge, unobservable or nonsensible, everlasting, and (probably) unchangeable. In just the same way, Aristotle takes his own universals to be the basic objects of knowledge; and he takes at least many of them to be everlasting, unobservable, and unchangeable. However, Aristotle takes Platonic forms but not his own universals to be separate, self-predicative, perfect paradigms" (Fine 1993, 25).

ignorance of the problems and difficulties, and no alternative is immune to objection. As presumptuous as the stark contrast between Forms and particulars may appear, especially when read as taking Forms to be nothing more than universals, an offhand rejection would be just as objectionable, not only in denying that the Forms are universals in any sense, but also in assuming that the usage in question makes them universals in every sense. Plato's Forms may not be universals in the modern sense, nor even in the Aristotelian sense, differing at least in being reified and transcendent albeit instantiable, but if they were not universals in some sense, how then could they be Forms in the relevant sense, revealed through Plato's repeated acknowledgment of a Form for every multitude of things with a group identity (*Republic* 596a; *Parmenides* 130d–e, 135a–d; *Timaeus* 51c)? Any version of the claim that Forms are particulars rather than universals, no matter how it is expressed, always comes across, on some level, as saying that universals are particulars rather than universals. That is a testament to the strength of our conditioning to associate Forms with universals, with either concept then constituting the proper complement for particulars.[10]

Yet the distinction between Forms and particulars is not the only meaningful if controversial way of articulating the relationship between Forms and the things of which they are Forms. Another option is to put the matter in terms of a contrast between Forms and sensible phenomena. That can be just as problematic in an entirely different way. A comparison of Forms with sensible phenomena may work well for concrete things, such as horses, cups, and tables, but not so much for ideal values, such as prudence, courage, and temperance; nor for ordinary properties, such as redness, largeness, and brightness; nor for universal relations, such as rest and motion, or same and other. Not all of these things qualify as sensible phenomena, at least not in the same sense. The case of the horse will easily pass any test of observationality, as will that of cups and tables and so on. To some extent, color and size and the like are also quite perceptible, though not when taken by themselves, like horses or cups or tables, and only in connection with the things we actually do perceive around us. At the opposite end from full observationality, however, prudence, courage,

---

10. F. C. White devotes considerable attention to Plato's conception of particulars, tracing the development of his views in that regard through a series of contributions to the literature, including one book (1981) and several articles (1976; 1977; 1978a; 1978b; 1982; 1988), all listed among the works cited in the bibliography at the end of the present volume.

and temperance, and the virtues in general, would be pushing the limits of what and how much we get through sense perception alone. Even if justice, for example, were invariably attached to something that is observational, say, a specific act or event, justice itself would still not be observational, and therefore, would not qualify as a sensible phenomenon the way that horses readily do. Observing justice always requires greater recourse to interpretation and evaluation than does observing horses.

There is no expression that perfectly captures the intended relationship between Plato's Forms and whatever they are the Forms of. All three formulations considered so far (Forms vs. things, Forms vs. particulars, Forms vs. sensible phenomena), and perhaps a few variations thereof (including looser references to Forms and their instantiations), are used without apology throughout this book. Such references are not intended to assert, represent, or sneak in without argument, a decisive position either on what the Forms are, that is, on their ontological status, or on what they are the Forms of, that is, on the nature and variety of the things instantiating them. They are intended merely as conventional references to a relationship all students of Plato invoke in one way or another, none being entirely satisfactory for everyone, but each being immediately recognizable by anyone. The establishment of any particular position regarding the ontology of Plato is reserved for dialectical development in subsequent chapters. But that is no reason to shy away, even at this early stage, from saying what a Form is. Plato's Socrates would surely admonish us thus: How can you know anything about the Forms, even whether they exist at all, unless you can say what a Form is?

1.3. What Are the Forms?

After a couple of millennia and several centuries, we still do not agree on an answer, but we now have quite a few good ones. Some of the most relevant contributions are mentioned at the end of this chapter, though covering all of them is no more necessary than it is possible. The aim of this section is to illustrate the most compelling approaches, together with the most interesting scholarship, since there is no particular consensus to speak of, nor any practical way of putting one together as a patchwork, synthesis, or distillation of the leading conceptions and analyses.

A consensus of opinion on what the Forms are remains hopelessly beyond reach where, as illustrated in the preceding section, we cannot even agree on whether they are (more like) universals or (more like) particulars, or possibly (more like) something in between, or perhaps (more like) something altogether different. I. M. Crombie (1963), for one, is certain that they are universals rather than particulars:

> The conclusion then of this discussion is that the forms were not perfect schematised particulars, they were universals or common natures. Or, to put it more precisely, the concept of a universal was the concept that Plato was trying to isolate and give expression to when he wrote about forms. (Crombie 1963, 270)

Grabowski (2008), as mentioned above, takes them to be perfect particulars:

> These considerations led Plato to posit the existence of Forms, not as abstract universals, but rather as *concrete exemplars* or *perfect particulars*, combining the rigidity and unchanging nature of mathematical truths with the perceptible quality of ordinary sensible particulars; or, at least, this is *likely* what he takes them to be. (Grabowski 2008, 10)

McCabe (1994), also mentioned above, comes closer to Grabowski than to Crombie, though she draws the comparison, not in terms of two different kinds of particulars, but in terms of individuals of one kind in contrast to individuals of another. Her primary distinction is between Forms as "austere (simple) individuals" as against particulars as "generous (complex) individuals" (McCabe 1994, 4; cf. 3–21, 25–52, 53–94), with the corresponding divisions also explicated in terms of a contrast between "intelligible individuals" and "sensible individuals" (1994, 78):

> Sensible individuals, first of all, are conceived in a *generous* way such that each may (or must) admit a multiplicity of properties. Forms, by direct contrast, are conceived in an *austere* way so as to exclude altogether any multiplicity or variation; they are "themselves by themselves," *auta kath' hauta*. (McCabe 1994, 78)

Yet it is entirely possible to speak of Forms, and even to define or describe them, while at the same time explaining how they differ from the things of which they are Forms, without once invoking universals, particulars, or individuals of any kind. Consider how Richard ("Red") Watson (1995) accomplishes this:

> Platonic Ideas are perfect, eternal, unchanging archetypes existing independently in the realm of Being, as opposed to changing ordinary things in the realm of Becoming. Each Idea is a model, exemplar, or paradigm that exhibits the perfect expression of the structural or ordered pattern or plan of a kind of thing. An Idea is an archetype that has being and can be apprehended. It is a hylomorphized set of structural relations essential to and exhibited by things of its type. It is not an abstract notion of an unexemplified set of relations which would be empty and unreal. Rather, each Platonic Idea is a perfect, real (ideal but existing) paradigm of a type of thing. (Watson 1995, 5)

Although he explicates the transcendence of Forms, or their separation, in the usual way, Watson neither endorses nor rejects a dualism of "worlds" as such, speaking instead of two different "realms," which could be taken either in exactly the same sense as "worlds," for a realm could conceivably be a world, or in the entirely different sense of "domains," possibly in indication of different spheres of influence within a single continuum. His emphasis on a radical difference and separation, however, suggests that he may, in fact, be thinking of realms in terms closer to worlds than to domains jointly constituting a single world:

> And further, even though the realms of Being and Becoming—and thus Ideas and things—are in many respects radically different and separate from one another, Ideas and things do resemble one another in a very straightforward way. Ideas are archetypes, perfect exemplars, patterns, or plans; things are imperfect manifestations or exemplifications of those same archetypes, patterns, and plans. (Watson 1995, 7)

More importantly, note that Watson is able to avoid identifying the Forms as universals, particulars, or individuals of any kind, only by describing them as something even more fluid and more difficult to classify, namely as archetypes, paradigms, patterns, and so on, any one of which could still qualify either as universals or as particulars, and certainly also as individuals, given that something's being an archetype, paradigm, or pattern neither requires nor prevents its being a universal, particular, or individual. Despite some temptation to interpret archetypes and the like as particulars, in which case they cannot be universals, though they might well be individuals, particularization of that sort is not imperative to account for what they are or what they are for. If the primary function of archetypes is to provide metaphysical grounding for exemplification, there is no good reason why they cannot be universals, or at least something very much like universals, and still serve in that capacity. Plato's conception of Forms is not so rigid as to preclude that possibility.

It may be objected that universals, as we commonly understand them, are abstracted from particulars, and are, in that sense, contingent upon particulars, because they come after them in terms of ontological priority, if not also with regard to temporal precedence, whereas archetypes and paradigms are just the opposite, given that they serve as models, which clearly places them before whatever is modeled after them. This is the kind of objection that Lloyd P. Gerson (2002, 91), for example, presents against associating Forms with concepts, the latter of which, much like universals, do not have the requisite ontological priority for the intended association. But the Forms need not be taken to be limited in that way, given that they are generally not taken to be limited in any of the ways that universals are, as evidenced most notably by the widely recognized objective reality of Forms (from Plato's perspective) in contrast to the controversial ontological status of universals.

The only reason that the problem arises at all is that the absence of formal definitions or clear instructions by Plato encourages us to develop heuristic interpretations of his Forms as being "just like x but without x's limitations of a, b, and c" in an effort to make sense of the Forms in terms that are more readily familiar to us. This approach is both acceptable and useful. It provides the justificatory context for the contemplation of Forms as universals, presumably in a reasonable way of central relevance, despite the ontological dependence of universals upon particulars, which could just as easily be accommodated in a list of exceptions exempting Forms from certain limitations ("a, b, and c" in the preceding formulation) as it could be brought up as a reason against the similarity of Forms to universals.

Gerson (2002) is not wrong to invoke ontological priority as an obstacle to the intended association, but removing ontological priority altogether from the domain of the intended association is not wrong either. The difference is a matter of interpretation. Plato could quite conceivably have anticipated the relevant features of universals without making them contingent upon particulars, in fact, possibly instead reversing that relationship to make particulars contingent upon Forms, which would thereby have escaped the standard impediment to their utilization as archetypes or paradigms. While too many such exceptions may eventually undermine the association intended, thereby eroding the grounds proposed for relevant similarity, that possibility has not yet weakened the scholarly tendency to construe the Forms as universals of some sort.

Watson does not push his own analogy very far in either direction, but his identification of Forms as archetypes is sufficient to suggest not just that he does not consider them universals instead of archetypes, which he obviously does not, but also that he does not consider them universals that are archetypes, or archetypes that are universals, which may not be so obvious. The reason to rule out any conception of "Forms as universals" as Watson's intended meaning is simply that the discussion of Forms in terms of universals is so popular that Watson would have been sure to lead with that had he considered the Forms universals as well as archetypes. While his silence on the matter certainly does not determine the matter, this would only be a problem if one were focusing exclusively on whether Plato's Forms are universals or particulars. Watson himself seems perfectly satisfied with identifying them as archetypes and leaving the matter at that, though his satisfaction is on firmer ground in epistemology than in metaphysics.[11] Either way, he manages to avoid direct engagement with the controversy over whether the Forms are universals or particulars.

The most interesting attempt to eliminate the problem itself, as opposed to merely avoiding the terminology, namely of universals versus particulars, is Nicholas Denyer's (1983) initiative to construe the Forms as "elemental stuffs" akin to chemical elements. Attributing the various interpretive problems surrounding Plato's conception of Forms to the historical tendency to treat them as universals, Denyer offers an analogical paradigm from chemistry as a solution:

> [A]ll the most troubling contentions that Plato makes about forms turn out to be either true or at least quite plausible if we

---

11. Watson (1995) is indeed concerned primarily with the epistemological perspective: "Nothing could be plainer. Plato took knowing Ideas, and, by projection 'knowing' things by way of Ideas, to be as unproblematic as—and just like—seeing things immediately in the unobstructed light of the sun" (Watson 1995, 7).

suppose that forms are meant, not as universals, but as chemical elements instead. Plato's theory of forms is not a grotesque misunderstanding of universals; it is a sober, intelligent, and largely true account of the elemental stuffs from which the world is made. (Denyer 1983, 315)

The central example is that of a gold ring, "my ring," as Denyer puts it in a fixed reference employed throughout the discussion (1983, 315–327). The relationship between Forms and the things of which they are Forms, Denyer submits, is comparable to the relationship between "my ring and gold, the element of which it is made" (1983, 316). Just as "my ring" is gold insofar as it is made of gold, that is, in virtue of its share in gold, so too are all things what they are in virtue of their share in the corresponding Forms. Gold itself, as an element, is just gold, pure and simple, whereas things that are made of gold, and called gold for that reason, are gold only in composition, and therefore only by association. The gold in something is not what that thing is but what it is made of. Accordingly, a gold object is not what it is, because of the gold; rather, it is the gold variety of whatever it is, because of the gold.

Denyer admits that the analogy breaks down at the subatomic level, where chemical elements incorporate fundamental particles in various combinations, as against the partless simplicity of Forms: "Plato's theory remains a plausible account of elemental stuffs only so long as we ignore the truth of atomism" (1983, 315). The analogy he is after in explication of Forms is not with the internal structure of chemical elements but with the way in which they account for the external structure of the world. While chemical elements are differentiated in accordance with the number of protons in their nuclei, they all account for our phenomenal experience of the world in the same way as Forms, with each object having a share in the element, or elements, with which it is associated.

Denyer's goal is not to prove that Plato's Forms represent the right approach to ontological and cosmological explanation, but to demonstrate that universals represent the wrong interpretation of that approach, regardless of what the right approach may be. What he thinks of Plato's approach, even under the right interpretation, is both frank and telling: "Sober and coherent, and also untrue" (Denyer 1983, 326). This is not a retraction of his earlier assessment of the "theory" of Forms as "sober, intelligent, and largely true" (Denyer 1983, 315) but an elaboration upon it in the context of prevailing paradigms in particle physics. His earlier endorsement is of the Platonic model as a practical interpretation of how the world works, while his later opposition is to the same model as a scientific explanation of how the world works.

One may be tempted to press Denyer on whether the "elemental stuffs" he adopts as the analogical correlates of Plato's Forms function more like universals or more like particulars, which would be to ask the same question raised above in connection with Watson's "archetypes." But that would be to insist arbitrarily on framing the discussion in terms of a distinction between universals and particulars, despite the rejection of that model and the presentation of an entirely different one, and in the absence of direct evidence either warranting or requiring the implied Aristotelian framework. Acknowledging and rejecting the Aristotelian alternative from the very first sentence, Denyer presents his own solution as a "more charitable, less Aristotelian, way to interpret what Plato says about forms" (1983, 315).[12]

Aristotelian strands in Platonic interpretation, particularly with respect to Forms, are due not just to Aristotle's brilliance as a philosopher, nor simply to his position as a student of Plato, but also to the unavailability of established terminology for the conceptual analysis Plato was conducting and the provisional results he was communicating. As Crombie (1963) rightly notes: "Plato was developing the notion of an abstract entity or universal at the same time as he was developing the language for conveying the notion" (1963, 263).

Much of the disagreement over Forms, including what they are and how they work, comes from differences of opinion as to the purposes they serve. Why does Plato invoke the Forms? What does he do with them?

---

12. Watson (1995) and Denyer (1983) are not alone in describing the Forms as something besides universals (whether or not their being universals is ruled out in the process). Peter D. Larsen (2018), for example, without ever bringing up universals, construes the Forms basically as essences, whatever else they may happen to be. This is, of course, still consistent with their being universals, not to mention any number of comparable or compatible things, at least in the sense that the corresponding possibilities are mutually independent. Being an essence neither requires nor precludes being a universal (or an archetype, or a paradigm, or a pattern, and so on). Larsen himself is evidently cognizant of the inherent plasticity of his formulation, and sensitive to its broad compatibility with complementary accounts, which seems to be why he readily and repeatedly acknowledges in advance "whatever else" may be true of the Forms, while designating them primarily as essences, thus leaving open a host of parallel possibilities.

Where does he use them? These are not very difficult questions. But there are too many answers, most of them correct. Sorting them out will help put the foregoing considerations into perspective. Although gaining that perspective requires some repetition, it affords even greater insight, not unlike how the cosmological account of the *Timaeus* starts over from the perspective of necessity (47e–68d) right after covering the perspective of reason (29d–47e). Studying the functions typically assigned to the Forms will help us to understand the essence commonly attributed to them.

The evidence is clear: Plato uses the Forms to distinguish reality from appearance, to recognize permanence against change, to discern stability within flux, to prove continuity over time, to reconcile being with becoming, to uphold unity in plurality, to explain identity in difference, to establish objectivity in values, and to demonstrate the unity of the virtues. Even the most casual reflection on only the most salient patterns of dialectical development in the Platonic corpus will confirm that these answers are all correct, though there may be others that are correct as well. Yet commentators typically have a favorite answer, usually to the exclusion of other answers, and sometimes in outright rejection of other answers.

McCabe (1994), for example, regards the Forms as Plato's solution to the problem of individuation. She finds them relevant, not to the question of what there is, nor to that of what the world is made of, as is usually supposed, but to the entirely different question of what it is that makes anything an individual thing. She reads Plato as abandoning the foundational question of what there is, or what the world is made of, for the more pressing question of what it is that makes anything "one something" as she puts it. The reason for the transition, according to McCabe, is that the question of what there is, or what the world is made of, cannot be answered through the Forms, whose utter purity and partless simplicity precludes interaction either with each other or with anything else, which then leaves too much unexplained.

But why would anyone so passionately curious as to seek out the fundamental principles of metaphysics, as a persistent matter of course, that is, as part of a routine intellectual pursuit, ever abandon that search, even upon, nay, especially upon, discovering problems with the initial formulation of answers? Why indeed would Plato move on to an entirely different problem, instead of working on unfinished business, or doing both at once? Concern with the principles of individuation is consistent with concern with the ontological constituents of the world. The Plato we know was both industrious enough and competent enough to tackle all sorts of philosophical problems at the same time, even though it is not clear whether he actually solved any of them.

We have to assume, at any rate, that he tried, and therefore that his Forms were, at least in his own mind, good for something besides solving the problem of individuation. The Forms are flexible enough, if only because Plato makes very few ontological commitments, to accommodate the critical examination of a variety of philosophical problems, including ethical and epistemological ones, as well as metaphysical ones. The inherent flexibility of Forms, combined with their novelty, both in regard to rationale and with respect to terminology, is the main reason why Plato's ancient initiative continues to attract diverse attempts to explain the matter in more familiar terms.[13] That is also why concepts and universals are quick to come to mind in modern attempts to make sense of the Forms.[14]

The concept of "concept" was so alien, and that of "universal" so Aristotelian, that the language Plato had to work with did not have any words reserved specifically for either one of them, though it had at least a dozen words that were relevant albeit not quite equivalent to "concept,"[15]

---

13. Various aspects of terminology, both Greek and English, are discussed further in chapter 2 (section 2.5). Additional sources worth consulting include the following: Ademollo (2013, 41–85, especially 56–69), Baldry (1934, 141–150), Else (1936, 17–55), Herrmann (2007b), Taylor (1911, 178–267).

14. Helmig (2004; 2007; 2012), and Schumacher (2010) expanding on Helmig (2004), are notable for their examination of the place of Forms in the process of concept formation in knowledge acquisition, with particular emphasis on the role of recollection (*anamnēsis*) in Plato's epistemology. Gerson (1999a; 1999b), Thorp (1984), and Warner (1965) are prominent forerunners, providing points of departure as well as revealing areas of convergence.

15. Helmig (2012) recognizes more than a dozen words, including quite a few variations of each, as comparable ancient designations for what we now think of as concepts: "In Antiquity, several words can stand for a concept: *axiōma, archē, eidos / genos, ennoia, koinai ennoiai, epinoia, noēma, ennoēma, logos, katholou, katholou logoi, koinon, lekton, prolēpsis*. Some of these expressions can be qualified by means of adjectives such as *doxastos / doxastikos* (pertaining to *doxa*), *husterogenēs* (later-born or of later origin, that is, abstracted), *ousiōdēs* (essential), or *ennoēmatikos* (having the nature of a concept). These latter adjectives can, in turn, be used as nouns" (Helmig 2012, 14–15). He notes that the most important ones are *ennoia* (*koinai ennoiai*), *logos*, and *katholou*, identifying *ennoia* as dating back to Plato, while making the usual connection between *katholou* and Aristotle (Helmig 2012, 15).

including *katholou*, invented by Aristotle, or rather appropriated by him (*kata* + *holos*), in his customary distinction between universals (*tōn katholou*) and particulars (*tōn kath' hekaston*).[16] Yet the absence of a direct Greek equivalent in Plato's day for what we now mean by "concept," or by "universal," would not necessarily have prevented him from exploring the logic, language, and metaphysics of abstraction, particularly through concepts and universals, reified or otherwise, as one aspect of what he was doing with the Forms. Plato could well have been inventing, exploring, and reifying concepts and universals, all at once, as part of a single yet protracted philosophical process, given that neither he nor anyone else at the time was quite sure what to do with abstract ideas, if they had any interest in them at all.

Plato's Forms are certainly not, strictly speaking, either concepts or universals, but they do indeed seem to be what he came up with in trying to fill that conceptual void in his day and in his way. There are, of course, significant differences, both in essence and in function, between what Plato presented as Forms and what we now think of as concepts or universals. The most important difference, and one that is invariably at the forefront of discussion, is that the Forms have an undisputed claim to objective reality, whereas concepts and universals both divide philosophers in regard to their ontological status. Granted, plenty of philosophers also deny that the Forms exist, in fact, with no less conviction than they deny that universals exist, but nobody denies that Plato takes the Forms to exist. For his own part, Plato clearly bestows upon the Forms an existence outside the mind (*Parmenides* 132b–c), whereas we are still nowhere near a consensus on whether concepts and universals exist, except perhaps in a representational sense as mental constructs in our mind.

Other differences that are commonly acknowledged, for example, by Holger Thesleff, and by me, but also by various others, bring out a host of features common and peculiar to Plato's Forms. A typical list would indicate that the Forms are transcendent, intelligible, paradigmatic, perfect,

---

16. Plato's Forms do qualify as universals in the Aristotelian sense: "I call universal [*katholou*] that which is by its nature predicated of a number of things, and particular [*kath' hekaston*] that which is not; man, for instance, is a universal [*katholou*], Callias a particular [*kath' hekaston*]" (*De Interpretatione* 17a38–b1). The relevance to Plato becomes obvious, or is at least made explicit, as Aristotle himself construes Plato's Forms as universals in his own references and objections (*Metaphysics* 1038b35–1039a3, 1040b25–30, 1086a32–35).

immutable, simple, and unique.[17] Various combinations of these features, and, no doubt, yet others, are typically adduced in expository accounts of Plato's Forms or of his metaphysics in general (as in Press 2012, 173–175, 218–220). The list is not definitive, though it is sufficiently indicative. There will be those who object that certain features do not belong on the list, as well as those who detect omissions that do belong on the list, and yet others who may find some of the existing features either jointly redundant or mutually inconsistent. The aim, however, is to start with a comprehensive account taking stock of all the things Plato seems to say of the Forms, sorting it all out later through further reflection and comparative analysis. It is better not to neglect anything, even at the cost of some initial clutter, than to be too selective and miss the point from the beginning.

The one thing that such a list establishes beyond the slightest doubt, be it the very list just presented or any of the countless others put together by other commentators, is that the Forms are special. Whatever they are like, they are like a superlative version, not the exact same thing. That is why it will never do to object that the Forms are not concepts, or that they are not universals, in response to anyone attempting to explain what they are through those and similar analogies as points of reference. Modern comparisons between Plato's Forms and anything else, including abstractions, archetypes, categories, concepts, exemplars, kinds, particulars, patterns, properties, templates, types, and universals, are hardly ever intended to suggest that the Forms are exactly like one of those things. Anyone claiming that the Forms are essentially concepts, universals, or patterns typically means that we may, in order to make sense of the Forms in terms readily familiar to us, think of them as concepts, universals, or patterns that happen to have at least an objective reality, as well as several other features we must recognize if we wish to remain faithful to the texts.

The specific features may differ from one interpreter to the next, but the general sovereignty and ascendancy of the Forms does not. It is clear that Plato sees some sort of supremacy there, though it may be difficult to

---

17. The same list of characteristics, presented as essential features of Plato's Forms, can be found in chapter 2 (section 2.6), chapter 3 (section 3.4), chapter 4 (section 4.4), and chapter 5 (section 5.3). The list is neither my own invention nor Thesleff's, though it does reflect our mutual agreement. Many of the items find their way onto comparable lists by other scholars, who either add a few features or leave some out, usually doing both. In any event, the list is intended to be representative rather than exhaustive.

agree on a complete set of characteristics. In addition to being objectively real, the Forms have an ontological profile superior in various other ways as well to that of concepts, universals, patterns, and the like. First and foremost, they have a logical and ontological priority over the things of which they are Forms, as already touched upon in this chapter, whereas concepts and universals are abstracted from the things of which they are concepts or universals. Patterns, exemplars, and templates may not count as abstractions in the same way (as being abstracted from instances), but they, too, remain contingent upon the things to which they refer, given that they would not exist without anything specific to represent as a pattern, exemplar, or template. This gives the Forms an ontological independence, where neither their existence nor their essence depends on sensible phenomena. They also boast a causal efficacy and explanatory power, nowhere to be found in concepts, universals, and other analogues commonly invoked in trying to define or describe the Forms by analogy. They are the reason why the world is the way it is.

Yet none of this shows that Plato's Forms are not in any way like concepts or universals. It is perfectly acceptable, or at least not grossly inaccurate, to liken them to concepts or universals, or to any other reasonable analogue, in certain functional senses that help illuminate what they are and what they are good for. They are, for one thing, the results of Plato's thought experiments in abstraction and conceptualization in the process of dealing with specific philosophical problems, such as those enumerated above: distinguishing reality from appearance, recognizing permanence against change, discerning stability within flux, proving continuity over time, reconciling being with becoming, upholding unity in plurality, explaining identity in difference, establishing objectivity in values, and demonstrating the unity of the virtues.

Does that make them concepts, or universals, or the like? No, Plato clearly rules that out, or has Parmenides do it for him, denying outright that the Forms are thoughts or ideas (*noēmata*, cf. *Parmenides* 132b–c). But what is ruled out there is a contingent existence restricted to the mind. That is not the same as denying that the Forms are "überconcepts" or "superuniversals," as it were, the reified and superlative referents of concepts and universals, which then makes the Forms the transcendent correlates of concepts and universals, with an objective reality, ontological priority, and metaphysical supremacy normally not recognized in such things.

To be fair to critics defending the opposite perspective, we must acknowledge that their objection to construing the Forms as concepts or universals is rarely ever made in ignorance of the fact that those who construe them as such are aware of the difference between the objective reality Plato ascribes to the Forms and the open question through which we nowadays discuss the ontological status of concepts and universals. Their objection, or the strongest objection anyway, is not that the existence of the Forms is certain from Plato's perspective, whereas that of concepts and universals is controversial from ours, but that the Forms are depicted as determining reality, giving the world the structure that it has, whereas concepts and universals are determined by reality, representing the structure that is already there. We form concepts and identify universals insofar as we are able to make sense of the framework and details of the universe as observers whose inherent cognitive abilities, deficient though they may be, in all cases include pattern recognition, regardless of whether the corresponding pattern is an integral part of reality or a heuristic construction enabling us to explore and understand our world, the latter originating as a survival mechanism preserved and developed through natural selection. The Forms, in contrast, are ingrained in the very fabric of reality, independently of whatever we may happen to think of the world, and indeed, independently even of whether we ourselves happen to exist.

As true as it is that nobody, or hardly anybody, who explains the Forms in terms of concepts, universals, or patterns, contends that the Forms are nothing more than concepts, universals, or patterns, it is just as true that nobody, or hardly anybody, who objects to such an explanation objects to it on the grounds that the attendant analogy contradicts the objective reality of the Forms as against the lack of agreement on a comparable rationale for concepts and universals. Gerson (1999a; 1999b; 2002; 2004a; 2004b), to return to his viewpoint, rejects the explanation on entirely different grounds, fully granting that the analogy may be drawn in cognizance of the difference between the modes of existence, or the degrees of reality, attributed to Forms versus those attributed to concepts and universals. He objects instead that we cannot reasonably construe the Forms as concepts, because they would actually have to be, not mere concepts, but the things of which concepts are concepts, in order to do what the Forms are supposed to do. And what are they supposed to do? "As everyone knows, separate Forms are adduced by the Platonists to explain identity in difference, not concepts" (Gerson 1999a, 65).[18] As for

---

18. Gerson's focus on the role of Forms in the ancient approach to identity in difference is a common theme in his interpretation of Plato and Platonism. Examples

universals, those, like concepts, and unlike Forms, lack the ontological priority required to be useful in metaphysical explanation:

> The reason why forms are not universals is simply that forms are ontological explanatory entities and universals are not. Universals in fact do not explain anything ontologically precisely because they are ontologically posterior to that to which they are made to apply. That which is ontologically posterior cannot explain that which is ontological[ly] prior to it. (Gerson 2002, 91)

Gerson is absolutely right, but the appeal to concepts or universals in the process of defining or describing Forms need no more be made in ignorance of the special ontological and metaphysical status of Forms, including the full range of attributes that set them apart from anything else, than the same appeal is ever made in ignorance of the axiomatic existence of Forms. Dissenters rejecting descriptive and explanatory accounts in analogical terms invoking concepts and universals, if they are astute and fair enough to recognize that the type of description or explanation in question is never intended to deny the objective reality of Forms, must be prepared to acknowledge that such descriptions and explanations are also not intended to strip the Forms of any of the other features responsible for their ontological and metaphysical differences from concepts and universals, including their intelligibility, transcendence, immutability, and so on, and so forth.

It is not merely charitable but also intellectually responsible and methodologically obligatory of dissenters to accept that no serious scholar of Plato thinks that Plato's Forms are nothing more than concepts, universals, or patterns. But no agreement on that point will go far enough if it stops at the objective reality of Forms, proceeding to make an issue out of everything else that sets the Forms apart from concepts and universals and such. Whenever anyone likens the Forms to any of these things, or to any others in the vocabulary of professional philosophers, what they mean is that the Forms work like these things in relevant ways that may already be familiar to us, while in themselves retaining a superior ontological and metaphysical status consistent with the differences typically noted by dissenters.

---

include: Gerson 1990, 79; 1999a, 65; 1999b, 12; 2002, 88–90, passim; 2004a, 306, passim; 2004b, 237–239, 254.

Dissenters may surely object, and not without good reason, that if the Forms are so different from concepts and universals, then they are not really like concepts and universals. Perhaps they are not. But analogy is an instrument of comprehension. Likeness, in turn, is a function of perspective, a reflection of purpose, and a matter of degree. Of course, the Forms are not just like concepts or universals. And maybe they are not even sufficiently similar to concepts or universals for a convincing or meaningful comparison. Yet the conviction or the meaning is precisely what is in question here, which then makes it unreasonable to dismiss either analogue, or any others, without argumentation or demonstration. If the objective is to understand the Forms, it is best not to reject comparisons with other things, so long as they are not patently and completely irrelevant, given that Plato himself does not clearly state what the Forms are. They may not be much like concepts or universals, but that is only because they are not, in fact, quite like anything else. If we submit to that restriction, however, all we are left with for an explanation is that the Forms are just Forms. That is not very helpful, as it amounts to nothing more than an instantiation of Bishop Butler's tautological dictum that "everything is what it is, and not another thing."

As for my own view, it has already been stated twice in the course of discussion above. There is no harm in repeating it one more time: I take the Forms to be reified concepts or universals resulting from Plato's thought experiments in abstraction and conceptualization, constituting the methodological backbone of his lifelong dedication to the solution of philosophical problems, including, but not limited to, the ones listed above: distinguishing reality from appearance, recognizing permanence against change, discerning stability within flux, proving continuity over time, reconciling being with becoming, upholding unity in plurality, explaining identity in difference, establishing objectivity in values, and demonstrating the unity of the virtues.

The tripartite classification of Forms mentioned in the preface and outlined in the introduction, a recurring theme throughout the book, is thus indexed to the notion of universals. The way that Thesleff and I originally put it was that "Forms are what universals fail to be" (pp. 83, 117, n. 5, this volume), a playful allusion to McCabe's assessment that "Forms are what particulars fail to be" (1994, 60). This was our encapsulation of their ontological status as universals that are objectively real and transcendent yet instantiable, among other characteristics, fully illustrated in the original and duplicated here in the corresponding pages.

There is obviously some prima facie tension between transcendence and immanence, whereby the same thing cannot both transcend reality and be immanent in it, at least not in the same reality, nor in commensurate senses of transcendence and immanence in any reality. I find that tension exaggerated. I fully admit that the same thing cannot be both transcendent and immanent in a sense that retains the distinction while removing the contradiction. But some type of metaphorical reconciliation is quite conceivable, and it must indeed remain metaphorical to be at all reasonable, which then invites no amazement and requires no explanation. I see no problem with the possibility of Forms being instantiated in our phenomenal experience, despite being transcendent in themselves, because I do not consider the Forms themselves to become immanent when they are instantiated. I consider them instead to be, still and always, transcendent in and of themselves yet intelligible in a representational sense through the corresponding instantiation. Even the striking earthly manifestations of beauty (*Phaedrus* 250b–e) are just that, manifestations of beauty, and not direct encounters with beauty itself.[19] We are never in contact with the Form itself, at least not during our corporeal existence, no matter the strength of the instantiation, which then rules out the immanence of Forms in any sense contradicting the transcendence of Forms.

Our best bet for understanding the Forms, both in regard to what they are and with respect to how they work, is to look at how and where Plato uses them: philosophical reflection and dialectical development in epistemology, ontology, cosmology, ethics, and aesthetics, before these fields were even recognized as distinct divisions within philosophy. The solution to various problems in different fields invariably turns out to be contingent on the existence and essence of Forms, regardless of whether Plato discovered them or invented them. This is what makes them both the conceptual instruments and the most salient results of Plato's thought experiments. And it is also why they work more like universals in some

---

19. Although I do not consider the tension between transcendence and immanence to constitute a serious problem for Plato's metaphysics, further discussion is available in chapter 3 (section 3.4), chapter 5 (section 5.4), and chapter 7 (section 7.6). Readers interested in studying either transcendence or immanence in greater detail would do well to consult Fine, who takes up each phenomenon separately and with admirable clarity, first addressing transcendence through an essay on "separation" (Fine 1984; cf. 1985), and subsequently taking up immanence (Fine 1986), though naturally with some overlap in either case.

places, more like particulars in others, and more like patterns or paradigms in some places, more like properties or categories in others.[20] Different problems come with different solutions developed through different thought experiments, each one bringing a different feature of the Forms into the foreground.

Admittedly, the variation in experimentation may not be sufficient as an explanation or justification of all the apparent discrepancies in Plato's conception of Forms in one dialogue versus another, but it is definitely where all the Forms come from. Regarding specific inconsistencies, such as their amenability to interpretation as universals as well as particulars, depending on the context, it is entirely possible that Plato may have changed his mind one way or the other, or that I may be wrong to take the Forms as universals in some sense, or that others may be wrong to deny that they are universals in any sense. But the one truth that remains even if everyone, including Plato, is wrong about the Forms, is that they function both as the instruments and as the results of his thought experiments. The Platonic corpus may not constitute an organized catalog of thought experiments with definitive solutions to well-defined problems, but it does present compelling evidence of Plato's predilection for such experimentation as a methodological preference in philosophical deliberation.

Parallels in the scholarly literature, especially those that are comparable to invoking thought experiments as an analogical explanation of Plato's Forms, include Gerson (1990; 2002), McCabe (1994), and Harte (2019). Gerson, for one, clearly interprets the Forms in terms of their

---

20. Any given Form can, not just appear to be, but actually be several different things at once. The presumption in such cases is not necessarily in favor of a contradiction, which must be proven rather than assumed. Why should a Form not, for example, be a universal in some respects and a paradigm in others? A case in point is how Fine (1993) construes Plato's Forms as paradigmatic properties, or more simply, as properties that serve as paradigms: "forms are not meanings or particulars, but explanatory properties" (24); "they are properties and not particulars" (63); "forms are paradigms in so far as they are standards" (63); "forms are self-predicative paradigms in virtue of their explanatory role" (63). Of course, not everything said of the Forms can be true all at once. Explaining how, for instance, a Form might be both a universal and a particular would require further argumentation, if only because the latter two are typically considered to be opposites in some sense. That combination would certainly not be the easiest to explain or justify. The point, however, is that it is not necessarily wrong to think of Plato's Forms in terms of the various different things they may happen to resemble by analogy.

methodological purpose and explanatory power: "I have suggested that Forms are most properly viewed as entities postulated to explain data, not wildly dissimilar to the postulated entities of modern science" (1990, 39). The core data they are postulated to explain pertains to the familiar problem of identity in difference, representing Gerson's considered opinion on the purpose of Forms: "Plato's basic argument for positing hypothetical, explanatory entities called 'Forms' is that Forms alone are able to account for the data of identity in difference" (1990, 79; cf. 1999a, 65; 1999b, 12; 2002, 88–90, passim; 2004a, 306, passim; 2004b, 237–239, 254). Gerson agrees that apparent differences in how the Forms are portrayed throughout the Platonic corpus depend at least partly on the specific circumstances and requirements of the philosophical context: "For all I know, and depending on the principle of individuation employed, there are numerous theories of Forms, perhaps as many as there are dialogues in which forms are mentioned, explicitly or implicitly" (Gerson 2002, 87). Even though he and I do not fully agree on how the contextual requirements are met, that is, on precisely what the Forms are, we do have the same idea about where to look for an answer: "So, the answer to the obviously pertinent question, 'what is a form?' must be entirely constructed from the explanatory work a form does'" (Gerson 2002, 88).

Gerson and I also seem to be in agreement with McCabe and Harte on the matter of methodological procedures and implications. McCabe offers an unmistakably context-driven and function-oriented analysis: "Now obviously enough these [the Forms] are theoretical items—they are not sensible, visible, obvious objects, but constructs offered as explanations of particular problems (this stick equal to that; Alcibiades' beauty)" (1994, 78). Harte is just as explicit in her identification of Forms as theoretical entities: "Forms are theoretical entities in the sense of being entities whose claim to existence is justified or defended in light of the theoretical work they do" (2019, 458). Harte offers her assessment as a general observation of the dramatic Socrates in action, particularly in the process of fulfilling experimental requirements: "Socrates appears to reason here in the following (reasonable) way: where there is no theoretical work for Forms to do, there is no reason to posit them" (Harte 2019, 458; directing readers to McCabe 1994, 78–81, for further discussion).

Any interpretation of Plato's dialectical processes in terms of experimentation, hypothesis testing, or theory construction, or any other scientific analogue, even if it is conceived only as a metaphor for the actual methodology, raises the question of the theoreticity of Forms: Does Plato really have a theory of Forms? Or to put it in a way that we can at least hope to be able to answer: Does what Plato says about the Forms in his canonical works constitute a theory? This is open to question, but nothing in this book depends on an answer one way or the other. Nor is the question itself very important for a proper understanding of Plato. The answer typically turns on what is meant by theory, which then undermines the relevance of the debate, as it makes the question more about the philosophy of science than about the philosophy of Plato. The simple and incontestable answer is that Plato does have a theory of Forms, if we construe theoreticity widely and loosely enough to include any serious and systematic exploration of a concept, issue, or problem, and that he does not have a theory of Forms, if we construe theoreticity in strict conformity with contemporary standards of inquiry in the prevailing paradigms of the scientific method.[21]

However that may be, their role in thought experiments makes the Forms theoretical constructs of some sort. But designating them as constructs comes with the possible implication of a restriction to mental imagery, thereby undermining their customary claim to objective reality. It is clear that the Forms function as theoretical constructs, and just as clear that Plato considers them to be ontological entities that exist in and of themselves independently of any observation, imagination, or intellection. Can they be both? It is at least a possibility, not unlike the possibility of a theoretical particle posited by the physicist turning out to be a genuine part of reality in addition to representing speculative insight in exploring that same reality prior to discovery through empirical verification. In conformity with that possibility, then, and in order to avoid contradicting it without just cause, or at least to refrain from doing so

---

21. This assessment is grounded in my personal observations. Detailed discussions of the theoreticity of Forms can be found, among other places, in Annas (1981, 217–241), Gonzalez (2002), Hyland (2002), Sayre (1993; 2002), and Williams (2006). An overview of each of these entries, together with an analysis of the problem itself, is available in Alican (2012, 110–129). Some of the same considerations apply to the question whether Plato had a "doctrine" of Forms, which also tends to come up, though not with the same level of academic interest as the question of theoreticity. The disparity in scholarly attention is understandable: Plato may have engaged in theoretical reasoning, depending on the interpretation, but he was definitely not in the habit of promulgating doctrines, no matter the interpretation.

without argumentation, any references throughout this book to Forms as "entities" or "constructs," that is, as either one or the other, are accompanied, as a rule, by parallel (or at least parenthetical) references to each in terms of the other. Thus: "'entities' (or 'constructs')" or "'constructs' (or 'entities')"—with or without the scare quotes.

1.4. How Does It All Work?

Another avenue of disagreement among Plato scholars is the matter of how Forms are supposed to interact with particulars, or with sensible phenomena, or with whatever their metaphysical counterparts in the constitution of reality as a whole may properly be called. With regard to the Forms themselves, any scholarly dispute over their nature and function typically comes from opposing opinions on how best to fill in the gaps left by too little information in the primary sources. With regard to their interaction with the world at large, the focal point of any controversy lies in just the opposite direction, a plethora of information to be sorted out in hopes of identifying preference patterns in the Platonic corpus.

One aspect of the relationship was already discussed, toward the end of section 1.2, from the perspective of the contents of the two worlds traditionally assigned to Plato. The aim of the present section is to consider the structure of the relationship independently of the nature of the relata. The focus, in other words, is on the mechanics rather than the content, the latter of which is hereafter specified indiscriminately as things, particulars, sensible phenomena, and the like, using the standard terminology uncritically in the interest of exploring the relevant solutions without multiplying the problems.

The relationship between Forms and particulars confronts us through various different analogies, together with their attendant terminologies, none of them intended to be definitive, or rather none succeeding as such, thereby indicating that Plato was not able to work out a standard account to his own satisfaction, presumably because the relationship is not quite like anything we know and is therefore difficult to express in terms of the things we do know. The most general designation is "association," alternatively called "communion," "fellowship," or "partnership," among other things, all in translation of the same word (*koinōnía* at *Phaedo* 100d and *Republic* 476a), connecting the Forms with sensible phenomena in such vague terms that the reference serves not so much as an explanation of the relationship as it does as an assertion that there is a relationship, whatever it may be.[22] The same relationship is sometimes fleshed out through a relatively more specific reference, one invoking "presence" (*parousia* at *Phaedo* 100d), indicating that the Form is somehow present in the thing of which it is a Form, whereby the intended nature of the relationship gains some structure beyond an amorphous "association," though the corresponding mode of presence, presentation, or manifestation remains unclear.

From the opposite perspective, that is, from the opposite of the "presence" of the Form in the thing, and thus from the standpoint of sensible phenomena, Plato gives us the "participation" of the thing in the Form (*methexis* at *Parmenides* 132d; *metechein* at 129a, 132e; *metalambanein* at 129a), just as commonly described as a particular thing's "sharing in" the Form, and with some literary flair, as the thing's "partaking of" the Form. An alternative to "participation," with greater intuitive appeal, again from the perspective of sensible phenomena, is "resemblance" (*homoiōsis* or *homoiotēs* at *Parmenides* 129a, 131a, 132d–133a), or what is practically the same thing, "likeness" or "similitude," where the things in question are said "to resemble," "to be like," or "to be similar to" their respective Forms (translating *homoion* at *Parmenides* 132d–e, *eoikenai* at *Parmenides* 132d, and *proseoika* at *Phaedo* 74e). A conceptual analogue of "resemblance" (or "likeness" or "similitude") is "imitation" (*mimēsis*, including its various forms exemplified at *Cratylus* 423e, *Republic* 510b, and *Timaeus* 19d, 39d, 48e, 50c, 51b), where particulars are said to "imitate" (*mimeomai* at *Timaeus* 39d–e) the relevant Forms, which they may or may not be imitating in virtue of their resemblance (or similarity or likeness), given that a correlation between imitation and resemblance (or similarity or likeness) as processes or states of affairs does not make resemblance (or similarity or likeness) a necessary condition of imitation, nor imitation a sufficient condition of resemblance (or similarity or likeness).[23]

---

22. Stephanus numbers for specific Greek terms, here and elsewhere in the book, merely confirm and exemplify Plato's usage. They do not, in any case, constitute a complete catalog or comprehensive concordance. I generally refrain from prefacing relevant citations with "e.g." or "for example"—especially avoiding "cf., e.g." or "see, for example"—in order to keep the main text more readable, but all such references are indeed representative rather than exhaustive.

23. Allen (1960; 1965) takes a strong stand against confusing imitation with resemblance, as well as against conflating the two, contending instead that imitation, rather than

The abundance of explanatory models for the relationship between Forms and particulars makes it difficult to determine Plato's considered opinion on the matter, or even to ascertain with any certainty whether he had such an opinion, given that the actual relationship, not being like any other, would therefore have been difficult to capture fully in a single paradigm drawing on familiar elements. A likely alternative is that Plato embraced each paradigm, perhaps not equally, but also not to the exclusion of others, in virtue of each one's propensity to bring out an aspect of the relationship otherwise lost or inadequately represented through the others. Our own efforts to sort out the options typically come with an inclination to favor one over the others, habitually interpreting the available evidence in conformity with our natural preferences for a definitive answer, for example, by making too much of a rhetorically successful yet philosophically specious switch from "participation" to "resemblance" in the *Parmenides* (128e–132d), where the transition is not nearly as decisive as it may appear. This is where Plato moves from a direct relationship, where things participate in, partake of, or share in Forms (through *metalambanei* and variants at *Parmenides* 130e–131a), to an indirect association, where things resemble Forms (through *eoikenai* and variants at 132d, and *homoion* and variants at 132d–e). The reason why the move commands scholarly attention, as is the case with Sedley (2016, 12–14), among others, is that the relationship between Forms and particulars comes up in multiple dialogues, whereas the passage under discussion (*Parmenides* 128e–132d), including the transition from participation to resemblance, is the only place where the relationship comes under critical scrutiny, which then seems to indicate that this is the place to look for the definitive model, or at least for helpful clues in that regard.

The passage cannot, however, be invoked faithfully as the final arbiter of the precise nature of the relationship between Forms and particulars. This is because the apparently momentous transition from participation to resemblance is followed immediately by a rejection of this supposedly superior model, which then vitiates the basis for taking resemblance as the proper paradigm, if not also for continuing to favor resemblance over participation in a comparison limited to just those two models. The initial recommendation of the participation model comes with the Day Analogy (*Parmenides* 131b), where the dramatic Socrates elucidates the notion of

---

resemblance, is the model that Plato favors in explication of the relationship between Forms and sensible phenomena, with the latter imitating the former.

the presence of a Form in many different things at once, through the common conception of the presence of a day in many different places at once. Socrates presents this simile in opposition to the allegedly counterintuitive nature of the presence of one and the same Form in multiple things at the same time, and in rejection of the presumably equally counterintuitive nature of the participation of multiple things in the same Form. While this is a perfectly serviceable analogy, especially within the logical parameters of the discussion, Parmenides responds with great cunning and a bit of sophistry to replace it with an entirely different analogy that is vulnerable to objections that the original may arguably have survived.

Replacing the Day Analogy with the Sail Analogy (*Parmenides* 131b), where a different part of the sail is over each person in a group of people covered by the sail as a whole, Parmenides forces a disanalogous model on Socrates. The difference is that a day can be shared with infinite or indefinitely great participation, for as long as it lasts, whereas a sail provides only limited cover underneath, no matter its size or its structural integrity (how long it lasts). An immediate corollary to this disparity is that a day cannot be exhausted either by the number or by the size of the corresponding participants whereas a sail indeed can. Nothing that shares the same day as other things diminishes the amount of day available for those other things, but that is exactly what happens in the case of anything claiming a spot under the allegorical sail recommended by Parmenides as the appropriate analogy.

Socrates is thus compelled to acknowledge mereological problems, including the apparent divisibility of Forms, as well as the paradigmatic deficiency of presence or participation, where the whole Form can never be present in any one thing, nor anything participate in the entirety of any Form. Even if we overlook the questionable replacement of the Day Analogy with the Sail Analogy, as the dramatic Socrates proceeds to do (so as to create a contextual occasion for introducing an alternative along with further considerations), the model of resemblance lasts no longer against objections than does the model of participation it was supposed to replace. As a matter of fact, both models are followed by an infinite regress, an apparently vicious one that is considered decisive in either formulation (*Parmenides* 132a–b, 132d–133a), neither of which meets with any resistance from the dramatic audience, which means, in turn, that neither model proposed by Socrates recovers from the regress identified by Parmenides.

The first regress (*Parmenides* 132a1–b2) suggests that a new Form of largeness would be required in a never-ending chain of reasoning if the causal explanation for anything being large were in any way contingent upon its participation in largeness, or to the same end, upon the presence of largeness in that thing. What this means is that if the largeness of large things were a matter of their participation in largeness, or of the presence of largeness in them, then a second largeness would be required to explain and establish the largeness of the largeness by which the largeness of large things is supposed to be established, as well as the largeness of the large things left without a conclusive causal explanation in the first iteration, thereby invoking a third largeness for the second iteration, and so on to infinity.

The second regress (*Parmenides* 132d1–133a6) works the same way, except for its substitution of "likeness" for "largeness" as the focus of the relationship under consideration. It may appear, at first glance, to differ further in exploring both directions of the relationship as opposed to just one, specifically by addressing the relation of the Form to the things subsumed under it, in addition to the relation of those things to the Form corresponding to them, but any difference from the first regress in that respect is only apparent and not real. There are two directions, or dimensions, in either regress. The only difference is that the directions are asymmetrical in the first but symmetrical in the second. Any apparent discrepancy in structure between the first regress and the second regress, particularly with respect to the directional attributes of the relationship explicated through each, is best explained in reference to the asymmetry of "participation," where one thing's participation in another thing is neither equivalent to nor indicative of that other thing's participation in the first thing (though it is indeed representative of the other one's presence in the first), as against the symmetry of "resemblance," where one thing's resemblance to another thing in any way is direct confirmation of that other thing's resemblance to the first thing in exactly the same way. Even between an original and a copy, the original resembles the copy (in the same way) if the copy resembles the original (in any way).

The second regress extends in both directions and covers all bases, proposing explicitly that a new Form of likeness would be required in a never-ending chain of reasoning, not only to accommodate the likeness of like things to each other, nor only to acknowledge the likeness of like things to likeness itself, but also to establish the likeness of likeness itself to the like things said to be like each other in virtue of their likeness to likeness itself, that is, of course, if the causal explanation of likeness were in any way contingent upon a relationship with likeness itself. What this means is that, if the likeness of like things were a matter of, say, their resemblance to likeness, then another likeness would be required both to establish the likeness of like things to likeness itself and to establish the likeness of likeness itself to the things that are established as likenesses in virtue of their likeness to likeness itself, and yet another likeness would be required to account for the extra likeness invoked, and so on to infinity. The reason that Plato explicitly and meticulously extends the second regress in both directions seems to be that the symmetry of the relationship both demands and facilitates a full sweep of that sort. Despite any appearances to the contrary, however, the first regress also covers both directions, albeit only implicitly, and in one fell swoop instead of a full sweep, given that the emblematic presence of the Form in the relevant things is the analogical counterpart of the figurative participation of those things in the Form, even if the lack of symmetry obscures that reality.

To return to the matter of a logical, methodological, or philosophical precedence between the two models, the rejection of both in the relevant context makes it difficult to defend the second as attracting any kind or degree of loyalty, particularly from Plato, but also from impartial observers, over and above the first. Neither model stands out as a favorite over the other, nor even as a viable option in itself, let alone as Plato's preferred paradigm overall. This is not necessarily because the problem is decisive in each case, thus destroying both models, but because the objection is the same in each case, thus equalizing the threat: an infinite and vicious regress eliminating the dialectical context as a reason for favoring either model over the other.

There are some differences, however, in the sequence of presentation that may or may not be relevant to the relative viability and reliability of the models. For example, the first model is met with intervening opposition immediately before the corresponding regress objection, while the second model is followed directly by its own regress objection. This probably does not change the balance of their relative reliability, as the intervening opposition in the first case seems relevant in the second case as well, though it is difficult to say what Plato himself may have been thinking. To be more precise, the participation model (*Parmenides* 131b) is followed by mereological objections (131c–e) before the first regress (132a–b), while the resemblance model (132c–d) is preceded by a quickly dismissed third model (132b–c), where the Forms are likened to objects of thought, before it is followed by the second regress (132d–133a). The balance seems to be preserved, however, because the mereological problems in the first case, such as the question of which part of the Form is accessed by which thing participating in it (given that it cannot be the whole of the Form since that would leave nothing for any other participants), applies on the same terms in the second case, where we may ask which part of the Form is resembled by which thing resembling it (given again that it cannot be the whole of the Form since that would leave nothing for anything else).

It may perchance appear as if the participation and resemblance models were not equally resilient, or equally susceptible, to mereological problems, which might seem instead to undermine only the former and not the latter, but that would be a mistaken interpretation, even if it turns out to be the intended impression. The mistake in question would be in taking any particular's "participation" in the whole of the relevant Form as somehow constituting an exclusive claim, leaving nothing for other particulars to participate in, which is what the Sail Analogy is intended to illustrate, while taking a particular's "resemblance" to such a Form as not engaging the Form in any way precluding the possibility of parallel resemblance by countless other particulars, which is what the Day Analogy is supposed to show. The underlying motivation would be to take the participation model more literally than the resemblance model, while taking the resemblance model more figuratively than the participation model, whereas in reality both are entirely figurative, not relatively more so or comparably less so.

A temptation of that sort is understandable in light of the comparison between the Day Analogy and the Sail Analogy, where the introduction of the resemblance model might be interpreted as an effort by the dramatic Socrates, and possibly therefore by Plato himself, to revert to the Day Analogy, or perhaps to reassert what works best in that regard. While the possibility cannot be ruled out, it does not fit the dramatic progression introducing the resemblance model as a direct response to problems with the construal of Forms as objects of thought and not as a replacement for the participation model. Nor is it consistent with the introduction of the Day Analogy specifically in explication of the participation model, whereupon a reassertion of the same analogy by an entirely different model should at least have been free of intervening distractions of the sort introduced by the entirely superfluous Object-of-Thought Paradigm, which is not just incongruous with what is at stake in the particular context but also antithetical to everything Plato says of the Forms throughout the canonical corpus.

More importantly, the Forms have no parts, which then rules out mereological problems in either model, as it makes mereology irrelevant altogether.[24] The sheer intelligibility of Plato's Forms, to the exclusion of any sensibility, save for a metaphor here or there (e.g., beauty at *Phaedrus* 250b–e), precludes their availability both for participation and for resemblance in the ordinary sense of either term, thus requiring corresponding objections to be formulated in some other way, which cannot reasonably be presumed in advance to work out to the advantage or disadvantage of either model more than the other. With mereological considerations carrying no greater weight in one case than in the other, there remains no significant difference between the two models by way of critical evaluation, at least insofar as the dramatic and dialectical context of the dialogue is concerned, given that the associated regress objections, though more prominent than any other difficulty in either case, are likewise balanced out in a comparative assessment of the two models.

The difficulty is the same in each case, or at least remains methodologically comparable, because each regress is an instantiation of the Third Man Argument, an argument form deriving its name from a series of critical assessments of Plato's Forms in the testimonial evidence of Aristotle, who considers the relationship Plato ascribes to Forms and particulars to be undermined by a vicious regress. Aristotle's version proceeds with the example, not found in the Platonic corpus, of what makes a man a man, where the answer is participation in the relevant Form, which then requires another Form, and so on to infinity (*Metaphysics* 990b15–17, 1038b35–1039a3, 1079a13; *Sophistical Refutations* 178b36–179a10; *Peri Ideōn* [= Alexander of Aphrodisias: *In Aristotelis Metaphysica Commentaria*] 83.34–85.12). Both the success of Aristotle's objection and the

---

24. This is an admittedly naïve perspective grounded in nothing more than the inherent ontological simplicity of Forms, taken to be partless, precisely because they are simple, at least in that sense, if not also in others. The brevity of the inference may arguably be concealing nuances otherwise relevant to the comparison between simplicity and partlessness. Further reflection may thus be required for a firmer stand. I remain open to correction and suggestion. No better groundwork is available in that regard than Harte's detailed examination of the relationship between parts and wholes in Plato (Harte 2002, especially 64–73; cf. 73–89).

significance of its appearance in the *Parmenides* is a matter of ongoing scholarly controversy.²⁵

My own impression is that Aristotle ends up evaluating metaphorical relationships in terms of a literal approach to universal predication, whereas Plato himself puts the matter in terms of analogies with participation, resemblance, imitation, and so on, not one of which requires an extension of the analogy to the Form itself. Aristotle's objection is that the defining property of the Form predicated of a set of particulars in any causal explanation must also be predicated of the Form, together with the particulars in question, in order for the explanation to work in the first place, which then does not work at all, because the predication requirement cannot be retired at any point in the infinite regress activated by the logical and methodological subsumption of the Form itself under the same explanation (*Peri Ideōn* [= Alexander of Aphrodisias: *In Aristotelis Metaphysica Commentaria*] 83.34–85.12). While this is an insightful observation, it does not commit Plato to the absurdity of Forms participating in themselves, resembling themselves, imitating themselves, and so on, just because he takes sensible phenomena to participate in, resemble, or imitate the Forms. The underlying causality, explanation, or causal explanation need not be its own cause or explanation. The scope can reasonably be limited to sensible as opposed to intelligible phenomena (even

---

25. A seminal restatement and analysis of the problem by Vlastos (1954) in the middle of the twentieth century created something of an academic subdiscipline where both the volume of contributions and the level of engagement grew far beyond what can be covered adequately in a footnote. Even just the personal response of Vlastos himself to the scholarly reception of his own assessment would require serious study for a full grasp of the issues (see Vlastos 1954; 1955; 1956; 1965a; 1965c; 1965d–1966; 1969a; 1969b; 1969c; 1974; 1981). This is to say nothing of equally important work both preceding and following Vlastos. A fair sampling would include, but could hardly be limited to, the following contributions: Allen (1960), Barford (1978), Bestor (1978), Block (1964), Cherniss (1944, 226–234, 275–318, 375–379, 488–494, 500–505; 1957, 225–266), Clegg (1973), Cornford (1939, 87–95), Cresswell (1975), Devereux (1977), Durrant (1975; 1979), Fine (1993, 203–224, 225–241), Frances (1996), Geach (1956), Gerson (1981), Goldstein and Mannick (1978), Hathaway (1971), Heinaman (1989), Lee (1971), Malcolm (1981; 1991), Mates (1979), Meinwald (1992), Mignucci (1990), Moravcsik (1963), Nehamas (1973; 1979; 1982), Nerlich (1960), Otto (2017), Owen (1953), Pelletier and Zalta (2000), Prior (1983), Rankin (1969; 1970), Robinson (1942), Ross (1951, 85–91; cf. 161, 170–171, 230), Ryle (1939), Scaltsas (1989; 1992), Schweizer (1994), Sellars (1955), Sharma (2005; 2007), Sharvy (1986), Silverman (1990), Taylor (1915–1916).

and especially) where the latter are invoked in explanation of the former. Nor must the explanation be recursive.[26] It can be rejected, of course, but not because it is extended indefinitely, which is an interpretation rather than an implication, observation, or demonstration.

What makes complications associated with the Third Man Argument such an appealing objection is that Plato elsewhere speaks of the Forms as instantiating themselves, or as being predicated of themselves, and thus as embodying and exhibiting the properties they are otherwise responsible for effecting in and manifesting through particulars. This apparent tendency toward self-predication, a term originating with Gregory Vlastos (1954, 324), is then taken as additional confirmation for any regress of the sort coming up in the *Parmenides* (132a–b, 132d–133a).[27] But the corresponding instances of self-predication suffer from overinterpretation or, to call it what it really is, misinterpretation, which does not go unnoticed in the relevant literature. To cite an example from recent contributions, already partially reproduced in section 1.2, Sedley (2016) opposes this tendency as follows:

> This temptation should be resisted [the temptation of assuming self-predication whereby each Form is "an ideal model

---

26. Armstrong (1989) and I are in agreement that it is both reasonable and advisable to deny an infinite regress in the relevant context: "However, my idea is that the instantiation regress can be halted after one step. We have to allow the introduction of a fundamental tie or nexus: instantiation. But suppose that we have that a instantiates F or that a and b in that order instantiate R. Do we have to advance any further? I do not think that we do. For note that the alleged advance is now, as it was not at the first step, logically determined by the postulated states of affairs" (Armstrong 1989, 109).

27. While Vlastos (1954) is responsible for coining the term "self-predication," he identifies Taylor (1915–1916) as the first to recognize in print that self-predication is an implicit assumption of the Third Man Argument: "The credit for recognizing that this is an indispensable, though suppressed, premise of the Third Man Argument goes to A. E. Taylor" (Vlastos 1954, 324). Vlastos gives the relevant citation as "Taylor 1916, 46 ff.," but the pagination he provides is actually from the 1934 reprint of Taylor's 1915–1916 article. The same citation in reference to the original (see the list of works cited in the present volume) would be: Taylor 1915-1916, 250 ff. (= 1934, 46 ff.). It may be interesting to note, as an incidental remark, that Vlastos (1969c, 74, n. 1) later had second thoughts about the term "self-predication," at one time considering "homocharacterization" as a replacement, though eventually finding the original term too popular to replace or retire.

or exemplar which paradigmatically manifests the property in question"]. A Form, being the *one* thing shared by many diverse but like-named particulars, is a 'one over many': not a further particular but a universal. The sense in which the Form of, say, largeness is a paradigm against which all individual attributions of largeness are to be tested, and approved in so far as they resemble it, is not that largeness is a supremely large thing. It is that largeness itself, a universal, fully satisfies its own definition, and that other things are large precisely in so far as they too satisfy that same definition, that is, in so far as they resemble largeness itself. (Sedley 2016, 13)

I agree with Sedley. Plato does, for example, intimate that he considers the just itself (the Form of justice) to be just (*Protagoras* 330c), the beautiful itself (the Form of beauty) to be beautiful (*Phaedo* 100c; cf. *Phaedrus* 249c–250e; *Symposium* 210e–212c), and so on, but he does not present any such consideration in a sense that would encourage or justify an attempt to sleep on the bed itself (the Form of bed) rather than on the physical manifestation of it in the bedroom (cf. *Republic* 596b). Just as the bed itself is a bed, only in the sense that it is what it is to be a bed, so too is the just itself just, precisely because it is what it is to be just, not because it is itself the kind of thing that is just in the relevant moral or legal sense, and so too is the beautiful itself beautiful, simply because it determines and represents what it is to be beautiful, not because it is itself the kind of thing that has genuine aesthetic qualities or an overall aesthetic appeal, given that it is itself that quality, and itself that appeal.[28]

On the other hand, the problem under consideration is, and has long been, both too intricate and too important to dismiss out of hand.[29] The resistance I have offered constitutes a digression revealing my position rather than establishing it. The point is that the two regress objections

---

28. See Devereux (1977), Morris (1985), Prior (1980), and Vlastos (1974) for further discussion.

29. Problems associated with the so-called self-predication of Forms, not to mention the Third Man Argument, which has developed into a distinct area of specialization, may indeed be too intricate and too important to dismiss out of hand. But that does not mean that such problems cannot, upon due consideration, be simplified and dismissed with just cause, especially if their intricacy is illusory and their importance exaggerated, as suspected, for example, by Armstrong (1989, 108–110).

brought against the models discussed in connection with them are both manifestations of the Third Man Argument, which works no better or worse against one model than against the other. Since there are several more models, however, Plato could still be thought to have a favorite, even if it is not one of the two most obvious choices, each appearing in many places and both apparently rejected in the *Parmenides*, at least by the protagonist, though not necessarily by Plato himself.

Although the possibility of a favorite cannot be ruled out, the multitude of analogies, explanations, and terminologies is difficult to sort out with much confidence, either as exhibiting deliberate and sustained development on the part of Plato, or as constituting conceptual or philosophical progress in the subject matter itself, whether or not Plato was in active and successful pursuit of such progress. While it is possible that one model was abandoned for another, and furthermore, that this has happened more than once, there are simply too many models, each appearing in too many dialogues, for us to be able to map out a linear succession terminating in a final resolution. Even the participation model, which the dramatic Socrates of the *Parmenides* abandons in haste to switch to the resemblance model, comes up in various places besides the transition in the *Parmenides* (128e–132d), with other notable appearances including the *Phaedo* (100c, 102b), *Symposium* (211b), and *Republic* (402d, 476c–d). The only way to draw a compelling inference from the critical evaluation of either model in the *Parmenides* is to ascertain the order of composition of Plato's works in an effort to trace the development of all such models, together with the apparent affinity of the author for each one over time. Doing that may be even more difficult than figuring out the intended relationship between Forms and particulars, which would mean that the means contemplated puts the end further out of reach.

That being said, whatever can reasonably be inferred in that regard, despite falling short of conclusive evidence or demonstration, could be used to pick a model based on chronology. Yet even indubitable chronological conclusions can at best identify the last model discussed in the corpus, which need not be the best model conceived by Plato. It need not even be any better than any of the others. For example, the survival of the imitation model (already present in the *Cratylus* [423e] and the *Republic* [510b]) well into the final stretches of Plato's philosophical career, especially as evidenced by its domination of the *Timaeus* (19d, 39d, 48e, 50c, 51b), commonly acknowledged to be one of his latest works, makes that model a prime candidate for his favorite paradigm if chronology is a reliable indicator. Yet it is by no means certain that the dominion of the imitation model in the *Timaeus*, even with the neglect of other models in the same work, is not due to the contextual requirements of emphasis as opposed to a final and comprehensive change of view in regard to what is tenable and what is not in explication of the relationship between Forms and particulars. It is, no doubt, reasonable to look for evidentiary significance in the very last model used, but it is, at the same time, perhaps too easy to find it there in the absence of competition, even the implicit possibility of which could conceivably continue to be a respectable alternative in general, whether or not it is particularly relevant under the circumstances.

I am neither espousing nor opposing a developmentalist interpretation of Plato's philosophical output. The proliferation of paradigms for the relationship between Forms and particulars does not even come up, certainly not as a defining issue, in the debate between developmentalism and unitarianism. Although studying developmental variations between paradigms for that particular relationship may be possible, perhaps even enlightening, specific solutions would be no more or less reliable than answers to other (more typical) developmental questions, all of them remaining open, to various degrees, for various reasons. This is not a denial of the possibility that Plato's positions may have changed in significant ways over time, as may be expected of any philosopher, and indeed of any person. It is rather an acknowledgment of the fact that efforts to trace such a change through the composition order of the dialogues remains a highly controversial area of Plato scholarship.

Nothing in this book turns on the chronology of the dialogues. I do refer, from time to time, to "periods" in Plato's career, with his works presumably being divisible into early, middle, and late periods, among other possibilities (see Alican 2012, 148–188), but this is in conformity with terminological conventions rather than in affirmation of historical truths. Of course, even bare terminological conformity can suggest alignment with developmentalism as an interpretive framework, where the divisions coincide with significant changes in philosophical outlook, including what is done with the Forms before and after the *Parmenides*, what is done with the soul before and after the *Republic*, and what can be made of the diminishing presence of the dramatic Socrates as evidence of a distinction between Socratic and Platonic philosophy in the canonical corpus (Vlastos 1991; 1994). Hence the caveat: I neither believe nor reject the underlying story. I simply employ the associated terminology for convenience in reference.

Be that as it may, developmentalism as an exegetical platform grounded in philosophical considerations is not the only approach relevant to chronology. Stylometric studies exploring gaps and clusters in stylistic choices and literary tendencies constitute the empirical counterpart of the theoretical methodology of philosophical developmentalism. Stylometric conclusions appear to be better grounded than developmental ones, though they cannot reasonably be considered infallible, given that Plato is known to have revised his works extensively and repeatedly, and is likely therefore to have revised one after drafting another, and vice versa, and so on with all the dialogues. He is also quite likely to have worked on more than one piece at a time, possibly composing several shorter works alongside any of the longer ones, such as the *Republic* and the *Laws*, which then makes the temporal precedence of dialogues in any cluster of works not merely difficult to determine but irrelevant to consider. Even an audience opposed to any and all chronological platforms, however, will immediately recognize that commentators are not talking about, say, the *Euthyphro* or the *Republic*, when they refer to the dialogues of the "late" period. We owe at least that much of a consensus to stylometric studies, anchored to the testimony of Aristotle (*Politics* 1264b26–27) that the *Laws* comes after the *Republic*, together with the report of Diogenes Laërtius (3.37) that the *Laws* was barely finished at the time of Plato's death.[30]

We are thus assured of a few firm anchors, but they hardly add up to a comprehensive and definitive chronology showing the development of Plato's considered opinion on the relationship between Forms and particulars throughout his career. As already submitted above, the last thing said on a particular subject is not necessarily the best thing said on that subject. Nor therefore can it be presumed to be the one dearest to Plato's heart, or nearest to his mind, even if we could be reasonably confident in

---

30. Pioneers of stylometric studies include Campbell (1867; 1896), Dittenberger (1881), Lutoslawski (1897), Ritter (1910; 1931/1933), and von Arnim (1896; 1912). More recent developments can be followed through Brandwood (1976; 1990), Kahn (1996; 2002), and Ledger (1989), to cite just a few examples. The work of Thesleff (1982 [= 2009, 143–382]; 1989, 1–26; 1999, 108–116 [= 2009, 489–497]), including Thesleff and Loimaranta (1981), is particularly noteworthy both for substantive contributions to chronological studies and for critical assessments of the methods and findings of others working in the same area. Nails (1993; 1994; 1995) can also be consulted for insightful analyses of the merits of developmental theories and stylometric tests.

our estimation of what came first, what came last, and where everything else went in between.

No wonder, then, that we have not been able to agree on the relationship intended between the Forms and sensible phenomena. There is no solution to the puzzle because there is no puzzle. The models are not mutually exclusive even if they appear incompatible. They are all relevant in some way. More accurately, the models themselves may be mutually exclusive in their entirety, but only certain elements or aspects of each, rather than the complete details, or the precise patterns, were ever intended to be relevant to the relationship between Forms and particulars.

What we are dealing with here is a unique relationship that defies articulation through any one explanation or any single model. That is why so many different attempts are made. As a matter of fact, Plato admits as much himself where he makes the dramatic Socrates refrain emphatically from either naming or defining the relationship responsible for anything's being beautiful, one of Plato's favorite references in illustration of how the world works through the interaction of Forms and sensible phenomena: "nothing else makes it beautiful other than the presence of [*parousia*], or the sharing in [*koinōnia*], or however you may describe its relationship to that Beautiful we mentioned, for I will not insist on the precise nature of the relationship, but that all beautiful things are beautiful by the Beautiful" (*Phaedo* 100d).

1.5. Conclusion

The kind of conclusion that is both required and warranted at this point is not a deduction from what has been said so far, since this chapter is merely an exegetical and analytical anchor for the alternative interpretation developed throughout the remainder of the book, thus identifying points of departure rather than presenting, promoting, or defending a particular position. Nor is the kind of conclusion required and warranted here an overview of what is to come, since the preceding chapter (the unnumbered "introduction") is already dedicated entirely and exclusively to that end. The only thing that can be inferred with reasonable confidence from the expository and analytical coverage in this chapter is the absence of a unified view on the nature and structure of reality in Plato's outlook, save for widespread agreement on a dualism of worlds, despite vast differences of opinion on what is in them or how they are related. Hence, given the ongoing relevance of unresolved issues, the depth and breadth of the corresponding disagreement, and the sheer volume of scholarly contributions, concluding remarks are best reserved for suggestions for further reference.

Even the best of intentions, however, will fall short of a comprehensive effort toward that end, for the literature on Plato's Forms is enormous. Selective coverage, on the other hand, is not so much a reflection of an objective assessment of the best contributions as it is a revelation of personal predilections. A brief survey will help illustrate mine. Since what has made a strong impression on one student of Plato is likely to have done so for others as well, the corresponding entries will be readily familiar, obviating the need for an annotated bibliography. Skeletal lists organized around publication formats should work well as an academic roadmap of the intellectual inspiration behind this book. The items listed in this section are also included in the complete works cited at the end of the book.[31] Their partial duplication here should help isolate avenues for further exploration while emphasizing opportunities for fruitful consultation.

Beginning with scholarly monographs, the most memorable publications in English that are either directly or indirectly about the Forms include the following entries, though they are not exhausted by this list:

> Allen, Reginald Edgar. 1970. *Plato's 'Euthyphro' and the Earlier Theory of Forms*. London: Routledge and Kegan Paul.
> Blackson, Thomas A. 1995. *Inquiry, Forms, and Substances: A Study in Plato's Metaphysics and Epistemology*. Dordrecht: Kluwer Academic (Springer).
> Cherniss, Harold Fredrik. 1944. *Aristotle's Criticism of Plato and the Academy*. Baltimore: Johns Hopkins Press.
> Cherniss, Harold Fredrik. 1945. *The Riddle of the Early Academy*. Berkeley: University of California Press.
> Dancy, Russell M. 2004. *Plato's Introduction of Forms*. Cambridge: Cambridge University Press.
> Dorter, Kenneth. 1994. *Form and Good in Plato's Eleatic Dialogues: The Parmenides, Theaetetus, Sophist, and Statesman*. Berkeley: University of California Press.

---

31. Nothing that is not referenced elsewhere in the book is listed here in this section, since recommendations for further study or consultation are best restricted to actual study and consultation.

Fine, Gail Judith. 1993. *On Ideas: Aristotle's Criticism of Plato's Theory of Forms*. Oxford: Oxford University Press.
Grabowski, Francis A., III. 2008. *Plato, Metaphysics and the Forms*. London: Continuum.
Helmig, Christoph. 2012. *Forms and Concepts: Concept Formation in the Platonic Tradition*. Berlin: De Gruyter.
Kouremenos, Theokritos. 2018. *Plato's Forms, Mathematics and Astronomy*. Berlin: De Gruyter.
Malcolm, John. 1991. *Plato on the Self-Predication of Forms: Early and Middle Dialogues*. Oxford: Oxford University Press.
McCabe, Mary Margaret Anne. 1994. *Plato's Individuals*. Princeton: Princeton University Press.
Patterson, Richard. 1985a. *Image and Reality in Plato's Metaphysics*. Indianapolis: Hackett.
Penner, Terry. 1987. *The Ascent from Nominalism: Some Existence Arguments in Plato's Middle Dialogues*. Dordrecht: D. Reidel (Springer).
Prior, William J. 1985. *Unity and Development in Plato's Metaphysics*. London: Croom Helm.
Rickless, Samuel Charles. 2007. *Plato's Forms in Transition: A Reading of the Parmenides*. Cambridge: Cambridge University Press.
Ross, William David. 1951. *Plato's Theory of Ideas*. Oxford: Clarendon Press.
Sayre, Kenneth M. 1983. *Plato's Late Ontology: A Riddle Resolved*. Princeton: Princeton University Press.
Schipper, Edith Watson. 1965. *Forms in Plato's Later Dialogues*. The Hague: Martinus Nijhoff.
Shorey, Paul. 1884/1982. *De Platonis Idearum Doctrina atque Mentis Humanae Notionibus Commentatio*. Munich: Theodor Ackermann, 1884. English translation by R. S. W. Hawtrey, published with a preface by Rosamond Kent Sprague, as "A Dissertation on Plato's Theory of Forms and on the Concepts of the Human Mind," *Ancient Philosophy* 2, no. 1 (Spring 1982): 1–59.
Shorey, Paul. 1903. *The Unity of Plato's Thought*. Chicago: University of Chicago Press.
Shorey, Paul. 1933. *What Plato Said*. Chicago: University of Chicago Press.

Silverman, Allan Jay. 2002. *The Dialectic of Essence: A Study of Plato's Metaphysics*. Princeton: Princeton University Press.

Stewart, John Alexander. 1909. *Plato's Doctrine of Ideas*. Oxford: Clarendon Press.

Thesleff, Holger. 1999. *Studies in Plato's Two-Level Model*. Helsinki: Societas Scientiarum Fennica. Reprinted in his *Platonic Patterns*, 383–506. Las Vegas: Parmenides, 2009.

Journal articles and anthology contributions, even just the important ones, are too numerous for a list of manageable proportions. Any such list could easily extend to many times the size of the preceding one yet remain utterly incomplete. The scope of coverage in this category is therefore limited to the best options, after the turn of the century, for a general introduction to Plato's metaphysics, with a particular focus on the Forms, thus ignoring many excellent contributions toward the analysis and solution of specific problems related to the Forms. Ademollo (2013), Frede (2012), Gonzalez (2002), Harte (2019), and Sedley (2016) match that description, as they provide exceptionally useful overviews of the main themes and issues concerning the Forms:

Ademollo, Francesco. 2013. "Plato's Conception of the Forms: Some Remarks." In *Universals in Ancient Philosophy*, edited by Riccardo Chiaradonna and Gabriele Galluzzo, 41–85. Seminari e Convegni 33. Pisa: Edizioni della Normale.

Frede, Dorothea. 2012. "Forms, Functions, and Structure in Plato." Chapter 17 of *Presocratics and Plato: A Festschrift at Delphi in Honor of Charles Kahn*, edited by Richard Patterson, Vassilis Karasmanis, and Arnold Hermann, 367–390. Las Vegas: Parmenides.

Gonzalez, Francisco J. 2002. "Plato's Dialectic of Forms." Chapter 1 of *Plato's Forms: Varieties of Interpretation*, edited by William A. Welton, 31–83. Lanham: Rowman and Littlefield.

Harte, Verity. 2019. "Plato's Metaphysics." Chapter 19 of *The Oxford Handbook of Plato*, second edition, edited by Gail Judith Fine, 455–480. Oxford: Oxford University Press.

Sedley, David Neil. 2016. "An Introduction to Plato's Theory of Forms." *Royal Institute of Philosophy Supplement* (Supplement to *Philosophy*) 78, no. 1 (July): 3–22.

Highly regarded anthologies of previously published essays on Plato's metaphysics and epistemology, with considerable emphasis on the Forms, include a collection of twenty essays edited by Allen (1965), one of eighteen edited by Fine (1999), another of twenty-one by Irwin (1995), and a shorter one of thirteen by Vlastos (1971), with some mutual overlap in contents. Fine herself may be cited a second time in the same category, since in addition to the volume edited by her (1999), she has written enough on the subject to produce a collection of her own essays (2003), all previously published, five of them exclusively on the Forms. A relatively recent collection of eleven previously unpublished essays, plus an excellent editorial introduction, all exclusively on the Forms, can be found in Welton (2002). The entries in the anthology category thus add up to the following six collections:

Allen, Reginald Edgar, ed. 1965. *Studies in Plato's Metaphysics*. International Library of Philosophy and Scientific Method. London: Routledge and Kegan Paul.

Fine, Gail Judith, ed. 1999. *Plato*. Vol. 1: *Metaphysics and Epistemology*. Oxford: Oxford University Press.

Fine, Gail Judith. 2003. *Plato on Knowledge and Forms: Selected Essays*. Oxford: Clarendon Press.

Irwin, Terence, ed. 1995. *Plato's Metaphysics and Epistemology*. New York: Garland.

Vlastos, Gregory, ed. 1971. *Plato: A Collection of Critical Essays*. Vol. 1: *Metaphysics and Epistemology*. Garden City: Anchor Books.

Welton, William A., ed. 2002. *Plato's Forms: Varieties of Interpretation*. Lanham: Rowman and Littlefield.

Even a subjective and selective overview, such as this one, can be sufficiently indicative of the extent and quality of the secondary literature. The corresponding entries clearly add up to a rich platform of scholarship. Yet neither the representative sample here nor the entire population of publications on Plato constitutes a received view of his metaphysics, nor even just of his Forms.

With so much good work on the subject, that may come as a surprise. But disagreement of the highest caliber is exactly why Welton, cited above, was able to come up with the perfect title for an anthology on Plato's Forms when he brought together nearly a dozen entries, each with something different to say: *Plato's Forms: Varieties of Interpretation* (2002). This is not to ignore the countless scholars who hold a mutually consistent, and in some cases identical, view of Plato's Forms, or of his ontology, or even of the whole of his metaphysics. But those in agreement are certainly and overwhelmingly outnumbered by those who have an opinion on the matter. And no one opinion seems to rise above the rest in terms of scholarly reception.

One interpretive paradigm, arguably the only one concerning a major issue, that attracts enough support to make it a standard model in any sense, and by any measure, is the dualism of worlds attached to the variety of things. There have, of course, always been scholars who outright deny a dualism of worlds in Plato (see Ferguson 1921; Findlay 1974, especially xi–xii; Frede 1999; Nails 2013; Perl 1997; Robjant 2012; Smith 2000; 2012; 2019), but those who affirm it have consistently been in the majority, followed by those who take it for granted (thus accepting it without necessarily discussing or defending it) and by those who do not care one way or the other. The prevalence of the paradigm, though all too often adopted uncritically, nevertheless remains the closest thing we have to a consensus on or about Plato's Forms.

That is why it was important to devote this chapter to an illustration of the best representatives of the dualism of worlds, together with an overview of the various viewpoints on what is in those worlds, and on how it all fits and works together, before presenting and promoting the alternative of unitary pluralism in the rest of the book. This chapter thus constitutes a point of departure for subsequent methodological and philosophical development.

Chapter 2

Rethinking Plato's Forms

This chapter is a proposal for retracing the main lines of Plato's thought, doubling as a roadmap for reconsidering the formative features of his world, including the proprietary stock of conceptual tools he uses for building and maintaining it.[1] Developing an alternative interpretation of his philosophical vision, the central focus is specifically on what Plato does with the Forms. The guiding paradigm is the unitary pluralism of a hierarchically structured universe comprising interdependent levels of reality as a substitute for the traditional dualism of a world of Forms separated from the world of particulars. An integral part of the model proposed, representing a further departure from tradition, is a reorganization of Forms in three distinct categories: Ideal Forms, Conceptual Forms, and Relational Forms. The result is a recalibration of Plato's insights, tools, and methods toward a better understanding of his overall philosophy, especially his distinctive conception of reality and his unique perspective of the world. The initiative promises, in addition, to restore Plato's methodological trademark of systematic emphasis on that which is good, a dialectical predilection in articulation of a cosmological constant that cannot be accommodated through a separation of worlds.

---

1. This chapter was originally published as a journal article with joint authorship (Alican and Thesleff 2013): "Rethinking Plato's Forms," *Arctos: Acta Philologica Fennica* 47: 11–47.

2.1. Introduction

The dualism of Forms versus particulars is the most prominent theme in the study of Plato. Other issues have also been in the forefront, but the Forms have been at the center of attention, and Plato has often been defined by them. Unfortunately, the opposite does not hold: Plato has not, in any sense, defined the Forms. Thus, getting it right is both important and difficult.[2]

The traditional interpretation of Forms as uniform entities occupying a world outside our own is infelicitous in at least two respects: first in positing an extra world to make things work, second in compressing all abstractions, or too many of them, at any rate, into the concept of Form. The first problem is ontological extravagance, the second, the exact opposite.

While the tradition thus defined may not represent a united front dominating the field in unanimous agreement, it is both prevalent and dominant enough to constitute an interpretive institution. Opposition to it is certainly not a matter of chasing phantoms. On the contrary, what we have in the dichotomy of Forms versus particulars in separate worlds, together with the fungibility of Forms as a homogeneous group of abstractions, is a textbook interpretation of Plato's metaphysics.[3] Against tradition,

---

2. The literature on the Forms is vast. Studies with a broad coverage and general focus include: Ademollo (2013), Alican (2012, 87–110), Allen (1970), Blackson (1995), Dancy (2004), Fine (1993; 2003), Frede (2012), Gerson (2004a; 2004b), Gonzalez (2002), Harte (2019), Jackson (1882; 1882–1886), McCabe (1994, 53–94), Patterson (1985a; 1985b), Ross (1951), Schipper (1965), Sedley (2016), Silverman (2002), Stewart (1909), Thesleff (1999, 50–107 [= 2009, 434–488]). Studies of specific problems include: Malcolm (1991), Meinwald (1991; 1992), Nails (2013), Pelletier (1990), Rickless (2007), Rowe (2005), Sayre (1983; 1996), Scolnicov (2003), Teloh (1981), Vlastos (1954). These two lists may be rounded off by a collection of previously unpublished essays edited by Welton (2002). A conspectus of the global state of scholarship on the Forms can be found in Erler (2007, 390–406, 699–703). The final section of the previous chapter (section 1.5) provides additional references.

3. The designation "textbook interpretation" is a figure of speech rather than a measure of correlation. It generally does not call for documentation, unless the narrative it accompanies is at odds with what one might reasonably expect to find in an actual textbook. Despite a lack of agreement on details, however, what counts as traditional in Plato scholarship is no mystery. As for its reflection in textbooks, the famous one by Bertrand Russell, *The Problems of Philosophy* (mentioned in section 1.2 of the previous chapter), though perhaps not intended as a textbook in the standard sense, teaches us that "Plato is led to a supra-sensible world, more real than the common world of

then, and in defiance of its preservation in textbooks and classrooms, the purpose of this chapter is to recommend and pursue a course correction in Plato studies.

The first step of the correction is to liberate Plato from the burdens of a second world, setting him free to make the best he can of the only world he ever recognized: a single world with a sliding scale of reality where there is enough room both for Forms and for particulars, including their connection and separation in a manner consistent with the metaphysical demands of instantiation. This is a two-level alternative replacing the two-world standard. The founding principle is not that there are only two levels, but that Forms occupy one level, particulars another, in a hierarchical structure consisting of layer upon layer of ontological stratification, complete with a practically unlimited number of subdivisions, collectively representing a gradation of reality within and between the two primary levels. The result is not a strictly binary model of reality, an attempt to trade one sort of dualism for another, merely substituting the notion of level for that of world, but a unitary pluralism of ontological differentiation in a single world with a diverse population.

The second and final step toward the correct course is to distinguish between the inherently different kinds of Forms traditionally conceived erroneously as a uniform class of entities. Plato's experimentation with abstraction reveals, upon closer examination, three different categories of Forms, as opposed to a single breed covering every possibility, where candidates for Forms can be as diverse as justice, horseness, and motion. Taken up in detail later, the classification comprises Ideal Forms, Conceptual Forms, and Relational Forms.

---

sense, the unchangeable world of ideas, which alone gives to the world of sense whatever pale reflection of reality may belong to it" (Russell 1912, 144). A hundred years later, a prominent guidebook (*The Continuum Companion to Plato*) can still be found hesitant to introduce the Forms without reference, at least in scare quotes, to "what is often described as a 'two world ontology'" (Press 2012, 174). In between, something of the tradition has obviously survived. What that may be is captured rather well in an anthology on Plato's Forms, titled *Plato's Forms: Varieties of Interpretation*, where the editor's overview presents tradition as firmly embracing a two-world interpretation: "The most famous view associated with one of the greatest thinkers of all time is a view that seems to defy our common sense, to challenge our deepest beliefs about the very nature of reality; for it seems to tell us that the flesh-and-blood world of which we are a part, the world of change and time in which we pass our lives, is somehow 'less real' than a world we can only see in our minds" (Welton 2002, 1).

These two steps are best implemented through a single revisionist project bringing the fundamental elements of Plato's thought into better alignment. This is because they do not solve mutually independent problems in separate areas, instead explicating Plato's philosophical vision in the broadest sense, while making the corrections jointly necessary for a comprehensive sketch.

The reliability of the big picture is important not just for its own sake but also for getting the details right. A major cause for concern in that regard is the inadequacy of the prevailing patterns of interpretation to account for the axiological orientation of Plato's thought, that is, for the primacy of intrinsic value in his philosophical projects. Even though everything in Plato aims at the good, there can be no enlightenment, moral or otherwise, so long as the good resides in a different world, along with everything else that is fine and decent and noble. The aim here is to show that the big picture, revised as promised, restores Plato's devotion to value.

This is a bold undertaking that goes against the grain of interpretation in current scholarship. Although there is a good case for it, presented methodically in what follows, no amount of evidence pertinent to the present proposal for revision will add up to proof in the strictest sense of the term. The leading alternative, after all, is not itself based on proof but on a tradition dating back to antiquity.

The absence of proof, on the other hand, is not a license to replace tradition with a new perspective while dispensing with the need to provide reasons and reasoning. The acid test with respect to the monism versus dualism of worlds will be whether the unitary reconstruction advocated here makes better sense of Plato than the schismatic dualism that places the Forms in one world, and the particulars in another, leaving no room for an experience of value, which rests in the world of Forms with all the good stuff, not in the world of particulars where we dwell. The acid test with respect to the classification of Forms into three categories will be whether the variegation, which constitutes a natural fit with an already stratified reality, is more faithful to Plato than is undifferentiated abstraction confined to an alternate reality.

The reason that there can be no proof in the strictest sense, then, is that such tests are not evidentiary inferences or deductive conclusions but thought experiments, much like how Plato propounds his own philosophy. That said, the investigation of Plato's aims, methods, and achievements as thought experiments does not presuppose any particular pattern in his development as a philosopher or writer. Nor is the general initiative here helped or hindered by any given order in which the dialogues may have been written. This is not the place to argue against developmental accounts or chronological approaches, but ignoring them should give us no pause, as we can hardly be obligated to adopt them in passing.[4]

2.2. Stratification of Reality

Plato's philosophy has a distinct axiological orientation. His dialogues constitute a procession of thought experiments aiming at that which is good in itself, or what is the same, that which is desirable for its own sake (*to kalon, to agathon,* and the like). The attendant premium on value is difficult to reconcile with the attribution of metaphysically transcendent Forms to anything that is not explicitly good. The relevance of what is good to what is real, therefore, has a considerable bearing on the general interpretation of Plato. Yet it is easy to lose sight of that connection when discussing Plato's metaphysics as if it were a modern outlook.

Many scholars have, over the years, taken Plato's commitment to value-neutral Forms and trivial Forms as a given, or at least as a possibility. Some have even embraced not merely neutral and trivial Forms but also negative Forms, while others have expressed reservations on all three fronts.[5] Disagreement among philosophers is often buried under the terms used, some of them appropriated from ordinary language, some of them invented for the occasion. Reconsidering Plato's so-called theory of Forms,[6] primarily through a closer look at the dialogues, may help

---

4. Platonic chronology is a field of its own. Alican (2012, 148–188) may be consulted for an overview of problems and solutions. Thesleff (1982 [= 2009, 143–382]; 1989, 1–26; 1999, 108–116 [= 2009, 489–497]) should be preferred for a comprehensive survey combined with substantive contributions. Alican (2012, 185–188) and Nails (1995, 59, 134) are useful for general insight into Thesleff's views on the matter. Nails (1995, 58–61, 64, 76, 111–112, 131, 134, 203) is not to be missed for documentation of the main schools, major trends, and best achievements in Platonic chronology, all with the convenience of tabular presentations.

5. See Erler (2007, 397) and Guthrie (1978, 97–100) for references. See chapter 6 of the present volume for a discussion of negative Forms.

6. Ascribing a "theory of Forms" to Plato is becoming an increasingly delicate matter, with many scholars contending that he never held any such theory, and some holding that he never held any theory at all. Both groups in common dissent consider

resolve superficial disagreements and expose genuine differences. Chief among them is the gradation intended in a single world as against the polarization emerging in two worlds.[7]

The prevailing paradigm is the dualistic assumption of a unique, separate, and complete world of Forms that somehow corresponds to our own world, accounting for many of its features, or by some counts, for all of them, including change, variety, and diversity, but sharing none of its deficiencies. The difficulties in such an assumption are legion, the foremost of which is that Plato himself provides little ground for it in the dialogues. While the ideal state in the *Republic* (592a–b) and the cosmos in the *Timaeus* (28a–30d, cf. 51d–52d) may come to mind as corroborating examples, metaphysical dualism is not the only possible reading in either case.

We normally expect any world, whether actual or merely possible, and therefore any that might be metaphorical, to include change, variety, and diversity, as well as some indication of what is good and bad for the things within. None of that seems to be a feature of the world of Forms attributed to Plato. Such expectations are admittedly determined, at least in part, by the way our own world looks to us, which may not be what we can reasonably expect to find in all possible worlds, but we can rest assured that we can neither expect it nor extract it from any world of Forms as such.

---

the treatment of Forms in the canonical corpus to fall short of the conceptual and methodological rigors of theoreticity. A discussion of the relevant issues can be found in Annas (1981, 217–241), Gonzalez (2002), Hyland (2002), Sayre (1993; 2002), and Williams (2006, especially 154). A review of the literature, together with an evaluation of the possibilities, is available in Alican (2012, 110–129).

7. Some scholars tend to distinguish between ontological and epistemological versions of the two-world model. The nature of the present project leaves no room for bringing the epistemology of the question into the forefront. This is because denying a two-world ontology, as is done here, makes it contradictory to support a two-world epistemology, and superfluous to deny it, and therefore at least unnecessary, if not also distracting, to bring it up at all. An excellent source for the epistemological perspective is Smith (2000; 2012; 2019), who not only offers acquaintance with the literature but also contributes toward a solution. Nails (2013, 78, n. 3), for one, considers Smith (2000) to have settled the epistemological issue, having demonstrated, at least to her satisfaction, that the two-world model fails to account for Plato's epistemology. Yet as she admits, not everyone considers the matter closed. See Butler (2007) and Rowe (2005) for further discussion of the epistemology of the problem.

Even the preposterous immanence of presumably transcendent Forms has not convinced the proponents of dualism to consolidate their worlds in a single reality.[8] The world of sensible phenomena cannot be a replica of the world of intelligible Forms, certainly not if there is just one world, but even on the assumption that there are two, given that sensible phenomena cannot account for reality, remaining fully dependent on the Forms, not just for their own existence and essence, but also as part of any ontological scheme or etiological explanation.

Earlier fascination with recovering Platonic chronology, giving rise to the legend of Plato's development from immanentism to transcendentism, can also be set aside safely, now that Plato scholars are moving away, especially rapidly in recent years, from parochial patterns of interpretation dominating the field through most of the twentieth century. Much of the dogma handed down uncritically from generation to generation is either gone or on its way out.[9]

One that has proven persistent, however, is the dogma of "two worlds," which continues to distort the intellectual legacy of Plato.[10] The separation (*chōrismos*) of Forms from particulars was already being discussed in Plato's time, both by him and by those around him, as a logical problem.[11] But what if it was not an overwhelming problem for Plato? What if his universe was a single reality, as intimated in the *Timaeus*, a continuum

---

8. Standing out among the numerous treatments of this issue are Fine's articles on separation (1984) and immanence (1986), one each, and Devereux's single article (1994) on separation and immanence.

9. A progressive mindset was already in place by the end of the previous century. Consider, for example, what was fast becoming standard advice on how to read Plato: "the thought rightly attributable to the dialogues is likely to be something other than the traditional set of dogmas or doctrines, whether unitary or developing, that are found both in textbooks and scholarly writing, the philosophical system called Platonism" (Press 1993, 5). The backlash against developmentalism has been particularly strong, as illustrated in the front matter of the Hackett edition of Plato's *Complete Works*, whose editor finds it necessary, or at least useful, to "urge readers not to undertake the study of Plato's works holding in mind the customary chronological groupings of 'early,' 'middle,' and 'late' dialogues" (Cooper 1997, xiv).

10. This characterization of the two-world model as a dogma coincides with terminology (namely "dogma") also favored by Nails (2013).

11. See Plato's *Parmenides* and Aristotle's *Metaphysics* (987a29–b35, 1078b7–1079a4, 1086a30–b12) for original sources, Fine (1984; 1986) and Devereux (1994) for commentary.

of levels, somewhat as Plotinus saw it? These are not intended as purely rhetorical questions but as a springboard for interpretive possibilities, starting with direct answers in the next section.

2.3. A Two-Level Model

The two-level alternative advanced here in place of the two-world interpretation dating back to Aristotle (*Metaphysics* 990b34–991a3, 1079a32–34) is a thought experiment seeking firmer grounds for a proper explication of Plato's thought. The metaphor of levels, contrary to that of worlds, accommodates and facilitates the instantiation of Forms, without any contradiction between transcendence and immanence, while at the same time exposing a distinctively original value differential between a higher and lower order of entities or phenomena. The differences are considerable, the advantages compelling.

The underlying ontology is that of two main levels belonging together in Platonic harmony (*koinōnia*), like the sky over the earth in the worldview of Plato's contemporaries, or like gods and mortals, masters and slaves, reality and appearance, to place greater emphasis on the inherent hierarchy. It was natural for Plato to hold a two-level vision of a single world, an intuitive outlook always present in his thought but only indirectly reflected in what he said and wrote. This vision is, in all respects, prior to any theory of Forms. Plato is likely to have developed it early on, drawing on a combination of general Greek ideas and more explicit Presocratic thought.

The notion of a two-level vision in Plato was first conceived and articulated by C. J. de Vogel (1986, 50, 62, 145–148, 159–212, especially 159–171) and subsequently developed as an interpretive paradigm by Holger Thesleff (1993b, 17–45; 1999, 11–52 [= 2009, 397–436]).[12] The model can be illustrated particularly well through contrasts typical of Plato's view of reality. Imagine a representative set of complementary concepts, either assembled in a regular list or distributed along a horizontal separator as follows:[13]

---

12. Also relevant are Nails (2013, 78–87) and Press (2007, 159–171).

13. The example is from Thesleff (1999, 27 [= 2009, 411]; cf. 1993b, 21). See also Press (2007, 162).

one	same	stable	divine	soul	leading	intellect	truth	knowledge	defined
many	different	changing	human	body	being-led	senses	appearance	opinion	undefined

The concepts in question are not true opposites in the manner of those in Pythagorean and eastern thought. Plato employs his two-level vision in various ways and on various occasions. Take, for instance, his typical dialogue, where the discussion leader, representing the higher level, knows not just more than he reveals, but also more than everyone else, yet still profits from the contributions of his dialectical partners, all representing the lower level. Or take his typical irony, especially through Socrates, or his wordplay, where knowledge is covertly balanced against opinion, and reality against appearance. Or take the multilevel structure of his utopian society. The levels always operate together.

Consider the level of Forms. If transcendent Forms do not constitute a separate world, at least because such a radical separation precludes the possibility of a relationship, they must then belong to a different level within the same world. The level of Forms need not correspond to that of particulars in every detail, but it is not divorced from it either. They are two aspects of the same reality. One world, two levels—this may be as close as we get to Plato's vision of the abstract, where different terms and concepts are rarely, if ever, differentiated as perspicuously as we might wish.[14]

A two-level interpretation recommends itself for two reasons in particular. First, the imagery of levels comes with a complementary hierarchical structure within a single reality, which then stands as a cohesive whole where points, regions, and ways of contact are easier to grasp and defend, in contrast to the juxtaposition of disjointed and polarized worlds where any connection would be tenuous at best. Second, the two-level model readily accommodates Plato's orientation toward the good, owing again to its unitary hierarchical structure, whereas the two-world interpretation falls short in that respect as well, because it places the good in a separate world, thereby undermining the possibility of any conceivable connection with it or any sort of orientation toward it.

Moreover, the differentiation and order that can be had simultaneously in a single world with two levels is uniquely hospitable to a proper

---

14. Plato sometimes refers to a noetic *topos* outside the cosmos: *Republic* 509d, 517b; *Phaedrus* 247c–d, 248b. It is "over" us, as the sky is over the earth. See also *Timaeus* 50a–52e, where the "receptacle" is added as a third level.

classification of Forms, paving the way out of the cacophony in the variety of constructs passing for Forms.[15] In short, keeping things in the same world has its advantages. Fashioned after a communion (*koinōnia*) of sorts, as between anywhere upstairs and a correlative downstairs, the model is well represented throughout the canonical corpus. The most striking examples include the divided line in the *Republic* (509d–511e), the ladder of love in the *Symposium* (209e–212a), and the world-soul in the *Timaeus* (35a–36d).[16]

2.4. Classification of Forms

Any classification best begins with a definition. The term "Form," traditionally called "Idea," has misleading connotations in modern languages, some easily confused with Aristotle's conception of form versus matter. Worse, Plato's own terminology is hopelessly inconsistent. He never puts forth a clear and complete account of Forms. What we get instead is tentative visions, sometimes literally Socratic dreams, or suggestions proposed in different situations and at different times, all extremely difficult to sort out.

Since Plato does not impose terminological conventions, or issue methodological instructions, it is incumbent upon Plato scholars to figure out the central characteristics, and as many of the details as possible, of what has been handed down as Forms (or Ideas). A reasonable inference, following many interpreters since ancient times, is that a Platonic Form is a universal, yet always a unique one, and preferably a positive one, functioning as a defining characteristic, or standard model, of phenomena at the sensible level of our acquaintance with the world.

---

15. Plato's notion of the good was the cause of much perplexity in the fourth century. This was evidently due not just to what he made available through the dialogues but also to a notorious public lecture on the subject. See Alican (2012, 84–87), Cherniss (1945, 1–30, especially 1–13), Ferber (1984), Gaiser (1980), Ross (1951, 147–149, 186–187, 199–200, 204–205, 210, 244), and Thesleff (1999, 104–105, 164–165 [= 2009, 485–486, 531]). See chapter 6 (sections 6.1 and 6.2) and chapter 7 (section 7.3) for further discussion.

16. Other examples of a single reality with hierarchical levels in universal harmony (*koinōnia*) include: *Laws* 967d–e; *Phaedo* 100d; *Republic* 462a–464d, 477a–478e, 537c, 585b–c; *Sophist* 248a–e; *Theaetetus* 147d–e.

This preliminary inference is developed throughout the present chapter, but a few points of clarification might be immediately useful. Most importantly, Forms are "at least" universals, because they are invariably more than that, and because not all universals have corresponding Forms. The aphorism that "Forms are what particulars fail to be" can be adopted and adapted to assert instead that Forms are what universals fail to be.[17] This is not to deny that they are universals, but to affirm that they are indeed that, and always something more. Furthermore, though still in the same vein, the universal nature of Forms is part of what makes them unique, each one being just what it is, and not simply an example of a kind of thing called "Form." The "just itself," in Plato's thought, is not identical with what we now call "justice," but the latter term is a convenient and reasonable shorthand. Finally, the "positivity" invoked in the inference above pertains to what is valuable, significant, or interesting from Plato's point of view.

Explicating Plato's Forms in terms of universals, however, even if it is only to say that they are more than that, is open to misunderstanding. Universals no longer stand for the same thing they once did with Aristotle, thus leaving contemporary discussion far from a consensus. Nor does the conceptual and philosophical development between then and now add up, or average out, to a uniform understanding.

The customary observation that Plato reified universals does not go very far toward capturing what Plato thought to be a Form. The implicit question buried at the end of that statement ("what Plato thought to be a Form") is not even the right question. We cannot plausibly say what a Form is, as if it were just one thing, or exactly one type of thing, because the Form of justice and the Form of horse, to take just a couple of examples, are not really the same kind of thing, each one simply a Form. Plato seems to have experimented with abstraction in several different ways, ending up with different results, which are best classified in different categories or divisions.[18]

---

17. The elegantly abbreviated account that "Forms are what particulars fail to be" belongs specifically to McCabe (1994, 60), though the opinion expressed therein is not unique in the literature.

18. This does not imply any developmental conclusions, which must stand on their own, with the dialogues falling where they may in terms of chronological order. But it is quite telling in regard to the different types of entities tradition has handed down as Forms (or Ideas).

We have to keep in mind first that universals were yet to be discovered, or invented, depending on one's perspective, when Plato seems to have reified them, and second that Plato did not merely reify universals but almost deified them (in the loose sense of giving them "upper-level" qualities, not, of course, to worship them as divinities), and third that justice and horseness and everything in between are not reified or deified into the same kind of thing, or to the same extent, which then supports a broad spectrum of ontological profiles as the constituents of reality and of our experience of it.

The analogy with universals is a helpful starting point, doubling as a point of departure. Scholarly opposition to identifying Plato's Forms with universals is common enough. Some object because they find that universals fall short of Forms, others because they deny that universals exist, while recognizing that Plato considered the Forms to exist, yet others because universals are not individuals whereas Plato's Forms are, and the list goes on (see chapter 1, especially section 1.3, for further discussion).

As for the analogy itself, a good place to start is the praise Socrates receives from Parmenides for separating properties from the things of which they are properties (*Parmenides* 130b). This cannot be too far to reach from universals. The most salient point of departure is the importance Plato attaches to intrinsic value, not to be found in mere universals, nor in simply reified ones, whereupon the priority of value tends to disappear in the typically monochrome Forms discussed in much of the literature.

We may profitably recognize three distinct divisions among the referents of what are usually taken collectively as Forms:[19]

- Ideal Forms: These are metaphysically transcendent entities in the upper level of reality that embody the perfection of

---

19. The classification is silent on mathematicals (numbers and figures) because Plato himself is not clear on what those are. A common interpretation drawing on the testimony of Aristotle (*Metaphysics* 987b14-18, 1059b5-14; cf. "eidetic numbers" at 1080a23, 1081a23-25) is that Plato takes mathematicals to be a separate category between Forms and particulars. The assignment of an intermediate position may have been inspired by a late pythagorizing interpretation of segment (b) of the divided line (taken up further later in this section). Plato's interest in eidetic numbers also seems to have been a late pythagorizing experiment, as discussed in section 2.9 below (see Thesleff 1999, 91-107 [= 2009, 473-488]). Chapter 7 of the present volume provides comprehensive coverage of mathematicals as well as other intermediates.

qualities we aspire to in the lower level, as in justice, temperance, knowledge, and so on (cf. *Phaedrus* 247d–e). They have an axiological orientation culminating in the good. Put simply, they are charged with positive intrinsic value.

- Conceptual Forms: These are universals in the upper level of reality, manifested as particulars in the lower level, including concrete things (e.g., horse, ship, water) and their properties, qualities, or attributes (e.g., speed, size, color), as well as various phenomena broadly taken to comprise events, actions, and experiences, but excluding things that are either imaginary or inherently bad.

- Relational Forms: These are relational universal concepts, that is, correlative abstractions taken in contrasting pairs of apparently opposite but essentially complementary metaphysical categories together covering both levels of reality. They, too, are value-neutral in and of themselves. A good example is the pairing of rest with motion, and same with other, among the "greatest kinds" (*megista genē*) in the *Sophist* (254d–e).

Retaining the term "Form" as part of the name for each division serves as a reminder that the classification is a reorganization of what has long been discussed under this single name, though previously under the name of "Idea," still in vogue outside anglophone contexts. Ideal Forms come closest to capturing the essence of noetic perfection in what confronts us as Forms in the scholarly literature. They are objectively real paradigms of intrinsic value. Conceptual Forms and Relational Forms, in turn, represent strictly metaphysical experiments with abstraction, drawing on reification attempts outside moral, aesthetic, or religious domains.

A visual aid often makes complex thought more accessible. Fortunately, Plato provides one of the most memorable visual aids in the history of philosophy: the divided line (see Thesleff 1999, 31–32, 70–72 [= 2009, 416, 453–455]). His famous simile at the dramatic and philosophical center of the *Republic* (509d–511e) is in many ways illustrative of his two-level vision, subdivided into four segments. It can be taken as a cross-section of Plato's universe, with his ontology and epistemology in the foreground. It represents the hierarchy of all that he finds valuable.

86   ONE OVER MANY

Recall the four segments from top to bottom as (a), (b), (c), and (d).[20] If the segment of *noesis* (a) is understood to cover Ideal Forms, culminating in the good (*to agathon*), it is sensible to assign the segment of *dianoia* (b) to Conceptual Forms. Since Plato must have known that segments (b) and (c) are equal in length by mathematical necessity, it is reasonable to assume a close correspondence between the metaphysics of (b) and (c), the latter of which represents visible things (on the higher, more important, and more valuable of the bottom two levels): *zōa*, all that is *phuteuton*, even *skeuaston* of some value (510a), and geometrical figures, that is, visual illustrations (510c, 510e). These all have corresponding Conceptual Forms on level (b).[21] Relational Forms, rather than claiming a specific position on any one of the distinct levels, constitute a lateral projection of the structural representation in its entirety.

Even with the appeal to the divided line, however, much of the foregoing discussion introduces a predominance of conjecture over demonstration, which must now be supplemented with argumentation and documentation. The remainder of the chapter is devoted to fleshing out the proposed classification by showing how the proposal fits in with what Plato actually said, and to some extent, with how that has been interpreted.

2.5. Terminological Clues and Methodological Observations

The Platonic corpus is beset with ambiguity, inconsistency, and undeveloped lines of thought. This is nowhere more apparent and relevant than where the discussion turns to Forms, regarding which Plato is especially vague, laconic, and mercurial. A partial explanation of this is that the Forms were intended for philosophical rather than public discussion, and such discussion was best conducted orally, though it was often, and out of necessity, also captured in writing. The presumption of prior exposure to philosophy in general, and to the thought of Plato in particular, makes

---

20. We may imagine the line being drawn in the sand, or on a slate, before the dramatic audience. But we do not know just how Plato wanted the second cut to be made "in the same ratio" (*Republic* 509d). Nor do we know, therefore, whether the uppermost segment was meant to be the longest or the shortest. Interpretations have varied since ancient times.

21. See section 2.7 for the distinction between Conceptual Forms and mere concepts.

the delivery anything but straightforward from the perspective of outsiders, especially when reading a random passage in isolation without the minimum qualifications required for comprehension.[22]

Scholars traditionally look for linguistic clues to sort out Plato's conceptual apparatus. They typically begin with the terms *eidos* and *idea*, designations giving the Ideas, and later, the Forms, their modern name. Although the search for Forms, with *eidos* or *idea* as the descriptor, is a generic one, undifferentiated as to this or that division in the classification scheme here, it is far more likely to identify a Conceptual Form than it is to uncover an Ideal Form, and oftentimes liable to pick out nothing more than a concept, with no metaphysical overtones. Generally speaking, *eidos* and *idea*, as they occur in Plato's dialogues, approximate our notion of concept, but a concept is not a Form.

Some developmentalists have argued that *eidos* and *idea* became indicative of transcendence when Plato appropriated these terms to facilitate his experimentation with abstraction. This may well be true, but even if it is, it does not establish developmentalism as a definitive explanation of why these terms are never used in that way, and hardly ever in any way at all, in the so-called early period of Plato's career. The reason for Plato's conspicuously infrequent recourse to *eidos* and *idea* in the "early" dialogues, if such a cluster can be identified with any confidence, may be either that he had not yet developed an interest in abstraction, which would indeed support the developmentalist thesis, or that he had not yet started using these terms in a special sense indicative of abstraction, which would arguably also support the developmentalist thesis, though not as strongly, or that the corresponding texts were intended, by and large, for broader audiences liable to be alienated by esoteric terminology, as opposed to an inner circle of associates and students already familiar with Plato's usage, which would introduce an element of reasonable doubt regarding developmentalist conclusions.

It is true, in any event, that Plato uses the terms *eidos* and *idea* in a technical sense to refer to Forms. Yet he frequently uses them in their standard sense as well. How are we to distinguish, then, between the two occasions? The etymology of either word is of little help. They seem, in fact, to be practically synonymous, which makes it safe enough to focus

---

22. The *Symposium* was an exception, as may have been the *Phaedrus*, with the central issue in each concerning the heart of all theories of Forms, namely Ideal Forms. See Thesleff (2002, 289–301 [= 2009, 541–550]) for a discussion of publicity in Plato.

on the more common *eidos* for convenience. Originally, *eidos* just meant "shape" in the sense of "outward appearance," but it also, and still before Plato, signified a mental vision of the characteristic shape of something, thereby pointing to kinds, types, and classes. To Plato, it may sometimes denote an ideal shape, a model of sorts, and thus, implicitly, a concept of positive value. It remains unclear, however, to what extent this nuance was influenced by a budding theory of Forms.

Plato probably adopted the term *eidos* both for Ideal Forms and for Conceptual Forms in oral discussions of ontology and epistemology. The same may be true of *idea*. In either case, though, the result is not a systematic designation of Forms. Nor is it a reliable indicator of what Plato finds significant in metaphysical terms or valuable in ethical terms. The standard reference is to shapes and forms, but in a more abstract way than, say, *morphē* or *schēma*.[23] It is only after *eidos* and *idea* came to be employed for Ideal Forms, alongside their original usage, that they took on a philosophical connotation in addition to their original meaning.[24]

Going deeper into this complex of problems, we may infer that, in Plato's thought, pointedly abstract concepts automatically tend to be associated with the upper level of his universe, given its abstract nature. Insofar as concepts are common denominations of a group of phenomena accessible through the mind rather than through the senses (i.e., universals), they already claim some distinction, whereupon if they are conceived to be somehow real and important, and not imaginary, they merit a higher ontological ranking than their concrete manifestations. This possibility is developed further in section 2.7.

A more reliable way of tracing Plato's references to Ideal Forms is to search for his qualifications of universals with terms such as "(in) itself" or "as such" (*auto to, hauto, kath' hauto*, etc.). Similarly indicative are words for "that which really and always is" or "that which is true" (*ho estin, aei, alēthēs*, etc.) or "that which is pure" (*eilikrinēs*).[25] References to the thing

---

23. Note that *schēma* can be used for "concept," as in *Meno* 74b, *Sophist* 267c–d, and *Statesman* 277a.

24. This assessment is consistent with traditional interpretations (e.g., Ross 1951, passim), but its relevance to the chronology of the dialogues is doubtful, as discussed above in the main text.

25. Even a preliminary effort to enumerate such instances can quickly grow to cover a dozen dialogues: *Cratylus* 439c–d (*kalon, agathon*, in Socrates's dream); *Euthydemus* 292d (*epistēmē*, but in ironical context); *Hippias Major* 286d (*kalon*, 289d with *eidos*); *Laches* 194a (*aretē*, playfully personified); *Meno* 100b (*aretē*, cf. 72c); *Parmenides* 130b

(in) itself, or to the thing as such, almost always indicate an Ideal Form, as do allusions to what the thing in question "truly" or "purely" is. The *auto* qualification, in any of its distinctive formulations, emerges as the gold standard among terminological clues.

A somewhat less reliable mark of Ideal Forms is the characteristic reference to the relationship between Forms and particulars as a presence or partaking.[26] It is less reliable because it is also, at least occasionally, extended to Conceptual Forms and Relational Forms. Considering the use of terms such as *parousia*, *metechein*, and *koinōnia* (*Phaedo* 100d), it appears that the discussion of "participation" was not limited to Ideal Forms.[27] There may have been a religious background giving a specific connotation to Plato's employment of these words. The question of particulars "reflecting" or "imitating" Forms (à la *Parmenides*), on the other hand, seems to be of a different origin.

Ideal Forms are, in the first place, ideal qualities or capacities, both of gods and of human beings at their best (i.e., philosophers). This constitutes a normative benchmark pointing to the divine upper level as a model for ideal human conduct, but it does not make Plato's point of view a religious one (see Thesleff 1999, 12–15 [= 2009, 397–401]). Another obvious influence, in addition to moral considerations, is the Socratic search for universals through definitions,[28] which has traditionally been regarded as a feature of the "early" dialogues, though the prospects for dating them with any precision remain dubious and controversial.

(*homoiotēs*, see section 2.8), 134b (*to kalon, to agathon*); *Phaedo* 65d–66a (*dikaion, kalon, agathon . . . megethos, hugieia, ischus*), 106d (*zōē*, with *eidos*); *Phaedrus* 247d (*epistēmē*, seen by gods on their winged journey); *Philebus* 59b–c (the problem of *to alēthestaton*, being close to *ta aei kata ta auta hōsautōs ameiktota echonta*); *Republic* 435b (*dikaiosunē*, with *eidos*, cf. 435e, 517e), 479e (*to kalon, to dikaion*, cf. 505a, *hē tou agathou idea*, not sufficiently well known); *Sophist* 248a–b (assumptions of the *eidōn philoi*); *Symposium* 211b (Diotima's portrayal of *to kalon . . . auto kath' hauto meth' hautou monoeides aei on*). Note the context: The "upper level" eventually reached by the philosopher is like an open sea (*pelagos* at *Symposium* 210d). See also *Phaedo* 109c–d and *Republic* 611b–d. Perhaps we may imagine *to kalon* shining like a sun over the upper level (as in the *Republic*).

26. See chapter 1, especially section 1.4, for a discussion of the proposed relationships between Forms and sensible phenomena.

27. See: *Euthydemus* 301a; *Gorgias* 467e–468a, 498d; *Hippias Major* 289c–d, 294a; *Lysis* 217b–e; *Sophist* 247a.

28. Aristotle (*Metaphysics* 987b1–10) finds the roots of Plato's Forms in Socratic definitions. Dancy (2004, 23–208, 209–244), for one, explores this in great depth.

Candidates for Forms also include entities representing physical things (e.g., man, fire, water) and universal concepts representing either the properties of such things (e.g., tallness, hotness, wetness) or the relations between them (e.g., similarity and difference).[29] All this comes out clearly in the presentation of Forms throughout the *Phaedo* and in the aporia of Socrates in the *Parmenides* (130b–d). Both dialogues are explored further in the section on Relational Forms (section 2.8).

Forms for physical entities probably came later, as it is more natural to operate with abstractions grounded in properties or attributes, before doing so with the substances to which those properties or attributes belong. This is certainly true of ancient Greek, which is what is relevant here, but it also holds for other languages. While separating the equality from the sticks, or the tallness or largeness from the man, counts as a milestone in the history of our ongoing efforts to understand and describe the world around us, working with the remainder, that is, with the substances themselves, requires an altogether different operation of abstraction, marking the advent of kinds, types, and classes.

The roots of Ideal Forms are not in the *eidē* (or *ideai*) of physical things.[30] A potter's vision of a Grecian urn, for example, or a carpenter's of a bed, does not capture the reification potential that excites and motivates Plato. A painter's vision of either one of those is even less inspiring. Not even the external appearance of a demigod, a satyr, for instance, or Eros in the *Symposium*, stands to be sufficiently impressive. The playfully introduced *phutourgos* in the *Republic* (597d), representing the demiurge of the entities of segment (b) on the divided line, is certainly no cosmic Creator. All these, and much more, are eclipsed by Ideal Forms, though many such references can and might correspond to Conceptual Forms.[31]

---

29. The case of fire (*pyr*) is more complicated. Its significance for humans was beyond doubt from the earliest cosmologies onward. The *Phaedo* (103b–e) gives it a respectable position in contrasting it with snow (unpleasant and undesirable) but seems to treat only its property, hotness (*thermon*), and not fire itself, as a Form (see section 2.8). Yet the presentation of Forms in the *Timaeus* (50c–52d) covers all four of the traditional elements, including fire (51b).

30. Broadie (2007) rightly rejects (Ideal) Forms for artifacts in the early "Platonistic tradition," but she does not consider anything like the floating category of Conceptual Forms, which would have been useful in accommodating *Republic* 510a–b.

31. See section 2.7 for a possible approximation of Conceptual Forms (and, in general, of universals representing sensible phenomena) to Ideal Forms. See section 2.8

A question eagerly debated in the literature remains open here: Were Platonic theories of Forms more Socratic early on and less so later? That is to say, were they, in their beginnings, more dependent on the Socratic search for moral truth, or as is alleged just as often, on artists' and artisans' search for models? To put it differently, are they better captured by the *eidos* (*idea*) approach, as with Conceptual Forms, or by the *auto* approach, as with Ideal Forms? Since neither chronology nor developmentalism is of particular concern in the present discussion, an open-ended "both/and" resolution will help avoid straying far from Plato with a forced "either/or" choice.

The next three sections focus in greater detail on the different divisions of Forms in the order indicated above.

2.6. Ideal Forms

Ideal Forms epitomize Plato's two-level vision. They have always been regarded, both by Plato and by advocates or critics, as the most representative examples of Forms. The most detailed discussion of Ideal Forms as the philosopher's specialty can be found in the *Phaedo* and in the central books of the *Republic*. The contrast between "philosophers" and "others" is especially indicative (*Republic* 475e ff.). See the preceding section for explicit markers, terminological as well as methodological.

Ideal Forms are best described, following many other commentators, though possibly opposing just as many, as transcendent, intelligible, paradigmatic, perfect, immutable, simple, and unique.[32] The list as a whole applies only to Ideal Forms, but some of the features are also found in the other two types of Forms. In any case, the criterion of positive intrinsic value is peculiar to Ideal Forms.

---

for similar approximations of the dominant element in Relational Forms (the paired component typically listed first) to Ideal Forms.

32. The features listed here tend to turn up anywhere from journal articles and scholarly monographs to the expository sections of the growing stock of companions to Plato. One example is Grube's monograph, *Plato's Thought*, where the first sentence alone goes through several of the features on the list (1935, 1). *The Continuum Companion to Plato* (Press 2012) covers most of the same features in two short entries: one on the Forms (contributed by Sayre, 173–175) and one on ontology (contributed by Silverman, 218–220). As for philosophy textbooks, a popular one currently in its ninth edition describes the Forms as "independently existing, nonspatial, nontemporal 'somethings' ('kinds,' 'types,' or 'sorts') that cannot be known through the senses" (Soccio 2015, 133).

The list is fairly representative of how Ideal Forms are portrayed in the dialogues, but it is not decisive or exhaustive. Some of the descriptors may be redundant, and yet others may need to be added. For example, we can immediately add that Ideal Forms are eternal and incorporeal, though these two features may be said to be redundant with, or implied by, those already listed. Both eternality and incorporeality (sometimes just "invisibility") can probably be inferred directly from the original list, but Plato does make a point of mentioning them separately, for example, in the *Phaedo* (78c–80b).

Another important feature of Ideal Forms is an exalted ontological status representing ultimate reality, the cosmic embodiment of true being, in contrast to the contingent mode of existence in the lower, phenomenal level. The importance of this two-level feature is not just metaphysical but epistemological as well, since the ultimate reality in question, with the stability it embodies, constitutes our only hope of attaining knowledge, the kind grounded in universal truth, as opposed to settling for mere opinion or belief (*pistis* on the divided line), affording no greater reliability than the illusory objects of perception at our own level of existence.

Causality may be added as yet another feature, but the etiological function of Forms is a controversial topic. Nobody is sure how it works. Even so, Forms are often invoked, both by Plato and by commentators, either as causal agents or in causal explanations. There is much talk of communion, inherence, partaking, participation, and so on. Yet these concepts are not themselves all that clear. Nor do they all describe the same process or relationship. The Aristotelian "final cause" is not relevant either. A popular attempt at clarification, to cite just one example, is the Vlastosian One-over-Many Principle, but that just presents the Form as a unifying principle for a multitude of things of the same kind (Vlastos 1954, 320).

A detailed analysis of clear or potentially clear cases of Ideal Forms in the dialogues would reveal a focus on moral value, which usually goes hand in hand with aesthetic value.[33] This is because intrinsically valuable entities are, from a human perspective, good in an exemplary sense. Ideal Forms do not come with negative counterparts that are also Ideal Forms. To elaborate, beauty and ugliness are opposite attributes, or properties, just as beautiful and ugly are opposite existential states, or aesthetic judgments, but at that level, neither one is an Ideal Form, though both

---

33. Such an analysis, with the focus specified, and the depth and breadth required, has never been conducted, not even by W. D. Ross (1951).

do well as concepts (discussed in section 2.7 on Conceptual Forms). At the level of Ideal Forms, we are sure to find the beautiful right where Plato placed it, but we will find no sign of the ideally ugly throughout the canonical corpus.[34]

This account builds on the cumulative evidence of passages in many dialogues, as illustrated in the preceding section, since none of them alone offers a clear and complete record (see the conspectus in Erler 2007, 390–406). As Plato himself points out, this is a much-discussed matter (*poluthrulēta* at *Phaedo* 100b).[35] The abundance of discussion, of course, is not an indication that the matter, having been thoroughly examined, may now be put to rest, but that it is to be investigated further still.

Plato often emphasizes the difficulties awaiting philosophers in comprehending the Forms. Although the original reference is, dramatically, to Socrates and his associates, and by extension, to Plato and his associates, it holds up rather well in transference to modern scholarship. Two areas where the views sketched here differ pointedly from any consensus prevailing in the literature are: first, the positive intrinsic value attributed to Ideal Forms, a feature largely implicit in the foregoing discussion and exemplified further later on (section 2.10 on negative Forms), and second, the set of distinctive characteristics that belong exclusively to Ideal Forms, and not to other Forms, nor to concepts or abstractions that are not reified as Forms.

2.7. Conceptual Forms

2.7.1. Conceptualization and Formalization

What makes a Form a Form? Inadequate attention to this question has been one of the biggest stumbling blocks in the study of Plato since antiquity.

---

34. The ugly as an Ideal Form is nowhere to be found in Plato's dialogues. Mention of the ugly (*Euthydemus* 301b; *Hippias Major* 289c–d; *Republic* 475e–476a; *Theaetetus* 186a), often in contrast to the beautiful, is common enough, but it remains at the conceptual level, pointing at best to Conceptual Forms, though more likely to mere concepts. See section 2.10 and chapter 6 for further discussion of the possibility of negative Forms.

35. See Tarrant (2000, 43). Attaining certainty about *to agathon* is almost hopeless, as evidenced, for example, in *Parmenides* 134b–c; *Philebus* 64a–c; *Republic* 496a–497d, 505a; and *Timaeus* 29d.

Very few of the innumerable abstractions with which the human mind operates are Ideal Forms. This is clear enough from the criteria laid out in the previous section. Yet a great many universals outside the core of Ideal Forms have traditionally also been classified as Forms, both by Plato and by others. How do those differ from mere concepts? And what are the criteria for qualification as Forms?

Classical Greek was eminently suitable for abstractions, both for using the ones in hand and for creating new ones, often as derivatives, easily generated with the aid of the article *to*. For the most part, such abstractions have nothing to do with Forms. Even with the anachronistic term "concept" standing for all abstractions, or for all universals, including those representing imaginary phenomena, there is no clear distinction in Plato between concepts and the words (names, *onomata*) that refer to them.[36] The linguistic expression is crucial, however, not just for Plato but also for a discussion of concepts.

The linguistic expression is not merely "the thing" as Antisthenes and others have held.[37] Spoken or written names of things, including what we might call "concepts" as a general term for all abstractions, can always be expressed by words. If such concepts turn out to be "real" or "important" universals from Plato's perspective, we can expect him to place them in the upper level of his universe, in close proximity to Ideal Forms. Examples follow below, but the claim itself cannot be proven, nor its details fully worked out, given the silence of Plato.

Complicating matters to some extent, both Conceptual Forms and the dominant element in Relational Forms can, depending on the context, approximate to Ideal Forms, in which case they each appear to take on some of the associated features. This is not to say that these Forms themselves undergo a transformation, but that Plato comes to treat them differently. Nor is there a specific subset of features identified with Ideal Forms that tends to be taken on by the other two kinds when they do approximate to Ideal Forms. The resulting ontological ascent is an arbitrary tendency,

---

36. Examples abound in the *Cratylus* and the *Sophist*. The *Timaeus* (52a) makes it clear that Ideal Forms are *homōnuma* with particular things. But taken as words, concepts are naturally nouns, or substantivized infinitives, as in *to eidenai* (*Phaedo* 75d), rather than finite verbs. While words and denominations may vary, it is through them that the diairetic process may reach the Forms. See *Statesman* 261e-262b, 285a-287d.

37. Diogenes Laërtius (6.3) reports that Antisthenes "was the first to define statement (or assertion) by saying that a statement is that which sets forth what a thing was or is" (Loeb translation).

not a systematic process. The question of which features, or that of how many, does not have a set answer and must be decided on a case-by-case basis. Plato is seldom exact on the sliding scale of his two-level vision.

A telling example of Plato's treatment of concepts is the diairetic method, with which he and his younger friends experimented. An experiment along these lines may perchance end up at the level of Ideal Forms.[38] Normally, however, it remains on a more linguistic level through "division and collection," the dialectical process of separating and grouping concepts. The concept of angler, for example, can be divided, reconstructed, and combined with other concepts, but it never becomes anything like an Ideal Form. The method is likely to have been originally designed for definitional purposes, not as speculative or theoretical exercises in support of an ontological system.[39] Note that even Ideal Forms are concepts (in addition to whatever else Plato would have them be), both in their Socratic origins and from our own vantage point. The converse, of course, does not hold: Not all concepts are Forms, let alone Ideal Forms. Nor are they all suitable for formalization as such.

All the same, it is evidently a short step from concept to Conceptual Form. To be more precise, the step, short or long, is from our conception of concept to our understanding of what Plato might likely have considered a Conceptual Form. Otherwise, projecting all this back into Plato is mostly a heuristic device for sorting out what he was doing. The simple explanation, given the premise that there is a Conceptual Form for just about everything, or more accurately, for everything Plato somehow found real or important, is that anything Plato was willing and able to conceptualize ended up as a Conceptual Form.[40]

However, we should not make the relationship between concept and Form as fluent as all that. Not every concept picks out a Form, not even

---

38. The method of division and collection is clearly articulated in the *Phaedrus* (249b–c, 265d–266c). See also the *Hippias Major* (301b ff.), *Philebus* (16c–17a), *Sophist* (253c–e), and *Statesman* (287c). The dialectician knows how to proceed.

39. The *Gorgias* (462e–466e) provides some corroboration. See also Prodicus on semantic distinctions in the *Protagoras* (340a–341e, 358a–e) and the eristic games in the *Euthydemus*.

40. See the discussion of the divided line in section 2.4. Conceptual Forms, given their plenitude and their possibly exhaustive coverage of phenomenal experience, may be Plato's answer to Parmenides's emphasis on the importance of not dismissing or underestimating apparently trivial candidates for abstraction (*Parmenides* 130e). Trivialities, however, probably interested the Academy more than they did Plato (see the *Sophist* and *Statesman*).

potentially. Plato makes this abundantly clear in dialogues where the Forms play a central role, especially in the *Parmenides*. Although Forms belong in the upper level of Plato's universe, the lower level is not set aside for exact and complete replicas of them so as to produce a mirror image of the upper level. The continuity of the levels must be kept in mind, as must the correlation between Ideal Forms and the other two kinds.

As already mentioned (section 2.4), the divided line suggests a direct correspondence between segments (b) and (c). The latter consists of physical things manifested as neutral phenomena in terms of value. These are things that are neither good nor bad in themselves, only instrumentally so, if at all, though the text is silent on their possible misuse (*Republic* 510a). It is easy to infer, and prudent to do so, that segment (b) of the line represents Conceptual Forms, vague though the connection may be. And it is reasonable to claim, as demonstrated in section 2.10, that no Platonic Form stands for the bad, and none again for the trivial (see chapter 6).

Relative value, or importance, is key here. Not all concepts are interesting for Plato. Not even all Conceptual Forms are of equal relevance in his universe. Some are more important than others. This is largely a reflection of the differential importance already existing at the phenomenal level, where some things are decidedly more important than others, often but not always depending on who is doing the valuation. Given a certain threshold of significance, Conceptual Forms stand for epistemically reliable phenomena. They are not identified with conjecture or fantasy, as is segment (d) of the line, but they are also not associated with noetic knowledge. Plato seems to regard them as objects for opinion informed by rational thought (cf. *Republic* 475e–480a; the divided line at 509d–511e; and *Timaeus* 51d–e).

The two-level vision, with its sliding scales, allows concepts a partial approximation to Forms, denied by the customary (Parmenidean) "either/or" logic. Concepts may, as it happens, be used in contexts where they resemble Forms, taking on some of the features enumerated in the preceding section. They then acquire a higher dignity, so to speak, than ordinary concepts. They become Conceptual Forms. The acquired dignity, or metaphysical eminence, that marks their transformation also confirms their ontological status as suprasensible abstractions, perhaps with a few other impressive attributes, and thus secures for them a higher ranking in Plato's stratification of reality.

Working with a two-level vision of reality, Plato is likely to have intuitively designed Conceptual Forms relatively close to Ideal Forms, whether or not he explicitly used the term *eidos*.⁴¹ The same applies to the less common *idea* (e.g., *Phaedo* 104d; *Phaedrus* 246a), though the connotation of Ideal Form is perhaps more prominent in that case.⁴² Plato was comfortable with ambiguity, as his use of play and irony suggests (see Thesleff 2017). No wonder the term *eidos* can stand for an Ideal Form as well as a Conceptual Form.⁴³ To place the terminology in the context of the divided line, we may observe that *eidos* is used in a broad sense for invisible objects (*Republic* 510c), and for classes of visible ones (510d), all the while pointing to the process of abstract conceptualization (511c).

Sometimes we find markers other than *eidos* indicating the approximation of a concept to a Form.⁴⁴ It is often impossible for us, and probably was for Plato as well, to say precisely when a concept receives the connotation of a Form. Take, for instance, *to dikaion*. In Greek, it is sometimes synonymous with *dikaiosunē* (righteousness as an ideal human virtue), but

---

41. Here are some instances (among a vast assortment) of *eidos* in reference to Conceptual Forms, easily mistaken for Ideal Forms, if the criteria for the latter are not taken into account: *Cratylus* 389a-b, 390b (on the *eidos* of the carpenter's shuttle); *Gorgias* 503e (*dēmiourgoi blepontes pros . . . eidos ti*); *Republic* 596a (the apparent revelation that "we are in the habit of positing a single *eidos* for the various *polla* to which we give the same name"), followed by 596b-608b (the rather playful example of the *eidos* and *idea* of "bed," made by the *phutourgos* and imitated by the carpenter, and the result, in turn, imitated by the artist); *Sixth Letter* 322d (*hē eidōn sophia*, including both Ideal Forms and Conceptual Forms as well as diairetic counterparts); *Sophist* 248a (*hoi tōn eidōn philoi*, referring to Academic radicals), 253d (on the dialectician distinguishing *eidē* in *diairesis*); *Statesman* 258e (on the statesman, king, master, and so on, as one); *Theaetetus* 148d (*dunamis*); *Timaeus* 51c (on the possibility of an *eidos* for every object). See the lists in des Places (1964, 159-161).

42. For this controversial issue, see Ross (1951, passim), Guthrie (1975, 114-121; 1978, 19-29), and the list in des Places (1964, 260-261). Note the possibly playful point at *Theaetetus* 203e, which is not directly concerned with Forms.

43. The parade example is *Republic* 445c. See section 2.7.2 of this chapter.

44. Examples of conceptual reification through designations other than *eidos* may be found in the following passages: *Parmenides* 133d-e (*autos doulos, ho esti doulos*); *Phaedrus* 260a, 261c-d (*ta ontōs agatha, to dikaion*); *Philebus* 59c (the pure, true, etc., and their cognates); *Republic* 401c (some craftsmen attempt to reach the *phusis* of *to kalon*, cf. 402c), 438c-439b (*epistēmē autē*, compared to thirst); *Seventh Letter* 342a-344d (the philosophical digression with the circle as an example of a Conceptual Form, cf. 342c); *Sophist* 235e (*alēthēs summetria*, cf. *Statesman* 284d, *auto t'akribes*); *Timaeus* 30c (*ta noēta zōia*, cf. 37c).

it also implies what is right, whether in general or in a given situation or simply in theory (cf. the German *das Rechte*). Or consider *to kalon*, or any of the many nuances of *epistēmē*. Such value concepts become easily identified with Ideal Forms if their reference is not clearly specified. The question of transcendence versus immanence is largely *non liquet*.

2.7.2. OPPOSITION AND POLARIZATION

Opposite terms invoking positive and negative values are commonly contrasted in Plato's works, but typically only as concepts, not as transcendent Forms. To some extent, this is a rhetorical device for intensifying their sense through juxtaposition. The tendency is to put the positive term first.[45]

Such cases usually have nothing to do with Forms, certainly not with Ideal Forms. We might, however, be tempted, on occasion, to regard the dominant member of a pair of opposites as representing a Form. Although this is more common with Relational Forms (see section 2.8), there are other occurrences of a comparable nature. In the existential digression of the *Theaetetus* (172c–179b), for example, the two *paradeigmata* of life (176e) primarily concern the general orientation toward models of behavior, not Ideal Forms. Still, at some point (175c), *autē dikaiosunē* slips in, together with its opposite, *adikia*.

Another example is *Republic* 475e–476e. Opening the discussion on true philosophers, Socrates contrasts the opposites *kalon* and *aischron*. Similarly, he says that each of the *eidos* (476a3) of *dikaion*, *adikon*, *agathon*, *kakon*, and the like, is one, but that (in *koinōnia*) their manifestations are many. He then centers on the philosopher's orientation toward *to kalon* (476b), taken explicitly as an Ideal Form. A reasonable interpretation is to take *eidos* at 476a only in the sense of a concept, which can naturally

---

45. There are many examples of opposition without reification, including, but not limited to, the following: *Charmides* 169b (*epistēmē* of *epistēmē* and *anepistēmosunē*), 174c (*epistēmē* of *to kakon te kai agathon*); *Lysis* 216d–218c, where the somewhat ironical discussion of opposites, including *to kalon* and *to kakon*, brings with it the term *parousia* (217b), yet without reference to Forms (cf. *Euthydemus* 301a-b); *Meno* 72a (manifestations of *aretē* and *kakia*); *Phaedo* 60b, 71a, 103b, and passim (opposites arising from one another, as *hēdu* from *lupē*, *dikaioteron* from *adikōteron*, etc.); *Republic* 402c (guardians recognizing *ta tēs sōphrosunēs eidē kai andreias . . . kai ta toutōn enantia*, certainly not implying Ideal Forms); *Sophist* 247a-e (some having a presence of *dikaiosunē* in their soul, others the opposite); *Symposium* 209b (begetting always done with *to kalon*, never with *to aischron*).

have opposites. This passage seems to illustrate the dramatic *apo skopias* reflection of Socrates, looking back, as if "from a lookout," over the dialectical ground covered, and declaring that there is one *eidos* of *aretē*, but an infinite number (of *eidē*) of *kakia* (445c).[46] Here, the term *eidos* is used with typical Platonic ambiguity. Uniqueness refers to an Ideal Form, plurality to various concepts (types, kinds).

Again, in the *Republic*, specifically in the final book, where we encounter one of Plato's proofs for the immortality of the soul (608c–612a), Socrates contends that everything susceptible to destruction has an inherent *to kakon* (*xumphuton*, 609a) that brings about its destruction. But the inherent evil of the soul, namely *adikia*, turns out to be incapable of destroying it. Plato never refers to a Form of the soul, though its contacts with the higher level are obvious (see sections 4.3 and 7.6). At any rate, this curious argument suggests that negative Forms do not reach the uppermost level of Plato's universe.

2.8. Relational Forms

Relational Forms are correlative universal relations representing complementary metaphysical categories responsible for the fundamental nature and structure of the universe, not in its minutiae, nor from a moral or aesthetic standpoint, but as a cosmic complex with an organic constitution. They can, in principle, be recognized, wherever they occur, as contrasting pairs of relational universal concepts.[47] Yet the fact that they may appear upon first impression to be little more than opposite terms can frustrate a search for them in any dialogue.

One obstacle to recognition is the ever-present possibility of false positives lurking behind the abundance of dialectical occasions for comparing and contrasting concepts, which often turn out to be just that, concepts and nothing more. The search can still be tricky, though, even upon correctly identifying works where Relational Forms are sure to be present. Two such dialogues, *Phaedo* and *Parmenides*, take us back and forth between mere

---

46. See, for example, *Philebus* 12c: many *morphai* of *hēdonē*, but only one term for it. See also *Sophist* 256e: many *eidē* of being, innumerable ones of nonbeing. The language used in the Cave does not reach the Forms (see Harte 2007).

47. See the discussion in Thesleff (1999, 74-90 [= 2009, 457-472]), where they are called "categories," following Plotinus.

concepts and actual Forms, in fact, covering all three categories of Forms, as the discussion shifts and the mode of expression switches, repeatedly and apparently whimsically, between the *eidos* label and *auto* expressions.

The *Phaedo* begins with Ideal Forms, each one stamped with the definitive *auto* designation (65d–66a) and imbued with positive intrinsic value. As noted above (section 2.4), neither of the other two categories of Forms is charged with intrinsic value. Yet the *Phaedo* is quick to bring Conceptual Forms into the mix, as Socrates mentions them in the same breath as Ideal Forms (65d). Relational Forms come later, initially through talk of similarity and difference (74a ff.), predictably standing out with their paired format. The format alone, however, can be misleading, as Conceptual Forms sometimes also come in pairs, albeit in metaphysically less significant ones. Conceptual Forms can, in fact, easily be confused both with Ideal Forms and with Relational Forms, a prospect that becomes especially relevant during the "second sailing" (*deuteros plous*) from 99c onward,[48] beginning as early as the contrast between *megethos* and *smikrotēs* (100e).[49]

Although the *Phaedo* employs the terms *eidos* and *idea* for apparently the same entities, particularly in its extended search for a plausible proof of the immortality of the soul, the focus is mainly on etiological and relational correlates (large and small, hot and cold, odd and even). The logic of the final argument is controversial (105b–107a),[50] as is the conceptual and dialectical groundwork building up to it (96a–105a), but what is important here is that the primary member of each relational pair (large, hot, odd) is dominant relative to its counterpart (small, cold, even).[51] Both are concepts, possibly also Conceptual Forms (either as *eidos* or as *idea*), but when presented together as a pair, they can easily be mistaken for Relational Forms. Making matters worse, the first member

---

48. The "second sailing" (*deuteros plous*) of the *Phaedo* (99c) probably draws on Plato's own autobiographical transition from fascination with teleological explanations originating in Presocratic philosophy to the development of hypothetical explanations through the Forms.

49. See Sedley (2007b, 82) for problems in taking *auto to ison* as just an Ideal Form. Relational Forms are manifested with sliding scales, as discussed further, later in this section.

50. See Alican (2012, 435–450), Denyer (2007, 87–96), and Erler (2007, 608–611).

51. See Thesleff (1999, 7–10, 11–25, 74–90, 120–121 [= 2009, 393–396, 397–410, 457–472, 501–502]).

in each pair has an additional tendency to appear, at least to the Greek mind in antiquity, as stronger and better, and hence, as closer to Ideal Forms, despite lacking the requisite intrinsic value.

The potential for confusion is considerable. The classification of correlative components in certain relational pairs as Conceptual Forms rather than Relational Forms, as exemplified in the preceding paragraph with large versus small, hot versus cold, and odd versus even, would seem to indicate substantial overlap between the two categories of Forms outside Ideal Forms, possibly even suggesting that Relational Forms are not so much a separate division of Forms as they are a subdivision of Conceptual Forms. They might then come across as little more than Conceptual Forms that happen to be paired up as complementary relations.

That would not, however, be an accurate interpretation. Relational Forms are inherently and categorically different from Conceptual Forms, even where the latter kind comes in pairs as well. The occasional overlap in format is not decisive. This is because Relational Forms do not represent just any combination of opposites, such as clean versus dirty, or loud versus quiet, but metaphysically fundamental structural relations paired as complementary contrasts, such as rest versus motion, or same versus other (cf. *Sophist* 254d–e). The ontological significance and cosmological function of Relational Forms jointly carve out a separate category for them among the Forms. The lateral perspective of Plato's two levels, as reflected in and through Relational Forms, thus opens up a new dimension for understanding the organizational structure of the universe.

To return to the practical assessment of difficulties in distinguishing between the various categories of Forms invoked in the dialogues, we must note that Plato's coverage of Forms is just as exhaustive in the *Parmenides*, and his presentation just as meandering there, as it is in the *Phaedo*. The discussion in the *Parmenides* opens with Relational Forms (128e–130a), such as one and many, similarity and difference, rest and motion, characterized by *auto* expressions (and *ho estin*) combined with the *eidos* label (*idea* also occurs, but *eidos* dominates). This start anticipates, at least dramatically, the Eleatic opposition between unity and plurality, and between permanence and change, through the Parmenidean notion of the One as the basis of reality, representing a philosophical problem that turns out to be the driving force of the dialectical portion of the dialogue (137c–166c).

Already impressed with the insightfulness of the young Socrates in separating Forms from sensible phenomena, Parmenides quickly comes to the point: What kinds of things have separate *eidē*? The full response of Socrates comes piecemeal in the form of replies to a series of more specific follow-up questions by Parmenides. The exchange between the two covers all three categories of Forms in succession as Parmenides presses Socrates on the matter of their ontological independence.

Relational Forms come first, recalling examples in the opening exchange between Socrates and Zeno, namely one and many, similarity and difference, rest and motion (128e–130a), which Socrates immediately acknowledges as having separate *eidē* (130b). These are followed by several examples that are familiar to us as Ideal Forms, specifically the just, the beautiful, and the good (130b), all of which Socrates again affirms in one fell swoop as having separate *eidē*. The problem arises with the uncertainty of Socrates regarding the status of physical objects, such as man, fire, and water (130c)—corresponding to Conceptual Forms in the classification scheme employed here—coupled with his conviction that trivial things, such as hair, mud, and dirt (130c–d), cannot have *eidē* of their own.

Something of an aporia sets in as Socrates openly expresses misgivings concerning his own responses, which jointly inspire him to question the consistency of accepting Forms for some things but not for others. This prompts the prophetic remark of Parmenides that Socrates will eventually, through philosophy, learn to appreciate the entire spectrum of things just considered, never treating any of them as unworthy of attention (130e). The semblance of a positive suggestion masks the underlying absence of either affirmation or denial that everything has a Form. There is no commitment, just encouragement. The invitation of the passage to embrace the full range of phenomena, despite having already repudiated Forms for certain types of things, and having done so with conviction, confirms the intricacies of a proper understanding and classification of Forms. However, we may still doubt Plato's own interest in trivialities.

Parmenides's subsequent elenchus operates chiefly with separate *eidē*, or transcendent Forms, as does the logical (philosophical) exercise that occupies the second part of the dialogue (137c–166c). The elenchus involves Relational Forms treated as Ideal Forms (though without neglecting the second, inferior member in the relevant pairs), in addition to proper Ideal Forms, such as knowledge, beauty, and the good (134a–c). Conceptual Forms also seem to enter into the picture (133c–d), but there are no clear examples of negative Forms.[52] As most interpreters agree, the

---

52. The curious pair of "being a master" and "being a slave" (*Parmenides* 133e) seems to point to Relational Forms. Yet the context is logical rather than axiological, which

elenchus can reasonably be taken as a preparation for the discussion in the *Sophist* of the *sumplokē* of *eidē* (259e), the interweaving process where Ideal Forms, Conceptual Forms, and Relational Forms cross paths as they enter into one another's domain.

The *Sophist* provides fertile grounds for Relational Forms. As already mentioned in section 2.4, and referenced again earlier in this section, Relational Forms come into play through the categories introduced as *megista genē* (254d–e), soon also termed *eidē* and *ideai*. The *Timaeus* (35a–36d), for its own part, utilizes Relational Forms as elements of the world-soul, which thereby takes on a cosmic mediatory function oriented toward the good. Drawing on these two dialogues, the list of examples from the *Phaedo* and the *Parmenides* can be expanded further,[53] bearing in mind that, despite coming in pairs of contrasts, the relevant entities are not polar opposites but correlative relations. They concern metaphysically significant concepts and phenomena, though they are not intrinsically value laden, which is an exclusive feature of Ideal Forms. They reflect the asymmetrical intertwinings of Plato's two-level universe, seen laterally, as it were. Their lateral reach and metaphysical significance together allow us to identify both members of each pair as Forms. The lower member is far from Ideal Forms, but its higher counterpart can sometimes masquerade as one.

Reflections on Relational Forms, especially on the first member of each pair, may indeed bring to mind Ideal Forms, as in Socrates's opening ponderings in the *Parmenides* (one, similarity, rest). Yet this would take us down the wrong track. They are, more than anything, "categories" or "kinds" (*genē* being a more appropriate term than *eidē*) covering the two levels (see Thesleff 1999, 74–90 [= 2009, 457–472]). The second member (many, difference, motion) can potentially be associated with bad things or evil qualities (see section 2.10), though it does not represent anything negative in itself. The *Sophist*, for example, invokes such concepts not only

---

is to say that the emphasis is on conceptual contrast rather than relative value, despite the implicit valuation in the master-slave relationship. Note also that the institution of slavery has nothing of the metaphysical significance characterizing Relational Forms, though it does have a forceful metaphorical relevance in this particular context.

53. An expanded list would include the following relational pairs: being (*ousia*) / being something (*einai ti*); one (*hen, monon*) / many, number (*polla, plēthos, arithmos*); sameness (*tauton*) / difference (*thateron, heteron, allon*); rest, stability (*stasis, hestanai, hēsuchazein*, etc.) / motion, change (*kinēsis, gignesthai*, etc.); bigger (*meizon, mallon*) / smaller (*elatton, hētton*); whole (*holon*) / parts, divisibility (*meros, meriston*).

to explain the *sumplokē* of *eidē*, originating in abstract concepts in the employment of language, but also to make room for negation (through "otherness").

The *Theaetetus* (185c–186c) is also open to misinterpretation in that regard, as the young partner of the dramatic Socrates suggests, with some encouragement from Socrates, that what counts as Relational Forms in the present classification constitutes a prerequisite for abstract thinking about the all.[54] The examples that follow are not Ideal Forms. They come in contrasting pairs of correlative relations, with the first member pointing to a higher level, and they lack important characteristics of Ideal Forms, most notably, intrinsic value (see section 2.6).

Unfortunately, Plato's indiscriminate use of the terms *eidos* and *idea* in the context of all three categories of Forms, combined with his occasional but potentially misleading introduction of Relational Forms with markers typically reserved for Ideal Forms (*auto* expressions), has had a snowball effect in conceptual confusion, as the clutter became perpetuated through contradictory interpretations throughout the history of Plato scholarship. A more comfortable, if less precise, alternative has been to label pretty much any abstraction a "Form," which can appear surprisingly authoritative with all the capitalization and scare quotes.

2.9. First Principles

A further source of confusion is the problem of the fundamental metaphysical principles (*archai, prōta*) Plato is said to have communicated orally: the one (*to hen*) and the-great-and-the-small (*to mega kai to mikron*), or the great-and-small (*tou megalou kai mikrou*), commonly invoked either with or without the hyphens. The-great-and-the-small is also known as the indefinite dyad (*he ahoristos duas*), not to mention comparable expres-

---

54. After abruptly displacing the good where one might expect to find it at the top of the divided line (*Republic* 509d–511e), the unhypothetical first principle of the all remains confined to that metaphor, never to be heard of again, at least not outside that context. Much of the modern literature is focused on whether the good and the all are somehow the same: either two aspects of the same thing, or two ways of thinking about the same thing, or outright identical. The scholarly debate to date seems to be leaning toward the identity interpretation. See Nails (2013, 88–101) both for a survey of the literature and for a challenge to the mainstream interpretation.

sions capturing its mathematical essence as being open (infinite) in both directions, toward greatness as well as toward smallness, toward more as well as toward less (see chapter 7, section 7.2.2).[55]

The place of these first principles in Plato's thought became a major concern in the 1960s as Tübingen scholars began to make inroads into documenting the credibility and importance of the so-called unwritten doctrines or teachings (*agrapha dogmata*), the purported outlet for the exposition and discussion of important matters not to be found in the canonical corpus, except perhaps in a rudimentary fashion requiring interpretation if not interpolation and extrapolation.

Recently, it has been argued that these two principles, together with a theory of ideal numbers (grounded in a Pythagorean mystical *tetraktus*, i.e., $1 + 2 + 3 + 4 = 10$, constituting the basis of arithmology and geometry), the latter of which Speusippus may have abandoned (see Aristotle: *Metaphysics* 1086a3–6), were a rather late pythagorizing experiment by Plato, in fact, an application of the two-level model (see Thesleff 1999, 91–107 [= 2009, 473–488]).

However that may be, Plato's first principles must not be confused with Relational Forms, nor can they be fully divorced from them, especially not structurally, as they essentially pair up unity and plurality as correlative relations through the interaction of the one and the-great-and-the-small. There is, in contrast, relatively little chance of their being confused with Ideal Forms or Conceptual Forms.

We know that some early commentators, probably members of Plato's Academy, came to take the-great-and-the-small as somehow symbolizing matter and evil (see Aristotle: *Physics* 203a4–16, 209b; *Metaphysics* 988a14–16, 1091b31–35). This trend corresponds to speculations about a metaphysically active negative psychic force, negative in the sense of bad or evil, which was an outlook on the rise in the Academy toward the end of Plato's life. Persian thought is likely to have been an influence there. Echoes of such speculations can be seen in new interpretations of the-great-and-the-small, especially on the strength of textual evidence in the introduction of a secondary (bad) world-soul in the *Laws* (896e–897d) and *Epinomis* (988c–e).[56]

---

55. See Reale (1990, 67–68), among others, for relevant terminological alternatives.

56. See the *Sophist* (268c–275c) and the *Timaeus* (48a) for a more genuinely Platonic background. See Nails and Thesleff (2003, 14–29) for why the *Laws* might not be so genuinely Platonic.

2.10. Negative Forms?

Any attempt to classify the Forms, or even simply to understand them, must deal with the question of negative Forms: Does Plato make room for negative Forms in his ontology? This question doubles as the subtitle of chapter 6, which offers a comprehensive discussion of the possibility of negative Forms. The aim of the present section is to acknowledge that possibility as a potential problem, while demonstrating that the model advocated here is sensitive to the issue and illustrating that its steadfast application reveals a solution to the problem.

The problem is not with the prevalence of negative concepts, for those are not Forms, though they are admittedly legion. What we must determine, rather, is whether there are any actual Forms that are negative, particularly Ideal Forms, such as the bad itself, the unjust itself, and the unholy itself. We can rule out negative Relational Forms, given that Relational Forms carry no intrinsic value, be it positive or negative. They come in pairs of value-neutral elements standing in a complementary relationship and jointly explicating fundamental universal categories. Despite the hierarchical nature of the correlation, the lower, or subordinate, element is not negative, especially not in the sense of evil. It is merely at a preferential disadvantage that may be psychological or cultural, whereby positive thoughts about the element typically listed first (because it is preferred) relegate the one listed second to a subordinate complementary status.

The focus must therefore be primarily on Ideal Forms, and by extension, perhaps also on any Conceptual Forms that may come to be associated with Ideal Forms. That is precisely where the problem can be expected if there are any negative Forms at all. Since Ideal Forms are, by definition, oriented toward that which is good and desirable, anything to undermine their goodness and desirability would overturn the classification espoused here. And menacing examples of apparently negative Ideal Forms are indeed available in the Platonic corpus. The critical reader may benefit from contemplating the salient passages.

The most conspicuous case is the beginning of the elenchus in the *Euthyphro* (5c–6e), where Socrates tries to elicit from Euthyphro a definition of piety, which creates an occasion for contrasting the holy (*to hosion*) and the unholy (*to anhosion*), using markers suggesting an Ideal Form (*auto, idea, eidos*, cf. 15d). Plato is teasing his audience here. Even ancient critics must have noticed the terminological slide where the otherwise reliable Bodleian manuscript reads *hosiotēta* at *Euthyphro*

5d4, perhaps as a reflection of an attempt to refer the entire sentence to *to hosion* rather than to *to anhosion*. And note the play with refined terminology (7c, 9d, 11a, 12c, 13e, 14c), indicating that the dialogue is not as early as some modern commentators have assumed.[57] It is not very likely that Plato would have believed in an Ideal Form for *to anhosion*. He seems even to have been in some doubt about *to hosion*, traditionally included among the cardinal virtues, as in *Protagoras* 329c and *Phaedo* 75d (with *auto*). In the *Republic*, for example, it is not a central virtue but a part of *dikaiosunē* (443a).

Another passage for consideration comes in the *Republic* (402b–403b, 409b, cf. 476a), where Socrates asserts that guardians-in-training must learn to recognize both the *eidē* of *sōphrosunē, andreia*, and so forth, and the *eidē* of their opposites. What is meant here is the various manifestations of such qualities, not the qualities existing in and of themselves as Ideal Forms. Both the positive and the negative correlates in question are just concepts, dispositions, or behavior patterns. The *megista mathēmata*, which include Ideal Forms, come later (503e, 504a).

The *Phaedo*, to expand on what has already been said about it above (section 2.8), is one of the most tempting places to look for negative Forms. The dialogue appears to bring together everything distinguished here as this or that type of abstraction, which upon closer inspection, may or may not call for designation as a Form of any kind. And the temptation to look there is intensified by the dialogue's preoccupation with opposition, repeatedly contrasting one concept with another.

For all that, however, negative Forms are nowhere to be found in the *Phaedo*. An introductory section on Forms mentions only Ideal Forms (65d–68d). The first argument on immortality (70c–72e) is concerned with opposition at the level of particulars rather than Forms. The second argument (72e–77a), drawing on recollection, does not even operate with

---

57. Scholars assigning a remarkably early date to the *Euthyphro* are too numerous to acknowledge with full publication details. To cite just one example, Ledger (1989, 224–225; cf. 229) places the *Euthyphro* in second place overall, preceded only by the *Lysis*. For further examples, see Thesleff (1982, 8–17 [= 2009, 154–163]), who provides a conspectus of chronologies cataloging 132 attempts at establishing the production sequence of the Platonic corpus. One of those attempts belongs to Thesleff himself (1982, 16 [= 2009, 162]), reflecting his earlier work (1967 [= 2009, 1–142]), but see Thesleff (1982, 204–205, 223–226 [= 2009, 351–352, 369–371]) for his later views, specifically on dating the *Euthyphro*.

opposition. The third argument (78b–80b), an argument by analogy, commonly known as the affinity argument, proceeds with pairs of relational universal concepts: noncomposite and composite, constant and changing, invisible and visible, soul and body, and so on.

This just leaves the final argument (105b–107a), where the prime candidate for a negative Form would seem to be death. The well-known conclusion of the argument is that the soul, as the bringer of life, does not admit death, as the opposite of life, because, so we are told, the soul's connection with life is interminable: Life is not simply a phase the soul goes through, but an inherent characteristic, or essential attribute, of the soul. This association firmly places the soul in the upper level, but there is no Form for it operative in the final argument (see section 4.3 of chapter 4 and section 7.6 of chapter 7).

The final argument is a highly controversial one (see Alican 2012, 446–450). But what is important for our immediate purposes is the nature of an asymmetrical contrast between life and death. The text bears out the interpretation of a Form of life (106d), but this does not mean that death is to be treated the same way. Even life is not quite like the typical Ideal Form (the just, the beautiful, and so on), leaving little room for its opposite to ascend to that level (see section 6.4 of chapter 6).

In the main, the *Phaedo* approaches opposition from the perspective of complementary relations as opposed to that of polar opposites. This makes them Relational Forms in the classification proposed and defended here. The primary elements (e.g., similarity, largeness, hotness, oddness, life), representing the upper level in each pair of contrasting universals, may approximate to Ideal Forms, but the corresponding counterparts (e.g., difference, smallness, coldness, evenness, death), representing complementary characteristics at the lower end, are not elevated to the status of Ideal Forms.

The *Phaedrus* (250a) mentions *to adikon*, but this cannot be an Ideal Form, as it is nothing more than a reference to an unfortunate turn away from righteousness in a soul that has failed in its cosmic journey toward the upper regions, where it was aspiring to dwell with the gods in the presence of Ideal Forms. *To adikon* is simply a negative concept. The later mention of a single *eidos* of *to aphron* must likewise be dismissed, coming as it does in the course of a brief commentary (265d–266c) on the method of *diairesis*, where the focus is on concepts or Conceptual Forms.

This is confirmed by the extensive *diaireses* in the *Sophist*, which presents a parallel case in point (246a–247e), as the Eleatic Stranger argues for the noetic and incorporeal *eidē* constituting true *ousia*. He offers as examples (247a–b) the presence of *dikaiosunē, phronēsis*, and so on, and of their opposites, in the soul to which they (as primary entities) give their character. Nevertheless, the evidence points to the abstract quality of concepts, not specifically to Ideal Forms, though the latter do serve as models.

Complementing any work-by-work commentary, as exemplified above with considerable brevity, a final set of observations cutting across multiple dialogues may provide additional insight into the question of negative Forms. A suitably wide-ranging theme for that purpose is the contrast between pleasure and pain. Pleasure is not, on the whole, regarded very highly by Plato. The most graphic reminder of this is the legendary chariot's unruly horse (*Phaedrus* 253c–254e), chastised repeatedly for seeking pleasure (cf. *Phaedo* 69b, 83b, and passim; *Timaeus* 69c–d). Occasionally, however, we do find hints of the possibility of an Ideal Form for pleasure. The *Philebus*, for example, sets great store by true pleasure throughout the dialogue, though the discussion only peripherally touches on the Forms. In the same spirit, the *Protagoras* (351d–357e) shows Socrates arguing that the art of *metrētikē* is a condition for reaching the good in pleasure (*hēdonē autē* 351d; cf. *Philebus* 55e; *Statesman* 283d). And the *Republic* (586b) places true and pure pleasure within reach of the wise. Yet even if there is an Ideal Form corresponding to pleasure, there is no such Form corresponding to pain, or to any other evil, anywhere in the corpus.

The search for negative Forms can go on forever, or at least until we run out of potential candidates in the canonical corpus, though exhaustive coverage in a brief commentary cannot be a practical goal. Readers interested in pursuing the matter further may appreciate the more extensive assessment in chapter 6.

2.11. Conclusion

The importance of Forms for proper insight into Plato has been somewhat overrated for centuries. But the question is an established part of his metaphysics and epistemology, where intuitive visions and strict reasoning come into play with equal vigor, and often also with equal subtlety. We have to make of it what we can.

A little reflection outside the received view immediately suggests that the various entities or constructs commonly known as Plato's Forms do not really belong together in a single category, for they do not all represent the same kind of thing. They originate in three separate attempts to explore abstraction from a philosophical perspective. These are distinct but overlapping efforts, modified as needed, either to develop new avenues of understanding or to rethink old ones, all part of a continuous thought experiment geared toward understanding a single universe with two ontological levels and countless subdivisions.

The building blocks of reality emerging from these separate attempts have come down to us as a massive collection of undifferentiated abstractions. Scholars have been content to treat this metaphysical heritage as a homogeneous collection of universals where each reification produces essentially the same kind of entity as any other. Breaking that habit promises to enrich our understanding of the main lines of Plato's thought. The revision required is to identify the proper divisions in the heretofore fungible Forms:

- Ideal Forms: noetic realities of superlative intrinsic value, especially moral value, but also aesthetic and religious value, as well as inherently valuable ideals and phenomena, such as knowledge and life, which are not themselves values.

- Conceptual Forms: universals to which Plato assigns objective reality, but not intrinsic value, though positive and negative connotations are both conceivable, the former by way of ontological ascent through approximation to Ideal Forms.

- Relational Forms: relational universal concepts reified in pairs of complementary metaphysical categories in the constitutional structure of the cosmos, the dominant element in each pair being capable of ontological ascent, much like Conceptual Forms.

Although these are not, strictly speaking, three different versions of exactly the same thing, retaining the designation Form is convenient for the continuity and consistency of discussion. The emphasis is on Ideal Forms, the other two being glorified concepts by comparison, as they fall short of the perfection associated with noetic reality.[58] They can take

---

58. The "glorified concepts" analogy is discussed further in chapter 3 (sections 3.4 and 3.5).

on some of the features of Ideal Forms, but not as a rule, and never the attribute of positive intrinsic value.

All three are more than concepts, abstractions, or universals, but it is not always easy to tell when Plato is talking about a Form and when he is talking about the corresponding concept. The difference between a concept and a Conceptual Form is significant, at least in terms of the second-order language we use in trying to figure out what Plato is doing, but the same thing can sometimes be treated as a concept and sometimes as a Conceptual Form. Plato can move in a flash from hot thing to hotness to the hot itself, and it is not always easy to see which sense is in the forefront, but it is clear that there are important differences. The same holds for Ideal Forms and Relational Forms, especially for the dominant element in each pair of the latter.

There will naturally be reservations regarding the proposed paradigm, not least because the proposal rejects metaphysical dualism in favor of unitary pluralism, but very likely also because it envisages a division of Forms into separate classes, and perhaps particularly because it favors one class over the others. The plausibility of preferential treatment, however, is supported by a powerful vision: the imagery of what awaits the soul of the philosopher upon the completion of its cosmic ascent (*Phaedrus* 248a–249d). When the enlightened soul joins the gods in adulation of the Forms, it will behold justice, temperance, knowledge, and such (247d), not horseness or wetness or muckness. Plato's poetry is all about Ideal Forms—transcendent, intelligible, immutable, and altogether precious, all culminating in the good. Among mortals, philosophers alone are able to ascend to their level.

As for Plato's first principles, the one and the-great-and-the-small, those seem to have been a late pythagorizing experiment elaborating on the gradation of reality forever under scrutiny. We do not know enough about them to incorporate them as essential ingredients in a working model of Plato's overall vision. They seem plausible, but not compelling. While the model here does not rule out first principles, or any other aspect of the Tübingen Paradigm, it makes no room for negative Forms. This is because Plato himself does not embrace negative Forms, following a course between neglect and disdain, as he denies negative concepts access to the noetic level, which is inherently opposed to negativity.

The present reconstruction of the conceptual apparatus Plato uses to make sense of the world has the additional advantage of bringing out the axiological orientation of his worldview. This is an area where the simple contrast between Forms and particulars is more of a hindrance than a convenience. That black-and-white contrast is both a legacy and a shortcoming of the traditional interpretation of Plato as a thoroughgoing metaphysical dualist. The solution is to abandon the dualism of worlds in favor of the asymmetrical and complementary hierarchy of levels, providing all the room necessary for ontological stratification in correlation with the texts, without any of the problems typically accompanying the traditional interpretation.

Chapter 3

Rethought Forms

How Do They Work?

This chapter is a critical evaluation of Holger Thesleff's thinking on Plato's Forms, especially of his "rethinking" of the matter, as he puts it in the title of his most recent contribution.[1] It develops a broadly sympathetic perspective through dialectical engagement with the main lines of his interpretation and reconstruction of Plato's world. The aim is to launch the formal academic reception of the outcome, which Thesleff cautiously and modestly presents as a "proposal"—his teaser to elicit a reaction,

---

1. The "rethinking" in question is actually a collaboration between Holger Thesleff and me, reproduced as chapter 2 of this book and originally published as a journal article with joint authorship (Alican and Thesleff 2013): "Rethinking Plato's Forms," *Arctos: Acta Philologica Fennica* 47: 11–47. The critical evaluation in the present chapter first appeared in the same journal as the original article but as an independent project (Alican 2014): "Rethought Forms: How Do They Work?," *Arctos: Acta Philologica Fennica* 48: 25–55. The reason that the latter is structured more like a commentary on Thesleff than like a follow-up to our mutual work is that Thesleff's insight into the matter predates our formal collaboration, with his pioneering efforts both deserving and inspiring acknowledgment. Thesleff's personal initiative unfolds through several of his earlier works: Thesleff 1989; 1993b; 1999 (= 2009, 383–506). My own efforts intersect with his initiative in two places: Alican 2012 (cf. 87–110, 110–129) and the present volume, parts of which were originally published as Alican and Thesleff 2013 and Alican 2014, 2015, 2017a, and 2017b, as explained in the preface and elaborated in the introduction.

positive or negative. The exegetical focus is on tracing the inspiration and reasoning behind his "two-level" model of Plato's ontology, which, in turn, supports his tripartite classification of Forms. The critical focus is on identifying potential areas of misunderstanding and supplying any explanations, analyses, and arguments that may enhance the clarity of the respective positions.

3.1. Introduction

Thesleff is difficult to ignore and easy to misunderstand. He has something to say about practically everything we are accustomed to discussing in regard to Plato and a few things we are not. He also has a proclivity for going against the grain of mainstream interpretation. That is why I have taken to calling him a maverick, both in person and in print (Alican 2012, 185–188). He has yet to correct me on that. His outlook on the Forms alone reveals why he has not voiced an objection: He *is* a maverick. And he is comfortable with that label. One would have to be to produce and promote the ideas that he does.

Thesleff's positions are always fluid, his work always in progress. What we get in his books and articles are snapshots of an ever-developing viewpoint. To some extent, this is true of all academic work, but with Thesleff, it is the common denominator of his intellectual output. That makes it all the more difficult, and that much more important, to keep up with his investigation of any given subject. The aim here is to explicate his unorthodox approach to Plato's ontology, with particular emphasis on what he does with the Forms.

3.2. The General Enterprise

The most striking feature of the general enterprise is its ontological elitism. Thesleff does not recognize every abstraction in Plato as a Form. Nor does he take what we normally regard as Platonic Forms to be, one and all, the same kind of thing, each one simply a Form, like any other. He sees a fundamental difference between, say, the Form of horse and that of motion, and further, between either one of those and the Form of justice—examples likely to be familiar even without specific references. He proposes rethinking Plato's Forms with a view to preserving the variegation present in the original as opposed to perpetuating the uniformity prevailing in the literature.

His rethinking inspires a tripartite classification consisting of Ideal Forms, Conceptual Forms, and Relational Forms. This arrangement comes with caveats reflecting uncertainties in the dialogues themselves. The following provisions in particular are important for a thorough appreciation:

- The tripartite classification is a thought experiment, as is Plato's own approach to philosophical problems.[2] There can be no proof in the standard sense.

- The taxonomy has little to do with chronology: To affirm differences between types of Forms is not to affirm developmentalism.[3]

- The three divisions are decidedly different from one another, so much so as to resist being brought together under the unifying rubric of Forms, a label retained for convenience and familiarity.

- Despite fundamental differences, one kind of Form can, depending on the context, take on the characteristics of another, specifically with certain Conceptual Forms and Relational Forms coming to resemble Ideal Forms.

We may add to these what would be the most important condition of all, though not directly about the Forms: the understanding of Plato's philosophical vision in terms of a sliding scale of reality represented by the metaphor of two levels in one world. This is Thesleff's alternative to the traditional two-world interpretation where the Forms reside in one world and particulars in another. The caveat here is that the focal point of Plato's metaphysics is not the relationship between Forms and particulars,

---

2. Thesleff uses this model to make better sense of Plato, who was in the habit of using his own models, among them, the Forms, to make better sense of the world.

3. See Thesleff (1982 [= 2009, 143–382]; 1989, 1–26) for his views on chronology. Admittedly, Plato may have come up with different types of Forms as a result of different thought experiments conducted at different times. Yet the resulting variety functions as an organic whole, not as a succession of increasingly better models of exactly the same thing. One category of Forms is not an improved version of another (see chapter 2, sections 2.1 and 2.2).

nor the diversification experiments with Forms, but the stratification of reality in a hierarchical ontological structure consisting of a higher and lower level and untold layers in between. Forms and particulars, not to mention the different kinds of Forms, are distinguished through this two-level vision, which is not merely a heuristic tool for understanding Plato but an outlook actually present in Plato.

This means, among other things, that Thesleff's classification of Forms is an initiative to tidy up the most important features of Plato's ontology rather than an attempt to provide an exhaustive catalog of Forms recognized in the scholarly tradition. But even after we make allowances for any and all caveats, Thesleff's account leaves us with questions that can fruitfully be pursued further and problems that cannot fairly be left entirely to Plato:

- What is the difference between Forms and concepts?
- What is the difference between Forms and universals?
- What is the ontological status of Forms, or to elaborate, what is the mode of their existence and the nature and implications of their reality?
- How does the ontological status of Ideal Forms differ from that of Conceptual Forms and Relational Forms?

The first three questions cannot be answered without expanding on them to distinguish between the kinds of Forms envisaged. And that is what gives rise to the fourth question. To be fair, Thesleff answers all these questions. But his answers can leave the reader wondering, for example, what exactly the difference is between horseness and justice, the former presumably a Conceptual Form, the latter definitely an Ideal Form. Horseness lacks the positive intrinsic value characteristic of (common and peculiar to) Ideal Forms and therefore present in justice. Apart from that, both horseness and justice are universals that exist in reality and outside the mind, thus pointing to a shared ontological platform. Roughly speaking, it would seem that both horseness and justice are the same kind of thing from an ontological standpoint, differing only in their axiological dimensions. We may then press Thesleff more generally on whether Ideal Forms really do differ from the other two kinds of Forms in any way other than the presence or absence of positive intrinsic value.⁴ This goes to the heart of his classification scheme, and we would, accordingly, do well to examine the main organizational principles behind that arrangement.

Despite the various uncertainties, always embraced unapologetically, Thesleff's perspective comes with several clear and strong commitments:

- Universal Nature: All Forms are at least universals, a provision allowing Forms to work like universals while having a greater claim to reality.⁵

- Objective Reality: All Forms are objectively real in the sense that they are ontologically independent, both of minds and of particulars, thus requiring neither cognitive correlation nor phenomenal manifestation for their existence, which is thereby free of perception, intellection, intuition, imagination, or instantiation.

- Discriminatory Reification: Some Forms are more real, so to speak, than others, or at least exhibit an ontological eminence surpassing others, depending on the relative value and importance Plato attaches to the corresponding concepts.

- Ontological Ascent: Forms with a lower ontological standing (Conceptual Forms and Relational Forms) can sometimes approximate to those of the highest ontological standing (Ideal Forms).⁶

---

4. The notion of positive intrinsic value in Forms naturally brings to mind the possibility of negative intrinsic value in Forms. Thesleff devotes considerable attention to the question of negative Forms (the bad itself, the ugly itself, the unjust itself, and so on), primarily with a view to establishing that there are none, or more specifically, that Plato does not countenance any. This is a developing theme in Thesleff's individual work (1999, 63–67 [= 2009, 447–450]) as well as in our collaboration (see chapter 2, section 2.10). Chapter 6 of the present volume is dedicated entirely to the question of negative Forms.

5. Recall that "Forms are what universals fail to be," a friendly amendment to McCabe's dictum that "Forms are what particulars fail to be" (1994, 60). See chapter 1 (section 1.3) and chapter 2 (section 2.4).

6. The term first appears in chapter 2 (see section 2.7 for discussion and development, section 2.11 for recapitulation). See sections 3.4 and 3.5 of the present chapter for elaboration.

- Etiological Function: All Forms are causally efficacious, functioning as causes, reasons, or explanations of sorts for the phenomena they represent.

The commitments enumerated here contain the answers to the questions posed above, especially in consideration of the caveats mentioned in the beginning. It may be helpful, all the same, to retrace such connections to make sure they are intact. This chapter is dedicated to doing just that, not necessarily by taking up each of the foregoing questions exactly as expressed, but by inspecting the vantage point Thesleff recommends for a clear view of the world as Plato saw it.

3.3. The Stratification of Reality

Thesleff's primary mission in Platonica is to replace the traditional two-world interpretation with a two-level alternative.[7] Perhaps his greatest contribution to Plato scholarship has been his campaign to unite the disparate worlds of the noumenal and the phenomenal in a single world with two levels and an indefinite multitude of subdivisions in a hierarchical stratification of reality.[8] The possibility and plausibility of bringing Forms and particulars together in a single world convinces him to lay to rest the thoroughgoing metaphysical dualism shaping the reception and presentation of Plato through the ages.

Thesleff locates the origins of the two-level model in the work of C. J. de Vogel but accepts responsibility for having developed it as an interpretive paradigm.[9] He embraces the model as the root of all Pla-

---

7. Other notable reactions to the tradition of two worlds in Plato include: Brentlinger (1972), Broadie (2004), Ferguson (1921), Nails (2013), Nehamas (1975), Robjant (2012).

8. A note on ontological versus epistemological frames of reference may be in order: In advocating his two-level model over the two-world model, Thesleff is concerned exclusively with the ontology of the matter. This is not the only possible approach, nor even the only actual one, and he is sensitive to the difference (see chapter 2, section 2.2). He finds the epistemological perspective irrelevant to his own project and refers readers primarily to the work of Smith (2000; 2012; 2019) but also to contributions by Butler (2007) and Rowe (2005). See further: Fine (1978; 1990) and the reaction to Fine by Gonzalez (1996).

9. See de Vogel (1986, 50, 62, 145–148, 159–212, especially 159–171). Compare with Thesleff (1993b, 17–45; 1999, 11–52 [= 2009, 397–436]). See also chapter 2 (section 2.3).

tonic thinking, a philosophical vision more basic than, say, the so-called theory of Forms.[10] It is, in fact, this feature of his approach, namely its relevance and reliability as a standard of interpretation, that so excites Thesleff, who declares the two-level perspective a prerequisite to a proper understanding of Plato.

Other fundamental perspectives, however, could also be at play here. Opposition, to name one, is a prime candidate. Thesleff admits this, or more accurately, he invokes and publicizes it, wherever he discusses the two-level model (see chapter 2, section 2.3), which he presents as the culmination of a preoccupation with opposition relations shaping the sociocultural mindset. It will be useful, therefore, to consider how the Greek conception of opposition may have influenced Plato's thought, particularly in leading him to develop a two-level outlook.

Although pursuing this in any detail here may be somewhat distracting, a rewarding distraction of that sort is to be found in the early work of Geoffrey (G. E. R.) Lloyd, a younger contemporary of Thesleff. During the period that Thesleff was moving from Pythagoras to Plato, Lloyd came out with a series of contributions (1962; 1964; 1966) to our understanding of the role of opposition in Greek philosophy, with emphasis on tracing its roots in Greek thought in general and demonstrating its growing hold on Greek philosophy in particular. According to Lloyd (1962), cultural preconceptions regarding opposition were prevalent in ancient Greece, among other places, with a strong impact and traceable influence on early philosophical ruminations ranging from the Presocratics to Aristotle.

Thesleff's work (1993b, 21; 1999, 7–10, 11–25 [= 2009, 393–396, 397–410]) is largely in agreement with that of Lloyd in regard to the emergence and development of opposition as a paradigm in Greek philosophy, though Thesleff (after his early work on Pythagoras) has remained more strictly focused on Plato, with Lloyd concentrating partly on Aristotle and mostly on Greek science. Inspired by what Plato did with the opposition framework he inherited, especially with the complementary contrasts he evidently preferred to polar opposites, Thesleff urges us to abandon the two worlds of the metaphysical dualism traditionally attributed to Plato in favor of two levels in a single world.

---

10. The theoreticity of Plato's Forms is a thorny question. Thesleff does not explore the matter personally, instead referring readers to a selection of substantive discussions (chapter 2, section 2.2): Annas (1981, 217–241), Gonzalez (2002), Hyland (2002), Sayre (1993, 167–199; 2002, 169–191), Williams (2006, 148–186).

The unitary pluralism of a two-level paradigm has the distinct advantage of removing the embarrassing conflict between transcendence and immanence in the traditional interpretation, where presumably transcendent Forms are supposed to be somehow immanent as well, fulfilling their transcendence in one world, their immanence in the other. This is embarrassing because it gives us one world for Forms, and another for content, while desperately attempting to sneak all Forms into the very world to which they do not belong. All it can reasonably promise is a world of Forms, none of them instantiated, and a world of sensible phenomena, none of them differentiated, thus leaving us with the odd combination of empty Forms and Formless things. The two-level solution unites everything in the same world.

Ironically, the leading objection to the two-level alternative also lies in the question of transcendence: If there is just one world, as the model stipulates, what exactly do the transcendent Forms transcend? And where do they do this transcending? Does transcendence not require a separate world? These all amount to the same question. It is, in any case, an open question. Yet it deserves recognition and discussion—even without a definitive solution.

We face a similar problem today in the choice between a universe and a multiverse as the proper interpretation of reality. Modern physics is increasingly favoring a multiverse, at bottom, a plurality of universes. While physicists assure us that this is a possibility—that what we have been exploring as the universe is actually just one of many (possibly infinitely many) universes that are not accessible to us—the assurance, or even flat-out proof, is not convincing, nor even relevant, if what is meant by "universe" in the first place is the totality of everything that exists, the whole of reality, accessible or not, whereupon the postulated "multiverse" adds nothing to the concept of "universe." Under a holistic interpretation, the scenario of a multiverse beyond the universe is not even meaningful, let alone being tenable. Yet under the alternative interpretation where the universe is only the part of reality that we have so far been able to explore, observe, and contemplate with the science, technology, and philosophy available to us, it is both meaningful and useful to think about what lies beyond the universe. It seems, in the end, to be a matter of perspective, a matter, that is, of what we mean by "universe" (what we take to be the referent of the term).

Thesleff's levels are like that. While Thesleff himself does not present any of this as a matter of perspective, instead asserting unequivocally that his own view is right, and anything in contradiction wrong, if the analogy were nevertheless extended to his case, he would come down on the side of the universe as opposed to the multiverse. He assigns a single world to the whole of reality, while handling diversity in levels. What others divide between two different worlds, he distributes throughout one world with two main levels and multiple sublevels.

But can two levels in one world accommodate the division between material and immaterial reality? That is the question here. And it is not the same question as whether it makes more sense to speak of a plurality of worlds or of a plurality of levels within a single world. Those who postulate a second world do so for no reason other than to make room for Plato's notion of transcendence, which they take to require an existence outside the familiar world of space and time. Thesleff, in contrast, combines everything, including any transcending to be done, in one and the same world. The two-world interpretation is entirely consistent with what we normally understand by transcendence, while falling short in explaining how the two separate worlds are supposed to account for the correspondence Plato sees between Forms and particulars. The two-level interpretation supports a curious sense of transcendence, with everything still belonging to the same world, where nothing can quite properly be said to have transcended anything, at least not in the ordinary sense of the term (as going beyond that which is transcended), but it is, for the very same reason, fully responsive to all manner of connection and correspondence between Forms and particulars.

What, then, is the answer? Can two levels in the same world accommodate the distinction between the physical and the abstract? Not if we think of the difference in terms of polar opposition. Nothing can reconcile reality with what lies beyond it. This is because nothing lies beyond reality. On the other hand, the physical does not necessarily exhaust reality. Perhaps the proper distinction, then, is between reality as we know it and reality as it is. Thesleff's recommendation is to think of such distinctions (material vs. immaterial, sensible vs. intelligible, etc.) in reciprocal terms, as in the interdependent contrast between upstairs and downstairs.[11] In this sense,

---

11. Thesleff typically explicates this distinction, or rather relationship, perhaps a communion (*koinōnia*) of sorts, with an abundance of examples, not just his own but also Plato's. Some of his favorites (chapter 2, section 2.3) are the divided line in the *Republic* (509d–511e), the ladder of love in the *Symposium* (209e–212a), and the world-soul in the *Timaeus* (35a–36d). See the following discussion through the end of the present section (including the corresponding notes) for the use he makes of the divided line.

some apparent opposites are not just compatible but also complementary, neither one being comprehensible without the other.

This is an exploratory response to the puzzle of transcendence in a single world. Thesleff's actual response is more elegant: Engaging me in private communication, though certainly not in a confidential context, he denies the problem altogether, as he takes "transcendence" in a weaker sense than the standard philosophical or theological notion of a reality outside or beyond the world. Under his interpretation, the relevant sense of "transcendence" is not, pace my playful label to mark the difference, a "curious" one invoking an otherworldly existence, without any other world to speak of, but a weaker one obviating the need for a duplication of worlds.[12] Thesleff's response is appropriately defiant, leaving no room for a problem to be solved. No solution is otherwise possible where the very nature of Forms places them in a different world while nevertheless requiring their presence in the same world.

The exploratory remarks immediately preceding Thesleff's own response demonstrate the significance of his promotion of complementary over contradictory opposition. They may not demonstrate how to remain in the world, the only one there is, while leaving it behind, but they do illustrate what goes on in Plato's world. Thesleff has been in the habit of using a visual aid to probe Plato's world, which he believes to be built on the relevant (complementary) sort of opposition. The design is simple, a line going through a list of ten pairs of contrasts as follows:[13]

---

12. This is consistent with Thesleff's ever-vigilant approach to transcendence in Plato. He has long denied a "transcendence" beyond the world, as it were, and has for this reason favored the use of scare quotes for the term itself: "It is natural, also, to infer from the two-level vision that all 'Ideas' (whatever terms used [= 'Ideal Forms' in chapter 2]), are (in spite of the κοινωνία between the levels) somehow 'transcendent,' i.e. distinct (χωρίς) from and pointedly primary in relation to sensible things (though they are certainly not 'beyond being'): being 'divine,' invisible and attainable by intellect only, they belong entirely to the higher level in Plato's vision" (Thesleff 1999, 58 [= 2009, 442]; cf. 55 [= 2009, 439] n. 97; 62 [= 2009, 446] n. 111). It is important to remember, however, that this distinction is still within the sliding scale of a single reality where neither end is cut off from the other in complete isolation or polar opposition. The *chōrismos* here is not a hard "separation" (or "separability") but a soft "distinction" (or "distinguishability"). See section 3.4 of the present chapter.

13. The visual aid in question can be found in several of Thesleff's works, either in the precise form presented here, as in chapter 2 (section 2.3) and chapter 3 (section 3.3), both duplicating Thesleff (1999, 27 [= 2009, 411]), or in a variation, as in Thesleff (1993b, 21). See also Press (2007, 162).

| one | same | stable | divine | soul | leading | intellect | truth | knowledge | defined |
| many | different | changing | human | body | being-led | senses | appearance | opinion | undefined |

The vertical alignment of the correlative elements in each pair of contrasts depicts an asymmetrical relationship, basically a sociocultural valuation pattern (of which the list is representative rather than exhaustive), developing into philosophical insight, with the top component considered superior to the bottom, but neither one contemplated apart from the other. The illustration is not so much about the Forms as it is about the more basic opposition paradigm Thesleff believes to have led Plato to develop his two-level outlook, which, in turn, supports and encourages the distinction between Forms and particulars, or which, from our perspective, helps explain that distinction. The distinction between Forms and the things of which they are Forms makes more sense in a single reality divided up in this manner than it does in two separate worlds, where the Forms would be without substance, the things without Form, and each without a frame of reference to identify it as what it is.

Thesleff's visual aid is, in a sense, a simplified version of the more popular one in Plato, the divided line of the *Republic* (509d–511e). Thesleff is, in fact, quite fond of the original simile, embracing it both as evidence of Plato's two-level vision and as a model for his (Thesleff's but also Plato's) classification of Forms. The four segments of Plato's divided line correspond to subdivisions in the two main levels of Thesleff's scheme, placing the Forms in the upper level, particulars in the lower.[14] To put it in Plato's terms, Ideal Forms belong at the top, right after *to agathon*, at the level of *noesis*; Conceptual Forms come next, at the level of *dianoia*; and Relational Forms constitute a lateral projection of the overall partition scheme. The lower two segments of Plato's line are reserved for physical things, at the level of *pistis*, and for images or shadows, at the level of *eikasia*, together corresponding to the single (but freely divisible) lower level of Thesleff. Details are best left to the next section, dedicated exclusively to the classification of Forms.

---

14. This is another occasion to remember that Thesleff presents the two primary levels as a metaphor for a comprehensive stratification scheme with an indefinitely large number of subdivisions. Wherever he refers to either of the two main levels, or to both at once, he means to include any and all subdivisions without specifically mentioning them.

3.4. The Classification of Forms

Thesleff's stratification of reality is the impetus for his classification of Forms. This is not to say that the divisions he proposes are peculiar to the two-level model of Plato's world. They are not. But what he does with the Forms is a natural extension of what he does with Plato's ontology.

Having long contemplated distinctions between the different kinds of entities collectively regarded simply and indiscriminately as Forms (1989; 1993b; 1999 [= 2009, 383–506]), Thesleff has settled, in his latest thinking, on a classification scheme with three divisions (chapter 2, section 2.3): Ideal Forms, Conceptual Forms, Relational Forms. All three are universals with objective reality. They are, as Thesleff puts it, at least universals, which leaves open how much more they can be, and what exactly each might be. It turns out that they are decidedly different things. They differ not only in the aspects of reality to which they correspond as universals but also in the qualities that make them what they are as Forms.

In terms of their range over sensible phenomena, (1) Ideal Forms constitute noetic realities of superlative intrinsic value serving as axiological paradigms; (2) Conceptual Forms cover types, properties, events, actions, and experiences; and (3) Relational Forms embody complementary metaphysical categories manifested as pairs of contrasting abstractions illustrating the fundamental nature and structure of the universe through correlative universal relations. In a sense, albeit a simplistic sense, Ideal Forms account for values, Relational Forms for relations, and Conceptual Forms for all other universals, be they types, properties, or anything else relevant to our phenomenal experience.[15]

As for what these Forms are qua Forms, Ideal Forms differ from the other two kinds through a host of features, including transcendence, intelligibility, and comparable refinements familiar from the long tradition of Plato scholarship.[16] Ideal Forms are the fantabulous entities associated with the gods, and accorded a status bordering on divinity, described

---

15. This is a simplistic account in the sense that Ideal Forms are not just values, Relational Forms are not strictly relations, and Conceptual Forms are not merely concepts. Each is the Form of the corresponding manifestation, not that manifestation itself.

16. The full list includes seven features identifying Ideal Forms as transcendent, intelligible, paradigmatic, perfect, immutable, simple, and unique (see chapter 2, section 2.6). These are commonly recognized features in the literature as opposed to personal discoveries or innovations. Additions, deletions, and modifications are always a possibility.

with great enthusiasm in the *Phaedo* and the *Phaedrus*.[17] In comparison, Conceptual Forms and Relational Forms come across as little more than glorified concepts. They exist, to be sure, but evidently not as anything so special as Ideal Forms.

The "glorified concepts" analogy runs the risk of understatement. It must be understood to include not just ontological independence but ontological eminence as well. As vague as that may sound, it captures the superiority of the lesser two types of Forms over things that are not Forms at all. The upper level of Plato's world is not just for Ideal Forms but for all Forms. Everything else belongs to the lower level (with the exception of intermediates, which enjoy a fluid presence cutting across both levels, as discussed in chapter 7). Furthermore, the eminence in question is not strictly ontological but broadly metaphysical. At the very least, these "glorified concepts," in addition to their objective reality, boast a causal efficacy of some sort. All Forms, no matter which of the three divisions they may belong to, function in an explanatory capacity on a cosmic scale, though it is not clear whether this is a logical, cosmological, psychological, or yet some other kind of explanation. The lack of specificity in this regard is not a shortcoming of Thesleff's account but a feature of Plato's. Thesleff acknowledges a causal role for the Forms, but he does not pursue it in any detail, partly because he has a greater interest in ontology than in cosmology, and partly because he does not think we can get very far with a reconstruction of Platonic etiology.[18]

---

17. *Phaedo* (78b-80b): the analogic argument where the soul is likened to the gods and the Forms, implying that the latter two are themselves comparable in some way. *Phaedrus* (246e-249d): the cosmic journey of enlightenment where the soul of the philosopher (248a-249d), together with the gods (246e-247e), eventually beholds the Forms.

18. Thesleff is not impressed with our prospects for discovering a coherent account of causality, causation, or causal explanation in Plato. He does recognize the various attempts in the canonical corpus—where causality is examined in the Forms, in the soul, in the demiurge, and even as a category of its own (*Philebus* 23d ff.)—but he also notes the absence of a connection toward a unified perspective (Thesleff 1999, 102 [= 2009, 483]). He finds the approach unclear even where the focus seems to be exclusively on the Forms (see chapter 2, section 2.6), adding, in fact, that there is no such restriction to Forms. What may appear to be about the Forms is more generally about the levels: "To put it somewhat aristotelically, there is a 'causal' relation between the levels, even more manifestly than between Forms and particulars" (Thesleff 1999, 30 [= 2009, 415]). Yet even then, observes Thesleff, "one cannot claim that the upper level is always or predominantly 'effecting' the lower level phenomena" (1999, 102 [=

The relevance of metaphysical eminence (ontological as well as cosmological) across the board in the upper level of reality is best reflected in Thesleff's allowance for the possibility of ontological ascent. This is a process (or phenomenon) through which the boundaries break down between Plato's presentation of Ideal Forms, on the one hand, and his presentation of Conceptual Forms and Relational Forms, on the other. Any Conceptual Form can, in principle, approximate to Ideal Forms, thereby coming to resemble them in every way except in the possession of intrinsic value. And the same holds for the dominant (more valuable or more important) element in the asymmetrically paired correlative universal relations constituting Relational Forms. Hence, the string of features normally reserved for Ideal Forms, including the qualities of transcendence and intelligibility, ceases under ontological ascent to be a means for differentiating between Ideal Forms and the other two types.

Ontological ascent opens up interesting possibilities, engendering greater flexibility within the classification scheme, but it also comes with implications that may be interpreted as complications. This is at the center of the discussion in the next section. At this point, it is best to proceed with a closer look at the system itself, taking stock of some of the more basic features of the different categories of Forms.

To start with, what makes Ideal Forms so special? They may seem, upon initial consideration, to be little more than moral exemplars, that is, paradigms of human excellence, but they are indeed more than that. First, they are more than paradigms: They are real entities albeit ones that transcend sensory experience, therefore being accessible through the mind alone. They also have some sort of causal or explanatory relevance, as already mentioned, though we need not dwell on that further, as moral

---

2009, 483]). He is equally cautious about what to make of the foundational principles of the unwritten doctrines. Rejecting the Tübingen tendency to take the principles as "'causes' in the Presocratic sense, which would mean stressing their 'material' and 'efficient' aspects," he interprets the subordination of the-great-and-the-small to the one as an indication that the principles "combine the 'formal' and 'final' aspects of Aristotelian causes" (Thesleff 1999, 101–102 [= 2009, 483]). He makes no commitments in this regard, offers no assurances. He warns that this is not so much about Plato as it is about Aristotle: "But of course 'aetiology' is an Aristotelian issue" (Thesleff 1999, 102 [= 2009, 483]). Even his call for caution is cautious: "The question of how to apply Aristotelian 'causes' (or rather, aetiology) to this complex, can perhaps not be definitely solved" (Thesleff 1999, 101 [= 2009, 483]).

values of the ordinary sort may also be said to have causal or explanatory relevance insofar as they tend to be invoked as reasons for action, and thus cited as justification, by moral agents performing moral acts. Ideal Forms are, in short, noetic realities. Second, their connection with the phenomenal level of reality covers more than moral value, extending, for example, to aesthetic and religious value as well, and possibly also to other categories of value. As a matter of fact, the relevant division is neither between moral and nonmoral value, nor between aesthetic and nonaesthetic value, nor between religious and nonreligious value, but between intrinsic and instrumental value. Hence, even something whose essential nature is neither moral (justice) nor aesthetic (beauty) nor religious (piety) can be an Ideal Form. The Form of knowledge comes to mind (*Parmenides* 134a–e; *Phaedrus* 247d–e), as does the Form of life (*Phaedo* 106d).

As for the other two types of Forms, the fact that they are both, in many respects, relatively less valuable (or less important, or less significant, and so on, all with reference to Plato's discernible outlook), and as it seems, equally less valuable, should not be taken as an indication that they are merely variations on a theme. They are different sorts of things and they play different roles in Plato's attempt to make sense of the world around him. Relational Forms are not a subdivision of Conceptual Forms that just happen to be taken in pairs of opposites. They perform the distinctive function of collectively illustrating the constitutional structure of the universe (see chapter 2, section 2.8).

As with any classification scheme, two questions arise with respect to Thesleff's: (1) Is the taxonomy exhaustive? (2) How does it compare with alternatives? The answer to the first question is that the aim is not so much exhaustive coverage as it is holistic explanation. It is more important that each division be a verifiable or defensible reflection of the Platonic corpus than that absolutely nothing be left out. Thesleff has never been after a complete catalog of everything that may pass for a Form, but he has always been interested in making sense of the variety of entities (or constructs, depending on whether one sees Plato as discovering or inventing these things) that may be organized in accordance with Plato's ontology and his general philosophical outlook, preferably in a demonstrable correlation with both. This being so, his classification of Forms has been inspired and shaped by his two-level interpretation of Plato. Nothing that is not supported by this model makes it into the classification. Nor does anything that happens to be either too vague or too controversial for accurate assignment.[19]

The answer to the second question can only be developed on a case-by-case basis. This is a matter of comparing Thesleff's classification with whatever happens to be nominated in its place. While competing alternatives have not yet appeared in print in the form of a direct response, both actual and possible alternatives are available in much that has been proposed independently. Many of them can be found in generalist commentaries on Plato (companions, guidebooks, overviews), required by their nature to make the "theory" of Forms accessible to a wide audience. Richard D. Mohr (2010, 5), for example, divides Plato's Forms into five groups, which he takes to represent the "traditional" list of Forms: moral and aesthetic values (justice, goodness, beauty); mathematical concepts (three, odd, even, square, sphere); relations (double, half, large, small, octave, speed); "notions that range widely over other notions" (being, sameness, difference, motion, rest); natural kinds (earth, air, fire, water). Mohr is right to offer this as a "traditional" list. But nothing here contradicts Thesleff's model, which covers in three categories what Mohr's does in five.

Examples can be multiplied indefinitely with much the same result. Alternatives are unlikely to be opposed diametrically to Thesleff's classification, instead presenting different ways of arranging roughly the same items, perhaps coming up with a division or two that Thesleff handles at the level of subdivisions. A broader survey may prove more informative. A combination of both questions could, for example, be taken up in an alternative classification grounded in the distinction between transcendence and immanence. Instead of Thesleff's three divisions, we might have just two: transcendent Forms and immanent Forms. This would not necessarily be incompatible with Thesleff's scheme, as both transcendent Forms and immanent Forms could arguably be divided further into Ideal Forms, Conceptual Forms, and Relational Forms. Or perhaps the three

---

19. The prime examples are mathematicals (numbers and figures) and immanent Forms. Thesleff has no interest in mathematicals, first because he is not convinced of the subject's relevance to his primary project, second because he is not optimistic about a resolution in any event (see chapter 2, section 2.4). He likewise shows no enthusiasm for discussing the possibility or implications of immanence—the chief implication being "immanent Forms"—declaring the question "largely *non liquet*" (see section 2.7.1). Chapter 7 of the present volume lays out my own position on mathematicals as well as other intermediates.

divisions could be assumed to be under transcendent Forms and their manifestations under immanent Forms. Either way, the result would be an elaboration of Thesleff's model, not a contradiction of it.

The matter of transcendence versus immanence, however, is not so much a distinction between types of Forms as it is a debate on the nature of Forms, specifically on the possible phenomenal manifestations of Forms. Employing it as a means of differentiating between Forms, just because some dialogues speak of the "F" in us, and so on, seems to beg the question. That, of course, may not be altogether fair from the perspective of anyone collating practically endless examples of transcendent Forms and immanent Forms throughout the Platonic corpus, and wondering why they are both in abundance if they may not be taken as two different types of Forms.

A case in point is a discussion note by Raphael Demos (1948, 456–460), drawing and expanding on earlier work both by himself (1939, 179) and by Francis Cornford (1939, 78). Demos objects to interpreting the interplay between Forms and particulars as a correspondence between *what* and *that*, in other words, as a juxtaposition of essence and instance, thus equating whatness (structure) with universals, while leaving nothing but brute fact for particulars (1948, 456). He envisages Plato's Forms as combining elements of both universals and particulars. Although he does not claim to be advancing a classification scheme, his discussion is dedicated to elucidating the distinction between what he calls "Ideal Forms" (or "Abstract Forms") and "Empirical Forms" (or "Phenomenal Forms"). The difference is that the former are grasped by *nous* whereas the latter are encountered in sensory experience. Ideal Forms are transcendent, invisible, and abstract. Empirical Forms are immanent, visible, and concrete.

The question is whether the distinction by Demos deserves the recognition denied it by those who reject immanent Forms as a type of Form, not to mention those who contest the very possibility of immanence for Forms. It does not. While the question of immanence certainly requires our full attention, it provides no grounds for a classification of Forms. This is because transcendence is a defining characteristic of Forms, routinely so with the undifferentiated Forms of the Platonic tradition, which then precludes immanence as an alternative for anything that is supposed to remain a Form. When we begin to talk about the difference between transcendent Forms and immanent Forms, or between Ideal Forms and Empirical Forms in the terminology of Demos, we are no longer talking about two different types of Forms but focusing on two entirely different kinds of things. We are, in effect, talking about Forms versus things that would be Forms if they were transcendent instead of immanent.

This leaves open the broader question of immanence, that is, the question whether the immanence of Forms is possible at all. Does rejecting immanence as the basis for a proper classification of Forms require rejecting immanence altogether? It may not be a requirement, but it is a good idea. A Form is not the kind of thing that can be immanent, whether or not this is used as a basis for classification.[20] This position may seem to be undermined by the countless examples typically adduced in favor of immanence, starting with the parade example of the tallness, or largeness, in Simmias (*Phaedo* 102b–d), but all such talk is a metaphor for whatever the actual relationship may be between Forms and particulars, not evidence of Forms that are incarnate in the physical realm, which would be tantamount to evidence of Forms that are not Forms. A so-called immanent Form is no more a Form than the tallness in Simmias is Tallness itself (*auto kath' hauto*).

What, then, is the tallness in Simmias, if not a Form? It is nothing more than the instantiation of Tallness, an indication that the thing is in conformity and harmony with the Form,[21] that it is displaying the essential quality or defining characteristic of the Form, that, in this case, Simmias is tall. The proper explanation is not that Tallness itself (*auto kath' hauto*) is in Simmias, but that the physical relation of Simmias to Socrates, coupled with other relations of the same sort (as in Phaedo in relation to Simmias), helps us to understand (recollect) Tallness itself, which is not in anything at all. If the Form, any Form, were ever actually

---

20. Denying this claim, on the other hand, does not require holding that Forms are immanent instead of transcendent, just that they are immanent. Perl (1999, see especially 339, n. 1, 361–362), for one, argues that transcendence and immanence are not contradictory positions, crediting Fine with having already established this with her two articles, one each, on separation (1984) and immanence (1986). On this view, it would not be wrong to claim that Forms are transcendent, and it would not be wrong to claim that they are immanent, but it would be wrong to claim, as I do, that they are transcendent and not immanent.

21. This is a special kind of indication, bringing together the phenomenal and the noumenal, and combining empirical evidence with rational reflection, in what is best described as a "bridge" between the upper and lower levels of Plato's universe. See Thesleff (1999, 33 [= 2009, 417–418]) for the notion of bridges in Plato's stratification of reality. It is particularly noteworthy that he identifies Plato's Forms as the philosopher's "most explicit, ambitious and famous" attempt to bridge the levels.

in something, it would not require recollection, just observation, thus making *anamnēsis* redundant.[22]

It may be objected that the instantiation of Forms is just what is meant by the immanence of Forms, and that the tallness in Simmias falls under such immanence, and, in short, that it counts as immanence. The objection, then, would be that I have misunderstood the nature of immanence, whether or not I have understood the position of Plato. Either way, I do not see how we can all agree that it is not Tallness itself, but the quality of being tall, that is in Simmias and still disagree whether the Form is in the thing. Or perhaps we do not all agree on the first part of the apparent puzzle.

Gail Fine (1986, 73), for example, considers "being in the thing as a property" to be an acceptable sense of "being in the thing" and, accordingly, "the Form's being in the thing as a property" to be the relevant sense of "the Form's being in the thing."[23] I agree that the Form's being in the thing as a property would not necessarily mean that the Form is nothing more than a property of the thing, but I do not agree that the Form itself can actually be in the thing as a property. I deny, in other words, that "being in the thing as a property" is the relevant sense of "being in the thing," or even that it is an acceptable sense of "being in the thing," unless Fine is willing to concede that the construction is entirely metaphorical.

My interpretation is closer to that of Daniel Devereux (1994, 88; cf. 66, 73–74), who submits that what is in Simmias is the "immanent character of largeness," not largeness itself. Devereux's rejection of immanence for Forms turns on a distinction (in the relevant part of the *Phaedo*) between Plato's use of *eidos*, reserved for nonimmanent Forms, and his use of *idea*,

---

22. The reference to *anamnēsis* is only a reminder of the underlying epistemology, which, of course, does not constitute a demonstration of anything regarding the metaphysics. Thesleff himself is not very interested in the matter, regarding it as a mythic thought experiment with little if any relevance to anything outside the eschatological epistemology of the philosopher following the gods toward a rather mystical enlightenment (*Phaedrus* 246e–249d). Noting that recollection never took on a more important function, he deems it "unfortunate" that the experiment "became a standard requisite of Platonism" (Thesleff 1999, 86 [= 2009, 468]).

23. The quotation marks here introduce conceptual constructions rather than indicating direct quotations. See Fine (1986) for what she regards as the relevant sense of "being in" something (71–73), which then shapes how she understands the tallness in Simmias (74). Compare her account of the tallness in Simmias with the rendition of Perl (1999, 345–347).

reserved for the "character" that comes to characterize or to "be in" the sensible thing (1994, 70–71, including especially n. 15).[24] While I agree with this conclusion, I am merely reporting its linguistic justification, not confirming the supporting observation, nor endorsing the inference drawn from it. My own impression, unlike that of Devereux, was shaped independently of the Greek, based solely on the nature of immanence. I would have come to the same conclusion had the original been in Klingon.

Some manner of experimentation may be helpful here. What if the problem were a matter of conflating abstract and physical instantiations while trying to distinguish between transcendent and immanent Forms? I am not suggesting that there is, in fact, a meaningful difference between abstract and physical instantiations. I am asking whether we do perhaps proceed as if there were, given that the question of immanence tends to come up more in reference to properties than it does with respect to types. We invariably show far greater interest in the tallness in Simmias, for example, than we do in, say, the bedness in beds, or the shuttlehood in shuttles, whenever the discussion turns to immanent Forms. What may seem to be a legitimate distinction between transcendent and immanent Forms may instead be a confusion between abstract and physical instantiations. We usually have no problem (or at least not the same problem) with beds or shuttles as instantiations, but we tend to complicate matters with tallness as an instantiation, conjuring up the notion of immanent Forms as a separate ontological category in explaining how tallness comes to be instantiated, as if it could not be instantiated in whatever way beds and shuttles are instantiated. We may thereby be making more of the tallness in something, or of someone, than is required to make sense of the instantiation of Forms in general. The tallness in Simmias is the tallness of Simmias.[25]

An even better distinction (or perhaps a better naming convention for the same distinction) may be between simple and complex instantiations—or between full and partial instantiations, or direct and indirect instantiations, or defining and refining ones. The simple kind is when

---

24. See Allen (1997, 116–119) for agreement, Gonzalez (2002) for opposition.

25. I am not alone in this reading. Kahn, for one, finds it plausible: "The reference to 'the tallness in us' at *Phaedo* 102d7 was probably intended only as a linguistic variant for *our being tall*" (1996, 357, Stephanus notation modified for stylistic conformity). Allen makes a similar point about the instantiation of justice: "to say, for example, that there is justice in an action is merely another way, and an ordinary way, of saying that an action is just" (1970, 146).

the Form is instantiated precisely as what it is, the Form of bed as a bed, the Form of justice as justice, and so on. The complex kind is when the Form is instantiated, again as what it is, but in something else, as in the case of the tallness said to be in Simmias. There is nothing wrong with one kind that would not be wrong with the other. Yet while we normally do not think to bring up the bedness of the bed as a complication, a puzzling category between the Form of bed and the physical bed, we do this regularly with the tallness of Simmias, as if the latter represented an entirely different sort of instantiation.

There is actually just one sort of instantiation.[26] We are not clear on how it works. Nor are we in agreement. But many of us would probably be willing to grant that, however it works, it works the same way in all cases. It may or may not be a tenable phenomenon or process, but the instantiation of Forms should not pose special problems requiring articulation on a case-by-case basis, only general problems, if any at all.

Greater clarity may be had through a reconsideration of the proper correspondence between the elements compared in the foregoing examples. Some of the comparisons may seem to have been cast at the wrong level, resulting in the juxtaposition of disparate elements. The analogic counterpart of the bedness of the bed is not the tallness in or of Simmias but tallness as a quality.[27] It may help to think metaphorically of the Form of Tallness as somehow coming to be present in Simmias, but that is not

---

26. That said, the instantiation of Forms, and thereby the relationship between Forms and particulars, is explicated in various different ways, ranging from the nebulous "participation" of the thing in the Form, to the enigmatic "presence" or "inherence" of the Form in the thing, to the even vaguer "communion" between the two. This is often associated with the question of causality or causal explanation in Plato, especially in its bearing on the Forms. See my previous work (Alican 2012, 95–97) as well as chapter 1 (section 1.4) and chapter 2 (section 2.6) of the present volume. The point of claiming that there is only one kind of instantiation is not to deny the variety of attempts to account for instantiation, but to suggest that any model proposed to explain instantiation, whether or not that model works any differently from any other model, must work the same way when applied to beds as it does when applied to tallness (or to anything else for that matter).

27. The tallness of Tallness the Form is an altogether different problem, one receiving plenty of attention in the literature through the Third Man Argument. See chapter 1 (section 1.4) and chapter 7 (sections 7.2.3 and 7.2.4) for a brief overview and some discussion. The question on hand is not whether the Form of bed is a bed but whether the bedness of the bed constitutes a puzzle, a separate and unfathomable ontological category, in the relationship between the Form of bed and the physical bed.

the same as identifying a new (immanent) Form of Tallness to be distinguished from the standard (transcendent) Form of Tallness. There is just the one Form (for Tallness as for anything else) and it is transcendent. Its instantiation is not the same as the Form itself.[28]

This is not intended as a conclusive answer, or as a definitive account of instantiation, but as a possible explanation and justification of the refusal, both Thesleff's and my own, to recognize immanent Forms.[29] Whether or not the skeletal response sketched here is on the right track, it gives rise to an arguably more important question. Even if the response contemplated is correct in itself, and even if it captures Thesleff's thoughts on the matter, it brings us to a more fundamental matter requiring clarification. The prior

---

28. My dialectical discussion of the nature of immanence as instantiation is not a substitute for Thesleff's own answer. See his assessment of the opposition between tallness and smallness, presented in the broader context of his explication of the relationship between Forms and opposites (Thesleff 1999, 50–52 [= 2009, 434–436]). Both tallness and smallness are at best Conceptual Forms in his terminology. While it would be difficult (in the relevant context) to mistake them for Ideal Forms, note that they are also not Relational Forms (a mistake less difficult to make). The opposition between tallness and smallness does not make them a pair of Relational Forms, which are not simply pairs of opposite Conceptual Forms, but correlative universal relations of metaphysical significance, as discussed in the previous chapter (section 2.8) as well as the present chapter (earlier in this section).

29. Thesleff himself does not take an active part in the debate on transcendence versus immanence. Neither his "transcendence" nor his "immanence" is much like what one might expect to find in the literature: "It is a specific characteristic of the entities of Plato's first ('higher') level to be, somehow, inherent (rather than 'immanent') in the corresponding entities of the second ('lower') level" (Thesleff 1999, 30 [= 2009, 414]). The key to understanding his noncommittal perspective is his emphatic warning against making too much of the distinction: "It is again worth noting that there is no distinct gap of difference between the two levels in Plato's vision, no pointed χωρίς, no deep separation of the 'immanent' from the 'transcendent'" (Thesleff 1999, 63 [= 2009, 446]). His *koinōnia*, in turn, is no more demanding than his *chōrismos*. The balance, therefore, is steadier than would be required for a contradiction. This leaves Thesleff without much of an internal conflict, the absence of which also deprives him of a serious incentive to debate the matter. His tendency to remain outside the dialogue in the secondary literature extends to our collaboration as well (see chapter 2, section 2.2), where he is content to refer readers to the contributions of others (Fine 1984 and 1986; Devereux 1994; Nails 2013), though he does show a personal interest in relevant passages in the primary sources, for example, the complications in Plato (*Parmenides*) and the critique of Aristotle (*Metaphysics* 987a29–b35, 1078b7–1079a4, 1086a30–b12).

issue is not about transcendence alone but about the entire collection of features Thesleff attributes to Ideal Forms (see chapter 2, section 2.6). The potential problem is that transcendence, together with any other ontologically special feature, is accorded to Ideal Forms but not to the other two types of Forms, except under special circumstances through which they come to resemble Ideal Forms. The next section explains why this may appear to be a problem and examines whether it really is.

3.5. The Continuum of Abstraction

Thesleff's classification of Forms holds a certain potential for confusion in the details of the ontological stratification proposed. More accurately, the potential rests on just one detail that ties everything together: the provision of a gradation of reality, not only between Forms and particulars but also between different kinds of Forms and, further, between Forms and mere abstractions. The difference between Forms and particulars is par for the course, a common feature, if there ever was one, in the literature on Plato. The difference(s) between types of Forms is Thesleff's own contribution, and everything there is clear enough, which, at this point, is to endorse just the clarity and not necessarily the validity. The potential for confusion rests in the difference between Forms and mere abstractions, where Thesleff's distinctive classification of Forms stands to introduce further complications.

A concept, for example, is different from a Conceptual Form, the concept being less real, the Form more so, but we also find that a Conceptual Form differs from an Ideal Form in a similar way and to a comparable degree. We find, in other words, that a Conceptual Form is not transcendent or intelligible, and so on, except when it approximates to Ideal Forms. But in what way, then, is a Conceptual Form superior to a mere concept? The answer, not just for Conceptual Forms but for all Forms, is that the Form has an ontological eminence manifested at least as objective reality and causal efficacy, features common to all Forms, whereas what the Form represents, be it a value, a concept, or a relation, does not share that ontological eminence.

The answer itself is not problematic, but the assignment of objective reality and some sort of causal efficacy to all Forms, while reserving transcendence and intelligibility and other metaphysically privileged qualities for Ideal Forms, raises the further question of what kind of reality it is that is assigned to the other two types of Forms if not a reality that is transcendent and intelligible. What does it mean to say that Conceptual Forms and Relational Forms are objectively real? Just how real are they? We seem to be looking for a mode of existence corresponding neither to the physical reality of ordinary things nor to the conventional reality of abstractions nor to the perfect reality of Ideal Forms. It is difficult to imagine any type of Platonic Form with an existence that does not come with transcendence and intelligibility and the host of other features associated with Ideal Forms.

Note that we cannot evade the difficulty by backtracking and admitting that Conceptual Forms and Relational Forms are, after all, transcendent and intelligible and so on, for to do so would be to deny ontological ascent. Either they attain those qualities through ontological ascent, or if they have them in the first place, then there is no room for ontological ascent. And if they attain those qualities through ontological ascent, then they are not so special beforehand, not, in other words, much better than concepts.

A tempting response is that ontological ascent is precisely what accounts for the difference between concepts and Conceptual Forms (or between relations and Relational Forms, or between ideas or ideals and Ideal Forms), such that, without it, there would be no difference between a concept and a Conceptual Form (or a relation and a Relational Form, or an idea or ideal and an Ideal Form). But Thesleff clearly assigns ontological ascent to Conceptual Forms and Relational Forms that approximate somehow to Ideal Forms, thereby specifying when and explaining how these other two types of Forms come to possess features normally reserved for Ideal Forms (see chapter 2, sections 2.7 and 2.11). The same process cannot then be invoked to show that these other two types of Forms always possess those features (transcendence and intelligibility and so on).

This line of criticism is a bit pedantic. Thesleff is not all that demanding here. If we agree that Conceptual Forms and Relational Forms have legitimate claims to objective reality, which we might then flesh out as ontological independence (at least of the mind and of sensible phenomena), and if we recognize in addition that these two types of Forms have cosmologically significant causal roles, the cumulative evidence, that is, the base of agreement, could conceivably be sufficient, as suggested in section 3.4 of this chapter, to distinguish them from mere concepts and relations (and abstractions in general). This is indeed the central question—and the prime reason for the potential confusion regarding ontological ascent.

As far as Thesleff is concerned, we do not have to bother with the matter of causality, since we do not know what we would be getting into there. He is perfectly comfortable with objective reality, especially with full ontological independence, as representing a minimally acceptable sense of ontological eminence clearly not shared by mere abstractions. But as long as we are revisiting the response to the "glorified concepts" analogy entertained in section 3.4, a dispassionate assessment requires acknowledging that the ontological eminence claimed there for Conceptual Forms and Relational Forms, while establishing their superiority over concepts, leaves open the question whether they are nevertheless glorified concepts—difficult to rule out because the term "glorified concept" does not really mean anything, yet difficult to ignore because we all understand exactly what it means anyway.

The difficulties may be exacerbated by the modern convenience of using a metalanguage (relative to Plato in translation) that is an integral part of our natural language but was not a part of Plato's. The difference, to fill in the details, is between talking about Forms with a shared understanding of concepts and talking about them without one.[30] This is a controversial assumption, but it is not entirely untenable, despite recent studies suggesting that the actual gap was not as great as one may think and implying therefore that this way of putting it may be an exaggeration of the facts.[31] It is not, at any rate, an easy matter.

---

30. This is intended not as a judgment from a position of expertise but as a naïve exploration of the possibilities. If the statement is vulnerable, safeguards are certainly welcome as amendments. Perhaps, for example, the difference invoked here is better explicated as one between talking about Forms while drawing on a shared understanding of concepts (or of the process of abstraction) and talking about Forms with no recourse to a fully established and sufficiently common understanding of concepts (or of the process of abstraction).

31. The recent studies in question are those on Plato's understanding of concepts and on his notion of abstraction. Helmig (2004; 2007; 2012) is in the vanguard of ongoing research in this area. Schumacher (2010) is a good example of work drawing on Helmig. Gerson (1999a; 1999b), Thorp (1984), and Warner (1965) are forerunners worth consulting on the same topic. If it would not be presumptuous to speak of a trend here, one of the safest generalizations that can be made is that there is a growing consensus that we have to make a greater effort to understand Plato's approach to abstraction, using all the resources available to us, instead of confining the investigation to the letter of the text. Accordingly, the focus is oftentimes more on Platonism and the Platonic tradition than on Plato. We are encouraged to consult

The fact, for example, that Plato had a word (or two or three) for "concept" does not settle the issue one way or the other.[32] We know all too well how hard the Socrates of the so-called early dialogues has to work to get his interlocutors to understand the question whenever he inquires into the nature of what would now strike us as an ordinary concept.[33] If everyone in Socratic Athens, or even just the philosophical community there, had been comfortable with abstraction, we would not have had Socratic interlocutors giving an example of virtue as an answer to what virtue is (*Meno*), pointing to an instance of piety in response to what piety is (*Euthyphro*), and so on with other familiar examples in other memorable encounters. The existence of a word for something is not the same as a clear or common understanding of that thing, as confirmed by Plato's Socrates in reporting that he has yet to meet anyone who knows what virtue is (*Meno* 71c).

Nor is the problem restricted to moral concepts. Any scenario where it is necessary, or even merely useful, to explain that "Roundness" is not an adequate response to "What is shape?" (*Meno* 73e, 74b), or that "Whiteness" is not an adequate response to "What is color?" (*Meno* 74c), suggests that something is missing in the prevailing conception of abstraction. This is precisely what we have in the character of Meno,

---

Aristotle, other Academics, Middle Platonists, and Neoplatonists for clues on how to handle the gaps in Plato himself. The general lesson seems to be that a discussion of abstraction in Plato need not be restricted to the realm of Forms, which leaves room for an independent albeit related discussion of concepts.

32. Noting that ancient Greek had several words that can now be translated as "concept," though never claiming that any one of those refers precisely to what we typically take today to be concepts, Helmig (2012, 14–15) lists thirteen individual words and one pair of words, each and every one of them liable to be qualified by adjectives (also listed in full), which, in turn, can themselves be used as nouns. Among these, only *ennoia* is identified as already occurring in Plato, specifically at *Phaedo* 73c and *Philebus* 59d (Helmig 2012, 14, n. 6). This does not, of course, bring us, with reference to Plato, anywhere near a philosophy of concepts, or of abstraction, that can be distinguished from any philosophy of Forms. Nor does Helmig claim that it does.

33. Even if this were nothing more than a dramatic ploy to create an occasion for demonstrating how abstraction works, and not otherwise an indication that characters who do not understand abstraction are representative of actual people who did not understand abstraction, we would still be left with the fact that there was some use, in fact, a philosophical need, for a dramatic ploy to create an occasion for demonstrating how abstraction works.

who even after this very explanation, is still unable to demonstrate that he has understood what is being asked, as he declines to say what it is that is common to roundness and straightness and other things we call "shape" (*Meno* 75a–b). The various clarifications and instructions prove insufficient as Socrates has to go on to supply the answer as well. This is evidence both that Plato understood abstraction and that not everyone did.

To elaborate on the question of conceptual or linguistic differences between Plato's circumstances and our own, the problem is not simply that Plato was not able to work with abstraction, or merely that he was ill-equipped to do so, which he probably was in terms of the philosophical language he inherited, but also that he did not say enough about it to help us see exactly how he distinguished between concepts and Forms. We naturally use our own understanding of concepts to figure out what it is that Plato took to be Forms, since we are not able to use Plato's understanding of concepts toward that same end. We use terms like "concept" or "universal" or "abstraction" in our efforts to explore all possible shades of meaning between a Form and the thing of which it is a Form, but this may be a luxury or privilege, perhaps even an extravagance, that was not fully available to Plato. In the final analysis, Plato seems to have been at the forefront of a breakthrough in the conceptual, linguistic, and philosophical development of abstraction—thus engaged not in applying a familiar process but in inventing, exploring, or refining it—and we cannot sensibly expect from him the same discussion at the same level we are engaged in today.

This is not to say that Plato does not distinguish between concepts and Forms. He obviously does, though not very clearly. He would have otherwise had no occasion to convey a sense of hesitation regarding the assignment of Forms to man, fire, and water, while enthusiastically embracing Forms for justice, beauty, and goodness, and unequivocally rejecting them for hair, mud, and dirt (*Parmenides* 130b–d). He has a tendency to draw or imply distinctions, these and yet others, which we can appreciate from our perspective as a distinction between concepts and Forms.[34] In fact, recent studies on the subject both provide and

---

34. This brings up the question whether we might be reading our own perspective back into Plato's, but that cannot be all that is going on here, as it does not explain why not every concept or abstraction from our perspective is a Form from Plato's perspective. The selectivity in Plato is hard to miss, especially with Thesleff's approach, where there is a difference not just between concepts and Forms but also between different kinds of Forms.

recommend an examination of Plato's approach to abstraction in greater depth than the customary focus on Forms with little or no emphasis on concepts or concept formation.[35] What we keep debating is not whether there is a difference between concepts and Forms but what that difference is. And the difference is at once so plain yet so nuanced that we have to be guarded in what we say, which means that we usually do not end up saying anything very interesting.[36]

Efforts to explicate Plato's understanding of abstraction, beyond what we have long been discussing in regard to the Forms, focus on *anamnēsis*.[37] No doubt, just the mention of *anamnēsis* brings to mind a preoccupation with Forms. Yet the suggestion is not that we should divert our attention elsewhere, but that we should dig deeper here. Possibly the most exciting development in the relevant literature, for example, in the work of Lydia Schumacher (2010) expanding on that of Christoph Helmig (2004), is the thesis that Platonic *anamnēsis* is not a matter of recollecting this or that Form but of recovering the inherent intellectual ability, or capacity, for abstraction. Another way of thinking about this would be as the activation of a dormant cognitive faculty. Recollection, so the argument runs, *is* abstraction, particularly in the sense that it taps into our hardwired ability to make generalizations. On this interpretation, *anamnēsis* is not so much a matter of recollecting specific Forms as it is of recollecting what

---

35. See Gerson (1999a; 1999b), Helmig (2004; 2007; 2012), Schumacher (2010), Thorp (1984), and Warner (1965), among others, for further insight into Plato's understanding of concepts and abstraction.

36. This is better than not being able to say anything that is true. And the truth is not too far to reach. It is just difficult to articulate. That may be why we rarely end up saying anything more interesting than that Forms are not concepts. Here is one example: "Forms are rather the *objective correlates of thought*; they are not concepts or mental entities that are confined to human souls" (Helmig 2012, 50; cf. 2007, 306, for the same statement in almost exactly the same words). As unadventurous as this view may seem, its latest expression (Helmig 2012, 50, n. 43) is anchored, for good measure, to references to Cherniss (1944, 214–216, n. 128) and Lafrance (1984) in support of the hardly controversial claim that Forms are not concepts.

37. This is the so-called doctrine of recollection (actually more of a metaphor than a doctrine) introduced in the *Meno* (81a–86c), developed in the *Phaedo* (72e–77a), and invoked in the *Phaedrus* (249b–c). The separate occasions (*Meno, Phaedo, Phaedrus*) to utilize the "doctrine" (or merely to mention it, as the case may be) present mutual inconsistencies, at least in appearance, often inspiring efforts toward reconciliation, as in Allen (1959) and Helmig (2004).

to do with them, of how to use them to understand the world around us.[38] This is not the empirical abstraction espoused by Aristotle,[39] largely as an alternative to recollection, but a rational abstraction through the recovery and projection of an inherent intellectual ability, or innate cognitive faculty, as opposed to inert mental content.[40]

To return to the question of ontological ascent, any confusion regarding precisely where it belongs (and how it works) in Plato's metaphysics is a reflection or extension of uncertainties in the ongoing efforts of the philosophical community to work out the details of Plato's understanding of abstraction. We are all still participants in a collective work in progress. It is, therefore, not easy to ascertain whether Plato envisaged two different

---

38. There is still something to be said for the recollection of individual Forms, an established reading that cannot reasonably be dismissed offhand, even if the alternative broadens our horizons with respect to interpretive possibilities. The evidence is mixed. The *Meno* (81a–86c) can indeed be read as alluding to the recovery of the intellectual capacity for abstraction or even more generally to the activation of innate cognitive functions: Note the reference to discovering everything upon recalling one thing (*Meno* 81d). But the *Phaedo* (72e–77a) is replete with examples of specific Forms identified as objects of recollection: the equal (74a–75c); the greater and the smaller (75c); the beautiful, the good, the just, and the pious, with a loose and broadly inclusive reference to what seems like all Forms (75d; cf. 76d, 77a). The *Phaedrus* can go either way: It points to abstraction where it presents recollection as a process whereby the soul (of the philosopher) in its cosmic journey (248a–249d) forges a reasoned unity out of its various perceptions (249b–c). But it quickly degenerates into the recollection of specific items as it brings up the "sacred objects" seen before (250a). The emphasis on beauty, for example, is both unmistakable and unforgettable, especially as it is juxtaposed with justice and temperance, both of which are said to be more difficult to recognize in their earthly manifestations while beauty shines brightly (250b).

39. See Aristotle's *Posterior Analytics* (99b15–100b17) for his reaction and alternative to Plato's *anamnēsis*.

40. What is new or exciting here is not necessarily the construal of the object of recollection as an intellectual ability, or cognitive faculty, as opposed to mental content. The novelty, rather, is in associating that ability or faculty specifically with the process of abstraction. Otherwise, the same interpretation can be, and has been, cast in different terms. A good example, an alternative to the one on hand, is the approach of Allen (1959), who proposes that what is recollected is the power of inference, though he also retains the notion of the recollection of actual Forms: "The theory of Anamnesis is a theory of inference, and it rests on the intensional relations which the Forms bear to one another" (1959, 167). Allen even anticipates, and rejects, the abstraction account, maintaining instead that knowledge of the Forms is epistemically (and, for Plato, also temporally) prior to knowledge of particulars (1959, 169).

types of transformation, one from concepts into Conceptual Forms (or from relations into Relational Forms, or from ideas or ideals into Ideal Forms), the other from Conceptual Forms (or Relational Forms) into Ideal Forms.[41] He indeed may have. Or he may not have. The details of Plato's ontology are not cut and dried. Nor are they amenable to direct inference from assumptions or conclusions about his epistemology. As Thesleff claims, for the basic difference between mere abstractions from our perspective and Forms from Plato's perspective, we do not have much to go by except the demonstrable importance, significance, or value Plato attached to any given abstraction.[42] A value, concept, or relation has a Form corresponding to it if and only if it strikes Plato as being somehow important, significant, or special enough to have a Form corresponding to it. If we were to attempt to list all Platonic Forms, we would do well to stick close to the text of the dialogues. We could, of course, extrapolate from explicit examples that obviously recall others, but the further we tend to stray away from actual examples, the more we would be expanding the platform instead of exploring it.

3.6. Conclusion

What impressed Plato as important, significant, or special enough to have a Form corresponding to it is not as hazy a matter as the rather loose characterization here may seem to indicate. On any sensible interpretation, the relative value in question would have to be anchored to explanatory power. Plato, like any other philosopher, was looking to understand the world in which he found himself. But unlike most philosophers, he seems to have had to create or develop the conceptual apparatus required to carry out what might otherwise have been a standard philosophical project.[43] And his principal creation to expedite his own efforts is the interpretive paradigm of Forms. If that is true, then what impressed Plato

---

41. This is a different question from whether Thesleff would be justified (in terms of the internal consistency of his own position) in attributing to Plato both types of ontological ascent.

42. See chapter 2 (sections 2.7 and 2.11), chapter 5 (section 5.3), and chapter 6 (especially section 6.3 but also sections 6.4 and 6.5).

43. There is some truth, after all, to Whitehead's overworked estimation of Plato's position in the European philosophical tradition.

as important was whatever helped him explain the world. We already have some idea regarding the specifics, as we turn time and again to examples such as justice and beauty. But if any generalization were possible, this would be it, namely that the Forms help do philosophy, or at least that they helped Plato do philosophy. It is this simple principle that is at the heart of Thesleff's approach, guiding him both in differentiating between concepts and Forms and in formulating a classification of Forms, all in the same world as everything else.

Chapter 4

A Horse Is a Horse, of Course, of Course, but What about Horseness?

This chapter is a meditation on the philosophical preconceptions shaping the reception of Plato's metaphysics.[1] The central focus is on the dualism of a world of Forms existing separately from the world we know. The overarching aim is to explore the motivation for postulating that second world instead of making do with the one we have. While the approach is indeed exploratory, the underlying suspicion is that everything, Forms and all, belongs in the same world. The goal is not to prove that the Forms exist, nor to evaluate the proofs and objections on record, but to consider why and how they are supposed to exist, and what follows if they actually do. Dialogue toward a mutual understanding of why we think the Forms exist, and why we think they do not, might encourage a "second sailing" in waters where we have been unable to agree whether they do, and where they would if they did.

4.1. Bunny in the Clouds

My first encounter with Plato's Forms was a failure. I had not taken any classes in philosophy. Nor had I had any training in classical studies. I

---

1. This chapter originally appeared as an essay in a collection commemorating Holger Thesleff's ninetieth birthday (Alican 2015): "A Horse Is a Horse, of Course, of Course, but What about Horseness?," in *Second Sailing: Alternative Perspectives on Plato*, edited by Debra Nails and Harold Tarrant in collaboration with Mika Kajava and Eero Salmenkivi, 307–324, Commentationes Humanarum Litterarum 132 (Helsinki: Societas Scientiarum Fennica).

had heard of Plato but not of the Forms. Thus equipped with nothing but a blank tablet of a mind, I happened upon the "invisible things" of the *Phaedo*. I walked away from that experience without a whisper of an awareness regarding a separate world for the Forms. I had failed to notice an entire world.

Once I was told about it, however, I learned to recognize it when I saw it: first in the *Phaedrus*, then in the *Symposium*, later in the *Republic*, and with a little instruction, wherever it was supposed to be found. But I secretly suspected all along that I might be recognizing something that was not there, somewhat like agreeing to "see" the fluffy bunny people were always pointing out to me in the cloud formations above. All I ever saw was the clouds. That is perhaps why, in all the usual places where I was expected to see a division between two worlds, what I saw instead was a gradation of reality in a single world.

I liked the gradation. It made perfect sense. I did not understand why anyone would want to give it up for a binary division. I feared that much of the gradation, that is, most of the degrees of reality, would be lost through a separation of worlds. If one world were one extreme, I wondered, and the other world, the opposite extreme, would we not need yet another world for everything in between? Not if we could divide it all up between the first two worlds. But that, it seemed to me, would be like pretending that there was nothing between them to begin with, leaving us with a polarized reality from the outset. Where and why did all the differences in degree turn into a difference in kind requiring a division into separate worlds?

I did not know the answer then. I do not know the answer now. What I do know is that such a strong separation is not necessary to make things work. It is, of course, sufficient. It does make things work. The scenario of separate worlds serves its purpose, especially if the aim is to get rid of the Forms without repudiating them, or to retain the Forms without embracing them, thus treating them as an embarrassment to be hidden away and kept out of sight, much in the manner of the eccentric uncle living in the attic, or the crazy aunt locked up in the basement, the standard solution to such problems in B movies during the Golden Age of Hollywood. Yet one might reasonably expect a model of Plato's metaphysics to treat the Forms as something more than an embarrassment.

I came across such a model in Holger Thesleff's initiative to reject separation in favor of gradation, working with levels instead of worlds. This was his construal of Plato's ontology as comprising two main levels and a full complement of subdivisions collectively amounting to a stratification of reality in a single world satisfying all modes of existence and incorporating all grades and shades of reality. It was neither the only nor even the first reaction to a separation of worlds.[2] In fact, it was not so much a reaction as it was a positive viewpoint, a comprehensive platform for interpreting Plato. And that positive dimension was what attracted me to it.

My aim in this chapter is not to champion that perspective. Thesleff himself has already done that, later recruiting me to join him.[3] I intend, rather, to explore the basic intuition that would inspire any reader of Plato to favor one view over the other. That preference has never struck me as a reasoned conclusion of any sort, say, as the result of intensive study or careful deliberation. It has always impressed me as an intuitive grasp subsequently supported by evidence and argument.

We sift through the available evidence to justify the original intuition. That is what we do whether we favor gradation in a single world or opposition between two worlds. There is enough evidence either way to keep both sides happy. There is no proof in this. It is the bunny in the clouds, this second world. So, it may be worth our while to figure out why some of us see it and some do not. That stands to be more useful than attempting in vain to demonstrate either that it is there or that it is not. Even if we cannot settle the primary debate, we may be able to develop a better understanding of why we are engaged in it.

My own understanding, formulated well before becoming acquainted with Thesleff's, was that the second world was a heuristic device Plato's readers employed to make sense of the magic.[4] I am not talking about magic in the sense of sorcery, trickery, or illusion on the part of Plato. What I mean is that I found the Forms themselves to be magical, that is to say, delightfully different. Others, no doubt, may have found them

---

2. Reactions to a two-world ontology in Plato include Brentlinger (1972), Broadie (2004), Ferguson (1921), Nails (2013), Nehamas (1975), and Robjant (2012). Reactions to a two-world epistemology include Butler (2007), Fine (1978; 1990), Gonzalez (1996), Rowe (2005), and Smith (2000; 2012; 2019).

3. See Thesleff (1993b, 17–45; 1999 [= 2009, 383–506]) for his own thoughts, chapter 2 of the present volume for our collaboration (originally published as Alican and Thesleff 2013), and the rest of the book for my independent work (parts of which were originally published as Alican 2014, 2015, 2017a, and 2017b, as explained in the preface and the introduction).

4. A glimpse into my impression of the magic may be had in Alican (2012, 87–110).

disturbingly or provocatively different rather than delightfully so. And one reaction to what is both different and disturbing is to keep one's distance. Hence, a second world, one reserved just for the Forms.

Did the Forms not look a bit fanciful to me as well? They most certainly did. That part, I had not missed. I was enchanted through and through and had no doubt they were sprinkled with pixie dust. As fantabulous as the Forms seemed, however, I always thought that Plato envisaged them as making it easier for us to understand our world, not as requiring us to postulate another one, which we would likely understand even less.

I was not sure what to call my interpretation as against the two-world rendition, which I also did not know what to call, because it was presented to me as the only interpretation, thus without a name or an alternative. Not having an alternative, it did not need a name, or so it must have seemed. Without naming either one, then, I thought of mine as two aspects of the same reality. I did not think that Plato's Forms existed in one world while sensible phenomena existed in another. I thought that the Forms existed in one sense, sensible phenomena in another, quite apart from how many worlds there were, regarding which I happened to believe there was just the one.

That is still what I believe. And I now believe, in addition, that at least some of the disagreement, probably most of it, is grounded in what we make of existence as a metaphysical concept. There must be something in the way the Forms exist, or rather, in the way they are supposed to exist, that is uncomfortable, maybe even inscrutable, for some, but not for others. Some of us, I think, are predisposed to finding plenty of room for the Forms right here, while others see no option but to make room for them elsewhere, all the while, all of us being fully aware that they are not actually supposed to be anywhere. But if they take up no room, neither here nor there, why even bother with a second world? It cannot be just because something Plato once said sounded like a transcendent heaven (*Republic* 509d; cf. *Phaedrus* 247c–d). With all the metaphors to choose from, why pick the one that makes him sound like a lunatic? And even then, why take it literally?

I have no objection to a second world itself. I just do not think we need it for the Forms. Although that sounds like a fairly agreeable thing to say, I should confess, to be perfectly honest, that I actually do object to the idea of a second world, and to that of a third, and so on, which, to me, are all the same world, because the world is what there is. We only ever have what there is, not something else besides. Before we can get to anything else, it has to become part of what there is. There is never anything else. But this general outlook is not the point I am pressing here, even if, as admitted, I cannot truthfully deny being moved by it. My only concern in this chapter is specifically with whether we need a second world to accommodate the Forms, not with whether we can ever have a second world at all, which I am sure we cannot.

Despite this confession, I will try to be as receptive as possible to the general plausibility of a second world, responding instead to the specific requirement of one for the Forms. If I am shown a passage where the souls of the dead go to Hades, which is then purported to be (in) another world, I shall embrace that world of souls. If I am shown a passage where the gods dwell in the heavens, which is then said to be (in) another world, I shall revere that world of gods. I am not sure, though, whether the whereabouts of souls and gods would make for one more world or two more, thus possibly three in all, going up to four if we add one for the Forms. I am being deliberately difficult, of course, to make anything beyond one world sound sillier than it really is. No, there would be just one extra world. All the souls and gods and Forms, anything unfamiliar, would go there.

Yet even if I am being difficult, how is it that none of these things can be accommodated in the world we already have, but they can all be tucked away neatly in just one alternate reality? Why not an extra world for each kind of thing that does not seem to go with what we have here? Or are souls and gods and Forms the same kind of thing? Strictly speaking, they are not. But there seems to be a looser sense in which they might reasonably, or at least not unreasonably, be thought of as the same sort of thing, perhaps insofar as they belong in the same ontological category. If there is such a sense at all, it might well be in the way they are conceived to exist.[5]

Must we do this the hard way, speculating about things we do not know? Does Plato never say anything outright that could possibly be

---

5. Recall how the existence of the soul is compared in one part of the *Phaedo* (78b–84b) to the existence of gods and Forms, as if gods and Forms were the same kind of thing, or at least sufficiently similar to each other to justify such a comparison. That analogy is taken up in greater detail in section 4.3 of the present chapter, where the discussion turns to the corresponding argument of the *Phaedo* (78b–80b on the rationale, 80c–84b on the supporting imagery) for the immortality of the soul, not to evaluate the proof presented there, but to study the kind of existence contemplated in the process by Plato.

pointing to another world? On the contrary, he says plenty of things that *can* be read that way, and one or two things that *must* be read that way. But he swings the other way as well. That is what the debate has always been about. It cannot hurt to go beyond that to see if there is anything there. Variations in our approach to existence may well be the key to our disagreement.

With a focus on existence, a systematic study of Plato's ontology might seem to be in order. Fortunately, there are such studies. This one is not about what Plato thinks of existence. It is about what anyone might think of existence. That, too, can be relevant. It can help find common ground between those who are not satisfied with a single world and those who are not happy with a duplication of worlds. The reason why the corresponding conflict is fundamentally about existence is that it is the pressure that Plato's Forms put on the notion of existence that forces us, evidently only some of us, to imagine a second world. We need to understand, better than we do, why only some of us are thus affected.

4.2. Horses and Horseness

Whenever we deny that the Forms exist, we deny of them exactly what we affirm of sensible phenomena. We thereby deny something that nobody holds: "I can see the horse, Plato, but not horseness."[6] Indeed, none of us can. Antisthenes is not alone in his metaphysical predicament. Yet Plato is not troubled by the fact that horseness is nowhere to be seen. To trouble Plato, one would have to show that there is no such thing as horseness, not that horseness is not the same kind of thing as horses. One could also trouble Plato by showing that there is such a thing as horseness but

---

6. This would be Antisthenes addressing Plato. The quotation marks are not for exact quotation, not even in translation (as there are different renditions), but for imagined direct speech, inspired by the story of an exchange between Plato and Antisthenes, as reported, among others, by Simplicius (*In Aristotelis Categorias Commentarium* 208.28-32 [= SSR 5A 149 = Giannantoni 1990, 2.193]). The same basic plot, with Diogenes of Sinope replacing Antisthenes, and cups and tables replacing horses, can be found in Diogenes Laërtius (6.53 [= SSR 5B 62 = Giannantoni 1990, 2.255]). Susan Prince (2015, 428-445) offers extensive coverage of the relevant sources for the anecdote, particularly the Antisthenes version, which she presents with texts, translations, and commentary. The version featuring Diogenes of Sinope comes up later in chapter 7 (section 7.4) of the present volume.

that it exists only by convention and not by nature. That, however, is a roundabout way of saying that there is no such thing as horseness, the demonstration of which, I have already conceded, would be decisive. Plato would be the first to admit that horseness does not exist in the same way that horses do and the last to accept that either one does not exist at all. The task is to understand existence in context, not in space and time. That is what Plato's fabled response amounts to.[7]

But is that response fair and satisfactory or is it evasive and snarky? What if Antisthenes had come back with a rejoinder that never actually made it into the story? What if he had said: "Yes, yes, we know to call a horse a horse when we see it, but that still does not mean that there is anything other than this horse and that horse and that one over there and the one over yonder." What if he had added: "The only reason it occurs to you to speak of a horseness is the horses. If Poseidon were to take back the horses, there would be no horseness." This is not in character for someone reportedly complaining about not being able to see the horseness. But it does take us beyond that first step, which is where the debate gets interesting.

Given that we are still debating whether things such as horseness really do exist, even without anyone demanding to see the horseness, we obviously disagree on what it is to exist. Plato does not have to answer alone for that disagreement. He still has to give us more than horses, but we need to give him something in return. His responsibility to explain how horseness exists (if not as horses) does not absolve us of ours to explain how horses exist (if not through horseness). With Poseidon steadily losing credibility as a divinity, the Forms must be looking increasingly more tenable as an explanation.

A horse is a horse, of course, of course, but what about horseness? We should know by now not to ask Antisthenes. We know full well that he missed the point. Yet we keep echoing the same criticism. We remain just one step away from Antisthenes when we ask: "Okay, but do the Forms really exist?"

Almost anyone who is not a professional philosopher, and perhaps also a few professional philosophers, would rest easier with horseness

---

7. This is not Plato's actual reply, but it is close enough. His reply is reported to be that Antisthenes has the eyes required to see the horses, but not the mind required to grasp the corresponding horseness, in other words, that he can see well enough to make out horses but cannot reason well enough to figure out horseness.

existing the way horses do, not necessarily with a flowing mane of its own, but certainly with an existence on its own. They may not have to see the horseness to believe it, but they might still appreciate being assured that horseness exists no less than horses do when they fade out of sight on the other side of a hill.

We do not like for things to fade out of sight. We so fear the natural end to our own existence that we seek solace in a promised existence in some other realm after we cease to exist in this one. No wonder we do not want the Forms to exist in a funny way. We do not even want our souls or our gods to exist in that way.

That is why we have our souls dwelling with our gods, when they are no longer dwelling in our bodies, and our gods sending us books and messengers and offspring, as we wait for the reunion. If the gods can put in a personal appearance every now and then, even better. We need all the assurance we can get.

And we get plenty. We at least get what we need to keep talking to our gods, even when it is mostly a monologue. Happily, though, it is often more than a monologue. We want to hear something back. So, we do. We do not hear our gods the way we hear each other. But the connection, however it works, lets us know they are there. We know they "really" exist.

We normally would not bother to fortify the notion of "existence" with that of "reality." They are, for all practical purposes, mutually redundant concepts. Yet we sometimes combine them anyway, for example, in seeking confirmation: "Does Santa Claus really exist?" We also tend to combine them in emphasizing denial: "Santa Claus does not really exist." And we habitually do so with the Forms: "Do the Forms really exist?"

My answer to "Do the Forms really exist?" would be the same as my answer to "Do the Forms really, really exist?" and the same again as my answer to "Do the Forms exist?" It does not matter what that answer is. The point is that it should be, and in my case would be, the same in each case. It should be the same because each "really" is nothing more than a hidden demand for a confession that the whole thing is a sham. That demand, in turn, is anchored to a shared understanding of the difference between reality and fantasy: "Wink wink, nudge nudge, say no more, say no more. We can talk about leprechauns all you want, so long as we both know they do not really exist."

Scholars contemplating the nature of Forms and philosophers talking about the existence of universals rarely seem to be doing the same thing. There is something in the exchange on universals in a broad sense that sets it apart from the typical engagement with Forms in a Platonic context. There is, to be specific, a mutual toleration plain to see on either side of the debate on universals. There are signs there of a "wink wink, nudge nudge" kind of framework agreement, also imposed on Plato scholars, but seldom observed by them. This silent protocol breaks down when the existence of Forms comes up. Plato scholars do not wink back. Ignoring the overtures, they insist on a real debate, for they believe either that the Forms do exist or that Plato was not wrong to think so. Some of them might concede that the Forms do not exist, but none of them will agree that Plato was wrong to think so, given the material he had to work with to get across the points he wanted to make.

I am not denying that Plato's Forms can be, and sometimes are, discussed in the same way as ordinary universals. I am merely reporting that I personally feel an obligation to act surprised whenever I read a general overview presenting Plato, quite rightly, as having assigned to the Forms an objective reality outside the mind. It is almost as if each presentation came with a rhetorical question: "Can you believe what he is saying?" I, for one, can believe it, and almost always do believe it, making appropriate allowances for the customary play and irony in Plato. Because of all the false expectations, however, I never know whether I am allowed to praise Plato for anticipating and inspiring the subtleties of the modern debate or obligated to condemn him for making too much of what is, at bottom, little more than the natural capacity for abstraction, a capacity he famously taps through a kind of thought experiment to explain unity in plurality and identity in difference.[8]

I am expected to confront Alexius Meinong or Bertrand Russell without batting an eye. But I had better have an incredulous stare ready for Plato. That is the standard reception upon initial acquaintance:

> The "theory of Forms" is one of the most famous, most influential, and most controversial of all philosophical theories. It is also one of the weirdest, or at least so it seems to countless

---

8. A more extensive breakdown of the essential functions of Plato's Forms would have to include at least the following: distinguishing reality from appearance, recognizing permanence against change, discerning stability within flux, proving continuity over time, reconciling being with becoming, upholding unity in plurality, explaining identity in difference, establishing objectivity in values, and demonstrating the unity of the virtues. See chapter 1 (section 1.3) for further discussion.

undergraduates forced to learn about it in introductory philosophy courses. (Welton 2002, 1)

Undergraduates are not the only ones taken aback by an encounter with the Forms. Aristotle was evidently uncomfortable with them even after he graduated, and, no doubt, also before:

> Aristotle certainly thinks that Socrates and Plato share this view of the objects of the sciences, though Aristotle also thinks that these new objects of the sciences that Plato believed in were wrongly identified by Plato with certain extraordinary, even preposterous, entities, the Forms; while if we avoid such an overreaction, Aristotle continues, what we get are simply those (abstract) objects, universals, which are precisely what the objects of the sciences should be. (Penner 2006, 167)

In both of the passages just quoted, and in countless others like them, we get a hint of a metaphysical monstrosity that goes beyond the existence of the abstract. Sometimes, we get more than a hint:

> [T]he conception of forms as universals or as the meanings of general terms produces a baffled incredulity when we consider some of the things that Plato has to say about them. It would be outlandish enough anyway to be told that a universal is an object; it becomes positively outrageous when we are informed furthermore that the object which is the universal being a so-and-so is itself a very superior so-and-so, existing separate from and independent of the particulars it characterizes and causing them to have the nature that they do. Could Plato have seriously thought and meant things so foolish? (Denyer 1983, 315)

As a matter of fact, we almost always get more than a hint. The reason why the first two passages may only seem like hints is that the greater context is missing in each case. Hardly any commentary I have read merely mentions an abomination and leaves it at that. The misgivings usually run deeper than the sheer existence of Forms. What is shocking, or presented as shocking, is not simply that the Forms exist, nor just that they exist outside the mind, but more so that they exist as perfect paradigms after which sensible phenomena are patterned, the Forms themselves remaining forever changeless. There is so little agreement about what to make of the Forms that even this makeshift description will be found by some to be an understatement of the metaphysical extravagance they represent and by others to be an overstatement.

Whether through understatement or overstatement, or through avoiding both, it is hard to deny the extravagance. The Forms are splendiferous. So much so that the gods are in awe. The gods of the central myth of the *Phaedrus* (246e–249d) would certainly not be trekking out to the edge of the heavens to gaze upon these things just because they are there. No pilgrimage is ever made to behold the mundane. Things that exist, even things that really, really exist, will not, unless they provide some attraction other than their own existence, get Zeus and company out of Olympus to come take a look.[9]

Be that as it may, the shock value is not buried too deep in the metaphysical splendor. To be surprised, we need not even go into the glorious features that make the Forms worthy of the admiration of the gods. No, we are supposed to be surprised with far less. We are supposed to be surprised starting with their existence outside the mind:

> The problem [of universals] only persists if we acknowledge that sameness in difference requires an explanation and if we suppose that a Platonic solution to this problem is going to involve doing something weird with universals, e.g., positing them as existing on their own. (Gerson 2004b, 239)

The shock value in the contention that the Forms really do exist comes from the distinction that they would exist even if nothing else did. The sense of "real" existence here is existence with full ontological independence. Plato, it seems, has exaggerated the existence of the Forms, whatever else about them he may have exaggerated on top of that.

4.3. Modes of Existence

How does one exaggerate existence? What does that even mean? Plato often handles such questions with allegories and analogies. This works well because an indirect treatment of that sort turns out to be a strategically

---

9. All the Olympians make the journey except Hestia, who chooses, rather appropriately, to stay home (*Phaedrus* 247a).

advantageous way of taking a stand on the existence of abstract objects, especially for someone prepared to assign a greater reality to them than to concrete objects, and even more so for anyone doing so at a time when the leading candidates for abstract objects would have been gods.[10]

Abstraction itself seems to have been such a novelty, at least as a philosophical tool or topic, that Plato apparently not only worked with it but also spearheaded its development.[11] With anything novel naturally lending itself to metaphorical expression and explanation, allegorical articulation must have been the perfect medium for Plato to pass over all the patently real things around him to embrace those with a curious yet stronger claim to existence. This is not to suggest that the things around him, ordinary things, as they say, did not exist for Plato. They did. But the Forms ranked higher in his ontology.

We see this in the divided line dividing the *Republic* in two (509d–511e). We hear it from Diotima as she educates Socrates on love in the speech dividing the *Symposium* in two (209e–212a). We observe it in the cosmic journey of the soul in the great myth dividing the *Phaedrus* in two (246e–249d).[12] In each case, the division is not necessarily between two equal lengths of text but between appearance and reality, opinion and knowledge, and ignorance and wisdom. And even though there may seem to be a world of difference between appearance and reality, opinion and knowledge, and ignorance and wisdom, they are actually opposite ends of the same world, with many levels in between. Why else would Plato divide the same line over and over? Why else would Diotima lead Socrates up the ladder of love one step at a time? Why else would the ascent of

---

10. I do not mean to prejudge the question whether Plato's gods are material or immaterial, or both, or neither. Such a discussion cannot profitably be restricted to the traditional gods of the Greek pantheon. Nor should we focus exclusively on the demiurge. My concern here, at any rate, is with the gods in the analogic argument of the *Phaedo* (78b–84b), discussed further in the remainder of this section. A digression into the broader question of the nature of ancient gods is available in Alican (2018), a critical and comparative study of the development of religious thought with particular emphasis on the continuity between Greek polytheism and Abrahamic monotheism.

11. See chapter 3 (section 3.5) for my thoughts on Plato's contribution to the development of abstraction as a philosophical process and vision.

12. Even the myth itself is divided into two parts (*Phaedrus*): 246e–247e for gods, 248a–249d for mortals.

the soul be such a recursive struggle and, even upon repeated attempts, be possible only for the philosopher?

What we learn through the most memorable of Plato's allegories and analogies is that his reality comes in degrees. Thesleff, as mentioned above, is confident about where to go with that: a single world with two main levels and an indefinite multitude of subdivisions. That is his alternative to the two-world interpretation where the Forms reside in one world, sensible phenomena in another.

A gradation of reality can, of course, become more and more uncomfortable, abhorrent even, the further it takes us away from the reality we find familiar. But two separate worlds is no better, as the division merely shifts the uncertainty to the "other" world rather than resolving and illuminating it in this one. If the funny kind of existence is not exactly what we want, be it for ourselves or for our gods, then perhaps it is also not the kind of existence Plato's audience wanted, though Plato himself was evidently comfortable with it.

What we want is not very important, however, as we have to make do with what we get. That typically requires analyzing the kind of reality that is relevant in terms of the kind of reality that is familiar. Where the two differ, we try to find common features, and whether we find any or not, we try to express the difference as a similarity, at least in metaphorical terms. The unfamiliar thus becomes more familiar as it is placed in another "world," in a different "realm," and so on, thereby drawing on concepts we readily understand to create a context for those we do not. That is why we put up with a funny and fuzzy dialectic for souls and gods and such.

Just as we seek a familiar and reassuring interpretation of the kind of existence relevant to our souls and our gods, Plato seems to have tried to provide one for his audience, not just in regard to souls or gods, but in regard to everything that matters, most notably, the Forms. One especially rich stretch of dialogue that goes through everything that matters, including souls, gods, and Forms, is the *Phaedo*'s analogic argument for the immortality of the soul (78b–80b for the logical core, 80c–84b for the supporting imagery). There are many other places throughout the corpus where the discussion turns to souls, or to gods, or to Forms, and quite a few places where it concerns two out of three, but this is a rare occasion where all three of the fuzzy concepts intersect in a formal proof.

Given the prominence of Forms in Plato's thought, his philosophical output can reasonably be expected to come with a clear explanation of what the Forms are and how they work. But it does not. This is a common complaint that divides us as commentators as we go looking in various different places for the best account. Even when we all look in the same dialogue, we tend to focus on different parts or aspects of it. We need a better place to look, one that will not divide us, at least not as much as the alternatives. The analogic argument of the *Phaedo* is just such a place. The typical concern with the argument is, understandably, its success or failure as a proof of the immortality of the soul. I believe, in contrast, that it has more to offer as an account of the nature of Plato's Forms.

In all likelihood, the analogic argument was intended specifically as a dramatic vehicle to discuss the Forms, if only to say something about them by way of introduction and orientation. The possibility of a dramatic role is suggested by the absence, or weakness, of a logical one. The reason why it does not have an effective logical role is not just that it is a bad argument (which it is) but also that the main characters collaborate to expose it as a bad argument. The first thing Socrates says about the argument, immediately after he is done with the delivery, amounts to a confession that he himself does not think very highly of it (84c). This turns out to be just what his interlocutors were waiting for, with Simmias (85b–86d) and Cebes (86e–88b) taking turns picking apart the argument as soon as Socrates steps aside and clears the way. Hence, it is a bad argument acknowledged to be a bad argument. It is so bad that it serves as a segue into objections instigating the misology episode at the pedimental center of the dialogue (cf. 88c–89b for the actual misology, 89b–91c for the warning against it).

This is what makes me suspect a dramatic inspiration and expository motivation behind the analogic argument. I take it that I do not need to demonstrate that it is a bad argument, not just because it is an obviously bad argument, widely acknowledged to be so, both within the drama and outside it, but also because it is a bad argument for the immortality of the soul, whereas my interest in it lies in the insight it offers into what Plato may have thought about the Forms.[13] I take the argument to be something of an orientation session on the Forms. The session, such as it is, does not introduce anything like a proper theory, which is nowhere to be found anyway, but it does facilitate the interjection of a thing or

---

13. See Alican (2012) for an analysis of the analogic argument (418–424) and of the *Phaedo* in general (391–491).

two about the Forms without disrupting the natural flow of the dialogue. The audience of Socrates apparently does not need a formal lesson, as his interlocutors and auditors alike seem to be familiar with the Forms. The ensuing presentation, then, could have been intended for the audience of the dialogue itself.

Plato needs a creative way to reach his own audience, having abandoned the dramatic option to have Socrates do it for him through formal instruction. That is a need he fills through the semblance of an argument for the immortality of the soul. The parallel treatment between the Forms (78b–79c) and the gods (79e–80a) as analogues of the soul is an opportunity to make the Forms as familiar as possible to anyone who may otherwise be alienated. The soul, we are told, is similar not just to the Forms but also to the gods. Everyone, both then and now, has some idea what a god must be like. Regardless of whether our gods are revealed to us or created by us, no god goes unworshipped. And whether through revelation or through imagination, we all know what the gods are like: just like us, only better.

The parallel treatment in the logical core (78b–80b) of the argument is complemented by subsequent references to souls existing in Hades, to Forms implied (explicit elsewhere) to be accessible there, and to gods inclined to hang out with both (80d–81a, 82b–c, 83a–b). This may appear to lend credence to the postulation of a separate world for the Forms (where souls and gods dwell as well). But any talk of a different world as such is a metaphor for a different mode of existence in one and the same world. Recall the gradation of reality in the divided line, in Diotima's speech, and in the ascent of the philosopher's soul.

This is admittedly not the only conceivable explanation, nor even the only plausible one, for the motivation behind the analogic argument. Another is that Plato needs a dramatic foil for the misology episode, which means that he needs a minor win for the antagonists, which, in turn, requires a disposable argument for the protagonist, who thus serves up the analogic argument. Another is that Plato proceeds with several bad arguments leading up to one good argument (at least from his perspective), specifically that the analogic argument is one of three bad arguments setting up the fourth and final argument (96a–107a, or 105b–107a, depending on the focus), which does seem to enjoy greater support among the main characters. Another is that the *Phaedo* contains nothing but bad arguments, which would mean that the analogic argument is not special in that regard and, hence, not in need of explanation in the present context. But none of this means that an opportunity to say something about the Forms never crossed Plato's mind as he conjured up this argument. Each of the three scenarios considered as an alternative explanation is compatible with the partial elucidation of Forms as a possible motivation. All I am claiming, at any rate, is that this is a sensible interpretation.

Perhaps the greatest clue to the dialectical infirmity of the analogic argument is the pervasive theme of fear, namely the fear of death. This is the same fear we display today in connection with our own existence. The ancient manifestation of this existential angst permeates the dialogue with repeated references to the fear of death, invariably identified as common yet groundless. One such juncture is where Socrates affirms that the philosopher is not afraid of death (63e–64a). He goes on to elaborate on the reason, which, we soon find out, is that the philosopher's entire life is a preparation for death (63e–69a). A defining moment in the course of elaboration is where Socrates equates the resentment of death with the resentment of wisdom and declares the fear of death the height of folly (67d–68c). These references take death as the separation of the soul from the body, thus romanticizing it as the liberation of the true self, set free to work toward the purification of reason.[14] On the other hand, what the main interlocutors want to know, as many of us also do, is what happens to the soul after its separation from the body: Is its liberation also its termination?

Cebes becomes the first to voice this concern as he presents the fear of death, not as a fear of separation from the body, but as a fear of ceasing to exist altogether upon that separation, much like a dissipating puff of smoke (70a–b). Simmias repeats the same concern later (77b), indicating the failure of two prior arguments (the first two proofs) advanced in response to Cebes. There is meaningful emphasis on the fact that they are both talking about a common fear, hence not a personal feeling or outlook, nor a philosophical consideration, but a natural disposition in ordinary people. The opinion of the many is hardly ever to be trusted in Plato. Sure enough, Socrates identifies this common fear as a childish and irrational one (77d). But Cebes insists on proceeding as if they themselves were afraid, or as if the fear belonged to the child within each of them (77e). And this is what sets up the analogic argument.

---

14. Other references to the fear of death include: *Apology* 29a–b, 39e–41c; *Gorgias* 522d–e; *Phaedo* 58c–59a, 70a–b, 77a–78e, 84a–b, 85a, 88a–b, 91c–d, 95c–d; *Republic* 386a–b.

The argument is designed to show that the soul is decidedly different from things that are susceptible to destruction in the manner of the dispersal of a cloud of smoke, and that it is reassuringly similar to things that are not susceptible to that sort of destruction, dissolution, or disintegration. But the comparison does more toward communicating the nature of Forms, particularly in regard to their mode of existence, than it does toward establishing the immortality of the soul. The confirmation for this is not just the logic of the argument but also the nature of the conclusion. Even if successful, the argument would establish only the likelihood, and not the certitude, of the immortality of the soul, which has nothing to recommend it beyond that analogy. One thing's being like another in some respects does not entail its being like the other in any other respect.

Note that the conclusion would still not be satisfactory even if the argument were perfectly sound or exceptionally strong. It may be good news, for those who seek immortality, that the soul is like the Forms in their most impressive features. But what if the soul were like the Forms in every relevant way? What if the soul were like the Forms in every conceivable way? What if the soul were indeed a Form? Heaven forbid! The Forms are absolutely amazing, but nobody wants to be one. The Forms are not, after all, life forms. Even the Form of life is not a form of life. The Forms are simply not alive. That much, we know. The last thing we want the soul to be is a Form.

We want the soul to continue to exist, but we want it to do so as a living thing, in fact, as a rational being, preferably as the being it was prior to its separation from the body, minus the body. Much of this is stipulated as a formal requirement of the proof to be pursued: The soul must be shown to go on existing with certain powers or abilities, most of all, with an innate capacity for reasoning (70b). The soul must, therefore, possess intelligence. This is reiterated two proofs down the line, at the end of the recollection argument (72e–77a), where Socrates claims to have demonstrated not merely that the soul exists prior to birth but that it so exists with the prenatal power of thought (76c). The various twists and turns in the dialogue's dialectical development make it easy to lose sight of the negotiated emphasis on cognitive viability, which should nevertheless be regarded at least as implicit, especially where the focus turns to existence and its various modes.

The way of existence is the leitmotif not just of the analogic argument but also of the *Phaedo* in its entirety. The dialogue even opens with a reference to existence, or to presence, which is existence at a certain place at a specified time: "Were you there yourself, Phaedo?" (57a). The scope of the question is later expanded: "Who exactly was there, Phaedo?" (59b). The dialogue also closes with talk of existence, this time, that of Socrates (118a). He is no longer with us. Or is he? This is just the sort of thing we want to know. This is language we understand. In the beginning, we get the assurance that the narrator was personally present at the scene he will be narrating. In the end, we get the confirmation that the protagonist has left the scene, never to return. In between, we get the message that the Forms really exist.

And if we really get the message, we should get that what is most real about the protagonist is not what is left behind in the end. There is a part of Socrates that abides. But we do not know whether the part that abides remains the same without the part that is left behind. Perhaps all that remains is, much like a Form, real but lifeless.

Socrates never says that the soul is a Form. Could anything he does say be taken that way? That debate is still alive.[15] But it is possible to have too much of a good thing without being identical with it. And the analogic argument works in that direction. The portion of it where the soul is likened to the gods (79e–80a), independently of its affinity to the Forms (78b–79c), may provide some relief from the prospect of its being just like a Form. But even though analogic divinity may be appealing, especially for anyone concerned with life after death, we cannot be sure, since both analogies are there, whether we will end up more like a Form or more like a god.

Either way, though, the uncertainty is about the soul, not about the Forms. There is no question that the Forms get the royal treatment as they rival the gods as metaphysical benchmarks. Not only do they really exist but they do so at the highest level of reality. They really, really exist. Is this, then, how Plato exaggerates the existence, or reality, of the Forms? Arguably so. But the exaggeration, if there is any, is not as great as one might think.

---

15. See Bostock (1986b), Frede (1978), Gallop (1975, 213–215), Keyt (1963), Prince (2011), and Schiller (1967), among others, for the question whether the soul is a Form. See Barney, Brennan, and Brittain (2012) and Wagner (2001) for anthologies on Plato's conception of the soul. See chapter 7 (sections 7.4 and 7.6) of the present volume for further discussion.

4.4. Second Sailing

It is this aspect of Plato's world, namely its modes of existence, that Thesleff captures best. His Plato does not work with uniformly reified universals corresponding, as a homogeneous collection, to what we now call Forms (or Ideas), all residing in a separate world from the one we experience. He distinguishes between various different kinds of Forms and keeps them all in our own world. What we have heretofore recognized simply and without discrimination as Forms, says Thesleff, is instead a diverse assortment of ontological entities (or constructs) discovered (or invented) by Plato during his lifelong experimentation with abstraction.[16] The best fit he finds with the evidence of the corpus is a tripartite classification of Forms as such. Each representing a different thought experiment with abstraction or, more properly, a distinct episode of inspiration in a continuous process of experimentation, there are Ideal Forms, Conceptual Forms, and Relational Forms.

Ideal Forms are the reified analogues of value paradigms we commonly acknowledge in our experience in and of the world. The emphasis is on the nature rather than type of value: Whatever is intrinsically valuable has an Ideal Form corresponding to it. Whatever is not, does not. While the category is nearly exhausted by moral, aesthetic, and religious value, as exemplified, respectively, by the Forms of justice, beauty, and piety (among others), it also includes Forms such as knowledge and life, which are valuable in themselves albeit not in a moral, aesthetic, or religious sense.

Conceptual Forms account for the majority of Plato's other experiments with abstraction, primarily including types and properties (outside anything done with intrinsic value in that regard), but also covering events, actions, experiences, and various other phenomena to be evaluated individually (some of the latter possibly being redundant with types and properties). Examples are inexhaustible, ranging from the horseness denied by Antisthenes to the color of the horse he spotted while denying the horseness and the speed at which the horse was moving during the denial. The general idea, though this should not be taken out of context,

---

16. What counts as a discovery from Plato's perspective (and from that of anyone in agreement) could reasonably be considered an invention from a critical perspective. The Forms would be entities in the first case, constructs in the second.

is that "anything Plato was willing and able to conceptualize ended up as a Conceptual Form" (pp. 95, 253, this volume).[17]

Relational Forms are the metaphysical building blocks of Plato's world. They constitute a lateral projection of the two-level scheme through correlative universal relations manifested as pairs of contrasting concepts. What this means is that they are complementary metaphysical categories collectively responsible for the ontological and cosmological structure of our phenomenal experience. Examples include matching concepts familiar from the "greatest kinds" (*megista genē*) of the *Sophist* (254d–e): rest and motion, same and other. These are reciprocal relations, as Thesleff always pauses to emphasize, not polar opposites. While the contrast is asymmetrical, or hierarchical, with one element dominating the other (the dominant one listed first, for convenience), the internal hierarchy bears no real opposition, only joint coverage of reality.

This is a fair summary of the classification.[18] All three kinds of Forms occupy the upper level of reality, but Ideal Forms enjoy a higher ontological status than Conceptual Forms and Relational Forms. This is because features responsible for the shock value regularly invoked in the secondary literature—as in Welton (2002, 1), Penner (2006, 167), and Denyer (1983, 315)—are exhibited first and foremost by Ideal Forms, and only contingently by the other two kinds.[19] Nevertheless, Conceptual Forms and Relational Forms can approximate to Ideal Forms through a process of "ontological ascent" whereby they come to resemble them in

---

17. This does not mean that anything goes. The absence of external controls is not the absence of internal reasons. It is merely a reminder that reification is a reflection of value assignments by Plato and, hence, a matter of what Plato himself found valuable. The mechanics of Plato's reification tendencies are discussed as "conceptualization and formalization" in chapter 2 (section 2.7.1) and as a "continuum of abstraction" in chapter 3 (section 3.5).

18. The distinct categories begin to take shape as soon as Thesleff lays out his two-level model (1993b, 17–45; 1999 [= 2009, 383–506]), but they first appear in their present form in chapter 2 (sections 2.4, 2.6, 2.7, 2.8, 2.11) of the present volume. See chapter 3 (sections 3.2 and 3.4) for further exposition and exploration, including some critical reflection, though not with a revisionary agenda.

19. The provisional list of features in chapter 2 (section 2.6) comprises transcendence, intelligibility, paradigmaticity, perfection, immutability, simplicity, and uniqueness, with further references to eternality, incorporeality, and causal efficacy. These are elucidated in chapter 3 (sections 3.4 and 3.5) as signifying a distinctive "ontological [or metaphysical] eminence," some loosely unifying portion of which is broadly predicable of all Forms as a common denominator.

every way except in the possession of intrinsic value.[20] Although several qualifications concerning the relevant similarities and differences are missing from this overview, as are various other details of the classification, the skeletal core here is still sufficient, and certainly necessary, for a rudimentary understanding of what Thesleff does with the Forms in the two-level ontology he attributes to Plato.[21]

The key to understanding Thesleff, as he reminds us repeatedly, is his two-level model, not his tripartition of Forms.[22] Yet that model would be little more than shorthand for the traditional two-world interpretation if it were just another version of metaphysical dualism with indiscriminately reified universals at an upper level, wholly separated from any and all instantiations at the corresponding lower level and thereby completely ignoring everything in between. One of the most forceful ways in which Thesleff breaks that mold is his classification of Forms, not because that is obviously and indubitably how Plato does things, but because, without giving up any plausibility in terms of the evidence available, it affords greater explanatory power than the traditional alternative of a stark dualism with fungible Forms and matching particulars and not much of anything else.

The greatest contribution of Thesleff's two-level model is its natural propensity to account for the variety and variegation in Plato. While that alone makes for a richer ontology, it also identifies a fallible and flexible

---

20. Thesleff's allowance for ontological ascent can be traced back to his earlier work (1999, 69–73, 119 [= 2009, 452–455, 501]), but the concept is both named and refined later, specifically in chapter 2 (see section 2.7 for discussion and development, section 2.11 for recapitulation), with further elaboration and analysis in chapter 3 (sections 3.2, 3.4, 3.5).

21. A footnote will not make up for all the missing details, but had Thesleff seen this chapter prior to publication, he would have, no doubt, wanted me to state explicitly that imaginary things and negative values are categorically excluded from the classification. There are no Forms for fictional entities, none again for anything bad or evil (as discussed in chapter 2, especially sections 2.7.2, 2.8, 2.10). See chapter 6 for further elaboration on the possibility of negative Forms.

22. Thesleff is immovable on the primacy of the two-level vision in Plato: "The central position of the 'theory of Forms' in Plato's thought is easily exaggerated; indeed, Aristotle's criticism has made it appear as Plato's main doctrine. However, it constitutes only one aspect of his philosophic moves. The two levels as such, and the problems of their internal relations, always remained as foundations and frames in his thinking. The various themes and methods of the dialogues show plainly that many other aspects of his two-level vision kept in the foreground, indeed more prominently than any theory of Forms" (1999, 53 [= 2009, 437]).

Plato experimenting with abstraction. Thesleff's classification of Forms thus leaves room for at least the possibility of additional abstractions, or of other attempts at concept formation, which do not quite make it to the level of Forms, remaining instead at the level of concepts.[23] Hence, his recognition of indefinitely many subdivisions between the two main levels of reality is not a hollow formal allowance but a defensible practical assessment. The subdivisions themselves are real and operational. This is a fluid and fascinating world, liable even to hold a few surprises, not a regimented one polarized by Forms and particulars.

Also instrumental in breaking the mold of the thoroughgoing metaphysical dualism of the two-world model is the role Thesleff assigns to the Forms as "bridges" between the upper and lower levels of reality.[24] Themselves existing in the upper level of reality, the Forms fulfill this role through the familiar if controversial process of instantiation.[25] Their place in the upper level presents only a soft separation (*chōrismos*), balanced by a communion (*koinōnia*) of sorts, as reflected, for example, in the divided line (*Republic* 509d–511e) and the ladder of love (*Symposium* 209e–212a). Other bridges include "philosophy at large and dialectic in particular," with the "Philosopher" serving as a " 'daimonic' intermediate" between the two levels (Thesleff 1999, 33 [= 2009, 417]). Yet Thesleff nominates the Forms as the "most explicit, ambitious and famous" of Plato's "attempts to bridge the levels and explicate their internal relations" (1999, 33 [= 2009, 418]).

---

23. Plato, of course, is not equipped to make such a distinction between concepts and Forms. Or perhaps he is just not equipped to articulate it. Any attempt to do either would have to be from our own perspective. Some of the relevant possibilities and difficulties come up in chapter 1 (section 1.3), chapter 2 (sections 2.7 and 2.11), chapter 3 (sections 3.2, 3.4, 3.5), chapter 5 (sections 5.2 and 5.3), and chapter 6 (section 6.3). The main takeaway here is Thesleff's warning against saddling Plato with "anachronistic categories such as 'abstraction' or 'concept' " (1999, 54 [= 2009, 438]), a temptation he condemns as compromising modern insight into Plato's Forms.

24. The notion of ontological bridges dates back to Thesleff's original vision for the two-level interpretation (1999, 33 [= 2009, 417–418]).

25. Note that Thesleff does not make too much of the traditional debate over "transcendence" versus "immanence" (both habitually kept at a distance with scare quotes), preferring instead to balance the separation of Forms (1999, 62–63 [= 2009, 446]) with their inherence in particulars (1999, 30–31 [= 2009, 414–415]). He has been coaching me privately not to get more excited about instantiation, especially in regard to working out the mechanics and sorting out the details, than is absolutely necessary to follow Plato (see chapter 3, section 3.4).

In the final analysis, no matter what Thesleff says, there will be room for disagreement over both the existence and the essence of Forms, not to mention the meaning of existence itself, that is, the proper definition of the term and a satisfactory explication of the concept. Thesleff has not, to my knowledge, deciphered the meaning of existence in any sense, unless he has been keeping it to himself. But he has clarified the essence of Plato's Forms at least to my satisfaction.

Ultimately, maybe secretly, we all mean the same thing when we assert or deny the existence of something, even if we disagree when we take up existence as a philosophical problem of its own. What is most exciting about Thesleff's approach is that it expands our understanding of the existence of Forms, telling us how they exist if they exist. He is abundantly clear about what that includes, what it does not, and what difference it makes.

Do the Forms really exist? We are still allowed to disagree about that, but not so much about why they exist, how they exist, and where they exist. Perhaps most important, we now know what to make of a world, indeed only one, in which they do exist, especially since it is the same one in which we do. Plato may have discovered the Forms a long time ago, but he certainly did not stumble upon them in a galaxy far, far away.

Chapter 5

Ontological Symmetry in Plato

Formless Things and Empty Forms

This chapter is a study of the correspondence between Forms and particulars in Plato.[1] The aim is to determine whether they exhibit an ontological symmetry, in other words, whether there is always one where there is the other. This points to two questions, one on the existence of things that do not have correlative Forms, the other on the existence of Forms that do not have correlative things. Both questions have come up before in the scholarly literature on Plato, but the answers have not been sufficiently sensitive to the intricacies of the questions. Nor have they been adequately resourceful with what little evidence there is in the original sources. The intention here is to make up for that deficiency, not just with better answers, but also with better insight into the questions.

5.1. Introduction

This chapter explores the evidence for ontological symmetry in Plato's metaphysics. The symmetry in question is that between Forms and things:[2]

---

1. This chapter was originally published as a journal article (Alican 2017a): "Ontological Symmetry in Plato: Formless Things and Empty Forms," *Analysis and Metaphysics* 16: 7–51.

2. Given that Forms are also things, at least in the sense that a Form is something rather than nothing, the reference here, as elsewhere in the book, is to Forms and other things, specifically to Forms and the things of which they are Forms: Forms

never one without the other. Is such symmetry necessary? Is it possible? Is it justified? Is it there? Is there anything outside the reciprocal ontology of the Forms from which things draw their essence (or get their name) and the things of which they are Forms?[3]

Imagine the relationship between Forms and things in terms of the admittedly imperfect metaphor of a river. What can we say about the water alone? What about the channel through which the water flows? We can reasonably say that the water can exist without the channel, and the channel, without the water. We may find each useless or incomplete without the other, but we do find each without the other. What about Forms and things? Are they ever found alone, one without the other, or are they useless, perhaps meaningless, possibly even inconceivable, without one another?

Imperfect metaphors abound. Another is that of a pillow. Both the casing and the filling can exist without the other, but a pillowcase stuffed with any kind of filler becomes something more than the sum of those two things taken severally, more so than might reasonably be said of the wind in my hair, the keys in my pocket, or the milk in my refrigerator. Are Forms and particulars like that in any way? Do they make an ontological pillow, or flow, perhaps, like a metaphysical river? Or do they work more like the wind in my hair?

An even better example of a tightly integrated organic union might be that of a fertilized egg, where the dynamics of the combination may be more evident, with the sperm fertilizing the ovum as part of the reproductive process. Might that be analogous, then, to how Forms and particulars account for reality? Or are the constituents of Plato's world more like the hydrogen and the oxygen that would still be real and abundant even if they were never to combine to make water?

To put it in theoretical rather than practical terms, must we hold with Kant that "concepts without percepts are empty, percepts without concepts chaotic," and with A. E. Taylor that this is exactly what Plato

---

and particulars, Forms and sensible phenomena, Forms and their instantiations, and so on. See chapter 1 (sections 1.2 and 1.3) for the rationale behind the nomenclature.

3. Alican (2012, 103–104; cf. 87–110, 110–129) offers a provisional assessment of the symmetry between Forms and things. Chapter 7 (section 7.4) of the present volume provides additional considerations of relevance, particularly through a discussion of the range of Forms.

had anticipated with Forms and particulars (1926a, 188)?[4] Taylor's position is that we must indeed hold this with Kant, and that we must, therefore, reject both Formless things and empty Forms in Plato.[5] Is he right? Does Plato allow nothing without a Form, and no Form without a thing?

The questions have been with us for a while. But the answers have yet to inspire a consensus.[6] This is partly because the questions are not as clear as one might think and partly because the evidence is not as strong as one might hope. That combination can be a formidable obstacle, especially when the questions are not answered directly through targeted studies but addressed in passing in the course of dealing with other issues, usually concerning the nature of the relationship between Forms and particulars as opposed to the symmetry of the correspondence or correlation between

---

4. This is a loose translation of Kant's (1781/1787) famous maxim: "Gedanken ohne Inhalt sind leer, Anschauungen ohne Begriffe sind blind" (KrV A51/B75). The standard translation is: "Thoughts without content are empty, intuitions without concepts are blind" (see Kemp Smith; Pluhar; Guyer and Wood). Taylor comes closer to the liberal translation in the main text above but reverses it in proposing that "the theory [of Forms] does full justice to both parts of the Kantian *dictum* that 'percepts without concepts are *blind*, concepts without percepts are empty'" (Taylor 1926a, 188).

5. Taylor takes a firm stand on this in a footnote to the passage cited above: "there are no 'forms' except those which sense-experience suggests, or, to use the language which will meet us later in the dialogue [*Phaedo*], there are no 'forms' which are not 'participated in' by sensible particulars" (Taylor 1926a, 188, n. 1). This is an extension of his longstanding conviction that "Plato's fundamental problem is essentially identical with that of Kant in the *Critique of Pure Reason*" (Taylor 1908, 37).

6. On the question of Formless things, the literature reveals a broad spectrum of positions. Nehamas (1973, especially 463; 1975, 108–109), Patterson (1985a, 123–129), and Sedley (2013), to name a few, are open to things without Forms in Plato. Cherniss (1944, 240–260, especially 244), Ross (1951, 24, 79), and Vlastos (1969b, 301), in contrast, deny that Plato has any room for them. Broadie (2007, 232–253) and Fine (1993, 81–88, 97–102, 110–116), remaining sensitive to both sides, each offer an assessment of the conflict between evidence in Plato and testimony by Aristotle, particularly in regard to Forms for artifacts (the rejection of which would mean the acceptance of Formless things). As for the question of empty Forms, the prevailing perspectives tend to be more polarized, with little orientation toward anything between adoption and opposition. Proponents of empty Forms include Fine (1984, 74–85), Maula (1967, 12–50), and Vlastos (1969b, 301). Opponents of empty Forms include Crombie (1963, 153–246), Lovejoy (1936, 45–55), and Rohr (1978, 268–283 [= 1981, 19–56]), in addition to Taylor (1926a, 188, n. 1), already cited in the preceding notes as well as the main text.

them.[7] But even with clear questions and complete dedication, the nature and extent of the evidence remains a problem. The direct evidence, limited to the Platonic corpus, is inconclusive at best, arguably not even there at all. We get some help from Aristotle but not enough to make up for what is missing in Plato.

The purpose of this chapter is to determine the best we can do with the evidence that we have. The best we can do begins with the least we can do: clarifying the questions. There are two: one concerning Formless things, the other concerning empty Forms. A preview now of the answers formulated in due course may help appreciate the clarification process building up to them.

The answer to the first question (section 5.3) is that Formless things are a matter of what we mean by "Form," a matter, that is, of what counts as a Form. To elaborate, working out the possibility and reality of Formless things requires accounting for the fundamental differences between different types of Forms, the variegation in which precludes a single answer covering all the reified universals familiar from the canonical corpus. The examples in the dialogues come with differences in kind admitting of categorization, and, in fact, requiring it. As a result, the question of Formless things depends ultimately on whether we are prepared to count all such varieties as Forms. The corresponding answer builds on the premises and conclusions of previous chapters, where Forms are divided into three distinct categories, comprising Ideal Forms, Conceptual Forms, and Relational Forms, but no familiarity with the earlier material is required to follow the development here.[8]

---

7. The leading issues are the separation of Forms from particulars (Fine 1984; 1985; Morrison 1985a; 1985b; 1985c; Vlastos 1987) and the immanence of Forms in particulars (Dancy 1991, 9–23, 53–56; Fine 1986; Matthen 1984), questions that are also discussed in conjunction (Devereux 1994; Perl 1999; Rist 1964).

8. The continuity acknowledged here with previous chapters was originally a reference to previous publications, because the present chapter was first published as a journal article (Alican 2017a), conceived and developed from the outset as an independent study able to stand on its own. As for the earlier work in question, the principal source was a collaboration with Holger Thesleff (Alican and Thesleff 2013), reproduced here as chapter 2, followed by personal contributions (Alican 2014; 2015), reproduced as chapters 3 and 4. Nothing outside the present chapter is required for following the analysis here of Formless things and empty Forms. The point is not to classify Plato's

The answer to the second question (section 5.4) is that empty Forms are possible, with the possibility, either practical or conceptual, being determined by factors other than the nature of the Form in question. Instantiation could, for example, be interrupted by accident or prevented by necessity. To illustrate the relevant contingency, the Form of poetry, if there is such a Form, must have been empty before we started expressing ourselves in verse and would have to become empty again if we ever gave it up. To illustrate the role of necessity, the Form of resurrection, if there is such a Form, seems to be empty now and would have to remain empty if raising the dead continued to be unworkable. The reality of empty Forms, beyond the bare possibility, depends on whether Forms that would be empty, if they existed, actually do exist. This is different from the more basic question of the existence of Forms. This one is specifically about whether circumstances that point to a vacancy in a certain Form, whether by accident or by necessity, suggest at the same time, and therefore instead, that there is no such Form.

Serving the prior aim of clarification, a preliminary section on the evidence precedes the two sections on the questions. To avoid any misunderstanding, it bears reiterating that both the questions and the answers are concerned with what Plato thought about the matter or, given the dearth of evidence, with what he may have thought about the matter, not with what we might now be able to make of it, invoking what we take to be Forms, or any modern counterparts we may find more appealing.

5.2. The Evidence

One Form for each multitude of things with a common name, which is to say, for everything of the same kind (*Republic* 596a). That is the extent of the guidance we get from Plato on the correspondence between Forms and particulars. There is plenty more on the relationship, but that is it for the correlation. We are told, for example, of a separation between Forms and the things of which they are Forms, each residing in a different

---

Forms as I do, but to take stock of their essential differences as Plato does. We may not be able to agree on precisely how he does that, but we should be able to agree that he does it. That is all the common ground required.

region of the world (*Parmenides* 134d; *Phaedrus* 247c–d, 248b; *Republic* 509d, 517b).[9] We are told also of Forms inhering in things, of things participating in Forms (or partaking of them), and of the two being in a communion of sorts (*Phaedo* 100b–102b; cf. *Parmenides* 130a–135d).[10] We are told even of Forms being recollected upon sight of particular things (*Phaedo* 72e–77a).[11] As vague as some of these details may be, they add up to quite a bit of information on the relationship between Forms and particulars, but they have no bearing on the numerical correspondence.

Nothing about the nature and mechanics of the relationship tells us whether there is a Form for everything and a thing for every Form. Neither does the general rule, however loosely stated or intended, that there is a Form for each multitude of things with a common name (*Republic* 596a). This is because the statement is silent on whether there are things (a multitude of things with a common name) for each Form and hazy on whether the formula of one Form for each multitude is an ontological

---

9. The traditional interpretation assigns two separate worlds to this dualism, often drawing on the testimony of Aristotle (*Metaphysics* 987b1–13, 1028b19–21, 1078b12–17, 1078b30–32, 1086a30–b11). See chapter 1 of the present volume for a detailed discussion of the prevailing dualism. The full spectrum of relevant positions in the literature would be difficult to capture in a footnote, but a few references might help establish representative benchmarks: Allen, among others, illustrates the traditional perspective, giving a concise overview of it in one work (1970, 149–154) and referring explicitly to a "doctrine of two worlds" in another (1997, 115). Thesleff (1999 [= 2009, 383–506]) reduces this dualism to two "levels" in one world. I agree with Thesleff, with some differences in emphasis, as discussed in the preface and introduction, and illustrated in subsequent chapters. Nails (2013, 78–87) regards the division into two worlds as dogma and rejects it, though not necessarily endorsing either Thesleff or me in the process. Smith (2000; 2012; 2019) addresses the epistemology rather than ontology of the problem.

10. The relationship between Forms and particulars is discussed in detail in chapter 1 (especially section 1.4). Among other commentators, Rickless (2007) is particularly helpful, employing a rich set of axioms, auxiliaries, and theorems (10–52; summarized: xxii–xiv; flowchart: xv) in a reconstruction of the argument(s) of the *Parmenides* (112–250).

11. This phenomenon or process, *anamnēsis*, is sometimes interpreted as the activation of an inherent intellectual ability, or the recovery of an innate cognitive faculty—governing "inference" in Allen (1959, 167) and "abstraction" in Schumacher (2010) expanding on Helmig (2004)—as opposed to the recollection of individual Forms. The *Phaedo* (72e–77a) has hardly any room for an alternative interpretation of that sort, especially not for a competing (either/or) alternative, but the *Meno* (81a–86c) does seem open to it. The *Phaedrus* (249b–c, 250a–b) can go either way.

commitment (one rather than none) or a mathematical equation (exactly one and not any other number) or a conceptual affirmation (unity in plurality). The rule is confirmed in other words, in other places, and illustrated elsewhere with examples, but not in a way that expands, explains, or enriches the information we already have in the original statement.[12]

What does the rule say? Does it express a perfectly reciprocal correlation such that Forms are never without things, and things never without Forms? Or does it affirm only that Forms are never without things and not necessarily that things are never without Forms? Or does it do just the opposite, affirming that things are never without Forms, while remaining silent on whether Forms are never without things? Is it perhaps merely a limiting condition whereby at most one Form, in fact, exactly one Form, if any at all, corresponds to a multitude of things of the same kind, which does not rule out cases where no Forms correspond to a multitude of things of the same kind, and is altogether silent on cases where nothing corresponds to a given Form?

The text itself points to a limiting condition as the proper interpretation. This is because the general formula of one Form for everything of the same kind, as reflected in the availability of a common name (*Republic* 596a), is followed immediately by a discussion of why there can be at most one Form for bed (596b, 597c–d). Among those who favor the restrictive reading, Julia Annas (2003, 86) claims that a limitation is not merely intended or implied but expressly stated. She considers the more common rendition of an unrestricted range of Forms to be grounded in a mistranslation. Verity Harte (2019, 463–464) agrees that the passage need not be translated with an unrestricted range of Forms, but not strictly that it must not be so, presenting an alternative, actually reviving an old one, that has no bearing upon the range of Forms: "for we are, as you know, in the habit of assuming [as a rule of procedure] that the Idea which corresponds to a group of particulars, each to each,

---

12. A case in point is the reference to "our perpetual claim that there exists an intelligible Form for each thing" (*Timaeus* 51c). A couple of passages in the *Parmenides* (130d–e, 135a–c) and the *Republic* (507b) are just as relevant. Cherniss (1944, 244) adds several other examples. These are all partial expressions of what has traditionally been called, originally by Aristotle (*Metaphysics* 990b13, 1079a9), the One-over-Many Argument, which is not fully articulated by Plato himself, except arguably in the *Parmenides* (132a) and the *Republic* (475e–476a). They are, more accurately, instances of a One-over-Many Principle. Commentary is endless. Fine (1980; 1993, 103–119), Matthews and Cohen (1968), and Sedley (2013) are a few examples.

is always one, in which case [or, and in that case] we call the group of particulars by a common name" (Smith 1917, 70; original brackets). Ravi Sharma (2006, 27–32) rejects the alternative in Smith and recommends the earlier (and still current) translation suggested in James Adam's note to *Republic* 596a5: "for we are, as you know, in the habit of assuming a certain idea—always *one* idea—in connexion with each group of particulars to which we apply the same name: lit. 'an Idea, one each' i.e. each being one" (Adam 1902, ad loc.).

However that may be, the problem is not that we cannot be sure whether the restrictive reading is correct, but that we cannot use it either way to answer the question of Formless things or empty Forms. Even if there can never be more than one Form for everything of the same kind, there might still be some things without a Form and some Forms without an instantiation.

The apparent absence of a unifying answer in the Platonic corpus is often a motivation, both in general and in this particular case, to turn to Aristotle for any insight he might be able to offer in regard to Plato's actual answers. But the evidence is mixed there as well. Aristotle can be helpful on specific points of interest, some of which come up in the course of this chapter, but he cannot settle the debate for us.

Regarding the general rule under consideration (*Republic* 596a), Aristotle seems, on at least one possible reading, to interpret Plato's concern to be specifically with natural kinds, not with types in general: "And so Plato was not far wrong when he said that there are as many forms as there are kinds of natural things (if there are forms at all)" (*Metaphysics* 1070a18–19).[13] This would then seem to rule out, on Plato's behalf, Forms for artifacts, if for nothing else besides.

Yet Aristotle's praise can be taken either way. Another interpretation, as suggested by Richard Bluck (1947), is just the opposite: Aristotle's acknowledgment that Plato was not wrong in saying there are as many Forms as there are kinds of natural things could have been a foil for Aristotle's (presumable) conviction that "but of course he *was* wrong in

---

13. Patterson (1985a, 117–145) suspects a broader connection between Forms and nature (expanding thereby on what it means to be "in nature" and including therein what it means to serve a "natural end") than a strict restriction to natural kinds. On his interpretation, even the Form of bed (couch) can be said to be "in nature" (123–124; cf. 125–126), though Patterson reminds us that the example may represent Platonic play (126).

saying there are Forms of artificial products" (Bluck 1947, 75). This is the reading Bluck favors (see chapter 7, section 7.4, of the present volume for further discussion). Together with other clues, it shapes his conclusion: "Plato did not reject Forms of any *artefacta*, and I do not think Aristotle ever intended to suggest that he had" (Bluck 1947, 76). Gail Fine, in contrast, is inspired to go in the other direction with exactly the same evidence: "If Plato recognized forms in both cases [natural kinds and artifacts], Aristotle would not commend him as he does" (Fine 1993, 83).

Both commendations work, though the Plato in Fine's (1993) scenario is somewhat more commendable than the one in Bluck's (1947) scenario from the perspective of Aristotle in either scenario. It may not seem less fitting to commend Plato for recognizing one thing while condemning him for recognizing another (as Bluck has it) than to commend him for recognizing the first thing and rejecting the second (as Fine has it). But the distinction is more properly between commending Plato for recognizing a truth while condemning him for recognizing a falsehood (Bluck's scenario) versus commending him for recognizing that same truth and rejecting the corresponding falsehood (Fine's scenario). The achievement or distinction to be commended is greater in the latter case without making commendation altogether inappropriate in the former case.

This is just the periphery of interpretive difficulties in appealing to Aristotle on this matter. Even if we could confidently discard Bluck's reading in favor of Fine's, we would have to contend with opposition from other things Aristotle says as well as from some things Plato says. To return to the example on hand, finding a Platonic rejection of artifacts in Aristotle's commendation of Plato contradicts the way Plato's thoughts run to Forms for beds and tables (*Republic* 596b, 597c–d), if only in an exploratory dialectical effort, immediately after introducing the generalization of one Form for each kind of thing.

Curiously, Aristotle himself acknowledges the evidently familiar and controversial Platonic supposition of Forms for artifacts, as he invokes the manifestly artifactual example of the Form of table in the course of critical commentary on the "theory" of transcendent Forms (*Metaphysics* 988a1–5).[14] This, in turn, seems to undermine Aristotle's separate testi-

---

14. As is often possible, and frequently done, it might conceivably be objected, though not very reasonably in this case, that Aristotle is talking about Plato in one instance and about Platonists in the other. Such a combination can be especially problematic when the collective reference to Platonists is understood to exclude Plato himself. In

mony that Plato rejected Forms for artifacts, as related in two different passages (*Metaphysics* 991b3–8, 1080a3–10), both citing houses and rings as examples of things that Plato found to be without Forms (the actual reference indicating either the author of the *Phaedo* or the proponents of that work or possibly both).[15]

There are no easy answers, whether within Plato or outside Plato. No matter what we are supposed to do with Aristotle's testimony, Plato's general rule could have been intended, even on its own evidence, without a restriction beyond types, broadly construed.[16] It would thus rule out nothing more than arbitrary multitudes, those to which we would not be able to assign a "common name" as required by the original statement: for example, the random things in my desk drawer, or better yet, those outside my desk drawer (comparable to "barbarian" at *Statesman* 262e).

More important, this "general rule" is not the only relevant consideration here. Even if the generalized guidance provided through it could be trusted as a precise formula for sorting out the correspondence between Forms and things, and even if we were clear on what was actually being said in that regard, we would still have plenty of work ahead of us, though the "rule" as properly deciphered would certainly facilitate progress.

To summarize the logic of the problem, there are only two distinct questions here: (1) The question of Formless things: Is there anything without a Form? (Is there a Form for everything?) (2) The question of empty Forms (uninstantiated Ideas): Are there any empty Forms? (Is there a thing for every Form?)[17] We cannot look up the answers. There

---

this case, however, the reference to Plato is beyond doubt in the first passage, and hard to deny in the second, where Plato is mentioned by name just before and just after the relevant portion. Fine warns that the reference to Plato may not be certain even in the first passage, though she personally finds it reasonable to include him there (Fine 1993, 289–290, in reference to n. 11 on 83).

15. Fine (1993, 83–85; cf. 85–88) and Broadie (2007, 232–235) may be consulted for further discussion of these two examples (houses and rings). With some reservations, they both take the examples to support the interpretation of Aristotle as reporting Plato to have rejected Forms for artifacts.

16. Note that Aristotle at one point attributes an unrestricted range of Forms to Plato (*Metaphysics* 990b6–8) in contradiction of his own testimony in illustration of various restrictions on the same range (*Metaphysics* 988a1–5, 991b3–8, 1070a18–19, 1073a17–22, 1080a3–10), as partly documented and briefly discussed in the present section. See chapter 7 (section 7.4) for details and elaboration.

17. This is for the sake of parallel construction with the first parenthetical question. A more perspicuous way of asking the second parenthetical question may be: Must each

is nowhere to look. Plato does not tell us anything either way regarding either question. Had he done so, neither question would have come up in the first place. Whatever the answer, we have to reason it out instead of looking it up. Still, that does not render the dialogues useless. We must try to extrapolate from what Plato says of things that are clearly not Formless and of Forms that are obviously not empty.

A notorious exception to the absence of a direct answer in the canonical corpus is the apparent availability there of an answer to the first question, the question of Formless things. This is where Socrates the character declares with great confidence that there are no Forms for hair, for mud, or for dirt (*Parmenides* 130c–d). If we are meant to extrapolate from there, the only thing we have to go by, other than our own intuition, is the characterization of these things as trivial (130c–d), from which we may, if we are so inclined, conclude with Socrates the character, though not with the blessing of the other characters, that trivial things ("undignified" and "worthless" things) do not have Forms.

This is an unequivocal answer to the question whether there is anything without a Form. The answer is yes. There is at least hair and mud and dirt.[18] And the answer would be definitive save for the attendant dramatic conflict: First, the speaker himself, namely Socrates, confesses in the same breath as he rules out Forms for these things (hair, mud, dirt) that he is troubled by the inconsistency of attributing Forms to some things but not to others (*Parmenides* 130d). Second, the answer meets with disapproval from the character Parmenides, whose assessment of the matter is that the young Socrates is not yet a proper philosopher, and that, once he is, he will no longer consider such things (hair, mud, dirt) unworthy of attention (130e).

Given that the answer by the protagonist is undermined both by his own misgivings (paradoxically, perhaps ironically, coupled with his

---

Form correspond to something, that is, to some multitude of things with a common name, as per the rule of the *Republic* (596a)?

18. Other candidates include man and fire and water (*Parmenides* 130c), which may or may not have Forms, depending on whether and how the dramatic Socrates resolves his ambivalence in that regard. Man comes up again at *Philebus* 15a without any apparent ambivalence, and the hesitation regarding fire and water is evidently gone in the *Timaeus*, unmistakably so for fire at *Timaeus* 51b (cf. *Phaedo* 103c–d, 105a, 105c, 106a–c). Hair and mud and dirt, in contrast, are ruled out with certainty (*Parmenides* 130d), even if that certainty (ironically?) comes with doubt, as Socrates questions the consequent coherence of the general position on Forms.

certainty about the matter) and by protest from another major character, there really is no answer.[19] And this goes beyond the usual difficulty of attributing the views of Plato's characters to Plato himself.[20] In this case, the character whose views are in question is troubled by the inconsistency of his own views, and troubled or not, he is opposed by another character, one more advanced, both in years and in experience, if not also in wisdom. Hence, there is no solution in the work itself, regardless of whether the answer, such as it is, may reasonably be attributed to Plato.

This is not the only conceivable reading, nor even the only reasonable reading, of the conflict between the young Socrates and the elderly Parmenides. Richard Patterson (1985a, 126), for one, presents a respectable alternative. He contends that making room for hair and mud and dirt is consistent with a restricted population for Forms, because the Forms countenanced in the process represent natural kinds, already recognized as Forms, rather than arbitrary predicates constituting an aberration in the mutually accepted ontological platform. In other words, neither Socrates's misgivings nor Parmenides's intervention is about assenting to a Form for everything. The conflict is instead about acknowledging a Form for everything already qualified to have a Form (as natural kinds

---

19. In fact, evidence to the contrary, which is to say, evidence against hair and mud and dirt as serious exceptions, starts to accumulate quickly, as Parmenides, in the briefest of passages (*Parmenides* 135a–c, anticipated at 133c), thrice attributes a Form to each thing: "Only a very gifted man can come to know that for each thing there is some kind, a being itself by itself" (135a–b); "a form for each one" (135b); "for each thing there is a character that is always the same" (135b–c). Further discrepancies await elsewhere, even outside the *Parmenides*, where we encounter Forms for other things that seem trivial, especially in contrast to justice and beauty and goodness, though perhaps not in comparison with hair or mud or dirt: for example, bed and table (*Republic* 596b, 597c–d); shuttle, awl, and tools in general (*Cratylus* 389a–d). Yet none of these would count as "undignified" or "worthless," which seems to be required for rejection, but not for hesitation.

20. The difficulty has only recently become a "usual" one. It does not trouble Diogenes Laërtius (3.52), for example, as he identifies four mouthpieces for Plato: Socrates; Timaeus; the Athenian Stranger; the Eleatic Stranger. For critical perspectives, however, there is no better place to start than the collection of essays edited by Press (2000). Thesleff (1993a, 259–266; 1999, 6 [= 2009, 392]; 2000, 53–66) is a good example of interpretations taking the drama itself to speak for Plato as opposed to affirming or denying that the task is assigned to this or that particular character.

seem to be)²¹ but denied one only out of inexperience on the part of the young Socrates.

This is plausible. So is my interpretation. Both are consistent with the facts of the matter. The fact that making room for hair and mud and dirt among the Forms is consistent with a restricted population for Forms (as Patterson rightly points out) does not mean that it is inconsistent with a push toward a Form for everything (which Patterson does not deny). If this is a tie or standstill of some sort, note that Patterson's reading makes the drama do less work than one where the young Socrates is confused about truly philosophical problems. If there is no qualitative difference (for there will certainly be a quantitative difference) in the population of Forms with and without Forms for hair and mud and dirt, then the misgivings of Socrates and the intervention of Parmenides are both insignificant—or at least less significant than (dramatic backdrop for) a philosophical question regarding the range of Forms, or what is the same, (dramatic backdrop for) a philosophical concern over the possibility of Formless things. That is what Patterson's interpretation amounts to, leaving us with a Socrates hesitating, and a Parmenides wincing, for no better reason than the detection of prejudice against the dignity (value) of things like hair or mud or dirt. That is not a bad reason, but it is not as compelling as the recognition of the range of Forms as a philosophical problem. My reading allows the author of the *Parmenides* to be a better philosopher than does Patterson's alternative.

As for the second question, Plato does not even give us a conflict to work out. In the case of Formless things, we know at least that he is thinking about the matter. In the case of empty Forms, we know next to nothing. More accurately, there appears to be nothing in Plato, save for a muted allusion to a Form of the ideal state (*Republic* 592b). The significance of that reference, together with the strength of the evidence it constitutes, is discussed in section 5.4, initially around the middle of the section, but mostly toward the end. There seems to be nothing else. I could have missed something, but others would have caught it. Eric D. Perl (1999, 351), for example, is confident that there is nothing there: "Nowhere in the dialogues does Plato mention any uninstantiated forms, or even suggest that there could be such forms."

---

21. I am neither endorsing nor opposing Patterson's (1985a) understanding of natural kinds. I am merely reporting what he, in this one case, counts among natural kinds (hair, mud, dirt).

A possible exception to the absence of evidence, in fact, a somewhat popular one, is the tendency, as in Samuel Rickless (2007, 20, n. 12), to take evidence for or against the separation of Forms as evidence for or against empty Forms. This is not to say that Rickless confuses the two possibilities, or the evidence for them, but that he finds the evidence in one case relevant to efforts to judge the other. In contrast, I side with Allan Silverman (2002, 19), who divorces the two issues, including the evidence for them. This is consistent with Gail Fine (1984), whose interest in empty Forms is grounded in and limited by her interest in separation. The extent of the connection she makes between the two is that instantiation does not undermine separation, and conversely, that the absence of instantiation is sufficient but not necessary for separation (Fine 1984, 44, 74).

The reason why we have not been able to get very far with the conflicting evidence for Formless things is not just that the conflict precludes a definitive solution, but also that it attracts some of us to one perspective and some to the other, instead of inspiring us to unite around a consensus regarding the uncertainty, particularly around an agreement that the uncertainty of the matter is itself a conclusion, possibly the most reasonable conclusion under the circumstances.[22] We may, oddly enough, be able to do more with empty Forms, where there is hardly any evidence either way, as opposed to clear evidence both for and against. The greatest conflict we encounter in discussing empty Forms tends to be with one another, which is usually easier to negotiate than a conflict with Plato, the unavoidable result of a positive or negative answer to whether there is a Form for everything.

5.3. Formless Things

It is only natural that both the evidence for and the evidence against Formless things should command attention and find support. There is, to

---

22. The point here is not that we ought to judge the issue entirely on the merits of a short stretch of dialogue in the *Parmenides* (130a–e), but that the passage in question is rich enough, especially in combination with further considerations (135a–c), though also exactly as it stands on its own, both to confirm and to contradict whatever position one might take on the matter. It can also be read, therefore, either as corroborating or as undermining any other relevant piece of evidence throughout the corpus.

be sure, clear if sparse evidence on either side. But what does it mean, as suggested above, to embrace the uncertainty as opposed to adopting one position over the other? It means that the uncertainty need not paralyze us, instead showing us where to look for a solution. The problem is that the evidence is mutually inconsistent, thus supporting contradictory positions. But what if there were a way to remove the inconsistency in the evidence and, thereby, the contradiction between the positions?

It is possible to do just that under any interpretation of Plato that recognizes meaningful variation in Forms. The interpretation advocated and employed throughout the present volume works particularly well in that regard. The solution it provides is a division of Forms into three categories in the upper level of a gradation of reality in a single world: Ideal Forms; Conceptual Forms; Relational Forms. The basic idea is that the entities (or constructs) traditionally identified as Forms (or Ideas) in Plato are not, one and all, the same kind of thing, simply a Form, undifferentiated in any way and fungible in every way.[23] Instead of the interchangeable representatives of a homogeneous collection, there are Ideal Forms, such as the just itself and the beautiful itself (*Parmenides* 130b; *Phaedo* 57d); Conceptual Forms, such as shape (*Meno* 73e–76e; *Philebus* 12e) and strength (*Meno* 72d–e; *Phaedo* 65d); and Relational Forms, such as rest and motion, or same and other (paired contrasts exemplified by the "greatest kinds," or *megista genē*, at *Sophist* 254d–e).[24]

The examples may be telling enough on their own, but a simple analogy in familiar terms may help visualize their relevance: Ideal Forms represent value paradigms (moral, aesthetic, religious, etc.), Conceptual

---

23. The characterization of Forms as "entities," with a parenthetical reference to "constructs," or any such explanation with the opposite arrangement, reflects the role of perspective. The Forms are entities if Plato discovered them, constructs if he invented them. On Plato's view, they are, of course, entities. His view, however, may not, and need not, be the same as ours. A stand on this is best not taken in silence. I refrain from taking one at all, not only in this passage, but also in the rest of the book.

24. These are just a few examples. They can be multiplied indefinitely, as illustrated in chapter 2. Note in general that Plato does not give us an Ideal Form with every *eidos* or *idea*, whereas he typically gives us nothing but that with *auto kath' hauto*. This is substantiated through arguments and citations in chapter 2 (section 2.5), anticipated in Thesleff (1999, 53–61, 113 [= 2009, 437–445, 494]). On matters of terminology, Greek or English, see also Baldry (1934, 141–150), Else (1936, 17–55), and Taylor (1911, 178–267). For a more recent perspective, see Ademollo (2013, 41–85, especially 56–69).

Forms comprise types and properties, and Relational Forms constitute the building blocks of reality as complementary metaphysical categories operating through correlative universal relations manifested as contrasting abstractions. Strictly speaking, they are not these things, but the Forms of these things. In other words, they are not themselves these things, at least not nothing more than these things, though they represent these things as the Forms of these things. And as Forms, they are all more than concepts or universals as we understand them today.[25] They exist outside the mind (as well as within).

To illustrate the main difference between a Form and an abstraction, with respect to just one of these categories, an Ideal Form is not just a paradigm of value but also an ontologically independent noetic reality constituting the very value (itself-by-itself) only imperfectly instantiated in our experience. The same difference, or something comparable, holds for the other two categories of Forms as well. The comparison is merely to facilitate comprehension, not to indicate textual confirmation. The Form of justice (the just itself-by-itself), for example, is something more than the concept of justice, but this is not a distinction to be taken up with Plato, who was busy at the time with the more basic distinction between justice and things that are just.

The original model is available in chapter 2, but a few details here may help orient readers without consulting the original in full:[26] First, Ideal Forms

---

25. This is to say neither that we now have a common understanding of concepts and universals nor that concepts and universals are the same thing. The point is merely that Plato took abstraction more seriously than we do today. He was more excited about it, and that is perhaps why he seems to have found a greater reality in it than we tend to do. The difference between Forms and mere concepts (or mere abstractions) is not something Plato discusses, but it may still be possible to say something about it without being anachronistic (see chapter 4, section 4.4; chapter 6, section 6.3). Attempts to do so can be found in chapter 1 (section 1.3), chapter 2 (sections 2.7 and 2.11), and chapter 3 (sections 3.2, 3.4, 3.5).

26. The model was developed in collaboration with Holger Thesleff. The preface and the introduction to the present volume jointly trace the history of our association while at the same time summarizing our common convictions and setting out our differences in emphasis. See chapter 2 for the original thesis presenting Plato as a metaphysical monist working with various different types of Forms in a single world, chapter 3 for elaboration on both the monism of worlds and the classification of Forms, and chapter 4 for further thoughts on just the monism. The monism in question is, in fact,

(section 2.6) concern intrinsic value of any kind, without restriction to a specific category (moral, aesthetic, religious, etc.), thus including anything valuable in itself, whereby knowledge (*Parmenides* 134a–e; *Phaedo* 68a–b; *Phaedrus* 247d), for example, qualifies no less than justice or beauty or piety. Second, Conceptual Forms (section 2.7) cover types (including, but not limited to, natural kinds) and properties, but they also include other abstract phenomena, such as events, actions, and experiences. Third, Relational Forms (section 2.8) are not, despite any appearances to the contrary, Conceptual Forms that happen to be opposites. They are complementary metaphysical categories paired up as correlative universal relations collectively constituting a cosmic blueprint of reality. The contrast between the matching elements (rest and motion, same and other, etc.) represents an explanatory vision with an etiological foundation as opposed to a logical contradiction or polar opposition. There are no true opposites in this context, only complementary contrasts in reciprocal relations, albeit asymmetrical and hierarchical relations, with one element dominating the other.

The eidetic features recognized by the model include, but are not limited to, transcendence, intelligibility, paradigmaticity, perfection, immutability, simplicity, and uniqueness (see chapter 2, section 2.6; chapter 3, section 3.4; chapter 4, section 4.4). These are attributes of Ideal Forms (chapter 2, section 2.6), though the other two types of Forms can sometimes appear to mimic, exhibit, and eventually possess the same features (one or more or all of them) as they approximate to Ideal Forms through a process of "ontological ascent." This is a term introduced in chapter 2 (sections 2.7 and 2.11) in recognition of the fluid boundaries between the three different types of Forms in terms of qualities Plato associates categorically with Ideal Forms but acknowledges sporadically in the other two types as well (see chapter 3, sections 3.2, 3.4, 3.5; chapter 4, section 4.4).

The process, or phenomenon, of ontological ascent is thus one of approximation and association. The ascent in question is not so much about the Forms themselves as it is about Plato's conception of them. This is because the dynamics of formalization and reification (the emergence of Forms from the ranks of what are now considered concepts or univer-

---

a unitary pluralism, combining a monism of worlds with a pluralism of the relevant population (see the introduction to the book). The rationale for the classification of Forms, together with the main features of the individual categories, is laid out in chapter 2 (sections 2.4 and 2.11) and scrutinized further in chapter 3 (sections 3.2 and 3.4).

sals) are a matter of value assignments by Plato, making it inevitable that ontological ascent should also proceed in conformity with such assignments, which is why Conceptual Forms or Relational Forms (especially the dominant element in Relational Forms) tend to resemble Ideal Forms in proportion to Plato's interest in them (in the ones doing the resembling).

The significance of these value assignments, that is, the relationship between what Plato found interesting and what he identified as Forms, comes up again later, both in the main text and in the corresponding footnotes, but for a sustained discussion, which is not necessary to follow anything here, see chapter 2 (sections 2.7 and 2.11), chapter 3 (sections 3.2, 3.5, 3.6), and chapter 6 (especially section 6.3 but also sections 6.4 and 6.5). One example of ontological ascent in accordance with valuation patterns would be how equality, a Conceptual Form, seems to be on a par with beauty, an Ideal Form, in terms of features indicative of ontological eminence (see chapter 3, sections 3.4 and 3.5), whereas bedness (the Form of bed) or shuttlehood (the Form of shuttle), also Conceptual Forms, are dwarfed in comparison.

The classification of Forms into separate divisions is underpinned by a stratification of reality into ontological levels: two main levels with a profusion of fluid subdivisions not limited to a specific number.[27] The hierarchy of stratification ranges from the good at the highest level of reality to images, not just physical things, at the lowest level. Hence, it is not a strictly binary division between Forms and the things of which they are Forms.[28] The simile of the divided line (*Republic* 509d–511e) is a good model for the structure envisaged.[29] The two main levels of the layout contemplated here correspond roughly to the top two and bottom two segments of the divided line, but the subdivisions here, an indefinite

---

27. The corresponding ontology is in chapter 2 (sections 2.2 and 2.3), with critical elaboration in chapter 3 (section 3.3) and a broad reassessment in chapter 4. The progression is constructive rather than corrective. Any development is in the spirit of confirmation and explication as opposed to modification. The rudiments of the basic framework can be traced back to Thesleff (1993b, 17–45; 1999 [= 2009, 383–506]).

28. The key to understanding Plato's ontology as explicated in previous chapters is neither the distinction between Forms and particulars nor the division of Forms into three categories but the unitary pluralism (or two-level vision) of Plato. The Forms certainly have a place in that vision, but they are defined by it rather than defining it.

29. The analogy originates in Thesleff (1999, 453–455 [= 2009, 70–72]) and appears here in chapter 2 (sections 2.3 and 2.4) and chapter 3 (section 3.3).

many, allow greater flexibility than explicitly recognized in the original line. All three categories of Forms belong to the top level, though Ideal Forms rank higher than the other two divisions. The most important difference is that Ideal Forms possess intrinsic value whereas the other two do not (see chapter 2, especially sections 2.4, 2.6, 2.11).[30]

The proposed classification has the manifest advantage of simultaneously accommodating the rejection of trivial Forms by the young Socrates and the acceptance of the same by the elderly Parmenides. More accurately, it makes sense and use of three elements in mutual conflict: the young Socrates's rejection of Forms for trivial things; the same character's misgivings regarding the generalizability of that rejection; the elderly Parmenides's warning against rejecting them. The vision of Plato's world adopted here points to a way out of this conflict: Trivial things may have Conceptual Forms. Even if they lack Ideal Forms, they are not necessarily Formless.

This means that everything, or well near everything, could have a Form insofar as each of the three divisions may be counted as Forms. That possibility, however, raises a question, as these divisions are not different varieties of a single thing Plato introduces as a Form. They are instead different answers he comes up with in his thought experiments exploring (discovering or inventing) abstraction. An Ideal Form is quite different from a Conceptual Form, and both, in turn, are altogether different from Relational Forms. The question is whether they are similar enough that there being an Ideal Form for one kind of thing, a Conceptual Form for another kind, and a Relational Form for yet another, counts as there being "Forms" for those kinds of things, and so on to the conclusion that there is a Form for everything for which there is some "Form" or other.

This is a fair question. But it is neither as difficult nor as important as it may seem. The point is not that there is a Form for everything in a sense that predicates exactly the same thing of everything to which it attributes a Form, but that there is room for it all in Plato's lifelong

---

30. This is an essential difference (a difference belonging to the essence of the objects of comparison, essential as against accidental) persisting even through the process of ontological ascent, whereby the other two types of Forms may otherwise approximate to Ideal Forms. See chapter 2 (sections 2.7 and 2.11), chapter 3 (sections 3.2, 3.4, 3.5), and chapter 4 (section 4.4).

experimentation with abstraction, a process that gradually reveals three different divisions in the things traditionally regarded, without further differentiation, as Forms. The divisions are similar enough to be categories of some one thing (as opposed to being altogether different things) and different enough to be categories of that thing (as opposed to being uniform examples of it). If nothing else, they are both similar enough and different enough that they collectively exhaust what has long been understood as Forms without distinction, as in the distinction between, say, justice and beauty and goodness, on the one hand, and hair and mud and dirt, on the other.

This is how and why the interpretive model is able to accommodate both the young Socrates's misgivings and the elderly Parmenides's intervention and subsequent encouragement. The question of the balance of similarity and difference between the three divisions, or categories, of Forms reflects a more manageable problem than pretending that justice and mud, for example, are the same sort of thing, and then wondering why the young Socrates is fascinated by one and not by the other. The interpretation suggested not only removes the inconsistency but also explains why the young Socrates is bothered by it and why the elderly Parmenides considers it a lack of philosophical insight and development.

The possession of Forms is, as mentioned earlier, indicative of value assignments by Plato. The primary emphasis in the proposed classification of Forms is therefore on what is valuable, significant, important, or at least interesting, all from Plato's perspective. This contingency, grounded in subjective value, is the same contingency whether the result is a genuine Form or an ambiguous abstraction, perhaps halfway between a concept and a Conceptual Form.[31] The distinctions we are able to make, with the conceptual and linguistic apparatus available to us, between a concept and a Conceptual Form, cannot be confirmed by anything to be found in the dialogues, where concepts and Conceptual Forms from our perspective may remain undifferentiated from Plato's perspective.[32] But that does not

---

31. Hair and mud and dirt (*Parmenides* 130c–d), for example, may arguably represent a halfway category of that sort. Or they might be Conceptual Forms. The difference is not cut and dried.

32. See the discussion of "conceptualization and formalization" (reification) in chapter 2 (section 2.7.1) and of the "continuum of abstraction" in chapter 3 (section 3.5).

undermine the conclusion that there is room in Plato both for affirming and for denying that there is a Form for everything.

This conclusion is consistent with the dramatic nature of the underlying conflict. We need not take the uncertainty regarding Formless things as a midcareer crisis, an association often made in textbook characterizations of the *Parmenides*.[33] The developmentalist tradition ignores the explanatory power of the dramatic chronology connecting the dialogues in the Platonic corpus.[34] The latter perspective, the corpus as drama, has been gaining support as an alternative to seeking out the most likely production order of the dialogues.[35] The young Socrates of the *Parmenides*

---

33. Any guide or companion to Plato, or even to Greek philosophy in general, will note, usually without endorsement or objection, the significance of the *Parmenides* as a possible turning point in the development of Plato's thought, particularly in regard to the Forms. Examples at random include Benson (2006, 180–182, 184; cf. 184–198), Kraut (1992, 14), and Shields (2003, 90), the first three volumes I consulted in my personal library to test the pedagogical hypothesis. See Jackson (1882–1886), Rickless (2007), Sayre (1983), Schipper (1965), and Stewart (1909), among others, for further insight into the problem itself.

34. This does not prove developmentalism wrong. Nor is that the intention. I am merely pointing out an alignment between the present perspective and one possible alternative to developmentalism, mainly for the benefit of readers who may already have an interest in the methodological analogy of the Platonic corpus itself as a dramatic unit of sorts. This is neither a refutation of developmentalism nor a vindication of the alternative. The reason why I avoid formal opposition here, even though I do indeed have reservations regarding developmentalism, is that I feel obligated to acknowledge the complexity of the matter as an ongoing scholarly controversy, which I do not presume to be settling in passing.

35. No effort to reconstruct the dramatic order of the dialogues can do without *The People of Plato* by Nails (2002, see especially 307–330, 357–367). While her prosopography is not a roadmap to the dramatic unity of the Platonic corpus, if only because it remains silent on the plausibility and merits of such a perspective, it does provide all the data one may need to carry out a project of that sort. Note that Nails herself opposes developmentalism, at least the developmentalism of Vlastos, as discussed in a separate work (Nails 1993). A good example of what to do with dramatic details, on the other hand, especially in regard to whether such details can be stitched together to uncover the structure of the corpus at large as an organic whole, is Zuckert (2009, see 1–19 for an overview). A useful tabular presentation of the dramatic chronology of the dialogues is available in Press (2007, 72–73).

is the youngest Socrates in all the dialogues.³⁶ At the other extreme, the oldest Socrates in the corpus, in fact, the oldest Socrates possible, is in the *Phaedo*, going through his last day on earth. Even without agreement on what goes in between, and in what order, it should give us some pause to note that Plato could have avoided dating these two dialogues so far apart dramatically had he needed or wanted to. He could have easily used an ageless Socrates, as often done with characters in serialized fiction, whereby we would have had to rely on other dramatic clues, if any, to ascertain the relative dramatic dates of the two dialogues. An ageless Socrates may not have been possible to implement in the *Phaedo*, at least not without an entirely different plot, but replacing the young Socrates of the *Parmenides* with an ageless Socrates would have been sufficient to obscure the difference between the ages of the two protagonists. Given that Plato has done just the opposite, going out of his way to make the Socrates of the *Parmenides* remarkably young, there is something to be gained from considering the reason and even more from figuring it out.³⁷

We must keep in mind, of course, as Nicholas D. Smith has reminded me in private communication, that interpreting the Platonic corpus as a cohesive dramatic unit, in and of itself, attributes a rather elaborate scheme to Plato, whose radical initiative would then have been conspicuous enough to merit mention both by his contemporaries and by his successors. The fact that no such report or discussion has come down to us from antiquity presents a difficulty for the plausibility of dramatic holism as a planned or intrinsic feature of the canonical corpus. Even if a grand scheme of that sort is out of the question, however, it is still conceivable for Plato to have deliberately cast the youngest Socrates in the *Parmenides* for maximum contrast with the oldest Socrates in the *Phaedo*, intending thereby to draw attention to the lifetime of devotion and experience required to

---

36. Zuckert (2009, 11) makes a good case for locating the youngest dramatic Socrates in the *Laws* rather than in the *Parmenides*. But even if she is right in her relative dating of the dramatic settings of those two dialogues, the *Parmenides* places great emphasis on the youth of Socrates, whose counterpart in the *Laws* receives no such attention.

37. Consider an analogy from popular culture: Batman looked to be about thirty-five years old when I was five. I have grown older. He has not. He still looks thirty-five as he thrills new generations with new adventures. Had I ever encountered a teenage Batman, or an elderly Batman, I would have thought, even when I was five, that something out of the ordinary was going on.

appreciate and understand the Forms, a symbolic message consistent with the arduous training program laid out in the *Republic*.

An immediately relevant possibility is that of an intentional effort to emphasize the personal, intellectual, and philosophical growth of the character Socrates. The ambivalent young Socrates of the *Parmenides* could well have matured into the confident old Socrates of the *Phaedo*.[38] This is not to say that the *Phaedo* is free of doubt and uncertainty. Confidence is not certitude. Socrates exudes confidence even as he declares the arguments of the *Phaedo* fallible. Any doubt or hesitation in the *Phaedo* concerns the immortality of the soul, not the existence of the Forms. The uncertainty attached to the final argument, favored over the others, is purely technical. It is about the reliability of a conclusion based on a hypothesis (107a–b). What is unacceptable is not so much the immortality of the soul, or the existence of the Forms, as it is the inference of the former from the latter, where the latter remains an unquestioned assumption. The soul may well be immortal, and the Forms may well exist, but we cannot be sure that the former is established by the latter, until we conduct a separate inquiry into the latter.

It is in this spirit that the Socrates of the *Phaedo* introduces the existence of the Forms as a grounding hypothesis (100a–b) for the final argument for personal immortality. The success of that argument depends ultimately on whether the Forms actually exist. Socrates fully admits and clearly articulates this in the end (107b), having already stipulated at the outset that the hypothesis and the inference are not to be evaluated together in one fell swoop (101d–e). His admission that the final argument must be studied further, so as to test the hypothesis itself, does not represent a lack of conviction. If anything, it shows confidence in the hypothesis. He does not merely admit that the investigation could or should be continued. He insists that it must be continued, encouraging his interlocutors to make the effort (107b).

Indeed, the last Socrates we know is neither ambivalent nor hesitant nor confused. The best explanation for the transformation of conflict and uncertainty into sagely serenity is growing satisfaction with the subject

---

38. This scenario has no implications for the production order, as the dramatic alignment between the two dialogues can be achieved regardless of which one was composed before or after the other. As it happens, though, evidence suggests that the *Phaedo* was composed before the *Parmenides*.

matter, in this case, the Forms. This represents Plato's own satisfaction with what is done with the Forms throughout the corpus as a whole. The invitation of Socrates to study the matter further is the invitation of Plato to do the same. The result of that study need not be precisely like the interpretive model adopted here. However, if it makes sense to speak of a result at all, especially one that stands in contrast to a correlative beginning, that alone favors a comprehensive explanation in the spirit if not the letter of the one provided here.[39]

5.4. Empty Forms

The question of empty Forms is no closer to a consensus of scholarly opinion than is the question of Formless things. The main obstacle in this case is not the inconsistency of the evidence but the unavailability of it. Yet the scarcity of evidence is not the only thing standing in the way of an informed answer. A prior obstacle is the absence of a standard interpretation of the question. We do not agree on what the question is, so we keep coming up with different answers. We might still end up with different answers even if we agreed on what was being asked, but we would then be in genuine disagreement, which is the proper starting point of dialectic.

The question of empty Forms is rarely discussed apart from those of transcendence and immanence. These, in turn, can be addressed either separately or jointly, but they are usually taken up together, even in studies devoted primarily to one or the other (as in Fine 1984 and 1986). Aristotle often turns up in such discussions, and rightfully so, as he seems to have initiated them.[40] Specifically, transcendence tends to be discussed in terms

---

39. I am neither affirming nor denying the possibility of progressive development in Plato's lifelong experimentation with abstraction. Nor am I confirming or rejecting a correspondence between the classification scheme here and any developmental or stylometric periods (early, middle, late) in the production process of the Platonic corpus. My divisions are not inferences from any particular order of composition for the dialogues even if they happen to coincide with such groupings.

40. Various misgivings regarding the Forms, as laid out in the *Parmenides*, would seem to constitute an exception to initiation by Aristotle, as they indicate origination with Plato himself. Yet we cannot be certain that Aristotle did not inspire or initiate

of what Aristotle reports Plato to have said about separation (*Metaphysics* 1078b30–32, 1086a30–b11), while immanence is typically examined through Aristotle's understanding of the place Plato assigned to the relationship between Forms and particulars among the variety of ways one thing can be said to be in another (*Physics* 210a14–24; cf. *Metaphysics* 991a9–19, 1079b12–23), with additional relevance to the ways one thing can be construed as part of another (*Metaphysics* 1035b32–1036a13).[41] Hence, any metaphysical tension between transcendence and immanence also shows up in the contrast between the separation of Forms from particulars and the presence of Forms in particulars.[42]

The scarcity of evidence (in the Platonic corpus) on empty Forms does not translate into a further scarcity of evidence (in the Platonic corpus) on transcendence or immanence. There is an abundance of relevant dialectical progression in the *Phaedo* alone and certainly a plethora of evidence throughout the so-called middle dialogues. Yet none of it is sufficiently enlightening. We are all familiar with the equality beyond the sticks (*Phaedo* 74c1), the largeness in Simmias (*Phaedo* 102b5–6), and any number of other examples that illustrate transcendence and immanence without quite telling us how either one works.

The corresponding passages, I trust, recall various others without further citations. The Forms, specifically Ideal Forms, despite their transcendence, make themselves available at the edge of the cosmos where

---

these as well. What is meant in the passage above, at any rate, is that Aristotle seems to have initiated the secondary literature.

41. Going through Aristotle to reach Plato, even where necessary, can be messy, if only because it is not always clear whether Aristotle is talking about Plato in particular or about Platonists in general. The two passages invoked regularly in connection with separation constitute a prime example (*Metaphysics* 1078b30–32, 1086a30–b11), as they refer to the successors of Socrates, which may or may not be a reference to Plato. Sometimes, such passages become clearer in conjunction with those that refer to Plato by name (e.g., *Metaphysics* 987b1–13). When they do not, we are left with nothing more than what is in Plato. Nails (2013, 81–84) rightly emphasizes the importance of sorting out not just whether Aristotle is talking about Plato or Platonists but also whether he is talking about Socrates the philosopher or Socrates the Platonic character (see 2013, 83, including the footnotes).

42. Such metaphysical tension is clear in Aristotle and perhaps originates there. Fine attributes this to Aristotle's assumption that "universals cannot exist uninstantiated" (1984, 39, 45; 1986, 94–95).

gods and souls (the disincarnate souls of philosophers) travel for a glimpse of their eidetic glory (*Phaedrus* 246e–249d). And immanence is what we are able to make of the same Forms and yet others in our attempt to apprehend them while we are still trapped in a physical body.

The general presumption against the compatibility of separation and immanence, though by no means universal, is a reflection of how these concepts are understood. The variety of interpretations make the presumption, where it exists, far from uniform. Some combinations seem to support the presumption, while others appear to undermine it. It will be helpful to consider the possibilities. Suppose that separation comes in degrees, and immanence in modes. As a rough illustration of possible combinations, suppose further that degrees of separation are mapped onto modes of immanence. What would the result look like?

Degrees of separation might range from numerical distinctness, under the weakest interpretation, to transcendence, under the strongest, with ontological independence as a possibility somewhere in between.[43] The two extremes probably mean just about the same thing to everyone, but ontological independence is best spelled out.[44] I take one thing to be ontologically independent from another if neither the existence nor the essence of the first thing depends on either the existence or the essence of the second thing. I therefore take anything to be ontologically independent in an absolute sense insofar as neither its existence nor its essence depends on either the existence or the essence of anything else. This is to define ontological independence in both existential and essential terms.[45]

---

43. As I am not trying to reconstruct Aristotle's position (on Plato's position), I do not feel compelled to explicate the results in terms of priority (ontological or explanatory). Among those who do that well, see Cleary (1988), Corkum (2008), Fine (1984; 1985), and Morrison (1985a; 1985b; 1985c). Here, ontological independence should suffice to capture the range between numerical distinctness and full transcendence.

44. Note that to place ontological independence in the middle is not to deny ontological independence in transcendence. What is intended for the middle here, by way of reviewing the possibilities, is ontological independence without transcendence.

45. This is just to fix the reference of the term, not to introduce a special definition to manipulate subsequent positions or arguments. A plausible sense of separation, at least a provisional one, can readily be captured through the notion of ontological independence, particularly through a combination of its existential and essential

The existential dimension can, whether instead or in addition, be elucidated in explicitly modal terms, though this is not strictly necessary, as the modality is implicit in what has already been said:[46] One thing is existentially independent from another if that thing can exist even if the other one does not, and if it need not and does not exist just because the other one does, which then means that anything is existentially independent in an absolute sense if it can exist even if nothing else does, and if it need not and does not exist just because something else does.

The essential dimension is clear enough as it is: One thing is essentially independent from another if that thing is what it is, and the way it is, regardless of what the other thing is, or the way the other thing is, and if it need not and does not change in any way just because the other thing changes in some way. Anything is essentially independent in an absolute sense, therefore, if it is what it is, and the way it is, regardless of what anything else is, or the way anything else is, and if it need not and does not change in any way just because something else changes in some way.

As for modes of immanence, the relevant range might extend from a shared property, at the weakest end, to numerical identity, at the strongest, with instantiation falling somewhere in between. The distribution of actual viewpoints, both for separation and for immanence, may well have a different range or median or both. This breakdown should nevertheless suffice for the discussion in progress.

The difference in strength between instantiation and a shared property (one such property) is not clear. While it may be clear that they are not the same thing, it is not so clear why one should count as a weaker relationship than the other. My intuition is that sharing one property represents a stronger connection than sharing none at all, while falling short of proper instantiation, the latter of which, in turn, suggests a connection strong enough to tell that one thing is a manifestation of the other. I would be happy to defer to metaphysicians on this matter, and would, in fact, prefer to do so. All I am trying to do here is to visualize the ways in which separation may be combined with immanence

---

formulations. But I remain open to alternatives and suggestions regarding how best to interpret either one.

46. Fine also defines ontological independence in modal terms (1984, 33, 35, 43; 1993, 51, 268–269, n. 28). Corkum warns against doing so (2008, 76, n. 8). Fine's version differs from mine. Corkum would oppose us both.

and to determine whether any of them would leave room for empty Forms.

Even those who oppose mixing separation with immanence will find some combinations more appealing than others. One option is to combine a strong interpretation of separation with a weak interpretation of immanence. Another is to do the opposite, combining a strong interpretation of immanence with a weak interpretation of separation. The optimal solution, if the path of least resistance qualifies for that designation, may indeed be to pair the strongest sense of one with the weakest sense of the other. Depending on where the resistance originates, however, a viable alternative may be to take a moderate interpretation of each concept.

The resistance invoked here concerns the perceptions of observers, not the mechanics of the model under discussion. I am not trying to coin a technical term ("path of least resistance"). I am merely trying to anticipate how (and how not) observers may be inclined to reconcile separation and immanence, which may naturally seem less than maximally compatible both in the strongest form of each and in the weakest form of each, hence pointing to a path of least resistance in the combination of the strongest form of one with the weakest form of the other, or perhaps suggesting something between the two extremes in either category.

My own view falls outside the range of optimal solutions. On the matter of degrees of separation, I come down on the side of transcendence.[47] On the matter of modes of immanence, I am satisfied with the admittedly vague notion of instantiation. A position outside the optimal range is not automatically wrong. The point of going through combina-

---

47. I am not alone in this. McCabe (1994, 101, n. 6) and Silverman (2002, 13) also state that they take separation as transcendence in this context. Prior makes the same commitment without using the word "transcendence": "As I use the term, separation presupposes not only the numerical distinctness of the Form from its participants, its ontological independence and priority, but also the claim that the Form is not to be found in the phenomenal world" (1985, 49, n. 33). Perl uses both terms (or derivatives thereof), without personalizing his commitment like the others, while still making his position clear: "As incorporeal, changeless, intelligible realities, the forms remain as transcendent to the world of physical, mutable, sensible things as the strongest proponent of separation could maintain" (1999, 361). Ademollo proposes outright to leave separation to Aristotle, focusing instead on transcendence (2013, 74–75). The fact that I am not alone, however, does not mean that I am unopposed, nor even that I am in the majority.

tions of views on separation and immanence is not necessarily to adopt or recommend the path of least resistance but to show where that path is, thereby facilitating the reader's assessment of where the present position is in relation to that.

I take the Forms to be transcendent.[48] And I take them to be instantiable.[49] One does not preclude the other.[50] The Forms are transcendent by necessity, that is, as an essential feature of what they are, but they are immanent by accident. While their transcendence is a part of their nature, their immanence is a reflection of rational insight into their existence and essence. This makes them inherently transcendent and accidentally immanent. The question is whether there is room for empty Forms in this combination of transcendence and immanence.

As already mentioned, there is no particular conflict of evidence in the case of empty Forms as there is with Formless things. Here, the evidence, at least the direct kind, is deficient rather than contradictory. At the same time, we must recognize that the problem of empty Forms is not entirely a matter of neglect or reticence on the part of Plato. It is not as if the only thing missing were an express commitment by Plato

---

48. More to the point, I take Plato to take the Forms to be transcendent, thus making them objectively real yet beyond sense perception, which gives them an independent existence outside our phenomenal experience. But "transcendence" can and often does take on different meanings even when the context is restricted to Plato. See, for example, the overview in Ademollo (2013, 74-83). Here, I am thinking specifically of the first sense (A) Ademollo considers, though I would be on board with a combination of his A (75) and his B2 (83), provided that nothing there is understood as a commitment to a separate world for the Forms.

49. A Form's immanence means nothing to me beyond its instantiation. Elsewhere, I deny immanence but still embrace instantiation (see chapter 3, section 3.4). The two positions are consistent (see chapter 7, section 7.6). Instantiation is not, in either case, anything more than a phenomenal reminder of the transcendent Form. The immanence denied, on the other hand, is the worldly presence of the Form itself. I am always open to immanence as instantiation in a representational sense that does not compromise transcendence. This, however, is not directly relevant to the question of empty Forms, which is not about whether a Form is actually in the thing as opposed to being merely reflected in the thing, but about what to make of either possibility in contrast to a Form's having absolutely nothing to do with anything in our phenomenal experience.

50. Among those who explicitly recognize the compatibility of transcendence and immanence, see Allen (1970, 147), Fine (1986, 94-95) with some qualification, and Perl (1999, especially 339, n. 1, 361-362).

regarding the correct answer to a perfectly clear question. The problem itself is unwieldy, difficult even to articulate, let alone to resolve.

What is an empty Form? Is it a Form that does not, at the moment, happen to correspond to anything in particular, or is it a Form that does not, has not, and will not ever correspond to anything in particular? To illustrate, is there a Form of mastodon, and is it an empty Form? And if there is no Form of mastodon, is this because there are no mastodons anymore? The difference here is temporal. But perhaps the question should be expressed in modal instead of temporal terms. Is an empty Form one that does not correspond to anything, or is it one that cannot correspond to anything? Are empty Forms a temporal phenomenon or a modal phenomenon? Is instantiation a physical relationship (because it is a temporal one) or is it a metaphysical relationship? Or is it perhaps a logical relationship (or even a psychological one)?

We need to distinguish at least between "past emptiness" and "present emptiness"—and perhaps also between either or both of those and "future emptiness." All three can be relevant:

- Past emptiness (backward vacancy): Was there a Form of mastodon before there were mastodons? Was the Form of mastodon empty before it came to be instantiated, namely at a time before there were mastodons?

- Present emptiness (forward vacancy): Is there a Form of mastodon at present? If there is, is it empty because of the extinction, or is it still in some sense instantiated by the fossil evidence confirming both existence and extinction?

- Future emptiness (forward vacancy): Switching from actual to possible extinction: Will there be a Form of elephant when there are no longer any elephants in existence?

This is just to lay out some of the options. These considerations do not exhaust the possibilities. Consider, for example, the question whether recreating a mastodon from naturally preserved genetic material would count as "refilling" (or "repopulating") an empty Form. The extended sequence would start with an empty Form before there were any mastodons, followed by an instantiated Form when the mastodons came into existence and roamed the earth for a limited time, followed by an empty Form upon and during their extinction, followed by an instantiated Form reactivated through genetic engineering, followed by an empty Form if and when they became extinct again, with the cycle highly likely to be broken for good at any point, though not inconceivable to be repeated indefinitely.

What we should be looking for is probably not past, present, or future emptiness but timeless or unqualified emptiness. Likewise, what seems most relevant is not a backward or forward vacancy but a permanent vacancy. David Armstrong (1989, 75–76), for one, understands instantiation without temporal restrictions.[51] He considers a universal to be instantiated if it is instantiated at any time in the past, present, or future. It need not be instantiated forever. It need not even be instantiated "right now." An uninstantiated universal, on this interpretation, is one that is never instantiated. Armstrong rejects uninstantiated universals, defined as such, which thus amounts to denying permanently empty Forms, but not temporarily empty Forms, the latter of which are not considered empty per se. Yet he does, albeit with some hesitation, attribute permanently empty Forms to Plato: "It appears to have been the view held by Plato" (Armstrong 1989, 76). I agree that instantiation need not be either current or permanent to count as instantiation, but I do not see Plato's Forms failing to fulfill such a liberal conception of instantiation.

Neither does Armstrong. He does not claim that justice and beauty, for example, or any of the other Forms we regularly encounter in the Platonic corpus, are permanently empty, or even that they ever are. He merely suggests, without citing examples from the texts, and relying instead on hypothetical cases, that Plato seems to be open to Forms that are permanently empty. One such instance is his discussion of "travelling faster than light" as a candidate for an empty Form, or for an "uninstantiated property," as he has it (Armstrong 1978, 64–65). Our best evidence and our current theories tell us that traveling faster than light is not something to be realized in practice. But does that mean that the corresponding Form is empty ("uninstantiated"), or does it mean that there is no such Form ("property")? Armstrong himself rejects the property, but he takes Plato to accept the Form, not, of course, this specific one (traveling faster than light) but those representing uninstantiated properties (or universals) in general (1989, 75–82).

The problem with burdening Plato with the Form of traveling faster than light is not just that the very possibility contradicts prevailing sci-

---

51. Rohr (1978, 268–269 [= 1981, 20–21]) also favors an unrestricted temporal frame of reference.

entific theories, nor merely that Einstein's theory of special relativity is an anachronism with respect to Plato, but also, and more importantly, that the reference to traveling faster than light invokes too many separate concepts to count as a single Form. It seems to comprise motion, velocity, radiation, and a traveler, hence, at least four things rather than one as usual. It is not pure and simple enough to qualify as a Platonic Form. The simplicity requirement for Forms receives ample attention below, where it is defined in terms of a unitary integrity devoid of impurities.

Armstrong's example nevertheless serves as a reminder that we may need to distinguish not just between Forms that are temporarily empty and Forms that are permanently empty but also between Forms that are not instantiated and Forms that cannot possibly or conceivably be instantiated (and perhaps even between Forms that cannot possibly be instantiated and Forms that cannot conceivably be instantiated). We already have some idea, from questions concerning mastodons and such, what a Form that does not (but possibly could) correspond to anything might be like. What, then, might a Form that cannot possibly correspond to anything be like? Is the Form of unicorn perchance such a Form?[52] Or to break up the loaded question: Is there a Form of unicorn, and if there is, is it an empty Form?

A question of this sort inevitably comes to mind, but it may not be the right question to ask. Plato does not countenance Forms for fictional things. Notwithstanding the difficulty of proving negative claims, it may help to think of this not as an explicit rejection that can be confirmed anywhere in particular, but as an implicit aversion and avoidance that is evident through and through, for example, in the divided line of the *Republic* (509d–511e). Fictional entities are denied not just their own Forms but any representation whatsoever in the divided line. Even the lowest level, *eikasia*, is reserved for images of visible things, hence for shadows and reflections, not for wholly imaginary things, which is what fictional entities are. Plato would not be inclined to assign Forms to things he does

---

52. The example is for our benefit alone. Unicorns in Plato's day may have been considered closer to fact than to fiction. Aristotle reports actual beasts that are comparable, at least in terms of the solitary central horn, to the unicorns we now speak of as mythological creatures (*Historia Animalium* 499b18–19; *De Partibus Animalium* 663a20–34). A more suitable example of mythical animals for Plato (and obviously also for Aristotle) would be centaurs (*Phaedrus* 229d; *Statesman* 291b, 303c) and satyrs (*Laws* 815c; *Statesman* 291b, 303c; *Symposium* 215b, 216c, 221d, 221e, 222d).

not consider to exist or, more accurately, to those he regards as existing only by convention and not by nature.

Hence, the relevant question about unicorns is not whether their Form is empty but whether there is such a Form in the first place. And the answer to that is negative. Had Plato allowed Forms for fictional entities, the question about unicorns would have been closer to that of mastodons, the main difference being their animation in principle, irrespective of their instantiation at present, since neither one currently exists. Moreover, it is not clear whether the case of unicorns constitutes an example of a Form that cannot possibly correspond to anything in our experience as opposed to that of a Form that simply does not happen to correspond to anything of that sort. One reason for hesitation might be that an actual animal answering to the present conception of a unicorn could someday either come into existence through evolutionary processes or be brought into existence through genetic engineering.

What about things that are not fictional but are still not instantiated? Consider, for example, the case of the chiliagon, or that of the ideal state (city), both brought up by Gregory Vlastos (1969b, 301), the latter also (and earlier) by Erkka Maula (1967, 35). Plato would presumably classify them both as empty Forms.[53] Each would be empty because nothing in our experience corresponds to either Form, provided that there are such Forms to begin with.[54] But just because we cannot in practice tell the difference between a chiliagon and, say, a myriagon, as suggested by Descartes in his Sixth Meditation, does not mean that nothing of that sort could exist.[55]

---

53. Vlastos construes Plato as rejecting Formless things and accepting empty Forms: "For Plato nothing could exist in space and time with a definite character, F, if there did not exist a corresponding F, while the converse would not be true at all. The existence of a specific Form, say, of a *chiliagon*, would of itself not offer the slightest assurance of its physical instantiation; not only the Form of the Ideal City (*Rep.* 592AB), but infinitely many other Forms as well exist which have been uninstantiated since time began and may so remain forever in Plato's universe" (Vlastos 1969b, 301).

54. Both examples come up again toward the end of this section and in the conclusion, where the case of the ideal state is taken up in greater detail, particularly in relation to the requisite simplicity, or unitary integrity, of Forms.

55. Descartes (1641) considers the nature of both figures, as well as the difference between them, to be open to intellection but not to imagination. He rules out neither the existence of the figures nor our comprehension of them. We understand what a myriagon is, no less than we understand what a chiliagon is, but we cannot visualize either one.

Nor does the utopian nature of the ideal state preclude all possibility of instantiation. The chiliagon and the ideal state, if they are proper Forms, seem to be examples of Forms that are not instantiated but not necessarily of Forms that cannot be instantiated. They do not expand the relevant possibilities beyond the examples of the mastodon and the unicorn.

In the case of the ideal state, we know for a fact that we are dealing with something merely difficult, not impossible, to realize: "Then we can now conclude that this legislation is best, if only it is possible, and that, while it is hard for it to come about, it is not impossible" (*Republic* 502c). This is because the ideal state is the just state, not the perfect state, unless justice is sufficient for perfection. Any justice to be achieved in this regard must be modeled after the Form of justice. That is why philosophers are best suited to the task of helping the state live up to its potential: "the city will never find happiness until its outline is sketched by painters who use the divine model" (*Republic* 500e).

Are there, then, no examples of Forms that cannot be instantiated? This may be a bad question—or a bad way of putting a good question. The nature of the desired exemplification remains vague. What exactly, are we to assume, is preventing the instantiation in question? Is the instantiation impossible or is it inconceivable? More specifically, is it inconceivable, and therefore impossible, or is it impossible in some other way despite being conceivable? And either way, if the instantiation is impossible or inconceivable, how could the Form itself be possible or conceivable? Modal reasons against instantiation should also work against reification, and even against conceptualization, the preclusion of which would then make the original question vacuous.

Is there even a difference, preferably a relevant one, between asking for examples of Forms whose instantiation is impossible or inconceivable and asking for examples of Forms that are themselves impossible or inconceivable? And if we are really talking about impossible or inconceivable Forms, especially inconceivable ones, how are we to come up with examples? Fractional integers, rectangular triangles, and liquid icebergs, to name a few, are not good examples. This is not because they are impossible or inconceivable. It is because they are, in each instance, spurious intersections of two separate Forms rather than paradigm cases of one that is empty or impossible or inconceivable. The examples can be multiplied indefinitely with the same result: eternal moments, concrete abstractions, silent sounds, and so on.

There may be objections and counterexamples but none that rules out the instantiation while validating the Form. Eternal moments, for example, are neither instantiable nor even meaningful.[56] A Hegelian, on the other hand, might be quick to nominate space as an example of a concrete abstraction, but space would then represent the instantiation of a concrete abstraction, the Form of which, if there is such a Form, could not consistently be considered empty, since it would be instantiated at least by space. The problem with silent sounds, which presents a contradiction, is the same as the problem with soothing sounds, which does not: Neither combination has a Form. One is instantiable (realizable in practice), the other is not, but neither one counts as an empty Form, because neither one qualifies as a Form, owing to the composite structure of the referent in each case. The presumption against the instantiation comes from the contradiction, while the presumption against the Form comes from the complexity—combination, modification, or contamination—which is no longer about the instantiability of a particular Form but about the simplicity of Forms in general. Silent sounds will not be instantiated in our phenomenal experience, due to the contradiction, whereas soothing sounds will be instantiated, because they are consistent with the way the world works. But neither one will have a Form, nor therefore will either one exemplify an empty Form, because their complexity precludes the possibility of eidetic representation, whether as an instantiated Form or as an empty one.

This emphasis on simplicity, or against complexity, appears to have certain exceptions, depending on the interpretation. One obvious objection is that even basic geometrical figures, such as circles, squares, and triangles, are not simple without qualification. They are all plane figures with an internal structure common and peculiar to each. They are thus composed of simpler elements in a predetermined pattern. If there are Forms for lines and angles, for example, then the Forms of circles and polygons will arguably be complex ones, if acknowledged at all.[57] Perhaps the notion

---

56. The notion of eternal moments may work as a metaphor, and there may be a Form for metaphors, but there would be none for literal metaphors, because there would instead be two (literality and metaphors), as is the case with eternal moments (eternality and moments).

57. Plato's interest in geometry is the stuff of legend (see Alican 2012, 41–43). Whether he acknowledges Forms for geometrical figures, however, remains an open question,

of angles can be explained through that of lines, and may therefore be partly redundant, but even lines have a derivative nature originating in points as their constituents. And we cannot do much with points alone. Or maybe we can, but we cannot afford to start from scratch, that is, at the level of points, every time we encounter a problem in geometry. We need additional units even if they are relatively more complex ones. In short, our standard conceptual apparatus for making sense of the world is not restricted strictly to partless simplicity.

None of this, however, voids the premium on simplicity in Plato's Forms. Explicating that premium can help eliminate apparent exceptions. The simplicity here is not limited to the absence of parts. As a matter of fact, it does not even require the absence of parts. The restriction is against unstructured complexity, the kind associated with modification or contamination, as in the combination of disparate items as opposed to the composition of organic structures. The complexity of the square (*Republic* 510d), for example, is significantly different from the complexity of, say, either silent sounds or soothing sounds. The square is a unitary whole; the other two are not. The cohesion of the square may be a matter of perception and convention, hence subjective rather than objective, but

---

particularly from the testimonial perspective of his most famous student. Aristotle portrays Plato as giving mathematical objects (both numbers and figures) an intermediate position between Forms and particulars (*Metaphysics* 987b14–18, 1059b5–14). This would normally constitute confirmation that Plato did indeed acknowledge Forms for geometrical figures, because intermediates are always intermediate between Forms and particulars, never simply intermediate without eidetic or sensible correlates. Yet Aristotle complicates matters by describing Plato as holding all Forms to be numbers (*Metaphysics* 991b9, 1081a12), which then precludes the possibility of geometrical figures being either Forms or intermediates. Geometrical figures obviously cannot be Forms if all Forms are numbers, but they also cannot be intermediates, for the very same reason, given that there can be no intermediates without a corresponding Form, all of which happen to be limited to numbers, according to Aristotle's testimony. Plato himself is not clear about the matter either. Even where he mentions the "square itself" and the "diagonal itself" (*Republic* 510d), the reference is ambiguous between invoking a Form and calling attention to a certain geometrical figure as distinct from the particular manifestation or illustration of it under discussion. This is a matter of longstanding controversy among Plato scholars. See Yang (1999) for a short list of notable references, together with a brief presentation of his own position, which challenges what he calls the "critical view" that the references in question are to Forms. Chapter 7 of the present volume considers the problem of mathematicals in greater detail, specifically in the course of examining Plato's position on intermediates.

that does not make it any less significant as an example of the distinction between things with a unitary structure and those without a unitary structure. Plato's Forms are unitary wholes, if not outright simple objects. An internal structure is allowed, but modifications or impurities are not.[58]

This is not to say that Forms cannot instantiate other Forms, just that they do not merge into a single Form when they do. Nor do they give birth to a new Form separate from the interacting originals. There are no complex Forms, certainly no such Platonic Forms, or more precisely, none in accordance with Plato's ontology in the canonical corpus. This, of course, does not preclude the possibility of empty Forms, only that of whimsical combinations. All manner of empty Forms, so long as each one is its own Form, may still be possible and conceivable. They could even exist without our awareness. As with many other things, the existence of an empty Form is not contingent upon our knowing about it.

Answers to what we can know in this regard should not be charged with settling the broader question whether types, properties, abstractions, or fictional entities exist. In a field of study where it is perfectly reasonable to claim that there are nonexistent objects (Parsons 1982), and equally reasonable to ask where they are (Hintikka 1984), an answer is best not attempted in passing, in the process of working out an altogether different matter, as in the possibility or reality of empty Forms in Plato. Nor should it depend upon formulating a general theory of existence, nor even merely upon establishing whether existence is a predicate. These are the best of questions. But they go to the heart of philosophy itself, having no special bearing upon Plato's Forms. And even if they were to be addressed in connection with the Forms, the place for that would be in discussing whether the Forms exist at all, not in deciding what to do with the empty ones.

How, then, do we separate the question of the possibility of empty Forms from that of the reality of Forms? Are we to determine whether, given what Plato says about Forms, there could possibly be empty ones? Or are we to determine whether, given what Plato says about Forms, he might be

---

58. Plato's favorite Forms, if we may judge the matter by where he focuses his efforts, have no internal structure at all: justice, piety, beauty, temperance, knowledge, and so on. Those that do are unitary wholes with a cohesive structure: beds and tables (*Republic* 596b, 597c–d); shuttles, awls, and tools in general (*Cratylus* 389a–d); and evidently all artifacts (*Seventh Letter* 342d), including houses and rings, as reported by Aristotle (*Metaphysics* 991b3–8, 1080a3–10), though not specifically mentioned by Plato.

open to empty ones? We do not have much of a choice. Given that Plato says nothing about empty Forms, we are going to have to take what would be reasonable to conclude about them as a proxy for what Plato would have said or may have thought. This is not always the best thing to do, but it may be the only thing to do here. If we all agreed on the reasonable, we would not disagree so often. Yet so long as we take care to construe the reasonable with sufficient regard for what Plato himself would have found reasonable, based upon the things that he does find reasonable, this should be an acceptable proxy. It is, after all, not far from Plato to be reasonable.

We are not completely lacking in resources. As is often the case when we find ourselves without direct evidence, or without enough of it, we can turn to Aristotle for help. In this case, we have to reach a bit further, to an Aristotelian commentator, Alexander of Aphrodisias. Alexander (*In Aristotelis Metaphysica Commentaria* 81.25–82.7) reports that Aristotle, in his now-lost work *Peri Ideōn*, construed Plato as being committed by implication, though not by declaration, to the existence of Forms for some things that have ceased to exist, such as dead persons, as well as for some things that never did exist, such as centaurs and the Chimera. The point there, however, is not that, because of the alleged implication, we would be safe to assume that Plato had actually made room in his ontology for such Forms, but that we are compelled to conclude that what Plato says about Forms in general is productive of such infelicities, thereby undermining the tenability of his overall position on Forms.

The offending implication is to be sought in the Object-of-Thought Argument for the existence of Forms, an Aristotelian reconstruction assigning, on behalf of Plato, a Form to every object of thought (see Fine 1988; 1993, 120–141). Any such implication is difficult to confirm outside this context. In regard to dead persons, it would be hasty to saddle Plato with corresponding Forms, as he never mentions personal Forms even for the living.[59] In regard to imaginary things, again, there is no talk of

---

59. Dead persons continue to exist as disincarnate souls, presumably until they are reborn with an earthly body, but it is not clear whether individual souls have Forms. I have not seen a case for it in any of the relevant places: *Laws* 891d–893a, 893b–896b, 896b–899d; *Phaedo* 70c–72e, 72e–77a, 78b–80b, 102a–107a; *Phaedrus* 245c–246a, 246a–257a; *Republic* 436a–444a, 608c–612b; *Timaeus* 34b–36d, 41a–44d, 68e–72d. *Alcibiades* 1 seems to present an exception where it invokes something like the "self itself" at 129b1 (*auto tauto*) and 130d4 (*auto to auto*). But it is difficult to take this reference (especially in its more literal translation as the "itself itself") as conclusive evidence of a separate Form for each soul, which is not established even

corresponding Forms, nor any tendency on the part of Plato to recognize the reality of such things, let alone the existence of Forms for them. This, of course, is entirely consistent with the original objection, where the crux of the charge is that, precisely because Plato is not open to Forms for these things, the implication that he is (through the Object-of-Thought Argument) vitiates his general outlook.

What is relevant for our purposes is not so much the implication itself as it is the silent premise that Plato did not welcome (or would not have welcomed) Forms for dead persons or fictional entities. If this were a reliable report or a reasonable assumption, either way, it would constitute evidence that Plato did not countenance empty Forms. And that is perhaps just what it is. But there is still room for doubt, or at least for confusion, because the anomaly is attributed not just to the implied commitment to the existence of Forms for things that do not themselves exist but also to a parallel commitment to the existence of Forms for things that are tokens as opposed to types. Perishable things, including those that have already perished, and individual things receive simultaneous emphasis in the elucidation of the problem. That makes it difficult to tell whether Plato is supposed to be uncomfortable because the postulated Forms are empty or because they are individuated.

The difficulty does not apply to the example of centaurs, troublesome because centaurs do not exist, not because the example picks out a particular thing as opposed to a universal one. There is no specific centaur to speak of. The centaurs are a race or breed of legendary creatures. The Chimera, on the other hand, is a fictional individual rather than a fictional kind. It is therefore fully exposed to the ambiguity between not qualifying as a real thing and not qualifying as a type of thing.[60] The same ambiguity is

---

in the *Phaedo*, where the matter remains open to interpretation, despite meticulous exploration of the connection between the soul and the Forms. Had Plato thought that there were Forms for individual persons, the best place to make that clear would have been the *Phaedo*, where three of the four arguments for the immortality of the soul turn on its relationship with the Forms: the recollection argument (72e–77a for the argument, 77b–84b for objections and replies), the analogic argument (78b–80b for the logical core, 80c–84b for supporting imagery), and the causal argument (96a–107a or 105b–107a, depending on the focus). See Alican (2012) for an analysis of these arguments (413–418, 418–424, 446–450) and of the *Phaedo* in general (391–491).

60. The centaurs and the Chimera also come up together in the *Phaedrus* (229d), where their juxtaposition recalls just such a distinction between fictional kinds and fictional individuals (see Fine 1993, 127; Thomas 2008, 636).

present in the case of dead persons, say, a dead Socrates, which counts both as having perished and as being particular.

To be fair, there is no ambiguity in context. Both perishables and particulars are identified as problematic candidates for Forms. The ambiguity emerges only in attempting to sort out the specific examples in terms of whether they represent things that do not exist or things that do not exist as types or natural kinds. No doubt, the context of the objection would have been more enlightening in relation to the problem on hand had we been given only the example of a species that had perished instead of including that of an individual that had perished. Nevertheless, the Aristotelian scenario related by Alexander still suggests that Plato was not open to empty Forms, as we cannot explain away the example of centaurs, least of all by claiming to have detected an ambiguity of the relevant sort in it. The suggestion may or may not be compelling, but it is there.

Unfortunately, Plato himself says nothing about empty Forms. But he says enough about Forms in general to enable inferences about empty Forms. Gail Fine (1984, 74–78), for one, considers artifacts a candidate for eidetic vacancy. Her thinking can be generalized as the postulate that the Forms of artifacts can and do exist, and hence remain uninstantiated, both before and after the artifacts themselves are in existence.[61] But Fine (1984, 76) herself focuses only on their existence before the emergence of the instantiating artifacts (which is sufficient to discuss or demonstrate separation) and not additionally on their existence after the possible disappearance of those artifacts. She notes that any Forms for beds and shuttles, for example, and for artifacts in general, if there are such Forms, would have to exist not just when but also before the artifacts themselves are in existence, that is, before the first physical bed or shuttle is constructed.

This makes the Forms temporal, as does Fine's acknowledgment of the alternative (which she adds is unlikely to have been maintained by Plato) that the Forms of artifacts come into existence at the same time as the artifacts themselves (1984, 76, n. 73). We know, in contrast, that the Forms exist outside time, as evidenced by the fact that they were already

---

61. Fine (1984) does not claim that artifacts have Forms (nor even that Plato says they do). She merely explores the implications of the assumption that they do (or that Plato says they do). Broadie (2007), in turn, opposes the assumption itself, laying out some of the main reasons for rejecting Forms for artifacts (which then precludes empty Forms for them), together with a critical survey of the early history of that rejection.

in existence when the demiurge created time (*Timaeus* 37c–39e).[62] Time is, in fact, a creation fashioned after the Forms.

Yet making the Forms temporal is not necessarily wrong. Plato, we see, wavers between Forms that are created, unique to the *Republic* (597b–d), and Forms that precede creation, explicit at least in the *Timaeus* (30c–31a, 37c–39e).[63] We cannot be certain whether his Forms are infinitely durable (or perhaps just extremely durable) or simply atemporal. But maybe we do not have to have a direct and definitive answer in the original sources just to sort out the precedence between Forms and artifacts. Whether the Forms are atemporal or infinitely durable, the possibility of their emptiness would not be precluded by contingencies concerning artifacts, which are neither atemporal nor infinitely durable.[64]

Is it not possible, then, for there to be empty Forms? It is indeed possible. The *Timaeus* confirms not just a possibility but also a reality.[65]

---

62. Specifically, we know that "the model was itself an everlasting Living Thing" and that "it was the Living Thing's nature to be eternal" (*Timaeus* 37d). Thus, the Forms (or whatever answers to the description of that "everlasting Living Thing") were the model for the creation of time, and they were therefore in existence "when" time was not, that is, "before" time was created.

63. Even though the textual evidence leaves us with a contradiction between the *Timaeus* (30c–31a, 37c–39e) and the *Republic* (597b–d) on this point, what we know of Plato's Forms in general provides additional insight: If the Forms are transcendent, then they must exist outside spacetime and therefore outside time. For if they are transcendent, yet are not outside spacetime, what then do they transcend, and where and when do they do the transcending? Reflection on this question would seem to favor atemporality over durability or longevity.

64. See Patterson (1985b) and Whittaker (1968) for various interpretations of the eternality of Forms.

65. One can always dismiss inconvenient details or implications in the cosmogony of the *Timaeus* by invoking the ostensibly fragile credibility of the report as a creation myth. But that is not a self-sufficient appeal. It requires argumentation. The matter of how seriously we are to take the "likely story" (*eikōs muthos*), or "likely account" (*eikōs logos*), of the *Timaeus* (29b–d ff. passim) has yet to be settled. While the tension between metaphorical and literal interpretation is an ancient one, the balance in scholarly dialogue has been shifting from allegory to philosophy (or at least to philosophy through allegory). Taylor (1928, 18–19) and Cornford (1937, 24–32, 34–39), for example, both favor a less literal reading, though Cornford takes issue with Taylor for identifying the likely story as a bricolage of existing theories. Vlastos (1939, 71–73; 1965b, 401–419) and Hackforth (1959, especially 19), in contrast, move away from deliteralization, finding a greater commitment by Plato to the story offered. More

The Forms precede the cosmos, and therefore pretty much everything, given that the cosmos is fashioned after the Forms (*Timaeus* 30c–31a, 37c–39e). They are thus empty until sensible phenomena come into existence. What are these primordial Forms the Forms of? Presumably of everything. Otherwise, we would have to settle for an amorphous batch of Form-stuff, positively lacking in structural differentiation, and unable thereby to initiate cosmological individuation. Whatever may be the "everlasting Living Thing" serving as a model for the demiurge's creation of time (*Timaeus* 37c–39e), if it has anything at all to do with the Forms, then it has that to do with all Forms: "For that Living Thing comprehends within itself all intelligible living things, just as our world is made up of us and all the other visible creatures" (*Timaeus* 30c–d).

Fine (1984, 79) points out some interesting exceptions to uninstantiated Forms in the context of the *Timaeus*. The Form of fire, she observes, cannot reasonably be counted among any Forms existing uninstantiated prior to the creation of the cosmos, because, so the story goes (*Timaeus* 53b), there were already "traces" of fire in the chaos preceding the cosmos.[66] The same may be said of the other traditional elements, air, water, and earth (*Timaeus* 53b), though Fine (1984, 79) focuses specifically on fire, probably not to exclude the rest but to minimize clutter where one example will do just as well as four. Other exceptions she notes include justice and goodness, which, Fine argues (1984, 79), would have been instantiated even before the creation of the cosmos, because they would have then been instantiated at least by the demiurge (before any [other] moral agents and moral acts), who is said to be just and good (*Timaeus* 29a, 29e–30b).

What if justice and goodness (or any other Forms) came before the demiurge? Would they not then be empty Forms, not being instantiated by anything at all, including the demiurge? They would be until the demiurge came along, but this is not a good counterexample. One might object that, if both the demiurge and the Forms (of justice, of goodness, and of whatever else) preceded time, and were both eternal in that sense,

---

recent contributions include Brisson (2012, 369–391), Burnyeat (2005, 143–165), and Sedley (2007a, 93–132, especially 98–107).

66. Fine later places greater emphasis (2003, 293) on what she originally presents as an implicit distinction (1984, 79) between the "traces of fire" mentioned and "sensible fire as we know it." The discussion here is compatible with her observation at either level of emphasis.

then neither one could have come before the other, because there would never have been a time when either one did not exist. At least in this sense, the demiurge could arguably have always instantiated whatever it instantiates prior to the creation of time. But this objection is no better than the counterexample it targets. Both tend to come up, but they both rest on the independent problem of whether succession is possible (or conceivable) without time, or perhaps more generally on whether anything at all can happen outside time. Neither the counterexample nor the objection to it does anything to solve that problem.

We do not know whether justice and goodness (Fine 1984, 79) would have been the only moral Forms that were not empty before the cosmos came into being, since we are not told very much about the demiurge, whose nature may (or may not) happen to be such as to instantiate other moral Forms as well, conceivably even all of them. The point, however, is not to explore Forms that are never without instances but to explore those that are the opposite, namely those that are, in fact, without instances. And the *Timaeus* seems open to that possibility, even with a just and good demiurge preceding the cosmos.

The question of empty Forms depends, in the end, on what we want to know. We all agree, no doubt, that an empty Form is a Form that is not instantiated. There is no room for dissent there. That is the core definition. But the reasons for the emptiness, not to mention the actual circumstances, including the duration if applicable, together with any prospects for reversal, and yet other details, all stand to make a difference.

The immediate problem is that we are not clear on what the question is. Actually, that is not entirely accurate. We usually are clear, just not in harmony, or in agreement. We are clear on different questions, and consequently, keen on different answers. That makes us clear as individuals but divided as a community of interested scholars.

The underlying problem is that we are regularly torn between emptiness and existence as the relevant possibilities for the Forms in question. In other words, we are never quite sure whether problem Forms are just empty or simply do not exist. The confusion is hardly ever about whether a Form already agreed to exist is or is not empty. And it is even less likely to be about whether a Form that would be agreed to exist, even if it were empty, is or is not in fact empty when it is not instantiated. It is instead about whether the scenario being contemplated precludes just the instantiation or the Form as well.

The two possibilities jointly present a perplexing puzzle terminating in a logical impasse. The examples we come up with invariably require, or at least invite, a judgment, not just on whether the relevant Forms are empty but also on whether they exist. These do not unfold as a sequence of mutually independent considerations: Does the Form exist? Check! Is it empty? Check! They turn out to be competing conclusions, with any evidence that the Form is empty also suggesting that it does not exist. That being so, they complicate matters as they provide no more inspiration to deny the instantiation of any given Form in a problem scenario than they do to deny the existence of the same Form in the same scenario. This is not because they are in every case equally plausible alternatives, but because the uncertainty in any case is sufficient to leave us undecided. They thus leave us adequately inspired to do both, yet utterly unable to do either one with any confidence. Even more likely, they inspire some of us in one direction, others in the opposite direction.

The potential for confusion is there regardless of the complexity of the scenario. Simple scenarios come with a temporal frame of reference in which things that used to exist no longer do. In that case, the corresponding Forms, if they still exist, are most certainly empty. The Form of mastodon, as already discussed, is empty right now, as would be the Form of elephant if the existing elephants were to disappear. These are easy answers to easy questions. Yet they come with reasonable doubt. It might be reasonable, or not altogether unreasonable, to deny the existence of such Forms and thereby also the possibility of their being empty. One could object, for example, that things that do not exist do not have Forms, and further that things that are extinct are, in fact, things that do not exist. This is not an untenable position even if there is a case to be made for the contrary view that a Form does not cease to exist just because its contents or participants do.

At the opposite end from the simple scenarios, the questions are still not difficult, just more complex and perhaps a bit contrived. The same ambiguity awaits there. The scenarios become enigmatic as their specifications begin to stretch the imagination, as in the polygon that has too many sides, or the state that is run too well, or the object that is moving too fast. In each case, the excess is to an unworkable extreme: The chiliagon is supposed to have too many sides to imagine; the ideal state, too much justice to realize; the superluminal starship, too great a speed to subsist (retain mass and remain coherent). The common problem is the notion of a Form that cannot possibly or conceivably be instantiated. The answers are easy there as well: The corresponding Forms, if any, will surely be empty. Yet it is not clear that there would be any Forms answering to these descriptions. Even if such Forms cannot possibly be instantiated, one could, for much the same reason, deny not just the instantiations but also the Forms themselves, especially if one is committed to keeping the discussion focused on Plato's Forms as opposed to universals from a modern perspective.

As intimated earlier in this section, immediately upon introducing the ruminations of Armstrong (1978, 64–65), the example of traveling faster than light points to a structural complexity bringing together too many elements to constitute a single Form. One way around that difficulty, and hence a reason not to dismiss Armstrong's example out of hand, is to use "starship" as shorthand for the otherwise busy combination of elements in the original example. Starships routinely come with warp engines enabling superluminal travel. They thus qualify as unitary wholes without conceptual modification, because it is not necessary (since redundant) to add that they happen to be able to travel faster than light. Continuing references to "superluminal" starships are for emphasis and not for substantive qualification of the starships themselves, which are already superluminal. Although our acquaintance with starships is restricted largely to science fiction, especially to *Star Trek*, recourse to warp technology in Starfleet should not be much of a stretch where we are already discussing unicorns. What the starship illustration shows, at any rate, is not that Armstrong's original example works, but that its failure need not come from its complexity, which could conceivably be ironed out through conceptual consolidation, as in using the unitary notion of a starship to stand for the more complex and less structured one of traveling faster than light.

Conceptual consolidation may be conceivable in other cases as well, but it does not guarantee a Form for any of them. The chiliagon, for example, already comes with a unitary structure providing ontological coherence and is not in need of any consolidation of the kind imagined and effected through the image of a superluminal starship. Yet it suffers from the same apparent ambiguity between not being instantiated and not having a Form. The ideal state, on the other hand, does not seem to be amenable to conceptual consolidation, but it appears nevertheless to stand as something of an anomaly among the examples considered so far. It is difficult to place the ideal state in the same category as either the chiliagon or the starship traveling at warp speed. While we may be unable to decide whether chiliagons and superluminal starships lack Forms or have Forms that lack instantiations, the evidentiary context precludes the first alternative in the case of the ideal state. We could even dismiss the other two examples as irrelevant from Plato's perspective, but the ideal state is among his fondest interests. It would be almost heresy to deny that Plato would countenance a Form for it. As a matter of fact, he appears to be doing just that at the end of the ninth book of the *Republic* (592a–b), as Maula (1967, 35) and Vlastos (1969b, 301) remind us. And the Form for this ideal state would have to be empty for the same reason that the Forms in the other two examples would be empty if they existed.

If this is the proper reading of the related exchange between Socrates and Glaucon on the ideal state, we would seem finally to have an answer to the question whether Plato held a specific position on empty Forms. He evidently did, openly embracing that possibility through the example of the ideal state. But the evidence is not as conclusive as it may seem. Heresy becomes appealing, perhaps even compelling, as the assignment of a Form to the ideal state contradicts the simplicity and purity of Forms, discussed above in connection with other examples. The ideal state is a complex or derivative notion invoking not just statehood but also ideality (however defined), and accordingly, combining two Forms rather than exemplifying one, or else tampering with a proper Form to create an imposter redundant with the original.

This is like combining a type with a property where the property is not just one of many accidental attributes imaginable but presumably also one that cannot be realized. Various kinds and degrees of complexity may be accommodated, or at least debated, in contemporary discussions on universals, but Plato makes no allowance for such complexity in Forms. Even if there is a Form for statehood, or perhaps especially if there is one, there should not be a separate Form for the ideal state.[67]

---

67. An alternative reading is that there is just one Form for the state, which, being a Form, naturally happens to be an ideal one, with any degeneration or corruption confined to its phenomenal manifestations. On this reading, the Form of the state is, by default, the Form of the ideal state (which is nothing other than the just state, since the ideality Plato attributes to the state is, in fact, justice) because there is no other (less than ideal) kind among the Forms, only among the ones established in practice. This might overturn my objection that the ideal state is not simple enough a notion to be considered a Form in and of itself. But this unified Form of "state = ideal state (just state)" would no longer serve Maula (1967, 35) and Vlastos (1969b, 301) as an example of a Form that is not or cannot be instantiated, as it would instead be an example of one that is badly or imperfectly instantiated, rather like every other

And it is patently counterintuitive for there to be a Form for the ideal state but none for statehood. Introducing a Form for the ideal state is like reserving a Form for the longest line, or the largest circle, or the greatest pleasure, not only in the sense that these things are not instantiated in our phenomenal experience but also in the sense that the longest line is still a line, the largest circle still a circle, and the greatest pleasure still a pleasure. None of them should have an additional Form as a superlative. Nor should the ideal state.

Yet there it is, the Form of the ideal state, tantalizing us at *Republic* 592b. There is no mention throughout the canonical corpus of any other superlative Form redundant with its ordinary counterpart, but we have to make peace with the fact that there is mention of what looks very much like a bona fide Form earmarked for the conceptually redundant and phenomenally uninstantiable ideal state.

The complexity of that Form, however, if it really is one, is not the only consideration against taking it seriously as a Form. Another reason for suspicion is the lack of dramatic support. A difficult and significant interpretive judgment concerning a major philosopher is best not indexed to a hasty generalization from a single passage in his intellectual output. What is even worse in this case is that the problem is not merely with the quantity of evidence but also, and more so, with the quality. It is dramatically discordant, and therefore philosophically disconcerting, that in our best evidence for a Form of the ideal state there should be absolutely nothing of the irrepressible confidence typically reserved for talk of Forms. The celestial pattern for the ideal state is suggested only as an understated possibility, with both speakers expressly affirming no more than a likelihood (*Republic* 592b). The thrust of the passage is that we should strive to achieve the ideal state, and thereby to instantiate it, no matter the odds against its realization. This can, if it must, be interpreted against the grain of evidence, as a complex (combined, modified, or contaminated) Form that happens to be empty, but the ambivalence is hard to miss.

Form we know. If the Form of "state = ideal state (just state)" must be empty simply because phenomenal manifestations of statehood are always less than ideal (not quite just, or what would then be the same, not perfectly just), then all Forms must be empty for analogous reasons. Yet the Form of the equal (*Phaedo* 74a–75e), for example, is decidedly not empty, despite being notorious for how everything that strives to be like it (like the equal itself) inevitably comes up short in instantiation.

The standard dramatic template for discussing Forms is a spectacle with fanfare. Plato provides plenty of that elsewhere: "Do we say that there is such a thing as the Just itself, or not? We do say so, by Zeus" (*Phaedo* 65d). That is how Plato normally introduces a Form. He guides and excites his audience. The passionate endorsement in the exchange just quoted is motivated not by a special devotion to justice but by a general appreciation of Forms. We find the same spirited agreement even where the question is about whether we shall say there is such a thing as the equal itself: "Indeed we shall, by Zeus, said Simmias, most definitely" (*Phaedo* 74b). This overly theatrical combination of conviction and enthusiasm animates the customary confirmation for the existence of Forms. Simmias conditions us to expect it in all cases: "Nothing is so evident to me personally as that all such things must certainly exist, the Beautiful, the Good, and all those you mentioned just now" (*Phaedo* 77a). Yet the intensity is simply not there in the passage brought up by Maula and Vlastos as evidence of an empty Form for the ideal state: "But perhaps, I said, there is a model of it in heaven. . . . Probably so, he said" (*Republic* 592b). The evidence, of course, is still there. Despite the wooden delivery and halfhearted response, it still counts as an apparent reference to empty Forms (ignoring the aberrant complexity of the notion of an ideal state). But it is difficult to accept that as the final word on the matter.[68]

The final word may well be the uncertainty whether what is missing is the instantiation or the Form itself. The lukewarm confirmation ending the ninth book of the *Republic*, if it really confirms empty Forms, also confirms the uncertainty. But independently of the question of textual evidence, the idea of a Form that cannot possibly or conceivably be instantiated is itself overelaborate. Uninstantiated universals may be common in thought experiments, but not all universals from our perspective are Forms from Plato's perspective. Only the important ones are.[69] And those

---

68. Burnyeat agrees with me where he assures us, explicitly and without reservation, that "there is no such Form as the Form of the ideal city" (1992, 298).

69. As noted earlier (section 5.3 on Formless things), Forms are what Plato makes them out to be. His lifelong experimentation with abstraction springs from and operates with what he himself found valuable, significant, important, or at least interesting. See the role of Plato's valuation tendencies in chapter 2 (sections 2.7 and 2.11), chapter 3 (sections 3.2, 3.5, 3.6), and chapter 6 (especially section 6.3 but also sections 6.4 and 6.5). That is why we keep encountering the same Forms throughout the various dialogues invoking the Forms. And that is why we are confronted, over and over, with justice and beauty and goodness, and not with flights of fancy taxing the imagination.

without instances could hardly have been prominent enough for him to take notice. Plato may, if pressed, have to make room for some such entities in his ontology, but we cannot either rightfully or responsibly lay them all at his doorstep just because we detected something of an affinity in the case of the ideal state.

The real threat to dialectical progress here is that our failure to confirm a phenomenal manifestation for a Form undermines its existence even if it also supports its emptiness. A mitigating factor is that it does not do so equally well. This presents an opportunity to resist the doubt, or to work with it or through it, even as it lingers as a possibility. The inherent ambiguity does not rest on a precise epistemic balance. The possibility that what is missing is the Form rather than the instantiation is merely a reasonable doubt, a nagging suspicion at most. It should keep reasonable persons from concluding with confidence that they have discovered empty Forms, but it need not keep them from pursuing the possibility.

The alternatives are not equally plausible, at least not necessarily so. As indicated above, I am not in favor of disputing the existence of a Form just because its contents are emptied out or its participants are killed off. There is no end to that train of thought. There might even be a slippery slope in there somewhere. To claim that the Form of mastodon is gone, just because the mastodons are, could be the first step toward the extreme result that Forms blink in and out of existence, not to mention undergoing fundamental constitutional changes (in contradiction of their supposed immutability), to match the whimsical course of nature, including both the natural and the artificial phenomena and processes therein.

Granted, one could hold that Forms do not exist at all before they are instantiated and that they cease to exist when they are no longer instantiated. This need not automatically degenerate into a slippery slope. But the same ontological minimalist would then have to admit that Forms come back into existence upon reinstantiation, only to disappear again upon disinstantiation, thus revealing a radical metaphysical dependence of Forms upon sensible phenomena. What is wanted, in contrast, is an answer to whether ontologically independent Forms can be empty and whether they ever are.

It would appear that they can be and that they sometimes are. Yes, the mastodons are gone, but it is not as if they never existed. Why not mark that difference with an empty Form? Yes, the chiliagon seems too intricately nuanced to draw or imagine, but it is not as if it were not a proper mathematical object. Why not honor that distinction with an empty Form? And perhaps we are not having much luck thinking, or willing, objects into motion, but it is not as if the possibility were unimaginable. Why not allow an empty Form for psychokinesis? These may or may not be Forms, but if they are, they could easily be empty ones.

On the other hand, we should not have to assent to a Form, empty or otherwise, for everything we encounter through fantasy or science fiction. Perhaps we need to answer the question of empty Forms on a case-by-case basis, especially if we are to stick with what Plato himself would have thought. As we try, it is infinitely more important that we agree on what the question is, so that we may come together on where the problem is and ultimately on what the answer is.

5.5. Conclusion

The overarching aim of this chapter has been to enrich our understanding of Formless things and empty Forms in Plato. A guiding principle in the formulation and development of answers has been the clarification and refinement of the prevailing questions. There may be more to do in that regard. There always is. Yet the questions are now clear enough that we may adopt or reject any answers that have emerged in the process.

With respect to the question of Formless things, the answer must start with the Forms themselves. Sorting out the characteristics and implications of a thing without a Form requires reconsidering what Plato takes to be a Form and differentiating between the various constructs we have been in the habit of associating indiscriminately with his philosophical vision for Forms. They exhibit essential differences, and that, in turn, makes a difference in whether they are all the same sort of thing. No answer to the question of Formless things can be right if what we take to be Forms is wrong. Any sensible answer has to accommodate pertinent differences.

The ontology attributed to Plato in this volume constitutes just such an answer (developed in previous chapters). The basic profile is one of unitary pluralism in a solitary two-level world with three types of Forms—Ideal Forms, Conceptual Forms, and Relational Forms (see section 5.3)—all in the upper level of reality. What is true of one type could but need not be true of the others.

This classification not only clarifies the question of Formless things but also provides an answer to that question. The answer is that there is an Ideal Form for everything corresponding to that definition, a Conceptual

Form for everything corresponding to that definition, and a Relational Form for everything corresponding to that definition. Hence, the answer depends on what is meant by "Form." If these are all Forms, then, yes, there is a Form for everything. If they are not, if only Ideal Forms count, then, no, there is not a Form for everything.

This answer has the advantage of making sense (both dramatically and philosophically) of the conflict between the main characters of the *Parmenides* (as well as the internal conflict of the protagonist there) on whether there is a Form for everything. It does this by explaining how Plato could be content to leave us with a protagonist associating Forms only with things that matter, against an antagonist (or deuteragonist) recommending a Form for everything: Not everything merits an Ideal Form, but anything lacking an Ideal Form might instead be classified under Conceptual Forms or Relational Forms.

Plato's dialogues jointly accommodate all three categories of Forms, and this suggests that everything, no matter how trivial, could conceivably have a Form in some sense or other. The implication for Formless things is the removal of otherwise acceptable candidates from consideration. There is nothing, at least nothing among the actual examples we encounter in the dialogues, though not necessarily among any examples we might be able to conjure up ourselves, that cannot be associated with one of the three types of Forms identified here. This, we must keep in mind, is not a demonstrable solution, or a verifiable observation, but a "proposal" for consideration, a label of caution employed from the outset to acknowledge the absence of conclusive evidence and the presence of competing alternatives (also without conclusive evidence).[70]

Note that the tripartite classification allows but does not require everything to have a Form (in some sense or other). There may well be abstractions remaining at the level of concepts (the lower level of reality) and not quite making it to the level of Forms (the upper level of reality). Hence, the solution espoused here does not strictly rule out Formless

---

70. The introduction of unitary pluralism as a "proposal" starts with the original two-level model as the core paradigm: see especially the first four sections of chapter 2 and the first two sections of chapter 3. Recall that the classification of Forms is a "thought experiment": see chapter 2 (sections 2.1, 2.3, 2.11) and chapter 3 (section 3.2). This does not in any way trivialize the initiative, as Plato's own schemes and projects, including the so-called theory of Forms, are also thought experiments.

things, as the flexibility it introduces into the conception and discussion of Forms is consistent with the possibility, but not with the necessity, of a Form for everything.

This is not an oversight but insight, recognizing as it does that reification is a matter of value assignments by Plato (see section 5.3). Even if hair and mud and dirt, for example, have Conceptual Forms corresponding to them, there might be yet other things, perhaps even more trivial than these, that do not have any Forms whatsoever corresponding to them. This is neither to affirm nor to deny that hair and mud and dirt have Conceptual Forms. They could, and they might, but they do not have to. Both possibilities remain open. This is not a bad thing. But neither is further deliberation. Aiming for greater certainty and broader agreement would require combing through the dialogues to identify all the actual value assignments by Plato. That, however, would be to flesh out the details of the answer already given here rather than to reject it in its essentials.

In the meantime, a good reason for preferring this solution over the traditional alternative of a homogeneous collection of Forms representing the same thing in every context is that it makes Plato a more interesting and more resourceful philosopher without giving up anything to be gained by retaining the traditional alternative instead. The solution advocated here would be more compelling if we could be assured categorically that it was Plato's considered opinion instead of a reconstruction consistent with the evidence. But that is no reason to reject and no excuse to ignore the possibility. Any lack of certainty here is no greater than the prior, and indeed primary, one regarding what Plato thought about the existence and essence of Forms. Did he ever think they were real, and, if so, did he always think so? If we can live with the uncertainty there, we should be able to survive the one in the tripartite classification of Forms and in the implications of that for (and against) Formless things.

Comparable gains can be claimed for the section on empty Forms. There, too, the clarification process moves the discussion forward, exposing and establishing solution prospects that seem plausible: (1) The Form of mastodon, given that there are no longer any mastodons, is demonstrably empty; (2) the Form of unicorn, given that there have never been any unicorns, is assuredly empty; (3) the Form of the chiliagon, given that it has too many sides to distinguish it from a myriagon, or either one of those from a circle, is apparently empty; (4) the Form (if allowed) of the ideal state, given that it is too good to be true, is regrettably empty; (5) the Form of the superluminal starship, given that the requisite velocity cannot be attained, is evidently empty; and so on with any examples I may have overlooked, or any that may yet come up.

These answers are only provisional. But they collectively point to one that is conclusive: Empty Forms, as it turns out, are empty either because of a phenomenal contingency, as in the case of mastodons, unicorns, and faster-than-light travel, or because of a conceptual difficulty, as in several of the other examples. The first gives us contingently empty Forms, the second, necessarily empty Forms. The exact terms are not important. Another modal formulation might be accidentally empty Forms versus essentially empty Forms. In temporal terms, the first kind would be occasionally empty, the second, permanently empty. Between Forms whose phenomenal manifestations have been destroyed or inhibited (and are therefore circumstantially empty) and those that cannot possibly or conceivably be instantiated (and are therefore categorically empty), there are no Forms that just are empty, in other words, empty despite the absence of internal or external restrictions (physical, metaphysical, or logical) dictating such a vacancy.

The last reference is as difficult to verbalize as its referent is to visualize. A Form that is empty without reason, call it an "inherently empty Form" just to give it a name, would probably have to be something like the Form of beauty if it were never instantiated, not because of a practical or conceptual problem, such as the destruction of all things beautiful, but simply because nothing ever happens to instantiate it, as might be the case if nothing at all were ever beautiful. Inherently empty Forms, in contrast to contingently empty Forms and necessarily empty Forms, would be empty by design, yet for no reason other than the absence of a corresponding instantiation. Another name for them might be "naturally empty Forms" (or perhaps even "mysteriously" or "surprisingly" or "inexplicably" empty Forms). There are no such Forms. If there are any empty Forms, not one of them is like that.

This conclusion is consistent with the principles of classification for Forms under the model of interpretation employed throughout the present volume, where inherently empty Forms are ruled out because the status of Forms as Forms, especially Ideal Forms but also the other two kinds, reflects the importance that Plato attaches to the reification of their correlates among particulars. Forms of any kind are recognized as Forms if and only if their phenomenal manifestations seem important enough to Plato to attract his attention. This means that any Form, including that of beauty, is instantiated by default. This is because, given that the process of conceptualization and formalization in Plato proceeds with phenomenal value assignments by Plato himself, the things to which the relevant values are assigned will naturally instantiate the corresponding Forms.

This takes the mystery out of the puzzle. The rest are perfectly reasonable answers, though arguably not as exciting as they are reasonable, and perhaps even a little frustrating. It is not very interesting, for example, that the Form of mastodon is now empty, or that the Form of unicorn will always be empty unless we engineer the unicorns, or that the Form of faster-than-light travel must be empty if we are reading the universe right. It is also not particularly exciting that all Forms (perhaps with exceptions) were empty before there was anything other than Forms and a lone demiurge. As for the impossible or inconceivable instantiations, they may be more interesting, but the rigidity of the scenarios leaves no room for discussion. And all cases come with the vexing uncertainty whether what is precluded is the instantiation or the Form itself. Yet uncertainty hardly ever keeps philosophy from being worthwhile. It is probably just the opposite. And that explains any frustration that may accompany the uncertainty.

Perhaps we want to know something more than whether a Form that does not happen to be instantiated, or one that cannot possibly be instantiated, or one that cannot conceivably be instantiated, is or is not, in fact, empty. It just so happens that there is nothing more. Either kind, if it exists, is indubitably not instantiated and is therefore empty. That is the extent of the problem. The question is not even meaningful outside the context of Forms that used to be empty, those that have been emptied out, and those that have to be empty. The answer, then, is that there can be contingently empty Forms and necessarily empty Forms but not inherently empty Forms (the elusive hypothetical correlate of a Form that is, for example, just like the Form of beauty, except that, for no reason at all, it never happens to be instantiated).

This answer is only about the possibility. It points to Forms that would be empty if they existed, but it does not, in addition, show that there are such Forms. The question whether there are empty Forms turns ultimately on whether we are prepared (with good reason) to accept or reject the Forms that would in fact be empty if they existed, or more to the point, it depends on whether Plato would have accepted or rejected them.

Neither any lingering hesitation nor the inherent uncertainty, however, diminishes the progress made through the clarification process carried out in the corresponding sections and through the conclusions drawn on that basis. Although these questions, like any others, would benefit from further thought, any initiative toward that end will be more likely to build upon the present one than to tear it down.

Chapter 6

The Good, the Bad, and the Ugly

*Does Plato Make Room for
Negative Forms in His Ontology?*

This chapter questions the place of negative Forms in Plato's ontology.[1] And it does so against appearances to the contrary, given that Plato himself seems to acknowledge both positive Forms and negative Forms, that is to say, both good ones and bad ones. He may not say so outright, but he invokes both and rejects neither. The apparent finality of this impression is so strong that it creates a lack of direct interest in the subject: Plato scholars do not give negative Forms much thought except where the prospect relates to something else they happen to be doing. Yet when they do give the matter any thought at all, typically for the sake of a prior concern, they try either to support the textual evidence or to contradict it, indicating that the evidence does not stand on its own. The aim of this chapter is to determine why they tend to affirm or deny the obvious, how they try to confirm or dispute it, and what this says about Plato's position. The strategic vehicle is a comparative case study. The confirmation comes from Debra Nails (2013), who needs to embrace negative Forms to demonstrate that the unhypothetical first principle of the all is not identical to the Form of the good, something she cannot do unless Plato recognizes

---

1. This chapter was originally published as a journal article (Alican 2017b): "The Good, the Bad, and the Ugly: Does Plato Make Room for Negative Forms in His Ontology?," *Cosmos and History: The Journal of Natural and Social Philosophy* 13, no. 3: 154–191.

negative Forms. The contradiction comes from Holger Thesleff (2013),[2] who needs to reject negative (Ideal) Forms because the defining feature of his (Ideal) Forms is the possession of positive intrinsic value, which cannot be predicated of anything negative. Despite defending opposite views, or perhaps because of this, they jointly make up for any lack of interest in the scholarly community. I appreciate both yet side with Thesleff.

6.1. The Question of Negative Forms in Plato

Are there any negative Forms in Plato? This is a good question. Here is a better one: Why would anyone bother with the first question, given that Plato is widely known to speak of such things at least sporadically if not systematically, sometimes even bringing up the good, the bad, and the ugly all in the same breath, as he does, for example, both in the *Republic* (475e–476a) and in the *Theaetetus* (186a)?

A couple of caveats may help prevent misunderstandings even if the subject matter is clear enough as it is. First, the sense of negativity intended here is not logical negation (not-good, not-just, not-holy, etc.) but outright evil (bad, unjust, unholy, etc.). Second, the evil in question is not exclusively moral or religious evil but any manifestation whatsoever of negativity (ugliness, ignorance, pestilence, etc.). The focus, then, is on the possible connections between negativity, broadly construed, and Plato's Forms.

The negative is never too far to reach in Plato. It is always close at hand and typically under scrutiny. Further examples include talk of the just with the unjust (*Phaedrus* 250a–b; *Republic* 476a), the beautiful with the ugly (*Euthydemus* 301b; *Hippias Major* 289c–d), and the holy/pious with the unholy/impious (*Euthyphro* 5c–6e). The list can be expanded indefinitely, covering anything of any value amenable to any manner of opposition.

---

2. The work cited above for Thesleff (2013) is actually Alican and Thesleff (2013): "Rethinking Plato's Forms," *Arctos: Acta Philologica Fennica* 47: 11–47. A lightly revised version of that article is reproduced as chapter 2 of this book. The reason that I prefer to remain in the background in most of the present chapter is that the format of a case study comparing competing positions works best with a third-person narrative, at least in the earlier stages of comparison and contrast.

Is it not obvious, then, that Plato welcomes negative Forms alongside the positive ones? Evidently not. It must not be so obvious, since we keep asking the first question, or insist on answering it when no one has asked it. It is far enough from obvious that we routinely disagree on the answer. That is what makes the second question a better one. And that is the question I intend to explore in this chapter.

I do not intend merely to answer the question. The answer would fit on this very page with room to spare. I will, of course, answer it. But I will also demonstrate that, and explain why, we normally do not think about the matter at all, until it intersects with something we do happen to be thinking about.[3] And I will suggest that, and show how, confronting the second question can help us with the first question, even if that may seem counterintuitive because the second is inspired by the first. Finally, I will recommend an answer to the first question based on the answer to

---

3. This lack of direct scholarly interest concerns only the possibility of Forms for negative phenomena in the broadest sense. It does not extend to the matter of Forms for negations or to the problem of Plato's theodicy. Hence, when I speak of neglect of negative Forms in Plato, I do not mean to imply either that no one is interested in how Plato handles negation or that no one cares what Plato does with the problem of evil from a moral or religious perspective. Both issues are widely discussed, but neither one addresses the problem on hand. The first issue is about the logic, semantics, epistemology, or ontology of Plato's approach to negation, for example, in places where we encounter not-large, not-beautiful, and not-being (*Sophist* 258b–c), or in those where we find not-Greek and not-ten-thousand (*Statesman* 262d–e). Discussions, to name a few, include: Brown (2012), Lee (1972), Lewis (1976), O'Brien (2013), Prior (1980). The second issue, while it can be restricted to Plato's ethics, is more often about his theodicy, with questions typically centering on whether evil comes from the body or from the soul or from both. Noteworthy contributions include: Cherniss (1954), Chilcott (1923), Hoffleit (1937), Mohr (1978; 1980), Wood (2009). The question of neglect, on the other hand, arises specifically in connection with the broader focus of the present chapter on whether Plato recognizes Forms for bad things in general, that is, for negatively valued or so conceived phenomena: anything undesirable in any way for any reason. It is here that I note a relative lack of immediate and consequential interest, but even here the matter is not in a state of complete disregard. The most prominent of scholars have been known to comment, but only in passing, and not with a view to developing a solution: Cherniss (1944, 266–267; 1954, 27), Guthrie (1978, 97–100), Herrmann (2007a, 223–225), Reeve (2006, 84–85, 293, n. 34), Rist (1967, especially 289–293), Ross (1951, 167–168), Sedley (2013, 119), Vlastos (1965c, 6–7; cf. 1965d–1966, a complementary piece).

the second question, or more specifically, based on my analysis of possible scenarios giving rise to the second question.

These are not structural or logical parts of the chapter. They are, more loosely, aims I hope to achieve. That is what I mean by "exploring" the second question instead of merely answering it. As for the first question, we will probably never know the answer, and we will certainly never agree on it. That is why we have the second question.

Just how would one go about exploring a question beyond simply answering it? Since the second question is about why anyone would bother with the first question, I propose to examine what has already been said by those who have actually bothered with the first question. The most helpful answers will be those that either affirm or deny negative Forms in Plato. Any other answer, say, that the matter is not clear, even if correct, will not be as helpful, because we can already tell that the matter is not clear.

People who do find the matter clear usually have more interesting things to say, if only because they are willing to go out on a limb. Debra Nails (2013, 95–101) does this as she supports negative Forms in Plato, Holger Thesleff (chapter 2, section 2.10) as he rejects them. They are not out on a limb simply because they accept or reject negative Forms in Plato. They are out on a limb because of the way they do this, which is in each case a Platonic adventure well worth taking, as illustrated in what follows here. They are both perfectly clear on the problem and remarkably confident in their answers, which is a fitting combination for studying the opposition around negative Forms, whether in response to the first question or in connection with the second.[4]

Any attempt to answer either question stands to benefit from the prior consideration of a point of departure relevant to both: the distinction between the good and other Forms. The question of negative Forms,

---

4. My own answer to the first question, though it is not relevant at this point to what I am doing with the second question, is the same as Thesleff's (see the first two notes in this chapter), as laid out in chapter 2 (section 2.10) of the present volume. My agreement with Thesleff, not to mention my collaboration with him (Alican and Thesleff 2013 = chapter 2 here) becomes relevant only later, first in the adjudication process in section 6.4, then in the concluding remarks in section 6.5, both of which elaborate on my own thoughts on the matter. In terms of origination, however, Thesleff's personal initiative (1999, 63–67 [= 2009, 447–450]) predates our collaboration as well as my independent work (chapters 3–6, previously published as Alican 2014; 2015; 2017a; 2017b; and chapters 1 and 7, newly drafted for the present volume).

whether the first or the second, comes with a distinction between the bad and other (negative) Forms, parallel to the one between the good and other (positive) Forms. It is conceivable, perhaps even obvious to some, that Plato accepts negative Forms, the bad being one of many, if indeed there are any. But it is also conceivable, though possibly with greater dissent, that he envisages a hierarchy of negative Forms with the bad at the top. The scholarly inspiration for either view would likely come from what he does with positive Forms.

Plato, it is true, tends to bring up the good with the bad, sometimes with additional room for the ugly, reminding us today of the ensemble cast of a classic spaghetti western: *The Good, the Bad, and the Ugly*. Yet the good has a uniquely exalted position among the Forms. Plato's good comes with a status far more glorious than the edge given to the good in westerns, even where Clint Eastwood is the good guy. The *Republic* goes so far as to single out the good as the greatest object of study (*megiston mathēma* at 505a) among the greatest objects of study (*megista mathēmata* at 503e, 504a). Since the greatest objects of study are the Forms, the good is thus the most important of the Forms (*Republic* 504d–e). To cite just a few examples, the good is greater than justice and the other virtues (504d), more valuable than knowledge and truth (509a), and more substantial than "being" (*ousia*), which then gives it a superlative mode of existence (509b).

The interpretation of the "good" as more substantial than "being" is just one rendition of the corresponding passage. The original reference, *epekeina tēs ousias* (*Republic* 509b8–9), simply places the good "beyond being" without explaining what that means. One reading, contradicting the one here, takes the identification of the good as "beyond being" to strip the good of its own being, though not thereby of its existence altogether, for something that does not exist can hardly be good, let alone serving as the good. Another reading, confirming the one here, takes the identification of the good as "beyond being" to indicate nothing more than the good's superiority over being, still leaving the good itself with an existential claim to being, the same way that Zeus is himself a god despite being the king of gods, which simply makes him superior to all the rest, without removing him from their ranks.

While nothing in this chapter turns on figuring out Plato's precise meaning, I do assume without argument, and without consequence, that placing the good beyond being no more voids its being, or precludes its existence, than performing beyond expectations fails to meet expectations, or going above and beyond the call of duty constitutes a dereliction of duty.⁵ I thus take the supremacy of the good to be unproblematic in that regard. The good is clearly a superordinate Form. Nothing else is. Or to stick to the verifiable facts, the good is the only superordinate Form identified as such in the Platonic corpus. And Plato is known to have made a fuss over it in person as well.⁶

That being so, how could Plato have been comfortable invoking the good as if it were just another Form, as he plainly does in many places, for example, in the passages referenced in the opening paragraphs of this chapter and in comparably general discussions of the good (as a Form) outside the central analogies of the *Republic*? The answer, by no means universally accepted, is that he had no choice. Comfortable or not, he had only one Form for the good. He might at times have found cause for mentioning the good among other Forms without making a spectacle of it. But having loudly trumpeted the supremacy of the good, both orally and in writing, he probably saw no reason to fear being misunderstood in that regard. We are not supposed to be confused by his references to the good (as a Form), thinking he meant one thing at one time, something else at another. It is all the same superordinate Form of the good, sometimes putting in an appearance with ordinary Forms relevant to the topic on hand.

An alternative answer is that Plato had two Forms for the good rather than one. Lloyd P. Gerson (2015, 225–242), to cite a recent example, holds that Plato must, and does, employ both a "superordinate Idea of the Good" and a "coordinate Form of the Good" in order to meet the

---

5. Anyone interested in a definitive solution will find the literature practically endless, dating back at least as far as Plotinus, who quotes the relevant passage (*epekeina tēs ousias*) more than any other passage in Plato, and even more than any other in general, citing it thirty-one times by the count of one careful reader (Halfwassen 2014, 192). Among recent contributions, see Baltes (1997) for a seminal statement of the position that the good is beyond being in a comparative sense preserving its own being, and Ferber and Damschen (2015) for a formal proof of the opposite position that the good is beyond being in an absolute sense contradicting its own being (see Ferber 2017/2018).

6. The reference here is to Plato's notorious public lecture on the good. The earliest known source is Aristoxenus (*Elementa Harmonica* 2.30-31) drawing on the testimony of Aristotle. Current commentary includes, but is not limited to, Alican (2012, 84–87), Cherniss (1945, 1–30, especially 1–13), Ferber (1984), Gaiser (1980), Ross (1951, 147–149, 186–187, 199–200, 204–205, 210, 244), and Thesleff (1999, 104–105, 164–165 [= 2009, 485–486, 531]).

different needs described here. Our disagreement is important in itself but irrelevant in the context of this chapter. The focus here is on the possibility, reality, and perhaps also psychology of the negative counterparts of Forms, quite apart from how many there would be if there were any. Yet anyone interested in the quantitative question, that is, in the purported duality of the good, can pursue the matter further through an abundance of references in Gerson's piece. The use he makes of Proclus is especially informative in that regard (Gerson 2015, 230–235).

There is nothing inherently inconsistent about taking the good listed among ordinary Forms to be the same good invoked elsewhere as a superordinate Form. This is not to deny the possibility of evidentiary reasons against doing so, independently of the question of consistency, but questioning the consistency of doing so is like refusing to acknowledge the Bible as a holy book so long as it sits on the same shelf with ordinary books. We can surely tell the Bible apart from other books no matter how they are shelved or stacked. Superordinate though it may be, the Form of the good is still a Form, and, in fact, still the same Form, regardless of how many others are present, much like how the Bible is still the same book even when it is placed right next to pulp fiction, and still holy then, if it is holy to begin with. A unifying perspective of that sort affords the most consistent view of the good.

What would be the most consistent view of the bad and of negative Forms in general? The good might still be considered the only superordinate Form, with ordinary Forms coming in positive, negative, and neutral varieties. Alternatively, the bad could be assigned a special status among negative Forms, similar to the one for the good among positive Forms. One would be in keeping with what Plato says about the good (the supremacy of the good thereby prohibiting us from assuming the same for the bad); the other would be in keeping with what he does with the good (the supremacy of the good thereby inspiring us to do the same with the bad). This evinces a subtlety in the possibility of negative Forms. Is this the possibility of a random collection of ordinary negative Forms, or is it the possibility of a negative superstructure with the bad at the top of a systematic negative hierarchy?

It may be tempting to object that the good has a special place among all Forms, not just among the positive ones, leaving no room for a comparable place for the bad among negative Forms, nor among all Forms. But that will not do. It is difficult to see the good as having anything to do with negative Forms (if there are any), and it is outright contradictory to take it as having the same thing to do with negative Forms (if there are any) that it has to do with positive Forms. A negative hierarchy is not an abomination. We need good reasons to rule it out. The fact that it is not mentioned by Plato is not a good reason. Not everything accepted by Plato need be mentioned by Plato.

To repeat, I am not concerned, at least not immediately so, with the question opening this chapter, not, that is, with whether there are negative Forms in Plato (be it at random or within a system). I am concerned, rather, with the one right after that, the question why it would occur to anyone to ask the first question, or to answer it unprompted, given that the answer seems to be in plain sight with abundant references by Plato to what appear to be negative Forms. Since the textual evidence, the direct kind anyway, is about ordinary negative Forms, with a superordinate Form of the bad requiring extrapolation, I will be pursuing the (second) question only as it pertains to ordinary negative Forms.

I am not against investigating the possibility of a special role for the bad. It is just not necessary for what I am doing here. Otherwise, it is only sensible to consider all the possibilities where we are not sure of the reality. Nails (2013), for one, has already explored this particular possibility. I myself will be content to consider negative Forms without regard to whether they are somehow shaped and sustained by the bad as the organizing principle and driving force of a negative hierarchy. This is because the second-order question with which I am concerned is not about a superordinate Form of the bad, since the direct and possibly obvious evidence, conclusive or not, is about ordinary negativity.

So, why indeed do we ask whether there are negative Forms in Plato in full awareness of passages pointing to negative Forms in Plato? The immediate motivation is either to reinforce or to reject the obvious: the appearance of negative Forms. But why do either? If Plato seems to be talking about negative Forms, why not just leave it at that? We do not bicker and dicker over the presence of positive Forms in Plato. We do not, when Plato seems to be talking about positive Forms, ask whether he is really talking about positive Forms. Why lock horns over the negative ones? Is it because there are more references to positive Forms than to negative Forms? Or is it because there seems to be a greater conviction behind the references to positive Forms than behind those to negative Forms?

I think it is neither. The typical motivation for asking (and for answering) the first question is not a reaction, favorable or unfavorable, to putative negative Forms in the texts. The typical motivation is the solution of an altogether different problem, whatever it may be, that either requires or precludes negative Forms. This is manifested in the tendency to raise the question of negative Forms as part of an effort to promote a pet theory on a related but different matter that turns on whether there are negative Forms in Plato. The pet theory can be a general interpretation of Plato or a particular position resting on a general interpretation of Plato. In either case, the outlook on negative Forms thus remains indexed to a general interpretation. Scholars are typically not moved to study Plato's references to what seems to be negative Forms out of a genuine or immediate concern with whether his intention really is to countenance negative Forms. How, then, can we verify what they say about the matter?

There is no verification. That is to say, there is no verification beyond going through Plato's specific references to putative negative Forms and attempting to determine whether the referents really are negative Forms. But we can do all that equally well (which happens to be not so well) outside the context of anyone's general interpretation of Plato. The question here is whether to accept the implications of the general interpretation for the specific problem. The only relevant consideration in that respect is whether we are persuaded: Can we trust what generalists say about negative Forms, suspecting all along that they will be inclined to say whatever makes their pet theory work, with no special regard, or at most a lesser one, for what may actually be true of negative Forms?

I believe we can. Let us not exaggerate the potential for bias in the service of vested interests. Generalists will, I imagine, be all the more careful with details and implications precisely because their own thesis is so special to them. They will want to avoid proceeding on the basis of questionable assumptions or hasty generalizations. Their particular position on negative Forms will indeed be in conformity with their general position on Plato's thought, but that is not a good reason to reject the latter, which is not a bad reason to accept the former.

Much of what we do with Plato is about trying to understand one thing without undermining what we thought we understood about another. This is not, if I may continue to speak for all of us engaged in Plato, because we are particularly slow or sloppy. It is because Plato is not sufficiently forthcoming with his thoughts. Although the Platonic corpus is not systematic philosophy, the actual interests and thoughts of its author cannot possibly have been as arbitrary as his combined output makes them out to be. A general interpretation will therefore be useful insofar as it exposes a basic outlook underlying the competing perspectives in the Platonic corpus while uniting the complementary ones. A general interpretation that works, especially one with great explanatory power, can be an acceptable proxy for a special theory on a specific topic.

This does not mean that we must accept whatever a general theory, even a good one, assumes or implies in regard to negative Forms. Nor does it mean that between any two general theories, let us say good ones, we must favor the one that is more general. What it does mean is that we ought not to reject a position on negative Forms just because it was not conceived specifically as a solution to the problem of negative Forms. And between any number of equally appealing positions, or in this case, metapositions, we have to decide which one has greater explanatory power, not which one is more general (though the same one could be both).

Does this constitute circular reasoning? Perhaps it does, at least to some extent. It follows a winding spiral, but it does not end up in a vicious circle. We are to decide what to do with certain details based on what a successful general theory tells us to do, while judging the success of that theory by whether, among other things, it is able to make sense of those details. However suspicious this approach may seem, it is not necessarily problematic. It can turn into a problem if handled badly, but it does not start out as one by design. It is, in fact, a common feature of one way of trying to understand Plato.

There is nothing wrong with trying to figure out Plato's overall philosophical outlook on the basis of what he says about certain issues (given the prohibitively exhaustive and jointly inconsistent catalog of everything he says about every issue), while also trying to determine what he says about certain issues with the help of what we make of his overall philosophical outlook. This is both acceptable and helpful so long as the set of issues invoked while going in one direction is not identical to the set of issues clarified while going in the opposite direction. And it may be acceptable even then. A circular method of interpretation could arguably be judged by its propensity to predict or explain relevant episodic details, especially bits and pieces that competing methods of interpretation do not explain clearly or convincingly.

We cannot afford to dismiss the spiral of evidence as circular reasoning if we are unable to get very far with the linear kind. But we also do not have to give up a close reading of relevant passages. The point is that a holistic approach works, not that nothing else does. It need not be followed exclusively, nor even very strictly.[7] It just ought not to be rejected out of hand.

That is how both Nails and Thesleff handle negative Forms. Each one proceeds with an assumption about negative Forms in conformity with their respective positions on a broader issue, that is, with their interpretations of Plato on a wider scale, but each one also introduces evidentiary benchmarks (in the form of passages in the corpus) to demonstrate that the assumption is consistent with the texts. Nails (2013) portrays Plato as reveling in negative Forms, complete with a hierarchy led by (the Form of) the bad, mirroring the better-known order of (the Form of) the good.[8] Thesleff (chapter 2) gives us a more conservative ontologist, wary of the negative and reluctant to make too much of it, least of all by countenancing Forms of that nature (section 2.10). Nails's Plato is open to all abstractions as potential Forms, which is why he does not weed out the negative ones. What this means is not that her Plato has a Form for every abstraction but that he is willing to consider them all without prejudice. He may (or may not) have other reasons to limit the population of Forms, but blocking the negative is not one of them. In contrast, Thesleff's Plato is preoccupied with (positive) value, eager to privilege the Forms that possess it, and ready to dismiss or discount the ones that do not. That is the basic difference between them.

Nails may be said to have the easier job because Plato already appears to endorse negative Forms, at least insofar as he seems here and there to be talking about them. By the same token, Nails may be said to have the tougher job if only because whatever she says (about negative Forms) will tend to be interpreted as confirming the obvious (regarding negative

---

7. Even Quine warns against exaggerating holism, at least his own holism, specifically by taking it to preclude empirical inquiry altogether: "I must caution against over-stating my holism. Observation sentences do have their empirical content individually, and other sentences are biased individually to particular empirical content in varying degrees" (1986, 427).

8. Nails does not insist on a superstructure of negative Forms versus a superstructure of positive Forms. This is my interpretation of a part of what she does in her approach to negative Forms (Nails 2013, 95–101). However, my assessment of her demonstration that Plato accepts negative Forms does not depend on this particular interpretation, which is therefore discussed only incidentally at the end of the chapter (section 6.5), where it would no longer be disrupting the discussion in progress.

Forms). In an important sense, however, neither one has this job at all, since each one sets out to do something else entirely.

In the final analysis, alignment with or against either Nails or Thesleff will not be a matter of whether they do a good job with negative Forms. If we were in a position to judge that, we would not need to mine their derivative input for primary insight. It will instead be a matter of whether they enrich our understanding of Plato. Even if they both do so, and certainly if they both do so equally well, a choice will be necessary, for their views are mutually inconsistent despite the absence of a direct contradiction. It will then be a matter of whose Plato is closer to our own. And since the only sense in which we can have our own Plato is distributive rather than collective, I will be summoning my own where necessary.

I do not mean to ignore other contributions. But these two stand out with the depth and gravity of their stake in the matter. My aim, in any case, is not to survey the literature. It is to show that and how and why the question of negative Forms tends to be treated as a derivative problem, and more importantly, to see if anything in that treatment can be adopted toward a better understanding of the primary problem. A focused case study is better suited for that task than would be a sweeping survey. To return to the distinction in the beginning of the chapter, this means exploring the second question for insight into the first question.

6.2. Embracing Negative Forms with Debra Nails

Nails (2013) finds plenty of room for negative Forms in Plato. She finds it all in the course of developing a separate argument (88–101) that requires negative Forms (95–101) as a premise.[9] Her main concern is with a problem that works out the way she wants only if Plato countenances negative Forms. It could possibly go her way even without negative Forms, but that is a detail best left for later, especially since negative Forms make her argument stronger than otherwise.

Fortunately, the default position on negative Forms happens to be that they do belong in Plato's ontology.[10] Yet Nails expands on the default

---

9. A critique of this argument may be found in Franklin (2013, 102–109), but the objections there are not relevant here.

10. The acknowledgment of a default position may not seem consistent with the search for an answer, but it is actually quite consistent, given that the aim of the chapter is to answer the second question (why we keep confirming or challenging the default

position instead of merely drawing on it. She not only presents evidence and arguments in support of negative Forms but also takes issue with the common objection that negative Forms (e.g., the bad, the ugly, the unjust) are nothing more than privations of positive ones (e.g., the good, the beautiful, the just). She finds that objection inconsistent with the texts (2013, 96). Her own reading is that Plato ranks negative Forms right up there with positive ones, holding them on a conceptual and methodological par with their more popular counterparts.

Nails thus maintains not just that there are negative Forms in Plato but also that their claim to being a Form is just as valid as the corresponding claim of positive Forms. Positive or negative, a Form is a Form is a Form. Hence, the ugly, the unjust, and any other negative Forms are all Forms in their own right, not privations of their respective counterparts among positive Forms. The bad, however, stands out: It is not an ordinary Form. Nor is it merely the absence of the good. It is, like the good, a special or privileged Form. To borrow the adjective favored by Nails, it is a "robust" Form (2013, 96, 99, 100).

Convinced that negative Forms are more than the ontological residue of imagining away the positive ones, Nails illustrates her position through the framework of opposition in Platonic metaphysics. She distinguishes between two basic manifestations of opposition in Forms (Nails 2013, 96): Some Forms are opposed to each other as the extreme ends of a continuum (e.g., motion and rest, sameness and difference, hot and cold), while others are mutually exclusive with no gradation in between (e.g., life and death, odd and even, finite and infinite). The main difference, beyond the association of mutual exclusiveness with the second group but not with the first (at least not explicitly so), seems to be that the paired elements in the first group (but evidently not those in the second) "might well be described as privations of one another, though neither need be considered negative" (Nails 2013, 96).

What does this mean for negative Forms? We get a better idea through the position Nails assigns to the good and the bad in her classification. She places the good and the bad in the first category (2013,

---

position) rather than, or at least before, the first question (whether there is a default position at all). The sense in which the acceptance of negative Forms constitutes the default position is that, despite the fact that Plato scholars are typically not concerned with the subject unless and until it affects something they are concerned with, there is prima facie textual evidence in support of it and no particular evidence in contradiction of it.

96). Given her earlier distinctions, this would seem to suggest (1) that the good and the bad are not mutually exclusive, and (2) that the good and the bad may possibly be privations of each other, though neither one need (for this reason alone) be considered negative (against the other as positive). Since she also acknowledges that "there is a vast range of the neither-good-nor-bad (NGNB)," we know further (3) that the good and the bad are not jointly exhaustive. We can combine the first and third implications, leaving the second one as it is in its essentials: (1) the good and the bad are neither mutually exclusive nor jointly exhaustive; (2) the good and the bad can (but need not) be privations of each other without either one being negative.

The second implication worries me. For one thing, acknowledging that the good and the bad may reasonably be considered privations of each other (and presumably just as reasonably not) seems strategically to be the opposite of what Nails ought to be doing, given that she does not want the bad (or any other putative negative Form) to turn out to be a privation. For another, adding that this, the possibility of a symmetrical privation relation, need not make either the good or the bad negative, also seems inimical to what she should be promoting, namely negative Forms. If neither the good nor the bad has to be negative, then neither one has to be a negative Form, and if neither one has to be a negative Form, then why are we talking about them, and where are the negative Forms? Without anything negative established in the scenario, the context is not about showing that a negative Form counts as a Form in its own right as opposed to a mere privation. It is instead about showing that some Form bearing an opposite, but itself not necessarily a negative Form, counts as a Form in its own right as opposed to a mere privation (and that the same holds for its opposite). Furthermore, the bad would, it seems to me, have to be considered negative if anything at all can be. How can the bad not be negative? It is the very embodiment of the negative. It is the common denominator of negativity. And it is, according to Nails herself, the sole explanation of destruction (2013, 94, 99, 100).

Perhaps I am misinterpreting what Nails is saying. Her reluctance to diagnose the negative might, in this context, indicate simply that, even if the good and the bad were privations of each other, which they are not (according to Nails), it would still not be clear which is the substantial element and which the privation, and hence, also not clear which is the positive element and which the negative. That is not quite it. Nails does not seem to be saying either that it would not be clear which is the substantial element and which the privation or that it would not be clear which is the positive element and which the negative. She seems to be saying that neither one would have to be negative even if each were the privation of the other. The only commitment she actually makes in that regard is that "neither need be considered negative" (Nails 2013, 96). This would correct my first mistake, my construal of Nails as admitting the possibility and reasonability of taking the bad as a *mere* privation of the good, just because she admits the possibility and reasonability of taking the bad as a privation of the good (in placing the good and the bad in a category of examples that "might well be described as privations of one another" [2013, 96]).

I do not know whether Nails would agree with any of this, but her correction of my mistake would probably have to run deeper, just as the mistake seems to do. The mistake to be corrected may be as basic as my supposing that the bad as a privation of the good would be a privation rather than a Form as opposed to a privation that is (or has) a Form. This would be a fundamental disagreement: whether a privation can also be a Form (or whether a privation can have a Form). I doubt that we can settle that debate here as an incidental concern, but even the recognition of it as the source of our disagreement on related issues would be a step toward constructive dialogue. Either way, there is still the matter of what would be my second mistake, my construal of Nails as leaving room for a bad that is not negative, or more specifically, a negative Form. I might here have distorted an otherwise innocuous general observation that a privation need not be negative (whether or not the bad actually is). Maybe that, too, would resolve itself upon the resolution of the more fundamental question at the root of our disagreement.

Yet even with all my misconceptions corrected, we might still disagree on the correlation between negativity and privation, despite agreeing that not all privations are negative. I would be inclined to think that the assignment of the status of privation proceeds from the prior identification of a positive element against which the privation is considered negative. It is not the other way around: We do not neutrally, that is, dispassionately, pair elements that are privations of each other, proceeding from there to value assignments. There might be cases where we do start out by pairing elements that are privations of each other, but those would be cases where we consider neither element negative, and where there would, therefore, be no value assignments to be made. The contrasting elements in the first cluster of passages Nails presents are excellent examples of privation without valuation: motion and rest, sameness and difference, hot and cold (2013, 96). But the cases where one element is positive and the other negative do not get their value assignments after a neutral identification of the privation relation. What happens instead is that we first sort out the good (the positive) and the bad (the negative) and then decide that the bad is a privation of the good (if we actually do believe that the bad is a privation of the good). What is the problem, then, if the examples Nails provides are excellent? The problem is that her good and her bad do not belong in that category of examples. The good *is* good and the bad *is* bad. The question of value does arise.

Let us grant Nails all of her claims and see what follows: The good and the bad are neither mutually exclusive nor jointly exhaustive, and neither of them has to be negative even if each one is the privation of the other. The upshot of all this, together with the supporting evidence (Nails 2013, 96–99), seems to be that the bad is a Form in its own right and that this is the case with negative Forms in general. Does this really follow as a conclusion? Yes, there is a strong presumption in its favor, emphatically so as Nails turns to citation, but there is also some clutter, which may admittedly be peculiar to my reading as opposed to her writing: If the good and the bad are not jointly exhaustive, then neither one alone can be the privation of the other (thus validating the original opposition of Nails), regardless of whether they are mutually exclusive, and regardless of which one, if either, might be negative. This is because the absence of the good stands to leave us not just with the bad but also with the neither-good-nor-bad as Nails correctly and repeatedly points out. She does not seem to need all her initial claims, though invoking them all does not damage her position.[11]

None of my objections so far overturns Nails's opposition to privation as an explanation of negative Forms, which, on that explanation, do not count as Forms. Any attempt to prove her wrong would have to contend with the examples she adduces from the Platonic corpus (Nails 2013, 96–99), especially since her main point against the privation interpretation is that "the texts do not allow it" (96). She organizes the relevant citations in two

---

11. The identification of a category where paired elements "might well be described as privations of one another, though neither need be considered negative" (Nails 2013, 96), becomes superfluous where the elements in question are not jointly exhaustive and therefore cannot be privations of each other, at least not in the sense of either one alone representing what is entailed by the absence of the other.

separate clusters, which together cover most but not all of her references to Plato. The first cluster (97), comprising six passages, one each from six dialogues, constitutes evidence that Plato found a reciprocal relationship between knowing the good and knowing the bad. The second cluster (97–99), comprising nine passages, all from the *Republic*, illustrates that "the good and its results are kept distinct from the bad and its results" (97). The first cluster supports her claim that negative Forms are Forms in their own right and not mere privations of their positive counterparts. The second cluster may also be said to do that, at least with some of the references, but its main function is to fortify her broader position against equating the unhypothetical first principle of the all with the Form of the good. That is what she is really after.

Nevertheless, it is still possible to say something relevant about her perspective on negative Forms without engaging her at the level of specific examples. Let us go back to basics: What is the motivation? Why does she need negative Forms? She needs them because Plato has to accept negative Forms alongside positive Forms if Nails is to establish her thesis that the unhypothetical first principle of the all is not identical to the Form of the good (2013, 88–101, especially 95–101). She cannot do this unless her Plato accepts and works with negative Forms, in addition, of course, to whatever else makes the world go round. Perhaps it could also be done in some other way, but this is the way she does it, and to be able to do it this way, she needs for there to be bona fide negative Forms, or rather, she needs for Plato to believe that there are bona fide negative Forms.

Under her interpretation, the Form of the good cannot account for harm or destruction, and that is why it cannot be identical to the unhypothetical first principle of the all, which can account for harm and destruction (and for everything else). The unhypothetical first principle of the all, then, covers more ground than the Form of the good. But it also covers more ground than the combined total associated with the Form of the good and the Form of the bad. This is because it alone includes "the vast range of the neither-good-nor-bad (NGNB)" (Nails 2013, 96). In some sense, the unhypothetical first principle of the all is equivalent to the Form of the good plus the Form of the bad plus everything in between or beyond, specifically "all those NGNB things made good or bad through their use" (Nails 2013, 99).

This is not the whole story. My summary so far is missing a key ingredient present in the original: the anthropocentricity of Plato's Form of the good, and for that matter, of his Form of the bad (if there is one).

Nails (2013) takes this up in several places: "Plato's form of the good is anthropocentric" (95). "Plato has a robust form of the bad, a form as intelligible as the others and yet—like the good—an anthropocentric form without application to the universe as a whole" (96). "[G]ood and bad are importantly, though not exclusively, anthropocentric" (100). This suggests that the unhypothetical first principle of the all covers not just the good, the bad, and the neither-good-nor-bad, but all that plus the nonanthropocentric senses of both the good and the bad (and perhaps also the nonanthropocentric sense of the neither-good-nor-bad if it, too, admits of that distinction).[12]

Right or wrong, this observation has implications outside the context in which it is presented. The anthropocentricity postulated seems to trickle down to places Nails does not discuss (because she does not need to for her immediate purposes). If the anthropocentricity of the good and the bad in Plato is part of what makes both the Form of the good and the Form of the bad less comprehensive than the unhypothetical first principle of the all, should it not pose an additional problem that neither the Form of the good nor the Form of the bad is as comprehensive as its own nonanthropocentric version would be? Under Nails's interpretation, Plato's (anthropocentric) Form of the good is too narrow not only as the unhypothetical first principle of the all but also as the (unqualified) Form of the good. It therefore does not work as the Form of the good it is purported to be. I am here observing rather than opposing what Nails is doing.

As for her own observation, anthropocentricity is an integral part of her opposition to the tendency to identify the unhypothetical first principle of the all with the Form of the good. It is so important that Nails could have based her entire case on this premise alone, had she been inclined to do so, without ever requiring a robust Form of the bad. She could have held the difference between the unhypothetical first principle of the all and the Form of the good to rest on the generality of the former and

---

12. Nails (2013, 94–96, 99–100) provides both reasons and references for her construal of the Form of the good as anthropocentric. I might add, without a personal inclination either way, that her position seems to be confirmed by the author of the *Seventh Letter*, who declares that "there is nothing worth mentioning that is either good or bad to creatures without souls, but good and evil exist only for a soul, either joined with a body or separated from it" (334e–335a).

the anthropocentricity of the latter. This is not an objection to Nails such that she should have done this instead. It is a note to the reader such that she could have done this instead. That is how relevant and important her observation is (especially for her own thesis).

On the other hand, had she done it that way, she would have ended up with a less significant difference between the unhypothetical first principle of the all and the Form of the good. She would have had to settle for an unhypothetical first principle of the all that is basically the Form of the good without an anthropocentric bias. And she would not have needed negative Forms for that. As it is, she does need them. It is to meet that need that she adduces textual evidence supporting the existence of negative Forms, particularly the Form of the bad but also others.

I am not convinced, however, that the evidence is conclusive. I will not challenge her examples one by one. They obviously support her position. It is the default position anyway. What I want to know is whether the reasoning that leads Nails to her position on negative Forms as genuine Forms successfully rules out the alternative that they are instead privations of corresponding positive Forms. The crux of her argument seems to be this:

> Since the good that opposes the bad and makes NGNB [neither-good-nor-bad] things good cannot cause harm or destruction, but harm and destruction do exist, there must be something else that harms and destroys. (Nails 2013, 99)

Why? Why must there be something else that harms and destroys? Nails and Plato have an answer:

> The bad is what destroys and corrupts, and the good is what preserves and benefits. . . . And do you say that there is a good and a bad for everything? . . . for the good would never destroy anything, nor would anything neither good nor bad. (Plato: *Republic* 608e4–7, 609b1–2, as quoted by Nails 2013, 99)

But that is not what I am asking. I am not asking why there must be something that harms and destroys. I am asking why there must be something else that harms and destroys. Might not the privation of the good work as an explanation of the bad, naturally covering harm and destruction as well, without requiring a separate cause dedicated to negativity: a robust Form of the bad?[13]

An apple a day keeps the doctor away. Take the apple away, the doctor comes to stay. Is this not a good explanation? It is admittedly not the best, but what exactly is wrong with it? There are, to be sure, better accounts of physical ailment. Yet if the absence of the apple is not the cause of harm and destruction, or in this case a sufficient explanation of disease, that is only because its presence was never the source of health in the first place, nor a sufficient explanation thereof. What we are facing is not an explanation that works in the first case but not in the second. What we are facing is an explanation that cannot consistently be dismissed in the second case unless it is dismissed in the first. Even if it is not a good explanation, or the correct explanation, it is a coherent explanation, because it attributes both the positive and the negative to the same cause, present in one case, absent in the other. This would not be the first time Plato came up with an explanation that did not strike our fancy.[14]

Ain't no sunshine when she's gone! Do we really need another explanation? Not if we want to enjoy the song. But if we want a weather report, we need more information, if not a different explanation. This one has limited value. Although we know not to expect sunshine when she is gone, there is no guarantee there will be sunshine when she is here, just an implication to that effect for those who want to see it. Nor do we know for sure that she is absent every time the sun is absent. We know only the converse, that the sun is absent whenever she is.

These are all gaps in the association, but they are easily fixed. The real problem is hidden underneath. Let us ignore the superficial issues and turn to the real problem. Let us assume, therefore, not that the song depicts a partial correlation, one limited to the mutual absence of the sun and the heroine, but that it draws on a complete causal relationship such that she bringeth forth the sun just as surely as she taketh it away.[15] That

---

13. Thesleff, it seems, would have joined me in this reaction even before our collaboration (chapter 2, section 2.10): "Evil is no active force: evil is imperfection and the chaotic state of lower-level tendencies getting the upper hand" (1999, 124 [= 2009, 505]).

14. Note by way of connection with chapter 2 (sections 2.6 and 2.10) that if Plato indeed holds Forms proper ("Ideal Forms") to have positive intrinsic value, he might well associate negativity with the absence of the positive, an absence that can all the same be filled partly by the neutral.

15. This is still poetic shorthand for the causal relationship, which can be expressed as the mutual satisfaction of the following conditions: (1) there is no sunshine when

must be what is meant anyway, given that we are talking, with poetic license, about someone so special. The problem, however, is that her absence is not as revealing as her presence. No sunshine. That, we know. But how do we explain the rain? Where does all the snow come from? What brings on the tornadoes and the hurricanes?

Suppose there ain't no sunshine and she's gone. Should we expect a drizzle or a blizzard? Or just overcast skies? It is hard to tell. It would help if we knew whether there's a bad moon on the rise. It might help even more if we knew whether there's trouble on the way. The absence of sunshine does not always mean we're in for nasty weather. But that is just when to expect it. Although it need not rain cats and dogs every time the sun is gone (as is she), it would indeed be more likely to do so (if at all) when the sun is gone (as is she). The poet probably intended the absence of sunshine as a blanket reference to conditions conducive to bad weather, ranging from scattered showers to biblical floods. But where is the poetry in that? We leave the art behind as we turn to the science, and vice versa, but we need not be ignorant of one just because we are focusing on the other.

Plato is a poet too. He knows very well that the absence of the good does not automatically translate into the presence of the bad. He trusts us to make that distinction—and to trust him to make it in silence. It is as a poet, I think, that he leaves it all to the good, and to its absence, not bothering to fill in the details with the bad. Nor do we need to invent a Form for the bad in order to work out those details. The possibility is there, but the requirement is not. If the absence of the good is no more likely, in any particular case, to leave us with the bad than it is to leave us with the neither-good-nor-bad, a Form for the bad is no more useful, or necessary, than a Form for the neither-good-nor-bad. Given that they both represent the privation of the good, and given that they do that better together than on their own, why would we ever need a Form for one but not for the other? I do not believe we need a Form for either. I believe we have all the Forms we need.

---

she is gone; (2) she is gone when there is no sunshine; (3) there is sunshine when she is here; (4) she is here when there is sunshine. From the opposite perspective, there is never a case when she is here but the sun is not shining, or when the sun is shining but she is not here. And none of this obviously has anything to do with the difference between night and day, instead representing a daytime difference between sunshine and its absence (obstruction).

6.3. Rejecting Negative Forms with Holger Thesleff

Thesleff rejects negative Forms in Plato.[16] He maintains that any and all apparently negative Forms are instead negative concepts or abstractions. Since Forms belong to the highest ranks of Plato's ontology, while mere concepts and abstractions do not, Thesleff thus stands out with a more restricted population for Forms than acknowledged by most other scholars.

But where exactly does Plato draw this distinction between Forms and mere concepts? Where does he explain the difference between abstractions that are Forms (or have Forms) and abstractions that are not Forms (or do not have Forms)? That would be nowhere.[17] Plato does not employ (or even have) a second-order language to describe Forms in terms of concepts or abstractions. We have to use our own if we are so inclined. Thesleff's point, on the other hand, is not that the distinction is explicit in this or that dialogue, but that it goes better with what we know of Plato than does a predisposition to accept absolutely anything as a Form.

We would not be able to get past the first few pages of the *Parmenides* if we were to assign the same weight to everything admitting of abstraction. That dialogue gives us a Socrates who is certain that there are Forms for justice, beauty, and goodness (130b), certain again that there are no Forms for hair, mud, or dirt (130c–d), but ambivalent as to whether there might be any for man, fire, and water (130c). The sample size may not be large enough to draw conclusions about the general population with any confidence, but the premium on value is hard to miss. Everything that makes the cut happens to be intrinsically good. Everything else is met with either hesitation or out-and-out rejection. The defining difference is intrinsic value. The only things the passage identifies as Forms are those that are good in themselves (valuable for their own sakes). If those lacking positive intrinsic value are at best held in abeyance, and just as easily

---

16. His most forceful stand is in Alican and Thesleff (2013), reproduced with modifications as chapter 2 (see section 2.10) of the present volume, though his resistance can be traced back to Thesleff (1999, 63–67 [= 2009, 447–450]).

17. I am not claiming that concepts and abstractions are the same thing. I am merely reporting that Forms tend to be compared and contrasted, and indeed even confused, both with concepts and with abstractions. See chapter 1 (section 1.3), chapter 2 (sections 2.7 and 2.11), chapter 3 (sections 3.2, 3.4, 3.5), chapter 4 (section 4.4), and chapter 5 (section 5.3) for what we might, in the absence of instructions by Plato, be able to make of the distinction between Forms and either mere concepts or mere abstractions.

dismissed altogether, why should there be, and how could there be, any Forms that carry negative value? Or to put it crudely, if hair, mud, and dirt are not good enough, how can injustice, ugliness, or evil ever qualify?

The answer I am fishing for, rather transparently at that, is that they never can. I am, of course, cheating. Such a controversial conclusion cannot be established with a single reference unless the message is beyond dispute. This particular passage remains open to interpretation. The restriction imposed on the population of Forms is not as authoritative as it might seem. We have evidence to the contrary, for example, in the character of Parmenides, who immediately opposes (130e) Socrates's inclination to reject Forms for "worthless" things such as hair, mud, and dirt. This then undermines the sole reason for invoking the passage as supporting Plato's rejection of negative Forms. We do not know whether to look to Socrates or to Parmenides (or to both or to neither) for what Plato thinks about the matter. It is clear, at any rate, that we are not to ignore the explicit warning of the older and wiser Parmenides. Even more indicative is the self-criticism of Socrates, who expresses misgivings about the consistency of attributing Forms to some things while denying them to others (130d). Must the assignment of Forms be so comprehensive as to leave nothing without a Form?[18] Whatever the answer to that question, there is too much dramatic opposition here to read this passage as a categorical rejection of negative Forms.

Yet the *Parmenides* is not the only dialogue to spurn negative Forms. The Forms mentioned in the central myth of the *Phaedrus* (246e–249d), each one favored beyond a doubt, and all of them positive without exception, are entirely consistent with the ones eagerly accepted as Forms in the *Parmenides* (130b). Beheld upon the completion of the cosmic ascent of the soul, these Forms include justice, temperance, knowledge, and such (247d), together with beauty (249d, 250b, 250d–e), which shines even more brightly than the rest, with glimpses of it available in our phenomenal experience as well. The list is representative rather than exhaustive. But it is easy to tell that hair and mud and dirt are not meant to be included. And there is no mention of man or fire or water. Nor is there an elderly sage warning us not to underestimate such things. They are not there anyway. All we have is the good stuff.

---

18. See chapter 5 for the possibility of Formless things (section 5.3) and empty Forms (section 5.4).

This is the sublime vision awaiting the soul (of the philosopher) upon its attainment of spiritual purification and intellectual enlightenment, not to mention the various gods, who are presumably already purified and enlightened to some extent even before the journey. Mortals and gods alike, the latter with greater success, travel to the outer edges of the heavens to behold the Forms in their full glory.[19] No wonder there is no room in the *Phaedrus* for any of the muck rejected in the *Parmenides*. Judging by the short list (justice, temperance, knowledge, beauty), nary a negative Form will be found there either. This is no place for negative Forms. And that, contends Thesleff, is because there is no place for negative Forms.

Thesleff does not allow any reification of negativity in his interpretation of Plato. But why should everything negative (e.g., injustice, ugliness, evil) be restricted to insubstantial concepts while positive phenomena (e.g., justice, beauty, goodness) are hailed as fully fledged Forms? And what are we to make of the various neutral abstractions that look like they belong somewhere in the middle, apparently qualifying as more than concepts, though hardly deserving designation as Forms? No neutral items we come up with, nor the ones that come up in the *Parmenides*, will be as good as the positive ones, but they are also not going to be as bad as the negative ones. Would they not need a category of their own then: "neither-Forms-nor-concepts," or more perspicuously, "not-quite-Forms-but-more-than-concepts," possibly to be abbreviated for convenience to something like "überconcepts"? Maybe so. Classification and specification can be useful, but a single category may not be enough. The category of the neutral in the *Parmenides*, for example, does not seem to be homogeneous, as it includes significant items, such as man, fire, and water, as well as insignificant ones, such as hair, mud, and dirt. If Thesleff is going to be insisting on a distinction between the positive and the negative, associating Forms with one, but not with the other, should he not tell us what to do with everything in between? He should. And he does.

Thesleff is not just suspicious of the negative. He is vigilant across the board. He can even be open to one neutral Form while rejecting another. He is picky. And that is what accounts for his opposition to the negative. We may, then, start with the negative, even though that is where Thesleff ends (see chapter 2, section 2.10). He does, after all, reject the

---

19. The myth (*Phaedrus* 246e–249d) has two distinct parts, starting with the gods (246e–247e) and moving on to human souls (248a–249d).

negative, lock, stock, and barrel, no matter how flexible or finicky he is about everything else. Indeed, let us ask why.

Thesleff's resistance to negativity is motivated by a vision of Plato's ontology that precludes negative Forms.[20] This may seem like a circular answer, but it is the actual reason. It is not a direct answer, as he has never been asked the question, at least not in print. Nevertheless, it is his position. Thesleff has to reject negative Forms.

The vision that dictates his rejection covers more than Plato's ontology.[21] It is, in essence, a general outlook on Plato's philosophical orientation, thereby observable in his ontology as well. And that outlook simply does not work with negative Forms. But Thesleff also prepares individual cases against some of the strongest candidates for negative Forms independently of the general outlook precluding negative Forms (chapter 2, section 2.10). Because of this overlapping coverage, it may at times be difficult to tell whether he is opposed to negative Forms because the cumulative evidence shows that Plato is opposed to them or because his own overarching perspective on Plato rules out negative Forms.

That, however, is not a problem. If we find Thesleff convincing, it should not matter whether it is because we find his overall interpretation compelling, and consequently stand ready to reject anything that contradicts it, or because we find his specific objections to prominent examples of negative Forms persuasive. The general vision may indeed be more effective than the specific objections, given that it is difficult to prove the negative, especially piecemeal: This one is not a negative Form, that one is not a negative Form, and so on to infinity.

---

20. The vision I have in mind, as elucidated below in the main text, is the unitary pluralism Thesleff and I have been championing, both separately and together, as the proper way of reading Plato. The inspiration originates as a two-level monism with Thesleff (1989, 4 [n. 14], 14 [n. 45], 24–25; 1993b, 17–45; explained: 20–22, 35–37; illustrated: 23–35; 1999 [= 2009, 383–506]), but the present formulation combining a monism of worlds with a pluralism of things begins to take shape in our collaborative account in chapter 2 (see especially the first three sections). The interpretive platform continues to unfold in subsequent chapters, expanding rather than either abandoning or merely retracing the main lines of the joint initiative.

21. Critics tend to be quick to find an anachronism in such statements. I am not suggesting that Plato himself distinguished between the various branches of philosophy, just that there is no harm in our doing so, even in discussing his philosophy.

Thesleff should not, in any event, be expected to present a case against each and every putative negative Form in the Platonic corpus. There are surely not as many reasons for rejecting negative Forms as there are candidates for negative Forms. One should be able to detect a pattern for rejection after a few key cases. And Thesleff does present quite a few key cases (chapter 2, section 2.10). They might even be sufficiently representative of the whole for readers to decide whether to side with Thesleff or to stand against him. I personally find the general vision more persuasive, or rather, persuasive enough not to require the specific cases to serve as additional proofs, better taken instead as supplementary considerations working in an explanatory capacity.[22]

Regarding the general vision, a skeletal sketch is all we need here. This is not just because the original is easily accessible and clear enough on its own (Thesleff 1989; 1993b; 1999 [= 2009, 383–506]; see chapter 2, section 2.10, in the present volume) but also because expository and critical commentary is readily available (chapters 3–5 here). Thesleff's Plato is not the thoroughgoing metaphysical dualist he is often made out to be. His Plato does not distinguish between the world in which we live and the world in which the Forms dwell. They are one and the same. Forms and particulars together outline a gradation of reality in the only world there is. This is the unitary pluralism of a hierarchical stratification of reality with two main levels and countless subdivisions in between (Thesleff 1993b, 20–22, 35–37; 1999, 11–52 [= 2009, 397–436]; see chapter 2 above, especially sections 2.2 and 2.3).

The Forms occupy the top level but not as a uniform class of entities. They are not simply one kind of thing, undifferentiated in any way. The intelligible phenomena we have come to know, one and all, as Forms, are actually a motley crew of ontologically distinct and distinctive constructs (or entities) emerging from (or discovered through) Plato's thought experiments in concept formation.[23] They are best taken up in

---

22. This is, in fact, exactly how the specific cases are intended. While my assessment may smack of privileged insight into intentions, it is nothing more than a reflection of our collaboration (Alican and Thesleff 2013 = chapter 2 here). See the end of the present section for more on the function of the specific cases.

23. The construct/entity distinction is a matter of perspective: Those who do not share Plato's commitment to the existence of Forms could well take them to be constructs conjured up by Plato in thought experiments. Those who agree with Plato that the

three categories: Ideal Forms, Conceptual Forms, Relational Forms (see chapter 2, section 2.4):

- Ideal Forms are the transcendent sources of unconditioned positive value in our phenomenal experience. The value in question is not limited to moral value as in goodness, or aesthetic value as in beauty, or religious value as in piety, instead being broadly consistent with anything of intrinsic value: for example, justice, temperance, knowledge (*Phaedrus* 247d). This makes Ideal Forms the objectively real and metaphysically perfect paradigms of all that is good in and of itself.

- Conceptual Forms are reified concepts with an ontological eminence falling short of Ideal Forms. They, too, are objectively real, but their phenomenal manifestations are not intrinsically valuable. Typical examples are types (e.g., man, bed, fire) and properties (e.g., tall, hard, hot), though the broad spectrum of actual cases may also include various other phenomena, such as events, actions, experiences, and possibly even mental states.

- Relational Forms are relational universal concepts reified as the ontological and cosmological building blocks of reality. They come in pairs of correlative universal relations representing complementary metaphysical categories, as illustrated by the pairing of rest with motion, and same with other, all familiar from the "greatest kinds" (*megista genē*) of the *Sophist* (254d–e). The apparent opposition is strictly complementary rather than contradictory.

These are types of Forms in the sense that they represent various episodes in Plato's lifelong experimentation with abstraction. The spotlight is on Ideal Forms. The other two can sometimes approximate to Ideal

---

Forms are objectively real could instead characterize them as entities discovered through such thought experiments. I leave the matter open here (by supplying parenthetical alternatives) because the existence of the Forms is not relevant to the question(s) I am exploring in this chapter.

Forms, under certain conditions, through a phenomenon or process called "ontological ascent" (see chapter 2, sections 2.7 and 2.11). But this does not blur the boundaries between the three categories. Most importantly, Ideal Forms are the only ones with intrinsic value. The other two may come to embody nearly all the features of Ideal Forms (chapter 2, section 2.6), but never intrinsic value, which is had either naturally (essentially) or not at all. Something that is not intrinsically valuable may come to be valued for something that is, perhaps eventually coming by association to be valued for itself, but that is not the same as its being valuable simply by virtue of what it is, that is, without the intermediation of the facilitating association.

It is this emphasis on value that precludes negative Forms. Negative Ideal Forms are out of the question since positive intrinsic value is a defining feature in their case. But that is not all. The emphasis on value is so extensive as to shape Plato's tendencies in reifying universals in the first place (see chapter 2, sections 2.7 and 2.11). Not all concepts are Forms, just the important ones. And the importance is the importance to Plato. He decides, because it is his "theory" (labeled as such by convention but actually more of an outlook than a theory). This explanation may seem simplistic. But that is how simple the matter really is. Forms come from among the concepts Plato finds universally important, significant, or valuable in some way or other. The odds are stacked from the outset against negative concepts. Perhaps some may turn out to be Conceptual Forms, but none can qualify as an Ideal Form, while Relational Forms are not even relevant in this context.[24]

The allusion to the possibility of negative Conceptual Forms is intended only in admission of the fuzzy distinction between concepts and Conceptual Forms.[25] It is not a standard feature of Thesleff's analysis of the negative in Plato. Then again, no attempt to separate concepts from Conceptual Forms in the Platonic corpus can be entirely free of doubt and

---

24. Relational Forms may perchance appear to be relevant because they come in pairs of contrasting elements, one of which is "dominant" in relation to the other. The contrast, however, is between complementary counterparts, not polar opposites. One "dominates" but the other is not negative. The most extensive coverage of the distinction is in chapter 2 (sections 2.8 and 2.10).

25. See chapter 2 (section 2.7.1) for a discussion of the ontology of concept formation in Plato as "conceptualization and formalization" (reification). See chapter 3 (section 3.5) for further analysis of the same process as a "continuum of abstraction."

hesitation. Thesleff admits, for example, that "anything Plato was willing and able to conceptualize ended up as a Conceptual Form" (pp. 95, 164, this volume). Does this include negative concepts? Not by intention, but it does seem open to that implication if one wishes to force the issue, since anything at all, and thereby negative concepts as well, would fall under an unqualified reference to "anything."

Against this implication, however, we must note, if we are fair, that the admission just quoted does not contradict the emphasis on Plato's value assignments and preference patterns. On the contrary, it exemplifies that emphasis to perfection and should therefore be interpreted against negative Conceptual Forms. For why would Plato have been "willing to" conceptualize what he did not find valuable?[26] And how could he have been "able to" conceptualize what remained below his threshold of significance, or importance, as negative concepts clearly would have been? Value, the primary qualification for proper reification, is not simply lacking but actually reversed in what would otherwise be negative Forms of any sort. Who would want a good-for-nothing Form? Worse, who would want a bad Form? Not Thesleff. And, so he tells us, not Plato either.

Hardly any hesitation, as in distinguishing concepts from Conceptual Forms, accompanies Thesleff's resolve to reject negative Forms: "Plato is evidently reluctant to speak of negatively valued conceptual Forms" (1999, 51 [= 2009, 435–436]; "conceptual" begins with a capital "C" from 2013 onward, as documented in chapter 2 of the present volume). While this particular observation is specifically in the context of *Phaedo* 105d, Thesleff's overall outlook shows him to be identifying a general tendency in Plato in addition to assessing usage in that passage (perhaps drawing on or confirming a previously identified general tendency in the process of assessing usage in that passage). He supplies the broader context for the observation before sharing the observation itself: "Here [*Phaedo*] as elsewhere Plato is unable to imagine a cosmic opposition of 'good' and 'evil'" (Thesleff 1999, 49 [= 2009, 434]). Note also that "Plato sees the conflict between opposites as a matter of the lower level" (Thesleff 1999, 50 [= 2009, 435]) and "takes it for granted that there is no antagonism or conflict of opposites on the higher level" (1999, 52 [= 2009, 436]). Since

---

26. Thesleff denies that bad or evil holds much interest for Plato (1999, 28 [= 2009, 412]). He claims that Plato is interested in just the opposite: "minimizing the significance of 'evil'" (Thesleff 1999, 32 [= 2009, 417], n. 63).

all Forms, and not just Ideal Forms, occupy the higher level, this leaves no room for negative Conceptual Forms.

Even if Thesleff could be read as somehow leaving the door open for (a few) negative Conceptual Forms, that would be as far as negative concepts could go, and it is neither certain nor likely, just conceivable from our perspective, that they would even make it that far. Thesleff is confident that he has enough evidence to conclude that there are "certainly no Ideas [= 'Ideal Forms' in chapter 2 above] (except in playful thought experiments) for negative notions such as 'violence,' 'ignorance,' or indeed 'evil'" (1999, 120 [= 2009, 502]). "Mark well," he urges, "there is no αὐτό τό κακὸν, αὐτό τό ἄδικον for Plato" (Thesleff 1999, 52 [= 2009, 436]).

As for cases where Thesleff goes through original passages with putative negative Forms in an effort to suggest alternative interpretations (chapter 2, section 2.10), they are not so much individual proofs or arguments against the possibility of negative Forms as they are systematic demonstrations of how to dig beneath the surface to avoid misinterpretation. They are intended as heuristic guidelines for reading examples that might otherwise be misconstrued as negative Forms. The idea is that the putative negative Forms we tend to come across in various dialogues are not proper Forms but abstractions falling short of Forms. To be plausible, this would have to be a general shortcoming, not a collection of random problems. In other words, the abstractions failing to qualify as Forms would have to have a common explanation for that failure. And that common explanation is the lack of positive value in the examples rejected. Positive value that is intrinsic automatically passes the litmus test toward qualification as an Ideal Form. Any other association with positive value, as well as the neutral absence thereof, is up for consideration in connection with one of the other two types of Forms. But outright negative value is not.

6.4. The Semblance and Structure of Negativity in Plato

My resistance to negative Forms is not reducible to the song and dance of my metaphorical response to Nails: Ain't no sunshine when she's gone. My suspicions, I confess, originated precisely at that level of abstraction, mainly as a devil's advocate. But they quickly matured through the dialectical orientation against negativity, particularly against systematic negativity and negative causal principles, in the general vision I have been advocating with Thesleff regarding a tripartite classification of Forms in the upper level of a monistic reality representing unitary pluralism.[27] Objective checks and balances, beyond any in the general vision mentioned, have also been instrumental. The ones I have in mind may not confirm my suspicions beyond a doubt, but they do keep me from feeling bad about remaining skeptical, or even in complete dissent, on the matter of ideal negativity.

One such example, prejudicing me against a singular superordinate negative force or Form, though not against any ordinary ones, comes late in the *Republic*. The relevant passage constitutes part of a proof (608c–612a) for the immortality of the soul, drawing on the major premise (609a–b) that the soul, like everything else, is susceptible to destruction only through its own evil and not through any other (and therefore not through a generic one).[28] Everything, we are told, has a specific evil common and peculiar to its kind, and that is the only way anything can be destroyed at all. These special patterns of destruction, then, leave no need, nor much room, for a broadly applicable destructive force.[29] While this particular appeal, if successful, works only against a cosmic destroyer, and not against specific negative Forms, in fact, confirming specific negative forces, other examples in other dialogues tend to be relevant in either case.

Another passage diverting me from idealizing the bad, be it as a supreme destroyer or as an ordinary one, is the scientific explanation of disease in the *Timaeus*: chemical imbalance at an elemental level (82a–b). This account, presumed obvious in the dramatic setting of the dialogue, is said to apply not just to disease but to decay, degradation, and degeneration in the broadest sense, actually to an "infinity of diseases and degenerations" (82b). As for diseases of the soul, even there, the cause is a privation, or at least a deficiency, specifically of intelligence, a shortage of which results in folly (*anoia*), identified as a disease, which, in turn, manifests itself either as madness (*mania*) or as ignorance (*amathia*) (86b).

The ultimate destruction, that of the soul, is envisaged in one part of the *Phaedo* as a breakdown or dispersal of sorts, hence again as a struc-

---

27. See chapter 2 for our collaboration and subsequent chapters for my elaboration.

28. See Alican (2012, 458–462) for further discussion of this proof (the "patterns of destruction argument" of the *Republic*).

29. There may still be both a need and some room for a broadly applicable destructive force if the way that destruction works is through the participation of these distinctive patterns of destruction (together with the unique evil inherent in each) in a superordinate Form of the bad (or of evil). In that case, this would not be a conclusive counterexample, and it could, in fact, go the other way.

tural problem arising without external intervention, and fully explicable internally within the local system in which it occurs. One of the dialogue's several proofs for the immortality of the soul is dedicated exclusively to alleviating the fear of such destruction (78b–80b for the main argument, 80c–84b for the accompanying mythos).[30] That sort of destruction, however, is not consistent with a universal principle of destruction, which, to be universal, must be effective beyond the things that come apart on their own.

Later in the same dialogue, after it is established, to apparent dramatic satisfaction, that the soul is not the kind of thing that is subject to dispersal or disintegration, because it has no parts or particles to break down or come apart, the discussion shifts to whether the soul can perish in some other way, whatever that may be. The destroyer then contemplated is death (*Phaedo* 105b–107a), a destructive force unique to living things, thus relevant only to the soul, with or without a body, and therefore not applicable to anything else, which is to say, not generically universal.[31] Hence, death is at most an ordinary Form, not a superordinate one, though it may not be a Form at all, certainly not an Ideal Form.

The role of death as a destructive force, even without universal relevance, may appear to contradict the position I am defending against ordinary negative Forms, but not so much when one considers the conclusion of the argument (*Phaedo* 105b–107a): Death fails! Not a single soul is ever destroyed by it, not one life ever extinguished. This is a resounding conclusion. It is also a compelling consideration against taking death seriously as a Platonic Form. Life is entirely successful in animating the soul, whereas death invariably fails to terminate it. Either death is not a Form or it is the only one that does not work.

Another striking example awaits in the *Symposium* (188a–b), where we learn that even love (Eros) can cause death and destruction, or possibly that only love can do so, though the latter interpretation is open to question. It may be objected, in either case, that this is the position of

---

30. A critical analysis of this proof (the "analogic argument" of the *Phaedo*) is available in Alican (2012, 418–424) as well as in two places in the present volume (chapter 4, section 4.3, and chapter 7, section 7.6). Each one of these provides a different perspective, though none in contradiction of the others.

31. See Alican (2012, 446–450) for further discussion of the corresponding proof (the "causal argument" of the *Phaedo*, often referred to simply as the "final argument") and Alican (2012, 391–491) for extended commentary on the *Phaedo* in general.

Eryximachus, whose appearance as a speaker is limited to a single dialogue, which then counts against the plausibility of his speaking for Plato. I will gladly concede this point if the alternative is to enter into a debate on how to pick and choose between the dramatic mouthpieces traditionally attributed to Plato, but I might then ask the opposition to demonstrate the reliability of its own witnesses for what Plato thought.

Whatever we are supposed to make of that, it is ironic, no doubt, that love should be a destructive force. And it is doubly ironic that the good doctor should even be speaking of destruction, given that his sworn duty is first and foremost to do no harm, and then to prevent it, or failing that, to reverse it. The dialogue's various references to Apollo (*Symposium* 190e, 197a) and to Asclepius (186e) are quite likely intended to emphasize that irony. The manifest irony here may only undermine the presentation of love as a destructive force, but the cumulative evidence moves me to question the attribution of a cosmic causality of any sort to destruction.

I do not claim that the foregoing examples show a Form of the bad (or of evil) to be inconceivable. I claim that they show it to be unnecessary, and hence, its requirement to be unjustified. Some of them, or perhaps all of them together, may even overcome, or at least escape, the challenge Nails poses: "The privation view cannot be right for Plato because the texts do not allow it" (2013, 96). The references Nails (2013, 96–99) provides do indeed support that conclusion. As is often the case in Plato, however, something that is not allowed in some of the texts might be allowed in others. That is what seems to be the case here.

That is why the subtitle of this chapter is "Does Plato Make Room for Negative Forms in His Ontology?" and not "Might There Be Any Room for Negative Forms in Plato's Ontology?" The same choice governs the opening question of the chapter: "Are there any negative Forms in Plato?" This is not the same as asking whether any negative Forms could conceivably be ascribed to the ontological scheme discernible in any of the dialogues. It is even less like asking without context whether there are any negative Forms at all. The question is whether Plato, in fact, recognizes them.

The reason I have avoided alternative formulations is not that I am against trying to figure out what to make of something left open in the Platonic corpus. If I were to rule that out, I myself would have very little to say about Plato. My intention, rather, has been to emphasize that the ideal is to determine Plato's own position. That is not always possible. But it is still better to keep working with what Plato said, building on it where both necessary and possible at the same time, as opposed to moving straight to what he should have said, which is typically a manifestation of what we think a reasonable person would have said under the circumstances.

When we are not sure what Plato's position is, we are often tempted to work out the most reasonable position as a substitute. Other things being equal, the most reasonable position is indeed a fitting tribute to Plato. Like most of us, however, Plato never once, I am sure, said anything that did not seem reasonable to him personally, at least at the time that he said it. While it is good to be charitable, and even better when it is needed, it may not always be required, or even appropriate. We have much to gain from remaining open to the possibilities. We should, for example, be prepared to work with less obvious alternatives if they fit the context better than those that seem more compelling from our point of view, or if they have greater explanatory power, especially in regard to the whole, or to a helpfully large or relevant portion of it.

That is the kind of choice facing us with Nails and Thesleff. Nails's answer is intuitively more appealing. Thesleff's answer has greater explanatory power. He tells us more about Plato than she does. Both Nails and Thesleff tell us what to do with putative negative Forms. And they both say what they say in connection with something more important they have to say. The difference is in this more important thing they are each after in the process of evaluating negative Forms.

Nails tells us that the unhypothetical first principle of the all is not (identical to) the Form of the good. There is room besides for a Form of the bad and for countless other things that are not covered either by the Form of the good or by the Form of the bad. This is informative. Thesleff tells us that the standard scholarly approach to Forms as a uniform metaphysical designation is an oversimplification ignoring philosophically significant differences. Forms come instead in three different varieties together occupying the upper level of reality in a unitary world where each variety constitutes a metaphysical category bearing a special relevance to the way the world is. This, too, is informative. I find myself better informed, or more extensively so, with Thesleff's answer. This is because I can do more with his answer than I can with Nails's. Assuming that Nails is right, I learn how to distinguish between the unhypothetical first principle of the all and the Form of the good. Assuming that Thesleff is right, I learn how to think about the Forms in general and thereby about the world according to Plato. The Forms have too much to do with how

Plato's world works for Thesleff's answer not to be regarded as having greater explanatory power than Nails's answer, that is, as telling us more about Plato.[32]

Plausibility, of course, is essential. Explanatory power is merely a tie breaker. We cannot condone the wildest theories just because they explain a lot. Nails's theory is far from wild while telling us something we (most of us) did not know or notice.[33] The reconstruction Nails offers is not just plausible, but also desirable, and even beautiful. A negative hierarchy of Forms is the perfect complement for a positive hierarchy of Forms. It is simple, straightforward, and elegant. Yet Plato is not obligated to be simple, straightforward, or elegant. Nor does he have to be reasonable from a particular perspective. There are different ways of being reasonable.

Thesleff's Plato is less predictable without being unreasonable. There is nothing unreasonable, for example, about favoring positive abstractions, discounting negative abstractions, and thinking hard about the neutral ones, eventually sorting them out on a case-by-case basis. It is our own predilection for closure, for structure, for symmetry, that prejudices us against an open, fluid, and asymmetrical scheme for the Forms. It may seem strange, from our perspective, that Plato should reject negative Forms while accepting their positive counterparts, but what is even stranger is to humor Plato on something as fanciful as the Forms, only to take him to task for leaving some out. If we are going to allow him the most outlandish ontological concoctions in the history of philosophy, we are going to have to let him handle them however he sees fit.

Asking whether Plato accepts both positive and negative Forms is not like asking whether he accepts both odd and even numbers. There is no independent criterion of truth in Forms as there is in numbers. The Forms are his show. The positive and the negative of it is his business.

---

32. It may be tempting to object that Nails, in addition to the distinction between the unhypothetical first principle of the all and the Form of the good, gives us negative Forms. She does. But what is at stake here is whether she is right to do so. We cannot decide the matter by making the outcome a part of that decision. And even if that were okay, any nominal advantage for Nails in confirming negative Forms would be offset by a correlative advantage for Thesleff in ruling out negative Forms, which is no less informative than accepting them.

33. I am not saying that she is right. I am saying that her thesis has substantial explanatory power provided that she is right.

Numbers, on the other hand, are everybody's concern. It is not up to Plato to judge the odd and the even, designating one series as numbers, the other as not. Concepts are closer to numbers in that regard. We do not need Plato's blessing to figure out whether there are both positive and negative concepts, not to mention neutral ones. The Forms, however, are not concepts. They are what he says they are. And he does not say very much. We have to fill in the blanks, but we do not get to impose our personal preferences. We cannot make him take the negative ones just because that is what we would do. We have to fill in the blanks the way we think he might, even when that is not the way we think is right.

This seems to be a good place to fulfill the earlier promise of summoning my own Plato where the alternatives are both acceptable on the basis of evidence, argument, and scholarship. My Plato reserves a special place for the positive that precludes the negative, not necessarily in our phenomenal experience, but certainly among the Forms. What may read like negative Forms, including the bad, are the rudiments of what we now call concepts. This is not to say that my Plato clearly distinguishes between concepts and Forms. He does distinguish between them, but not very clearly. What is quite clear, though, is that not every abstraction interests him. And this last bit is true not just of my Plato but also of the actual philosopher. Plato, the only one we have, was fascinated by some abstractions, not so much by others. He may well have decided that the Forms are too precious to be tainted with negativity.

A negative Form is not a positive Form with the charge reversed, any more than a dead person is a living person with the animation reversed. Or perhaps that is exactly what they both are, but neither one of them is then the same sort of thing as its analogic counterpart, nor even remotely similar to it. A negative Form is not a Form at all, just as a dead person is not a person at all. It might even be said to be the opposite of a Form, or the privation of it, much like how a dead person is what is left behind when the actual person is gone, leaving us at first with only a corpse, if that, and eventually with nothing more than a memory. Plato does not have to count as a Form the vacuous privation, or worse, outright opposite, of what he takes to be a Form. And he does not. This is what being a Form is all about: what matters to Plato.

We get the clearest glimpse of what matters to him in the central myth of the *Phaedrus* (246e–249d) mentioned earlier. The Forms are so special that even the gods trek out to the far reaches of the cosmos to gaze upon them (246e–247e). And the show is a rare privilege for mortals, very few of whom make it all the way out to this cosmic inspiration point as disincarnate souls (248a–249d). Everything worthwhile is there for all to see. The Forms we get to behold, if we manage to complete the journey (as good philosophers), are justice and knowledge and beauty and so on. There is no fire or water. There is no mud or dirt. And there is certainly no evil or ugliness.

6.5. The Relevance and Supremacy of the Good in Plato

I have decisively sided with Thesleff, but I have not really attacked Nails. I could position myself more vigorously against her, ending the chapter in steadfast opposition. This is not because I am particularly clever, but because the discussion is almost there anyway. Giving it a little nudge at the end may help emphasize just how wrong Nails is. And it might be better for me to do that here since I have unequivocally rejected negative Forms in collaboration with Thesleff elsewhere (chapter 2). What I have said here is basically a defense of what we say there. I could now make all of it work against Nails if I was ever able to make any of it work at all. But that would conceal an important part of what I think about the matter.

My understanding is that Plato rejects negative Forms while appearing inadvertently to accept them. This gives Nails perfectly good reasons (2013, 95–101) for concluding not just that Plato puts up with negative Forms but that he revels in them with flair, devising a systematic hierarchy with the Form of the bad at the top of a negative superstructure. Her own exposition is not quite so explicit, but the basic ingredients are all there. My reading is based largely on her assignment of an extraordinary status to both the Form of the good and the Form of the bad. Just as she identifies the Form of the good as a "superordinate" Form (Nails 2013, 95), an "extra-strength" Form (100), and a "superior" (to being) Form (95, 100), so too does she designate the Form of the bad a "robust" Form (96, 99, 100). While she does not, in so many words, say that this is all about a superstructure of positive Forms in contrast to a superstructure of negative Forms, both subsumed under the unhypothetical first principle of the all, she leaves us with exegetical elements that come together in precisely that arrangement.

This is borne out by her acknowledgment of "a hierarchy of forms, with the good at the top" (Nails 2013, 95), suggesting that what she is exploring with the bad, especially since she makes the Form of the bad the universal explanation of negativity, is a parallel hierarchy of negative Forms, with the bad at the top. Strictly speaking, she is after an account of "destruction" (Nails 2013, 94, 99, 100), not of "negativity," but she would need the bad to explain negativity no less than she would need it to explain destruction, which is a less general concept covered by negativity. However that may be, my interpretation of what she is doing here comes more from admiration than from opposition. If I have overstated the role she assigns to the bad, I have also overstated my admiration.

What Nails makes of negative Forms, with or without a negative superstructure, is consistent with the textual evidence, especially with the parts of it she brings to our attention in support of her thesis. I am nevertheless satisfied beyond a doubt that Plato rejected negative Forms, or from a different perspective, that he avoided making any, or from yet another, that he never detected any. How can I believe the opposite of what I have just admitted to be supported by perfectly good reasons? One explanation is that "perfectly good" is a figure of speech conveying adequacy rather than perfection. I happen to take the opposite view to be supported by even better reasons. Another explanation is that, even though I reject a negative superstructure of Forms, that is only because I reject negative Forms, not because I reject the structure itself in a possible world where there are negative Forms.

The scenarios in Nails and Thesleff are both plausible in the sense and to the extent that the textual evidence cannot be said with certainty to preclude either reading. The reason that I side with Thesleff against Nails, hence the reason that I believe Plato rejected negative Forms, is that I would rather give up a Plato recognizing negative Forms than to give up a Plato realizing and embracing the value inherent in the universe and supporting the structure required to accommodate that value. Negative Forms vitiate the moral, spiritual, religious, and aesthetic value Plato imputes to the universe in his vision of reality, as well as undermining the ontological, cosmological, and epistemological role he assigns to the Forms in the creation and constitution of that universe. The value in question, namely the good in the universe, is ingrained in its very essence. This is a world created by design and shaped in accordance with the dictates of reason and goodness. Negative Forms do not belong in such a world, which is best represented, or at least better so, by the evaluative reification patterns of the ontological model sketched here with a gradation of reality defined and held together by various different kinds of Forms, not one type or token of which is negative.

These are not my personal prejudices. I take my cue from the demiurge, who employs reason in the service of the good, and both in the creation of the universe, where the good emerges, without a rival, as the supreme causal principle (*Timaeus* 29d–30c). That is why I find a Plato operating with a richer ontology, one built on categories of universal value and significance, as against a homogeneous collection of indiscriminately reified abstractions, to be not just a better philosopher but also the actual philosopher who still has us discussing a thought experiment he introduced at the dawn of philosophy.[34] I am not willing to give that up for a more elegant philosopher, nor even for a more reasonable one.

I am not alone in saddling Plato with an organic connection between value and reality. Myles Burnyeat, to cite just one of the eminent scholars preceding me, stands firmly behind the same observation: "It is beyond dispute that in the *Timaeus* value is part of 'the furniture of the world'" (2000, 66). This line of furniture, to consult Burnyeat further, is evidently quite fashionable outside the *Timaeus* as well: "Plato, like Aristotle and the Stoics after him, really did believe there is value in the world as it is objectively speaking, that values are part of what modern philosophers like to call 'the furniture of the world'" (2000, 8). Let me add that, the craftsman being divine, and the Forms being perfect, the furniture comes out rather well. It is beautiful, functional, and practically indestructible. Every last piece combines good taste with expert craftsmanship and superlative materials. There is no negativity by design in Plato, and since the Forms are essential to the design of the universe, there are no negative Forms.

---

34. There is, of course, something to be said, at least with respect to Western philosophy, for identifying the dawn with Thales, or really with any of the Presocratics, or perhaps with a combination of them. There is no harm, however, in extending the duration of the dawn to include Plato. If we define it too narrowly, or push it back too far, we might have to make do, for our own part, with bumbling around in the twilight of philosophy. A dawn with Plato makes it plausible, at least for a while, to pretend that the sun is still shining.

Chapter 7

Between a Form and a Hard Place

The Problem of Intermediates in Plato

This chapter addresses the problem of intermediates in Plato, which is to say, it considers the possibility of a separate ontological category between Forms and sensible phenomena. The problem is grounded partly in the inadequacy of the evidence, which is scarce, tenuous, and testimonial, and partly in the incompatibility of that evidence with the standard interpretation of Plato as propounding metaphysical dualism, the strict application of which precludes the acknowledgment of a third category while affirming that there are only two. What makes the evidence a problem is that the testimony in question, originating in Aristotle with little confirmation elsewhere, is riddled with discrepancies and contradictions, while the matter never even comes up in the vast body of works by Plato. What makes the putative dualism of Plato a problem is that a strict enough rendition, which is all too common, confines Plato's world to a binary reality exhausted by Forms and sensible phenomena, which then presents a strong presumption against intermediates as an additional ontological category between the other two. The aim of this chapter is to provide a solution without reliance either on the testimonial evidence of Aristotle as a witness to intermediates in Plato or on the received view of Plato as a metaphysical dualist. The former appeal is insufficient to establish a commitment by Plato to intermediates but often turns up as the sole grounds of their acceptance on his behalf, while the latter appeal is insufficient to reject intermediates in Plato but frequently serves as the primary source of opposition in his name. The present initiative, in contrast to both, demonstrates that there is plenty of room for intermediates in Plato, more so than Aristotle ever imagined or reported, and that there is no sort of dualism in Plato that compromises the possibility of intermediates between Forms and sensible phenomena.

7.1. Introduction

Plato's position on intermediate ontological entities between Forms and sensible phenomena remains a controversial matter. There are two main reasons for the controversy. The first is that the evidence, which is entirely testimonial and specifically Aristotelian, incorporates various problems undermining its reliability. The canonical corpus of Plato neither confirms nor contradicts the possibility of intermediates, while the corresponding testimony of Aristotle comes with complications of its own, affecting its general accuracy as well as its internal consistency (see section 7.4).[1] The second is that traditional accounts of Plato's metaphysics are typically anchored to the exegetical parameters of a complementary relationship between Forms and sensible phenomena, where the dualism is dominant enough and polarized enough either to reject intermediates outright or to shift the burden of proof to their advocates. Both reasons present strong obstacles to scholarly agreement. They do so particularly well in combination because Aristotle becomes difficult to trust where his testimony is prone to internal contradiction, becoming especially problematic where it seems in addition to contradict Plato's metaphysics. A comprehensive solution requires meticulous attention to both problems.

The common reaction is to follow one alternative at the expense of the other, either accepting intermediates out of deference to Aristotle or rejecting them out of concern for a conflict with the dualism of Plato, if not for the specific problems in Aristotle's testimony, or the virtual absence

---

1. The problem is not that what Aristotle says about intermediates in Plato contradicts what Plato himself says about intermediates. This cannot be a problem, because Plato says nothing at all about intermediates, at least not in a way that makes it clear that he is talking about intermediates. The problem is that what Aristotle says about intermediates in Plato contradicts other things Aristotle says about Plato, as well as undermining some things Plato says about those other things Aristotle says about Plato (see section 7.4).

of evidence in Plato's works. This chapter challenges both tendencies, recommending caution against blindly accepting Aristotle's testimony, but favoring intermediates nevertheless, favoring them, in fact, with a broader scope of application and relevance than reported by Aristotle in restricting intermediates to the objects of mathematics, namely arithmetical numbers and geometrical figures, jointly known as "mathematicals" (*Metaphysics* 987b14–18, 1028b19–21, 1086a11–13, 1090b32–1091a5; see section 7.2 for further documentation and section 7.4 for evaluation). While there is nothing wrong, as a rule, with trusting the testimony of Aristotle, especially in regard to someone he knew so well, there is something suspicious about testimonial information that radically changes what we thought we knew, instead of merely expanding or elaborating on what we already knew.[2] Yet it is just as inappropriate to ignore the problem altogether in a haste to preserve the reputation of Plato as a metaphysical dualist operating with a polar opposition between the world of Forms and the world of sensible phenomena.

To be perfectly clear, I am not claiming that metaphysical dualism, or any kind of dualism, for that matter, requires mutually exclusive and jointly exhaustive elements precluding the reality of a third kind of thing on top of the two kinds already acknowledged to exist. There are certainly looser variations of dualism. I am claiming only that a rigid division of reality is a common assumption in the traditional employment of metaphysical dualism in articulation of Plato's philosophy, even if the modality of metaphysical dualism as a philosophical outlook does not itself require such a rigorous interpretation as a matter of course.

The general tendency in the received view of Plato is not just to emphasize the Forms and sensible phenomena as the constituents of reality

---

2. I admit that the absence of a certain view in the Platonic corpus is not proof that Plato himself never held that view. Yet I submit that there is an interpretive danger in the opposite direction as well, namely in the tendency to associate Plato with any theory whatsoever, so long as it does not directly contradict anything in the Platonic corpus, such a contradiction being all too conveniently avoided if the theory in question is not there at all. That is why I myself refrain from claiming to prove that Plato embraced intermediates, instead suggesting merely that he left plenty of room for them in his works. The problem with invoking Aristotle toward the same end is not just the leap of faith required in the absence of evidence in Plato but also Aristotle's drastic limitation of the room Plato left for intermediates, a category which Aristotle asks us to believe Plato restricted to mathematicals (see sections 7.2 and 7.4).

but to impose a radical separation on them so that the Forms end up in one world as against sensible phenomena in another, with the two worlds representing all there is. Hence, even if I am wrong about the corresponding problem in Plato scholarship, it is not because I misunderstand the logic of dualism in general, or the structure of metaphysical dualism in particular, but because I exaggerate how strictly they are employed in the standard interpretation of Plato. Any such exaggeration, however, starts with the traditional separation of worlds, which are not only difficult to put back together but also wide open to interpretation as a polarized dualism exhaustive of reality.

The starting point adopted in this chapter is reality as a unitary whole. The main methodological apparatus is an interpretive model where intermediates constitute a natural corollary, not a menacing threat, to the worldview of Plato, though not to the received view of Plato, which is in need of modification anyway, largely for independent reasons that work out to the advantage of intermediates (see section 7.6). Plato's world is not black or white. It is both and more. His reality comes in shades, often with a degree and kind of structure indicative of hierarchy. The model employed here combines a monism of worlds with a pluralism of things, where a unitary whole exhibits a gradation of reality between an upper level reserved for Forms and a lower level hosting sensible phenomena, with countless subdivisions in between.[3] This is the unitary pluralism advocated throughout the present volume as a single world with meaningful diversity.

The diversity is pervasive. Even what we have come to know as Platonic Forms are not just Forms, pure and simple, each one representing exactly the same sort of entity or construct as any other, and all thereby belonging to a homogeneous ontological category. There are three different types of Forms in Plato—Ideal Forms, Conceptual Forms, and Relational Forms (see previous chapters and section 7.6 of this chapter)—all subsumed under, and each aiming at, the good, that is, the Form of the good. The

---

3. The working model is introduced in chapter 2 and developed in subsequent chapters, including section 7.6 of the present chapter. The central idea of a two-level interpretation, however, dates back in essentials to the independent work of Thesleff (1993b; 1999 [= 2009, 383–506]), who, in turn, credits de Vogel (1986) with the innovation (see Thesleff 2009, xv; cf. de Vogel 1986, 50, 62, 145–148, 159–212, especially 159–171). Details of my collaboration with Thesleff are available in the preface and the introduction to the present volume.

Forms in each category in the upper level are instantiated by sensible phenomena in the lower level, while indefinitely many subdivisions, both in between and beyond, provide ontological and epistemological connections as well as supplying representational details toward a comprehensive picture of reality. Such subdivisions reveal philosophical possibilities rather than predetermined categories. The two main levels are prominently at the forefront of Plato's ontology and epistemology, with any and all subdivisions serving as a conceptual reserve for elaboration and exploration.

The premise of the present chapter is that this gradation of reality, including the overarching ontological structure, leaves plenty of room for intermediates between the two main levels. The claim is not that Plato must have countenanced intermediates because the unitary pluralism of a single world with a gradation of reality is demonstrably authentic while metaphysical dualism with a polarization of reality is indubitably false, nor even that unitary pluralism is patently superior to metaphysical dualism where neither one can be shown conclusively to be true or false, but simply that the notion of a single world with ontological stratification is consistent with everything else in Plato while at the same time constituting an ideal setting for intermediates. The aim is to weed out uncritical grounds both for accepting and for rejecting intermediates.

The solution cannot reasonably be entrusted either to the testimonial evidence of Aristotle or to the received view of Plato. Accepting intermediates in Plato becomes a bad idea when it is based entirely on Aristotle's testimony, because their explicit restriction (to mathematicals) in the Aristotelian corpus is just as difficult to explain as their effective absence in the Platonic corpus. Leaving the matter to Aristotle thus represents the very essence of uncritical acceptance, especially with a school of interpretation developing around how best to spin the discrepancies in his testimony (see section 7.5). Rejecting intermediates in Plato, on the other hand, becomes a bad idea when it is based entirely on their incompatibility with metaphysical dualism, since unitary pluralism is a viable alternative accommodating Forms and sensible phenomena as part of a single world open to other levels or aspects of reality. The legend of Plato's metaphysical dualism inspires uncritical rejection through an opposition between Forms and sensible phenomena that covers the ontological content of the entire world, or rather of both worlds, given the axiomatic duplication and separation of worlds under the corresponding dualism. A mutually exclusive and jointly exhaustive relationship between Forms and sensible phenomena would indeed be a good reason to reject intermediates but only upon demonstration of the validity of that interpretation and not through the mere assertion or postulation of it.

The remainder of this chapter is dedicated to showing that Plato's metaphysics works well with intermediates, independently of what Aristotle said about them (though his testimony is welcome where it is plausible), and that it works all the same regardless of the specious dualism often attributed to Plato with no greater authority than the unitary pluralism that fits the evidence at least as well as the mainstream interpretation.

7.2. Plato through Aristotle

The oral tradition in Plato was once the only tradition in Plato. It reigned as the received view when most of Europe was cut off from the original sources, though it was later demoted to an ancillary source of insight into the philosophy expressed in the dialogues themselves. Centuries before German scholarship first destroyed and subsequently restored the tradition, Plato was studied mainly through Aristotle, Aristotelian scholiasts, and Neoplatonic philosophers, whose collective testimony and commentary were filtered through and blended with the pedagogical ideals and conventions of Scholasticism.

The success of the Roman Empire, which brought about the gradual replacement of Greek with Latin as the lingua franca throughout the continent, left European culture in relative ignorance of Greek philosophy, not necessarily because the relevant works were themselves lost but quite decisively because scholarly reasons for literacy in Greek were lost. With the language of scholarship invariably following the official language of the state and the church, no matter the variety and popularity of the languages commonly spoken by the people, philosophy in the Middle Ages was conducted in Latin throughout the West. As a result, direct acquaintance with the works of Plato and Aristotle remained concentrated in eastern Europe and the Arab world, with western Europe restricted to the prospects available in Latin scholarship. While the isolation was not absolute, it was sufficient to undermine the transmission of Greek philosophy in general and the study of Plato in particular.[4]

---

4. Klibansky (1981) reminds us that the continental disparity in access to texts still allowed some continuity in the Platonic tradition in the West: "Thus, the history of Platonism presents at least three striking illustrations of the fact that, here as in other aspects of Renaissance culture, while the new materials and ideas coming from

Western access to the works of Plato was limited for centuries to a couple of partial translations of the *Timaeus*, one by Cicero, predating the transition from Republican to Imperial Rome, the other by Chalcidius, prepared in the fourth century. These were complemented later by relatively neglected translations of the *Phaedo* and *Meno* by Henricus Aristippus in the twelfth century, and subsequently by a partial translation of the *Parmenides* by William of Moerbeke.[5] Not only did Aristotle fare better during the same period, owing in large part to the availability of translations by Boethius of the logical works, but he also beat Plato by a couple of centuries in terms of the full recovery of their works as we now have them in the canonical corpus of each. The disparity in their popularity remained strong throughout the Middle Ages, with Plato beginning to catch up only during the Renaissance.

The Recovery of Aristotle in the West started in the twelfth century, spurred by growing opportunities for contact with the East, mostly through military campaigns and conquests, where manuscripts, collections, and entire libraries found their way into the West, both from the Byzantine Empire and from its Arabian and Persian neighbors.[6] The inflow of texts was complemented by an influx of scholars, which accelerated translation projects, initially from Arabic collections and subsequently from Greek originals. The first translation of the Platonic corpus in its entirety came in 1484 through the efforts of Marsilio Ficino (1433–1499), undertaking the project in 1463, under the auspices of Cosimo de' Medici.[7] The

---

Byzantium have to be considered, the continuous development within the Latin world must not be neglected" (1981, 30). Klibansky's point is well taken, but he is talking about continuity in the broadest sense of Platonism, with Christian scholars using Neoplatonism to patch up the holes left by a disruption in the study of Plato in at least some of Europe during at least some of the Middle Ages. See Lohr (2002, 15–17) for a contrast between the scholarly traditions dominating Europe before and after the social, political, and economic transformations revitalizing the intellectual milieux during the High Middle Ages, coinciding with the last of the so-called medieval renaissances (cf. 17–20, 20–21, of the same work for subsequent developments in two stages).

5. Background information can be found, among other places, in Hankins (1990, 4), Klibansky (1981, 29–31), Wilson (1996, 40, 86–87, 164, 213–215), and Reynolds and Wilson (2013, 121, cf. 246, 272).

6. Relevant aspects of the period are covered by Howlett (2016, 38–41), Klibansky (1981, 14–18, 19–21, 21–29), and Lohr (2002, 15–22).

7. Further details are available in Hankins (1990, 5), Howlett (2016, 46–48, 54–58, 165–172), Klibansky (1981, 312–314, 325), and Reynolds and Wilson (2013, 156).

availability of original works by Plato, simultaneously with testimony and commentary, the latter of which had previously been the whole of Platonic scholarship, laid the groundwork for centuries of disagreement on how to reconcile the differences.

7.2.1. Unwritten Doctrines

Aristotle's discussion of intermediates in Plato is an integral part of his testimony on the *agrapha dogmata*: the unwritten doctrines, teachings, or opinions of Plato.[8] These doctrines constitute a cluster of extremely important views at the heart of Plato's philosophy that we get only from Aristotle, or mainly from Aristotle if we count the evidence of lost reports by others, because Plato supposedly discussed them only orally and never in writing. Disclosing beliefs purportedly dearest to Plato, but conspicuously absent from the Platonic corpus, Aristotle thus becomes indispensable for a proper understanding of his teacher. The unwritten doctrines are not a random collection of unrelated ideas by Plato but various aspects of a profoundly mathematical metaphysics that transcends any hints or traces of such a foundation in the dialogues.[9] A proper assessment of intermediates in Plato requires not just an awareness of the corresponding passages in Aristotle but also an appreciation of their place and function in the unwritten doctrines as a whole.

---

8. The exact term, *agrapha dogmata*, comes up in only one place in Aristotle, specifically in the form of *ta legomena agrapha dogmata* ("the so-called unwritten doctrines" or "those doctrines that are called unwritten"): *Physics* 209b15 (though note the reference to "the lectures 'On Philosophy'" in *De Anima* 404b19–21). The qualification "so-called" in this context points to a conventional reference in common use rather than indicating personal dissent, disagreement, or opposition in connection with either the term or its referent (see Szlezák 1993b, especially 172–174). Despite the isolated occurrence of the specific designation, there is plenty of information by way of testimony on the content of such unwritten doctrines, teachings, or opinions, as discussed above in the main text. As for the reference itself, while *agrapha dogmata* hardly constitutes anything like a technical term that Aristotle employs invariably and exclusively in reference to Plato's oral teachings, it is now used in just that way, and widely so, to cover everything Aristotle says about Plato that is not in the dialogues.

9. This is not to deny that Plato's metaphysics is mathematical but to assert that it is not mathematical in the same way and to the same degree that Aristotle makes it out to be. The point is not that there are no hints or traces of a mathematical metaphysics in the dialogues, but that there is not enough of it in the dialogues to make Aristotle's testimony in that regard look like a readily familiar report of Plato's work.

The insight to be gained through Aristotle, if he can be trusted as a reporter or historian, is nowhere more compelling than in Plato's metaphysics. The standard view among those who interpret Plato exclusively through his own works is that the canonical corpus, particularly the literary and philosophical masterpieces of the so-called middle period, assigns the Forms a singular position in the nature and structure of reality, polarized into a dualism of intelligibility versus sensibility. But this account of the master's teaching, to hear his greatest student tell it, is nowhere near the full picture, nor even very accurate as a partial depiction of it. It is deficient in several respects. Aristotle makes up for all of them.

To elaborate, testifying first and foremost that Plato's world, including Forms and sensible phenomena, as well as anything in between, supervenes upon the one and the-great-and-the-small as fundamental metaphysical principles, Aristotle thereby opens up (what is now) an alternative interpretation of Plato's philosophical outlook, placing enormous emphasis on its mathematical orientation, most notably on the reduction of Forms to numbers, while at the same time making room for intermediate constructs between the otherwise polarized world of intelligible Forms and sensible phenomena. Some of the novelty in Aristotle's testimony has faint traces in Plato's dialogues, but the connection is too weak, and the hints too vague, to constitute evidentiary confirmation, thus making Aristotle our primary guide for insight into three aspects of Plato's metaphysics that we do not get from Plato's dialogues, at least not without a strong imagination and an outstanding ability to read between the lines:[10] (1) Forms get their essence from the one and their matter from the-great-and-the-small, which jointly serve as the fundamental principles of reality. (2) Forms are essentially numbers. (3) The objects of mathematics, basically arithmetical

---

10. Theokritos Kouremenos may be consulted for a comprehensive account of the mathematical orientation of Plato's philosophy, including a rigorous demonstration of why all Forms are mathematical, in his recent monograph entitled *Plato's Forms, Mathematics and Astronomy* (2018). While Kouremenos does invoke Aristotle (30–36, 41–47), he works primarily with the Platonic corpus (mostly with the *Republic, Timaeus,* and *Laws*). The first chapter of the book is devoted entirely to the matter of "Platonic Forms as Forms Only of Mathematical Objects" (8–76). Two sections there are particularly relevant to the discussion here: Section 1.3: "Are all forms only forms of mathematical objects?" (50–68). Section 1.4: "The equation of forms with form-numbers, and their Principles" (68–76). The book's close reading of passages in the *Republic* complements the author's earlier study of parallel themes in *The Unity of Mathematics in Plato's Republic* (Kouremenos 2015).

numbers and geometrical figures, constitute an intermediate ontological category between Forms and sensible phenomena.[11]

Not everyone has been eager, however, to follow Aristotle's lead on what to make of Plato. The opposition to trusting Aristotle's testimony on Plato's philosophy finds its strongest expression in Harold Cherniss (1944; 1945), who was suspicious of Aristotelian testimony in general (see Cherniss 1935), and who was influenced and preceded by Paul Shorey (1884/1982; 1903; 1927; 1933) on the proper approach to Plato. Like many of their contemporaries, both were inspired by Friedrich Schleiermacher (1804–1828; cf. 1836) and Eduard Zeller (1839; 1844–1852; cf. 1876; 1883), who dismissed the unwritten doctrines in favor of the dialogues. John Burnet (1914), A. E. Taylor (1908; 1911; 1926a; 1926b–1927; 1963), and W. D. Ross (1951) may be cited among those recommending serious attention to Aristotle on Plato, though with critical scrutiny, trusting Aristotle implicitly on what Plato said, but not necessarily on what Plato meant.

The Aristotelian camp, on the other hand, draws its strength from Hans Krämer (1957; 1964; 1990) and Konrad Gaiser (1960; 1980), the founders of an influential movement reviving the importance of the oral tradition in understanding Plato. A negative review of Krämer (1959) by Gregory Vlastos (1963) initially undermined the revival in the United States, but the ideological and methodological platform, known originally as the Tübingen Paradigm but now more commonly as the Tübingen School, has consistently been attracting the interest and support of some of the world's finest scholars, including Thomas Alexander Szlezák (1985–2004; 1993a; 1993b; 1998), who became its leading exponent in Germany; Giovanni Reale (1975–1980; 1984; 1990), whose resounding advocacy in Italy inspired the alternative designation, Tübingen-Milan School; and J. N. Findlay (1974; 1978a; 1978b; 1983), who independently arrived at many of the same conclusions as the members of the movement (see Krämer 1990, 47). Accepting the appellation "Tübingen School" only with considerable qualification, and even then, only with great reluctance, Szlezák describes the corresponding tradition as "an international enterprise" boasting a presence in "over a dozen" countries (see Szlezák and Staehler 2014, 160).[12]

---

11. The objects of mathematics consist of arithmetical numbers and geometrical figures, though the general category can reasonably be construed more broadly to include mathematical properties (oddness, primeness, linearity, etc.), relations (equality, sequentiality, perpendicularity, etc.), and operations (addition, subtraction, multiplication, etc.).

12. The history of interpretive trends in Plato scholarship is difficult to cover in passing. Cherniss does an admirable job in the space of a foreword to one of his books (1944,

Despite the inevitability of going through Aristotle to document the unwritten doctrines of Plato, Aristotle was evidently not the only ancient reporter of the corresponding doctrines, at least not of all of them. Holger Thesleff, for one, is confident that Aristotle's attribution of various positions and convictions to Plato, especially the doctrine of the one and the-great-and-the-small as first principles, was corroborated by independent reports that are no longer extant:

> Aristotle is our earliest explicit witness for the theory of two Platonic Principles. The reliability of Aristotle has been much debated, and his accounts of the Principles and related questions may indeed look loose and inconsistent. But though some of the later sources simply reflect Aristotle's interpretations, he is not our only early witness. It seems rather clear that Theophrastus, Dercyllides and Alexander (of Aphrodisias) had direct access to writings by some other of Plato's pupils who, like Aristotle in his now lost *De Bono*, discussed the Platonic Principles more systematically: namely Speusippus, Xenocrates, Hermodorus, Hestiaeus, and possibly Heraclides. (Thesleff 1999, 93 [= 2009, 475])

Note that Thesleff is talking specifically about first principles, while the discussion here goes beyond that to include the reduction of Forms to numbers and the postulation of intermediates between Forms (numbers) and sensible phenomena. There may have been yet other ancient commentators whose now-lost testimonies once corroborated Aristotle on these matters as well, but the longer the list of items reported, the more surely Aristotle emerges as the sole source of the report in its entirety, and the more curious it becomes that so much of Aristotelian testimony of crucial importance can only be verified through works that either repeat what he said or are no longer in existence, with most candidates satisfying both conditions.

The reason that Aristotle's discussion of intermediates in Plato is best understood within the framework of his testimony on Plato's unwritten doctrines as a whole is not just that the question in fact originates in that broader context, but also that Aristotle's critical narrative, especially his appraisal of Plato's restriction of intermediates to mathematicals, and of

---

ix–xxv). Gerson (2014) may be consulted for a complementary survey and analysis from the opposite perspective seventy years later.

intermediation to mathematics, is closely connected with his confirmation of Plato's restriction of Forms to numbers. Those two revelations regarding Plato's philosophy are, in turn, grounded in and supported by the third, namely the priority of the one and the-great-and-the-small as metaphysical principles more fundamental than the Forms. The combined effect of the Aristotelian perspective is the mathematization and formalization of Plato's metaphysics beyond any system or structure evident in the dialogues. Even the commonly recognized mathematical turn in Plato's later career is not reflected in his works to the extent confirmed by Aristotle, certainly not with the implications brought out by Aristotle. Looking at the whole helps us understand Aristotle's viewpoint better than looking at only what he said about Plato's view of intermediates.

Consider an example close at hand in the skeletal breakdown above of Aristotle's testimony on Plato. The relevance of a holistic strategy becomes clear in the apparent discrepancy between restricting Forms to numbers and restricting intermediates to mathematicals, where the latter are understood to comprise arithmetical numbers and geometrical figures. Put simply, if Forms are restricted to numbers, then intermediates should also be restricted to numbers, not more broadly to the objects of mathematics, where geometrical figures also enter into the picture. A comprehensive engagement with Aristotle on Plato is useful in both detecting and resolving the discrepancy. Since neither restriction reflects Aristotle's own position, we cannot reasonably blame him for the inconsistency, which he may well be reporting exactly as he witnessed it, presumably in Plato but, depending on the passage, possibly also, and perhaps instead, in others. More to the point, however, the discrepancy itself is not as decisive as it may seem, given the reductionist perspective, common in antiquity, of assigning representative numbers to geometrical figures, with comparable assignments to various other phenomena.

Exploring structure through numbers was a Pythagorean tradition, shared at least in part by Plato, who was fascinated by the Pythagorean *tetraktus*, a geometrical model of the number series through ten, incorporating ten dots in four rows beginning with a single dot at the top and adding an extra dot in each successive row $(1 + 2 + 3 + 4 = 10)$.[13] The

---

13. Some of the more obvious examples of mathematical modeling in Plato include (1) the simile of the divided line (*Republic* 509d–511e); (2) the metaphysical breakdown of reality into four classes, namely "the unlimited" (*apeiron*), "the limit" (*peras*), their

Pythagoreans held the *tetraktus* sacred, invoking it in mystical as well as mathematical contexts, the most obvious of which was the representation of points by the number one, lines by the number two, plane figures by the number three, and solid figures by the number four. Plato may not have been on board with the Pythagorean association of points with the number one, apparently instead (though not definitely so) adhering to the Greek practice of starting the number series with two. Evidence suggests that he considered the point a "geometer's fiction," at least according to Aristotle (*Metaphysics* 992a20–22; cf. Crombie 1963, 442, 464; Ross 1951, 223–224). He seems nevertheless to have followed the Pythagoreans in depicting lines with the number two, planes with the number three, and solids with the number four (*Metaphysics* 1090b20–24; *De Anima* 404b18–27). He also appears to have employed an epistemological scheme drawing on the *tetraktus*, again on the evidence of Aristotle, where reason was represented by the number one (or perhaps just by the one, given the uncertainty surrounding Plato's views on whether one is a number), science by the number two, opinion by the number three, and sensation by the number four (*De Anima* 404b18–27).

There is no doubt that the philosophy of Plato had a mathematical orientation. And there is no doubt that we need Aristotle to appreciate the full extent of it. But the most salient revelation in Aristotle's testimony concerning Plato's unwritten doctrines is the identification of metaphysical principles more fundamental than Forms. This is a good place to start because it provides the structural impetus for the mathematization of the system.

7.2.2. Fundamental Principles

The testimony of Aristotle introduces a shift in emphasis from Forms to fundamental principles, or first principles (*archai*), ontologically and cosmologically more basic than Forms, and therefore more so than numbers, given that the Forms are numbers, according to the testimony. The shift is not a complete anomaly relative to the direct evidence since the Forms are not always in the limelight in the dialogues anyway. Yet the testimonial

---

mixture, and the cause of that mixture (*Philebus* 23c–27c); and (3) the elemental ingredients and processes described in the account of creation from the perspective of "necessity" (*Timaeus* 47e–68d, especially 53a–57d).

evidence on fundamental metaphysical principles goes beyond any visible development in the Platonic corpus. The principles in question are "the one" (*to hen*), as the formal principle, and "the great and the small" (*to mega kai to mikron*), or "the great and small" (*tou megalou kai mikrou*), as the material principle. This is the classical opposition between unity and plurality, a quintessentially Greek contrast, arguably already present in Plato at least through the relationship between "the unlimited" (*apeiron*) and "the limit" (*peras*) of the *Philebus* (23c–27c). Another name for the material principle is "the indefinite dyad" (*he ahoristos duas*), though not in Aristotle, who prefers "the great and the small," including a few variations (cf. *Metaphysics* N1, especially 1087b5–31), but decidedly not "the indefinite dyad," which seems to have come into parlance as a later development in the commentary tradition (cf. Plutarch: *Quaestiones Platonicae* 1001f–1002a).[14]

Aristotle's terminological preferences reflect his conceptual predilections. This is already evident at a general level in his giving Plato a formal principle and a material principle interacting in a hylomorphic framework of sorts in explanation of some of the metaphysics we get through the dialogues. Yet interpretive difficulties arise at every level of detail as Plato's ideas get filtered through Aristotle's philosophical preconceptions. Aristotle seems torn, for example, between "the great and the small" and "the great and small" as the name for the material principle, which indicates that he is torn between how many notions to assign to Plato as his material principle. The difficulty here is not that Aristotle sometimes slips up and forgets the second definite article, or gets carried away and slips in an extra one, especially since a conscious effort is required in Greek to switch between *to mega kai to mikron* and *tou megalou kai mikrou*. The difficulty, rather, is that Aristotle withholds or includes the second definite article, depending on whether he is focusing on the unitary character and holistic integrity of the material principle or highlighting its inherent duality to reveal just how confused and misguided Plato was. No matter how many

---

14. This is not to say that Aristotle never uses the term "the indefinite dyad" (*he ahoristos duas*), or anything like it, in any context. One counterexample to such an assumption would be (*Metaphysics* 1081a14–15): "Number comes from the 1 and the indefinite dyad" (*ho gar arithmos estin ek tou henos kai tēs dyados tēs aoristou*). Yet this does not change the fact that Aristotle regularly refers to the material principle either as "the great and the small" (*to mega kai to mikron*) or as "the great and small" (*tou megalou kai mikrou*), evidently with a preference for the former over the latter.

articles are used as filler, and no matter how all the words are arranged, the construction of a material principle out of "the great" and "the small" already smacks of dualism. Calling it "the great and the small" emphasizes the duality, as if they were two separate principles rather than one, while calling it "the great and small" minimizes the duality, as if they were two aspects or features of a single principle.

Aristotle himself uses "the great and the small" with greater regularity than "the great and small."[15] But whether he does so for the right reasons, and with the best intentions, is open to discussion. Even when he is not trying to make Plato look bad, along with a host of others, he often succeeds in doing so, and he certainly never attempts the opposite. A single material principle accompanying the single formal principle is both more sensible and more elegant than alternative interpretations. In all fairness to Aristotle, he does appear to acknowledge that Plato's material principle has a unitary nature drawing on "the great" and "the small" together as a single metaphysical notion (e.g., *Physics* 192a4–16; cf. Philoponus: *In Aristotelis Physica Commentaria* 182.9–184.14). Yet he remains troubled by, and critical of, the duality of "the great and the small" (*Metaphysics* 1055b32–1056b3, 1083b23–32, 1087b4–33, 1088a15–35; cf. Syrianus: *In Aristotelis Metaphysica Commentaria* 144.4–145.2).

Modern scholars tend to prefer "the great and small" because it approximates, at least in form, a single principle with a dual nature, thus avoiding the appearance of two separate principles (see Ross 1951, 176–205, especially 204–205). But that amounts to trusting Aristotle for something Plato said, which we are in no position to judge, only to correct Aristotle regarding what Plato meant. We must indeed give Plato a single material principle, if we wish to understand him through Aristotle, but that can readily be accomplished through the introduction of hyphens into "the great and the small," which is, in this naked form (without hyphens but with the repeated definite article), the alternative that Aristotle uses more often, hereafter rendered as "the-great-and-the-small." One could, of course, instead or in addition, capitalize the first letter of every word, or slavishly employ scare quotes, or do both at once, on top of all the

---

15. Preference patterns in the *Metaphysics* indicate that Aristotle invokes "the great and the small" (*to mega kai to mikron* at 987b19–20, 988a13, 988a26, 992b4, 992b7, 998b9, 1055b32, 1056a12, 1083b23, 1083b27–28, 1087b11–24 [= four times], 1088a22, 1089a35–36, 1091a10) at least four times as often as "the great and small" (*tou megalou kai mikrou* at 987b25, 1087b7–8, 1087b10–11, 1090b35–36).

hyphens. The precise protocol does not matter as much as the consistency of its application. The approach in this chapter (and wherever relevant throughout the book) is to use just the hyphens, except in quoting others who do something else.

While the one and the-great-and-the-small are at the heart of the unwritten doctrines, thereby providing the foundation for Aristotle's mathematization of Plato's world, the most puzzling manifestations of that mathematical orientation are the reduction of Forms to numbers and the introduction of intermediates, exclusively mathematical ones, between Forms and sensible phenomena. The next two sections on Aristotle (subsections in strictly structural terms) are dedicated to exploring those avenues of interpretation.

7.2.3. Forms as Numbers

Aristotle's interpretation of Plato's metaphysics, including his philosophy of mathematics, which is inseparable from his metaphysics, is in the form of bits and pieces of critical exegesis. One of the most telling bits is the following passage:

> Since the Forms are the causes of all other things, [Plato] thought their elements were the elements of all things. As matter, the great and the small were principles; as substance, the One; for from the great and the small, by participation in the One, come the numbers. (Aristotle: *Metaphysics* 987b18–22; Ross translation)[16]

The translation shows Aristotle moving from Forms in the first sentence to numbers in the second. That alone is an indication of the equivalence of Forms and numbers. But the connection is even stronger in the original, which says outright that Forms are numbers, or more precisely, that "the Forms are the numbers [*ta eidē einai tous arithmous*]" (*Metaphysics* 987b21–22). The full sentence can conceivably be read in a

---

16. The quotation bears repeating in the original in appreciation and illustration of commonly acknowledged difficulties in translation and interpretation: *Epei d' aitia ta eidē tois allois, takeinōn stoicheia pantōn ōēthē tōn ontōn einai stoicheia. Hōs men oun hylēn to mega kai to mikron einai archas, hōs d' ousian to hen: ex ekeinōn gar kata methexin tou henos ta eidē einai tous arithmous* (*Metaphysics* 987b18–22).

less literal sense as suggesting that the mathematical nature of the process of generation, specifically of the participation of the-great-and-the-small in the one, and hence of plurality in unity, shows that all Forms are numbers because reality itself is mathematical. While a metaphorical reading of that sort may not seem pertinent where the actual words specify that "the Forms are the numbers" (*Metaphysics* 987b21–22), the literal meaning is not as compelling or as straightforward as it may appear. Scholars are divided over not just how to interpret the meaning of the assertion but also how to translate the actual words.[17] Any hope of agreement must extend beyond the quoted passage to include other passages where the same association is made either directly or in passing.[18]

As things stand, however, the facts remain blurry, and the connections loose, a combination that places scholarly consensus out of reach. Consequently, the discussion is often couched in terms of Plato's "identification of Forms with numbers," or Plato's "association of Forms with numbers," apparently to avoid saying outright that, according to Aristotle, Plato says that Forms are numbers. The reference to an "identification of Forms with numbers," though its standard sense is indeed to take Forms to be numbers, can also indicate a looser association, which then makes the expression less committal, on the whole, than the assertion that Forms are numbers. The reference to an "association of Forms with numbers" is even more evasive, saying hardly anything more than that one thing has something to do with the other.

Among the numerous passages where Aristotle discusses any account of Forms as numbers, some are obviously not about Plato, most are not obviously about Plato, and many are not clear as to what they mean. But

---

17. Annas, for one, warns that "the expression is so uncertain that different scholars have responded by emending the text in different ways" (1976, 64): "The Greek literally goes: 'from these (the great and the small) by participation in one the Forms are the numbers.' It is apparently grammatically anomalous to have both Forms and numbers. Some (e.g. Christ, Jaeger) cut out the numbers, others (e.g. Zeller, Ross, Tredennick) cut out the Forms. Stenzel keeps both and reads it as an apposition; Merlan (2) defends this reading on the grounds that Asclepius read it and that it is supported by a passage of Plotinus" (Annas 1976, 64, n. 79, cf. 66).

18. Annas puts together a list of such passages almost entirely from the *Metaphysics*: 987b18–25, 991b9–10, 992b13–17, 1073a17–22, 1080b11–12, 1081a5–17, 1082b23–24, 1083a17–20, 1086a11–13, 1090a16–17, 1091b26 ff.; *On Philosophy* fr. 11 (Annas 1976, 64, n. 78). Adding that the passages vary in evidentiary value, she proceeds to sort them out in accordance with the variance (Annas 1976, 62–73).

it is hard to deny the meaning and relevance of the few passages that strongly suggest that Aristotle is pointing to Plato himself, if not also to others at the same time, as holding that Forms are numbers (e.g., *Metaphysics* 991b9-10, 1073a17-22). As against this, however, there is at least one passage where Plato seems to be disassociated from this practice of taking Forms to be numbers (*Metaphysics* 1028b19-27).

The recalcitrant passage proceeds with direct testimony naming Plato as positing three kinds of substance: Forms, sensible phenomena, and mathematical intermediates (*Metaphysics* 1028b19-21). Plato is then contrasted with Speusippus, who is said to have made "still more kinds of substance" (not implying acceptance of all the ones recognized by Plato, as we know Speusippus rejected at least the Forms): one, numbers, spatial magnitudes, soul. Both are followed by a reference (in apparent contrast to each) to "some" who say "Forms and numbers have the same nature," indicating that Plato and Speusippus do not hold this (Speusippus obviously so because he rejects Forms altogether), as it would have otherwise made sense to state explicitly that they did hold it (given that they were already identified by name in the same passage) instead of switching to the anonymous some-who-say formula of documentation common in antiquity. While Aristotle's less ambiguous testimony elsewhere (e.g., *Metaphysics* 991b9-10, 1073a17-22), affirming that Plato considers Forms to be numbers, may be adduced to reinforce and salvage the association, that would only confirm the presence of a troubling contradiction requiring an interpretive spin.

Adding to the inscrutable nature of the documentation, where any is offered at all, the meaning of the testimony itself is not sufficiently clear. What does it mean for a Form to be a number? If Plato takes numbers (and other mathematicals) to belong to an intermediate ontological category between Forms and sensible phenomena, how can he possibly take Forms to be numbers, the latter of which would not then be intermediate between Forms and numbers? What it means turns out, upon closer inspection, to be that Plato takes Forms to be ideal numbers as opposed to mathematical numbers, the latter of which can then be said consistently to belong between the Forms that are ideal numbers and the sensible phenomena corresponding to those Forms. But this is neither profound nor mysterious nor even interesting. It is just plain equivocation on what it means to be a number, which then remains an open question as if the Forms both were and were not numbers in the outlook thus invoked or outlined.

Aristotle never actually presents an "identification of Forms with numbers" as a fallacious inconsistency where Plato's or anyone else's positing two types of number makes numbers both intermediate and not intermediate. But that is where he gradually leads and inevitably leaves readers through a series of terminological shortcuts and omissions. Ideal numbers, or Form-numbers, as Aristotle also calls them, are not so much numbers, especially not as we understand them from our perspective, as they are Forms. Aristotle certainly knows the difference, as he seems to have invented the distinction. Yet he switches freely between Forms and numbers in his references to ideal numbers in Plato (among others).

Aristotle's portrayal of Plato as taking all Forms to be numbers is his way of saying that Plato limits the population of Forms to the Forms of numbers. There is no other way for Plato, or for anyone else, to hold consistently both that Forms are numbers and that numbers are intermediate between Forms and sensible phenomena. The digitization of Forms is the only reading that saves Aristotle's testimony, along with the view he thereby attributes to Plato, from self-contradiction.

Yet Aristotle makes it a point to report, over and over, and rather emphatically each time, that this or that philosopher, or an anonymous congregation of such thinkers, take Forms to be numbers—not explicitly Form-numbers, not specifically ideal numbers, just plain "numbers." He does speak elsewhere of ideal numbers, distinguishing them from mathematical numbers, so as to be perfectly clear about what he is saying, which then makes it all the more conspicuous, and therefore suspicious, that he leaves us with an unqualified reference to "numbers" whenever he reports that Plato, or anyone else, takes Forms to be numbers. What is worse is that he then goes on to discuss, as if to invite incredulity for confusion, what these same thinkers think of mathematical numbers, which he also refers to simply as "numbers." The overall result is that the reported association (of Forms with numbers) and the subsequent discussion (of numbers as intermediates) together look like either an accusation or a demonstration of equivocation, with Aristotle habitually combining two mutually independent and consistent perspectives as if he were exposing a blunder to be censured.

The difference between ideal numbers (Form-numbers) and mathematical numbers (quantitative numbers) is straightforward. Ideal numbers, on any interpretation, are nothing other than the Forms of numbers, which means that they are Forms rather than numbers, just as ideal colors are nothing other than the Forms of colors, which means that they are Forms rather than colors. Mathematical numbers, in contrast, are actual numbers, those used for counting, and employed in mathematical operations, thus making them the only numbers there are, whether in theory or in practice. To present ideal numbers as numbers, as Aristotle does when it suits his purposes, is to position the Forms of numbers as numbers, which is no better than trying to pass off the Forms of colors as colors, or the Form of horse as a horse.

Moreover, this type of association, intended or not, presupposes the self-predication of Forms, which is an entirely different matter. Regardless of whether Plato is stuck with a logical inconsistency in infinite regress scenarios associated with the self-predication of Forms, the place to discuss that would be in connection with the so-called Third Man Argument, which has been receiving plenty of attention all the way from Aristotle to current commentators, thereby making it more distracting than helpful as a nuance in a discussion about something else.[19] Aristotle's mixture of testimony with criticism clouds the testimony, especially where, as in this case, neither the central claim nor the attendant objection corresponds to anything that can be checked against the word of Plato.

7.2.4. MATHEMATICALS AS INTERMEDIATES

The final feature on the agenda concerning Aristotle's interpretation of Plato is his testimony that Plato takes mathematicals, and only mathematicals (as documented and discussed later in this section), to be intermediates between Forms and sensible phenomena (reported clearly and distinctly in *Metaphysics* 987b14–18 and 1028b19–21 but also rather obviously in 1086a11–13 and 1090b32–1091a5):[20]

---

19. The Third Man Argument turns up in Aristotle's *Metaphysics* (990b15–17, 1038b35–1039a3, 1079a13), his *Sophistical Refutations* (178b36–179a10), and his long-lost *Peri Ideōn* as reported in the commentary of Alexander of Aphrodisias on the first book of the *Metaphysics* (*In Aristotelis Metaphysica Commentaria* 83.34–85.12), all regularly invoked (especially the first two) in connection with Plato's *Parmenides* (132a–b or 132d–133a or both). A seminal assessment by Vlastos (1954; 1955; 1956; 1965a; 1965c; 1965d–1966; 1969a; 1969b; 1969c; 1974; 1981) is now a modern classic in the literature. Among countless discussions in the subsequent scholarly dialectic, Sharma (2005; cf. 2007) stands out with a corrective attempt to demonstrate that the Third Man Argument does not present the infinitely regressive self-predication of Forms as a philosophical blunder committed by Plato himself, instead emerging as part of the exegetical machinery of Aristotle's own interpretation of Plato within the greater framework of Aristotle's approach to metaphysics, particularly his categories of substance and attribute. See chapter 1 (section 1.4) for a brief overview of the controversy and for some discussion.

20. A fuller list of references would have to include the following, though still with no claim to being exhaustive: *Metaphysics* 987b14–18, 991a4, 991b29–30, 992b14–17,

Further, besides sensible things and Forms [Plato] says there are the objects of mathematics, which occupy an intermediate position, differing from sensible things in being eternal and unchangeable, from Forms in that there are many alike, while the Form itself is in each case unique. (Aristotle: *Metaphysics* 987b14–18; Ross translation)

Setting aside, at least for the time being, the question whether the testimony of Aristotle is true, that is, whether Plato really accepted intermediates, a natural reaction is to ask why an extra ontological layer of that sort would be required only in mathematics and nowhere else. This is not just a natural reaction to Aristotle but also the very reaction of Aristotle to Plato. Aristotle's critical opinion comes out best in the process of evaluating, as opposed to merely invoking, the presumed ontology of mathematical intermediates in Plato, finding them internally inconsistent because Plato does not stipulate a comparable provision for intermediation in other areas, which would have otherwise, namely through the demands of consistency, required correlative intermediates in those areas as well (*Metaphysics* 997b12–32, 1059b2–9; cf. 991a6–8). His objection is not that there are, in fact, intermediates everywhere, which Plato somehow failed to recognize in a haste to focus exclusively on the mathematical ones, but that intermediates anywhere would require intermediates everywhere, a prima facie condition of consistency, which Plato evidently neither fulfilled nor accounted for in his oral engagements.

Aristotle's objection is appropriate, but only if his report is accurate. The inconsistency he protests is either evidence of a blunder on the part of Plato or evidence of faulty testimony by Aristotle himself, whether through an erroneous restriction of an otherwise full range of intermediates in Plato or through an erroneous assignment of intermediates to Plato to begin with. As one of Aristotle's strongest critics in this regard, Shorey argues that Plato does not, pace Aristotle, countenance mathematical intermediates, precisely because it is inconsistent to do so without allowing intermediates everywhere, which Plato presumably did not do, at least as far as Shorey is concerned (1884/1982, 33; 1903, 83; 1927, 214).

The two positions are mutually consistent: First, Aristotle can rightly insist that assigning an intermediate position to mathematicals requires

---

995b14–17, 997b1–32, 998a7–11, 1002b11–32, 1028b19–27, 1059b2–9, 1077a9–14, 1086a11–13, 1090b32–1091a5.

correlative assignments across the board in one's ontological scheme. He can therefore rightly press Plato on the matter, if Plato did indeed place mathematicals in a separate ontological category intermediate between Forms and sensible phenomena, while doing nothing of the kind in any other part of his vision of reality. At the same time, a critic (Shorey or anyone else) can rightly oppose this reconstruction of Plato on the very grounds on which Aristotle affirms yet criticizes it, namely on the grounds that the existence of mathematical intermediates, whether real or imagined, points to the possibility of all sorts of other intermediates, which are nowhere to be found in Plato. If it is problematic for Aristotle's testimony that the mathematical intermediates he attributes to Plato cannot be confirmed or disconfirmed in the vast body of Plato's works, it stands to be all the more problematic if no intermediates of any sort can be confirmed or disconfirmed in the Platonic corpus.

Why, for example, should there be an intermediate five between the Form of five and five apples, but not an intermediate red between the Form of red and red apples, as Shorey asks in a memorable display of objection by counterexample (1927, 214; cf. 1884/1982, 31–39; 1903, 82–85)? Shorey's red apples are only the tip of a single iceberg adrift in a glacial barrier of counterexamples. Once the color red between the Form of red and red apples is acknowledged as an intermediate on a par with the number five between the Form of five and five apples, we get to ask about intermediate sounds, scents, tastes, and so on without end, perhaps even wondering, not altogether unreasonably, about the intermediate apple between the Form of apple and the actual apples that grow on trees.

There is an easy way out regardless of the proliferation of counterexamples. We can side immediately with Aristotle, if we place any stock in his testimony, which indicates that Plato restricted intermediation to mathematics and intermediates to mathematicals (*Metaphysics* 997b12–32, 1059b2–9). All counterexamples then become irrelevant thought experiments as we assent to the veracity of what must be considered a firsthand report of the teaching in question.

The problem with siding with Aristotle, however, is that, given the paucity of evidence elsewhere, we would be deciding the matter almost entirely on the word of Aristotle. While Aristotle is one of the most prominent philosophers in history, as well as a member of the audience for much of what Plato taught, his testimony is rarely in the spirit of exposition, often coming instead as a peripheral sketch in the process of opposition. We cannot count on full disclosure when he is talking about someone else. Much of Aristotle's testimony, particularly on Plato, comes in a form suitable for criticism, whereupon we can never be certain we are getting the relevant facts, as fully and as accurately as possible, as opposed to selections torn out of context to fit Aristotle's particular purposes.[21] The fact that there is so much in Aristotle that requires us to revise or expand rather than confirm what we can gather about Plato from his own works is only one reason for caution in appraising and assimilating the testimony of Aristotle. This becomes an especially sensitive matter where the textual locus of the most profound ideas of Plato shifts from Plato himself to Aristotle, who then becomes our main source of insight into Plato, despite the fact that, on our best evidence, everything Plato ever put into writing is still available to us in the canonical corpus.

Aristotle takes issue with Plato's restriction of intermediates to mathematicals in a couple of places in the *Metaphysics* (997b12-32, 1059b2-9), though it is not clear in either passage, at least not from the text alone, whether he is talking about Plato or about other members of the Academy or perhaps about both. The first passage (*Metaphysics* 997b12-32) is a general reference to those "who assert the existence both of the Forms and of the intermediates with which they say the mathematical sciences deal" (*Metaphysics* 997b1):

> Further, if we are to posit besides the Forms and the sensibles the intermediates between them, we shall have many difficulties. For clearly on the same principle there will be lines besides the lines-in-themselves and the sensible lines, and so with each of the other classes of things; so that since astronomy is one of these mathematical sciences there will also be a heaven besides the sensible heaven, and a sun and a moon (and so with the

---

21. Katz (2013, 26-28; 2014, 344) reminds us, specifically with respect to Books M and N of the *Metaphysics*, though with further relevance as a general observation, that when Aristotle invokes the views of others, he does so in order to situate his own position among the prevailing ones, not to denigrate the opposing ones. While this is manifestly true, and consistently ignored, it is also true that the absence of malice is a poor substitute for faithful representation. What Aristotle says about the views of others, typically bringing them up only to recommend his own views over theirs, seldom adds up to a serviceable exposition. Aristotelian testimony, especially where it is the only evidence available, tends to be promoted beyond its evidentiary value no less than it tends to be derogated beyond its evidentiary shortcomings.

other heavenly bodies) besides the sensible ones. Yet how are we to believe these things? It is not reasonable even to suppose these bodies immovable, but to suppose their *moving* is quite impossible. And similarly with the things of which optics and mathematical harmonics treat. For these also cannot exist apart from the sensible things, for the same reasons. For if there are sensible things and sensations intermediate between Form and individual, evidently there will also be animals intermediate between animals-in-themselves and the perishable animals.— We might also raise the question, with reference to *which kind* of existing things we must look for these additional sciences. If geometry is to differ from mensuration only in this, that the latter of these deals with things that we perceive, and the former with things that are not perceptible, evidently there will be a science other than medicine, intermediate between medical-science-in-itself and this individual medical science, and so with each of the other sciences. Yet how is this possible? There would have to be also healthy things besides the perceptible healthy things and the healthy-in-itself. (Aristotle: *Metaphysics* 997b12-32; Ross translation)

The second passage (*Metaphysics* 1059b2-9) does not come with any contextual references whatsoever, not even in connection with anonymous proponents as in the first passage. It is simply about the position, without specification of either originators or subscribers:

Now evidently the Forms do not exist. (But it is hard to say, even if one suppose them to exist, why the same is not true of the other things of which there are Forms, as of the objects of mathematics. I mean that they place the objects of mathematics between the Forms and perceptible things, as a third class of things besides the Forms and the things in this world; but there is not a third man or horse besides the ideal and the individuals. (Aristotle: *Metaphysics* 1059b2-9; cf. 991a6-8; Ross translation; opening parenthesis closed outside the portion of text quoted here)

Although neither one of the two passages (and there are no others) criticizing the restriction of intermediates to mathematicals specifically names Plato, there is also nothing to rule that possibility out. Given that Aristotle unequivocally attributes mathematical intermediates to Plato, identifying him by name in passages where he discusses intermediates without explicitly criticizing their restriction to mathematicals (e.g., at least in *Metaphysics* 987b14–18 and 1028b19–21), he is indeed quite likely to be protesting Plato, if also others as well, in the two passages where he does question their restriction to mathematicals. Note also that, if the restriction had strictly concerned people other than Plato, mentioning Plato as an exception (perhaps through something like: "but, of course, Plato does not restrict intermediates to mathematicals") would have been a natural reaction, not only as part of a responsible effort to share that information but also as a respectable reason for introducing a relevant contrast for productive discussion. In other words, Plato's exclusion would have been newsworthy, which makes his silent inclusion more likely than his silent exclusion.

The absence of any such caveat in Aristotle suggests that Plato is at least included in the group if not intended as its sole or leading representative. If Aristotle is right, then Plato embraced mathematicals as intermediates but recognized no other intermediates. There seems, upon initial consideration, to be several different ways that Aristotle could be wrong: (1) Plato may have accepted intermediates of any kind, including, but not limited to, mathematicals. (2) Plato may have rejected intermediates of any kind, including, but not limited to, mathematicals. (3) Plato may have been indifferent on the matter of intermediates. (4) Plato may have been oblivious to the possibility, or to its significance, or both. The last three possibilities, however, are complementary subsets of the single and more general possibility that Plato did not accept intermediates of any kind. Whether he did not accept them because he rejected them, or because he did not care either way, or because he did not even see the difference, is not as important as whether he did or did not accept them. Hence, there are really only two ways that Aristotle could be wrong: Plato may have accepted all intermediates, or he may not have accepted any intermediates. There is no shortage of support for either alternative, nor for the Aristotelian evidence with which each of these two positions competes as an alternative.

Julia Annas (1975, 146–166), for example, sides with Aristotle, whose criticism of Plato for being inconsistent in positing intermediates in mathematics while refusing to acknowledge them elsewhere reinforces her reconstruction of the Aristotelian evidence as showing Plato to introduce mathematical intermediates (either discovering them or inventing them, depending on the perspective) specifically and solely to make up for the inadequacy of Forms as objects of mathematics. The inadequacy in question is that one cannot do mathematics with the Forms of numbers, any more than one can paint with the Forms of colors, or sing with the Forms of sounds, though nothing like the latter two cases ever comes up. Two plus three equals five, but the Form of two plus the Form of three does not equal the Form of five. With the intermediates thus becoming a specific solution to a specific problem, presumably unique to mathematics and irrelevant elsewhere, there is no question in the mind of Annas of Aristotle being wrong in either of the two ways mentioned above. He would not have misinterpreted Plato as restricting intermediates to mathematicals, because having thus developed intermediates explicitly to account for the possibility of mathematics, Plato would have had no reason to accept all intermediates, just as he would have had no reason to accept no intermediates.

Yet the first alternative, that of universal acceptance, is not too far to reach. Intermediates outside mathematics are even closer to the surface in Plato than are mathematical intermediates, though neither kind is easy to establish with any certainty. The account of causality driving the final argument for personal immortality in the *Phaedo* (96a–107a, or 105b–107a, depending on the scope of consideration) is probably the clearest illustration of intermediation both within and outside mathematics.[22] In fact, the reason that the *Phaedo* comes up so often in connection with Aristotle's testimony on Plato's philosophy of mathematics is precisely this rendition of intermediation, which draws on examples both from mathematics (e.g., three not "admitting" the even due to the essential connection between three and the odd) and from natural phenomena (e.g., fire not "admitting" the cold due to the essential connection between fire and the hot).[23] The

---

22. See Alican (2012, 431–450) for an exploration of causal intermediation in Plato's *Phaedo*, including a critical analysis of the final argument for the immortality of the soul (446–450).

23. Sophia A. Stone has been particularly productive in her search for intermediates in Plato's *Phaedo*. Her efforts range from journal articles (Stone 2014) to oral presentations, including a paper read at a workshop in Paris (Stone 2015), and another presented at a conference in Florida (Stone 2018). A revised version of the latter was subsequently published in volume 18 of *Plato Journal* (2018), together with a selection

oddness of the number three eventually finds its psychological counterpart in the life of the soul. Taking the life out of the soul turns out to be just as inconceivable as taking the oddness out of the number three.

The second alternative, that of zero acceptance, is no less tenable. Shorey (1884/1982, 31–39; 1903, 82–85; 1927, 213–218) is a classic exponent of this alternative, with his denial that Plato acknowledges any intermediates at all, fervently disputing Aristotle's direct testimony that Plato did so in mathematics. He cites and challenges what he identifies as the key passages referenced in support of the misconceived placement of intermediates between Forms and sensible phenomena: *Parmenides* 143a; *Philebus* 56 ff.; *Republic* 523d–526e[24] (Shorey 1884/1982, 33). Taking "numbers themselves" to be nothing other than Forms, he submits that the distinction between Forms and sensible phenomena is a strictly binary one: "In the same way that there is nothing interposed between 'the great itself' and a 'particular great man,' there is no third number situated between the ideal numbers and the particular numbered things" (Shorey 1884/1982, 33). He maintains that Aristotle himself believes in intermediates and erroneously attributes them to Plato, not with malicious intent but in an effort to fill a gap, which we cannot be certain Plato would have filled the same way (Shorey 1884/1982, 37–39).

All told, Shorey (1884/1982, 34–35) dismisses Aristotle's testimony on the grounds (1) that Aristotle struggled to understand what Plato was doing

---

of other papers from the same conference, dedicated exclusively to the problem of intermediates in Plato and organized by Stone herself in collaboration with Nicholas Baima. She and I have corresponded at length on where in the *Phaedo* to look for intermediates and how best to bring them out. We see eye to eye on the possibilities and share several conclusions on methodology, all arrived at independently. My own thoughts and findings date back to my formal study of causal intermediaries in the *Phaedo* (Alican 2012, 431–450).

24. Shorey shares his astonishment that Zeller is misled by this passage (*Republic* 523d–526e), which Shorey identifies as "the origin of the futile nonsense about mathematical numbers situated between sensible numbers and ideal numbers" (1884/1982, 33). His opposition is grounded in his conviction that Plato's reference in this passage to "numbers themselves" is a reference to the Forms of numbers, as opposed to numbers that are just numbers, being neither Forms nor sensibles. With Adam subsequently proposing precisely this interpretation in the notes to his own edition of the *Republic* (Adam 1902 [vol. 2], 114–115, n. 525d24), Shorey takes up the same passage in greater detail in a later paper (Shorey 1927, 213–218).

with concepts and abstractions; (2) that Aristotle often interpreted others, including Plato, in the light of his own views, and with technical terms of his own invention, which kept him from appreciating the intricacies of the actual source under investigation; and (3) that Aristotle was blind to Plato's use of humor and myth, either taking such passages literally or ignoring them altogether. He also offers a brief reconstruction of how Aristotelian testimony on Plato's metaphysical first principles superseding the Forms, namely the one and the-great-and-the-small, originates in Aristotle's failure to understand how Plato's Forms were supposed to exist at all if they did not exist anywhere in particular (in space and time). He argues that this puzzle of existence led Aristotle to assume that Plato's Forms were substances, in conformity with his own conception of substance, and to proceed, in general, in a manner enabling him to invoke Plato, as he was wont to do with many others, as a historical precedent for his own theory of causality (Shorey 1884/1982, 36–37).

Shorey thus recommends great caution in approaching Aristotle as a historian of philosophy. This is not because he finds Aristotle to manipulate the facts in deliberate distortion of the truth, or in open contradiction of it, but because he finds Aristotle to misunderstand the facts and to report what little he does understand only insofar as it promotes a particular point in his own philosophical agenda, whereby we can never be sure of getting an accurate or complete picture of the matter reported. Cherniss (1944; 1945) can be cited as another notable dissident, one with more of the same opposition as Shorey but with even keener observations, sharper objections, and an inimitable display of scholarship, all coming together in just the right ways to strengthen the prevailing opposition to Aristotle for insight into Plato.[25]

---

25. Even scholars who strongly disagree with Cherniss, including those who find his influence outright pernicious, tend to express a deep admiration for his scholarship. One example is Findlay (1974), who speaks of the "two brilliant and learned books" of "this Goliath of truly wonderful, but at times wonderfully misapplied, erudition" (455), applauding "his almost superhuman scholarship" and "his incomparable grasp of all the evidence" (473). Another is Gerson (2014), who cites "praeternatural erudition and the highest level of scholarship" as impressions inspiring him to "profoundly admire the work of Cherniss" (408), despite opposing his estimation of the value of Aristotelian testimony.

7.3. Aristotle as Historian

Was Aristotle a respectable historian of philosophy, or was he a bad historian of philosophy, as suggested, among others, by Shorey and Cherniss? This is not intended to prejudge the question whether Aristotle was a historian of philosophy in the first place (see Collobert 2002; Guthrie 1957; Lowry 1980; McKeon 1940; Stevenson 1974), or for that matter, whether he can reasonably be considered a historian in any sense at all (see Huxley 1972). In order to be a good historian, or a bad historian, one must obviously be a historian. But that is not what is at issue here. Whether or not Aristotle qualifies as a historian of any kind, we may still ask whether he got things right when he spoke of what others said. He need not have been a historian of philosophy in the standard sense for us to feel free to appraise the accuracy of his testimony on the views of his predecessors and contemporaries.

Where an appraisal is technically possible, and where the testimony turns out to be inaccurate, we should be able to say, without being accused of misunderstanding Aristotle's place in the history of ideas, or of being ignorant of the history of ideas itself, that his testimony is unreliable as a guide to the matter on hand, and even to call him a bad historian of philosophy if the discrepancies are great enough either in quantity or in quality, and certainly if they are substantial in both respects. Even if testimony by Aristotle does not fall under the history of philosophy, and thus cannot be evaluated by its standards, whether in intent, method, or outcome, his work is regularly referenced for information on the ideas of others, which he habitually presents in whatever way makes his own ideas look best, which regrettably has the makings of bad history.

A valid concern in any initiative to reconstruct Plato's philosophy through Aristotle's testimony is indeed the general reliability of what we get through Aristotle when he is talking about the ideas of others. There is a strong presumption in support of that reliability and an equally strong one against it. The presumption in support of it is that Aristotle's experience as a student of Plato, and as a member of the Academy, makes him an excellent source of information on every aspect of Plato's philosophy whether or not Plato ever put it into writing. Whatever the subject, if Plato uttered a word about it, Aristotle was in a position to know about it. The presumption against it is that Aristotle's testimony on Plato is sometimes inconsistent with what can be verified directly in

Plato, or checked indirectly against third parties, which then introduces an element of doubt into anything Aristotle says about Plato that cannot be confirmed either through Plato's own writing or through commentary or testimony outside Aristotle. The combined result is that these opposing presumptions support mutually inconsistent interpretations based on apparently reasonable generalizations.

The Aristotelian side of the conflict is held up not just by the positive implications of Aristotle's close association with Plato, and of his tenure at the Academy, but also by the negative intimations of Plato himself in revealing a general reluctance to share important aspects of his philosophy in writing. The strength of the main pillar, the positive implications, is the utter unpalatability of rejecting Aristotle's testimony out of hand, which would seem to make him either dimwitted, because he got important facts wrong despite close and constant exposure, or malevolent, because he got them right but misrepresented them on purpose. There is very little chance of the former being true, given the proven brilliance of Aristotle in contradiction of the possibility of persistent misunderstanding, and there is even less chance of the latter being true, given the standing threat of exposure by the other associates of Plato in the event of deliberate misrepresentation by any one of them.

The strength of the secondary pillar, the negative intimations concerning written work, is the direct connection with the ipsissima verba of Plato himself. Several sources in the canonical corpus indicate that Plato had a predilection for oral over written discourse in philosophy: *Phaedrus* (275c–277a), *Second Letter* (314a–c), *Seventh Letter* (341c–342a). While the corresponding passages do not confirm the veracity of any particular piece of testimony on any particular subject, whether by Aristotle or by anyone else, they do help explain why testimonial evidence in general would be relevant and could be useful. The common message seems to be, though it is not explicitly stated as such in each passage, that foundational insight into truth and reality requires dialectical exploration and discovery, which is best conducted through oral discussion as opposed to written communication, because the former affords endless possibilities for development while the latter ends with the last word on the scroll or tablet.

Not everyone recognizes all three sources as genuine works of Plato, but inauthenticity is not necessarily a mark of inaccuracy since the leading motive behind the creation of spurious works in antiquity was respectful imitation in demonstration of one's literary talents rather than malicious disinformation in execution of a destructive agenda. It has always been possible to get accurate information from an imitation falsely attributed to an author, especially where ancient philosophers were concerned, given that the forger was invariably at pains to emulate the author's style without distorting his philosophy. But even if this were not the case, the question of authenticity would apply to only one, or at most two, and definitely not all three, of the sources relevant here. While the *Second Letter* is considered spurious by most scholars, the *Seventh Letter* has as many proponents as opponents, and the *Phaedrus* typically goes unchallenged. All three confirm Plato's preference for oral over written disquisition in matters of philosophical importance. And since just one would have been sufficient, three in harmony prove to be more than enough.

The internal evidence of Plato's preference for oral over written engagement in philosophy is complemented by the external evidence of a public lecture by Plato on the good.[26] First reported by Aristoxenus (*Elementa Harmonica* 2.30–31) in reflection of the personal assessment of Aristotle, the lecture was evidently a mathematical presentation on the ontology of value to a crowd of ordinary people assembled instead with expectations of hearing about a more conventional conception of value, possibly hoping to learn about what is good in the sense of common morality, perhaps as pertaining to the identification and evaluation of things that are good in virtue of their role in human flourishing (*eudaimonia*).

---

26. The literature on Plato's lecture on the good is inexhaustible. Cherniss (1945, 1–30, especially 1–13), Ferber (1984), Gaiser (1980), Ross (1951, 147–149, 186–187, 199–200, 204–205, 210, 244), and Thesleff (1982, 201–202 [= 2009, 347–348]; 1999, 104–105, 164–165 [= 2009, 485–486, 531]), to cite a few of the most relevant scholars, comment with competence on its authenticity and implications. Ross collates the ancient sources as follows (1951, 147–148): Alexander of Aphrodisias (*In Aristotelis Metaphysica Commentaria* 56.33–35, 85.17, 250.17–20, 262.18–26), Aristoxenus (*Elementa Harmonica* 2.30–31), Asclepius (*In Aristotelis Metaphysicorum Libros A–Z Commentaria* 77.4), Philoponus (*In Aristotelis Physica Commentaria* 515.30, 521.10, 521.14), Porphyry (*Commentary on the Philebus*, a lost work referenced through Simplicius's *In Aristotelis Physica Commentaria* 453.25–455.14), Simplicius (*In Aristotelis Physica Commentaria* 151.10, 435.28, 453.25–455.14, 454.18, 503.12, 542.10, 542.12, 545.23, 545.24). Aristoxenus represents the earliest source available, with the others uncritically repeating rather than independently confirming his testimony, which then effectively reduces the stream of evidence to a single source. As discussed further in the main text below, however, limited documentation does not undermine the plausibility of the story, essentially an anecdotal account, which could easily have been exposed and falsified had Aristoxenus simply invented the legend.

Despite later tendencies to exaggerate some of the details and much of the context, the basic version in Aristoxenus, essentially a record of Aristotelian criticism, is a plausible account corroborated by circumstantial evidence, contradicted by nothing we know, and repeated by countless others.

The exaggeration in question is the tendency, without restraint or justification, to build upon the original report of the public lecture by Plato, which is perfectly believable as it is but sometimes blown out of proportion, typically in speculation of a series of such lectures as opposed to just the one that has ever been reported, or through the invention and introduction of various details never mentioned in the original. Cherniss describes this illicit "expansion of the evidence" as follows:

> Yet in most of the authoritative treatments of Plato, after a scholarly reference to this lecture on the Good, the singular becomes an unexplained plural within the paragraph, the lecture a whole series of lectures, and before the section has been finished we are being told that Plato gave "regular lectures," "systematic and continuous expositions in lecture form on some of the most important points in his doctrine." (Cherniss 1945, 2)

Positioning himself specifically against Burnet (1914), Field (1930), Hubert (1914), and Taylor (1926a), Cherniss interprets the corresponding expansion as a deliberate distortion of the facts to promote the Aristotelian perspective on Plato:[27]

> Here, then, is the reason why the single lecture on the Good which ancient sources mention is magnified and multiplied until it becomes a systematic course of oral instruction in the Academy. This systematic oral instruction is a hypothesis set up to account for those aspects of the theory of ideas which Aristotle ascribes to Plato but which are not found in Plato's writings. (Cherniss 1945, 10; cf. 1–30)

Even Gaiser, one of the most prominent proponents of the opposing Tübingen Paradigm, concedes the point, endorsing the authenticity of the one public lecture but not of a whole series of them:

---

27. Cherniss (1945) cites Taylor through the 1927 edition of the latter's *Plato: The Man and His Work* (Taylor 1926a).

Cherniss was right to protest against an "expansion of the evidence" and to deny that "regular lectures" could be deduced from Aristoxenus. The recent attempts by the Esoterics to use Aristoxenus as a witness to regular lectures on the Good were, I have to admit, mistaken. (Gaiser 1980, 16)

Note that Gaiser's concession is merely that the public lecture reported by Aristoxenus was indeed an isolated event. This does not rule out the possibility of lectures or oral instruction, whether on the good or on matters of comparable importance, in more intimate settings, with more receptive audiences, of the kind Plato must have enjoyed regularly in the Academy as well as in other scholarly circles.

Although the locus classicus of efforts at authentication is Aristotle's assessment of the lecture, as reported by Aristoxenus, the absence of independent confirmation through parallel sources is no reason to doubt that the lecture actually took place. Aristoxenus would no more have portrayed Aristotle in open criticism of a lecture that never took place (or one that took place but without any of the details indicated) than Aristotle himself would have been inclined to criticize a lecture that never took place (or one that took place but without any of the details indicated).[28] The storyline comes with too many witnesses to be a fabrication. It would have been foolish to make up a story, which if false in any way, could have been contradicted by just about anyone living in Athens at the time.

Supporting the authenticity of the lecture, Gaiser (1980, 9; cf. n. 12 on 29) directs our attention to the bibliographic evidence of contemporaneous confirmation, now lost to us, in the works of Xenocrates (Diogenes Laërtius 4.13) and Heraclides (Diogenes Laërtius 5.87). He also notes that the historicity of a public lecture by Plato on the good is supported by the evidence of widespread public familiarity with Plato's preoccupation with the good, as confirmed by various references in comic fragments—Alexis fr. 152 (II 353 Kock), Amphis fr. 6 (II 237 Kock), Philippides fr. 6 (II 303 Kock)—collectively indicating that Plato's good had become "prover-

---

28. Aristotle's opposition is not to the contents of the lecture but to the details of its promotion. Aristoxenus (*Elementa Harmonica* 2.30-31) does not say that Aristotle rejected, or even questioned, Plato's position on the good as articulated in the lecture. What he says is that Aristotle found the audience's frustration indicative of what not to do in public presentations, recommending instead that the speaker prepare the audience in advance as to what to expect.

bial for something of universal importance, but difficult to understand" (Gaiser 1980, 11–12; cf. nn. 21–23 on 29–30). "[T]he average theatre-goer in Athens," infers Gaiser (1980, 12), "had heard of Plato's Good," which is a compelling sign of publicity, eminently consistent with, though not conclusively demonstrative of, a public lecture on the good.

The problem, if any, is not historical support but evidentiary value. Although the legendary lecture is consistent with a preference for orality, it seems to contradict the pedagogical reasons for that preference. The central thesis of the mathematically oriented and philosophically overwhelming presentation seems to have been the unity of the good, purportedly established through a demonstration concluding that "the Good is One," which was apparently a source of sheer perplexity and utter frustration for the audience. One could conceivably and reasonably object, therefore, that while the very existence of a public lecture, together with the form of its delivery, seems to indicate a preference for oral over written philosophy, the particular circumstances contradict the presumed propensity of orality to promote a more effective learning experience, given that the lecture ends up producing confusion rather than enlightenment.

This is a good objection with a good answer. The objection has been made by Cherniss (1945), among others, and answered by Gaiser (1980), among others. While Cherniss (1945, 1–30, especially 1–13) objects that the evidence of the lecture contradicts any connection between orality and pedagogical efficacy, Gaiser (1980, especially 20, 25–28) responds that the motivation behind the public lecture, an isolated event as opposed to a regular practice, need not have been pedagogical at all. Gaiser's considered opinion is that the lecture was Plato's initiative to correct public misconceptions concerning the nature of his philosophy and the focus of Academic activity, probably one or the other if not both, largely in response to a deteriorating reputation in connection with perverted interpretations of his convictions and distorted reports of his activities. He maintains, without claiming certitude, that the lecture may have been conceived as a public illustration of the typical concerns of the Academy so as to show the people of Athens that the school was not a hotbed of subversive activity or breeding grounds for social misfits and political dissidents.[29]

---

29. Thesleff (1999, 104–105 [= 2009, 485–486]) offers an alternative interpretation that likewise constitutes a response to Cherniss (1945, 1–13) on the apparent conflict between the level of difficulty reported for Plato's public lecture on the good and the conviction attributed to him of the pedagogical superiority of oral over written dis-

Gaiser's response is both reasonable and persuasive, but Cherniss's reservations remain relevant nonetheless. The story of the lecture fails to confirm the testimony of Aristotle regarding unwritten doctrines, just as Cherniss says, though it does not necessarily contradict the testimony of Aristotle regarding unwritten doctrines, just as Gaiser says. Yet the case for orality as Plato's modus operandi, including the methodological explanation for that inclination, is neither predicated upon nor undermined by the evidentiary value of Plato's public lecture. The passages cited above from the Platonic corpus, namely the *Phaedrus* (275c–277a), the *Second Letter* (314a–c), and the *Seventh Letter* (341c–342a), already support the case on hand. They distinctly favor the spoken word over the written word in philosophical discourse, apparently on the grounds that oral engagement is naturally dialectical, thereby fostering comprehension and enlightenment. While the justificatory appeal to the dialectical opportunities in orality is not expressed precisely in those terms, that is the message intended, clearly so in the *Phaedrus* (276e–277a) and the *Seventh Letter* (341c, 343a), though not so much in the *Second Letter*, which is generally considered spurious anyway.

The same message can be found in various other dialogues in the canonical corpus, including the *Laws* (968c–e), the *Parmenides* (136e), and the *Republic* (536b–540c), which do not compare oral and written approaches to philosophy, but which do nevertheless emphasize the philosophical value and pedagogical virtue of dialectical training, thus confirming the justification indicated in the *Phaedrus* (276e–277a) and the *Seventh Letter* (341c, 343a) for Plato's preference for orality.[30] As Gaiser

---

cussion in philosophy. He considers the lecture a deliberate attempt by Plato, perhaps a Socratic stingray operation of sorts, to demonstrate the depths of what is required for moral enlightenment: "The problems of Plato's notorious public ἀχρόασις 'On the Good' can be solved reasonably well if one takes it to have been a single occasion when Plato wanted to make it clear to the Athenians that the question of τὸ ἀγαθόν is far too difficult for a couple of hours' lecture. Plato, I believe, was teasing his public" (Thesleff 1999, 104 [= 2009, 485]). He adds, on the next page, that any perplexity in the audience would have been restricted to the laypersons in attendance, thus excluding associates and students, who would have neither been taken by surprise nor therefore had any reason to take copious and meticulous notes, imagined by some scholars to have entered into circulation after the lecture, presumably as a direct consequence of it.

30. The three references (*Laws* 968c–e; *Parmenides* 136e; *Republic* 536b–540c) adduced here in support of the dialectical nature of Plato's philosophical and pedagogical orientation are from Gaiser (1980, 14–15), who invokes the corresponding passages, along

(1980, 20, 25–28) argues, this message is not contradicted by the account of Plato's failure to reach his audience during the public lecture, which Gaiser regards as an exceptional initiative very likely undertaken not to educate the public but to show them that the education in question is nothing to fear and, in the process, to correct any misconceptions about Plato's philosophical outlook and orientation.

What is definitive in terms of the immediate purposes of the present chapter is not the pedagogical correlation between Plato's public lecture and the purported motivation for the unwritten doctrines but the unequivocal and pervasive mathematical orientation of both. Even if the story of the lecture fails in every other respect, it does support the mathematization described by Aristotle elsewhere.

What is it, then, that forces a stalemate out of these otherwise persuasive considerations in favor of an Aristotelian interpretation of Plato's metaphysics? It is the demonstrable tendency of Aristotle, illustrated in the next section, to steer us wrong on details, even as he enlightens us on essentials. Be it through plain misunderstanding, deliberate distortion with full knowledge, or selective emphasis with no intent to deceive, Aristotle sometimes says things that are not true, especially in appraisal of Plato's

---

with the *Phaedrus* (275d–277a), to demonstrate that there are plenty of selections in the authentic works of Plato that corroborate the evidence of the arguably spurious *Seventh Letter* (which Gaiser himself does not reject): "Since the authenticity of the *Seventh Letter* has been doubted, it is important that the same position can be seen in the incontrovertibly authentic dialogues. As early as in the *Republic* (7, 536b–540c), Plato describes the long course of education which leads to apprehension of the Idea of Good only after decades of mathematical and dialectical training. Likewise in the *Parmenides* (136e), truth is said to be attainable only after prolonged education in dialectic—and this fact is not known to the Many. In the final section of the *Phaedrus* (275d–277a), Plato explains at length that the written word is not suitable for conveying ultimate knowledge, since this can only grow and ripen over a period of time. Finally, Plato makes the same point at the end of the *Laws*, his last work. The passage (12, 968c–e) runs: "precise and universal knowledge is only attainable through prolonged communion (πολλῆς συνουσία) of teacher and pupils. The essential concepts are not ineffable (ἀπόρρητα) in the sense of Mysteries, but are indeed 'unsayable in advance' (ἀπρόρρητα); that is, not before the student is able to grasp them for himself, after long practice in dialectic" (Gaiser 1980, 14–15, cf. nn. 32–33 on 31; Stephanus notation modified for stylistic conformity; italics added for the titles of Plato's works; paragraph breaks and footnote reference markers in the original omitted here).

philosophical positions, but also in connection with the ideas of others. No matter the reason, Aristotle's depiction of Plato's views is not always consistent with Plato's views, nor even with Aristotle's own articulation of them elsewhere.

Most of what Aristotle says in testimony is both accurate and consistent, but that provides little comfort, and deserves no compliment, where all of it should be accurate and consistent. The problem is not so much the magnitude or proportion of incorrect references and interpretations as it is the existence of any false testimonial contributions at all. A great many of them would be especially frustrating, as would be a few that are particularly egregious. But even one is too many where Aristotle is the only source. The presence of discrepancies in his testimony undermines the validity of the common and otherwise reasonable scholarly appeal to Aristotle's intellectual competence, together with his close and lengthy association with Plato, as a blanket argument against the possibility of his getting anything wrong in connection with Plato, or at least against the possibility of his getting something important wrong in that regard.

The problem that such reservations collectively present against the testimony of Aristotle, since they are grounded in specific discrepancies rather than methodological weaknesses, affects details rather than fundamentals. There is no doubt that the main lines of Aristotle's testimony concerning the unwritten doctrines of Plato are borne out as an interpretive possibility. The evidence considered thus far, as well as any that may be added to it in support, and much that has indeed been added in the ongoing scholarly debate, makes a rather strong case for the Aristotelian perspective. But the case thus made pertains more to the general plausibility of unwritten doctrines by Plato, that is, to the possibility that Plato developed certain doctrines that he kept out of the dialogues, than it does to the specific contents of any such doctrines.

Some of the specifics are, no doubt, also quite believably attributable to Plato, but the general plausibility of the existence of unwritten doctrines by Plato does not constitute a categorical justification of every last thing Aristotle ever said about Plato. Admittedly, the evidence of the metaphysical first principles, namely the one and the-great-and-the-small, is too strong to be dismissed just because it is not explicitly corroborated in the Platonic corpus. Yet we would not be unreasonable in scrutinizing the rest of what Aristotle says about Plato, especially in the course of presenting Plato as subscribing to an entirely mathematical metaphysical outlook.

While Plato's fascination with mathematics is evident in the dialogues, his thoroughgoing reduction of metaphysics to mathematics is a perspective we get only through Aristotle.

We should also note, against the tempting and rightful appeal to the intellect and integrity of Aristotle, that rejecting his testimony in the face of discrepancy or inconsistency, or even in the mere absence of corroboration or consistency, is not a matter of finding Aristotle stupid, ignorant, or malicious. Yes, of course, Aristotle would not have grossly misunderstood Plato, certainly not so much as to miss the main lines of Plato's philosophical orientation. And, of course, he would not have deliberately misrepresented Plato to make him out to be a bad philosopher who was wrong on an overabundance of philosophical questions. Even if Aristotle had never had a modicum of intellectual integrity, the natural pressure on any commentator to be truthful, lest he be exposed and ridiculed by other witnesses privy to the same information, would have been a strong and constant deterrent against a willful misrepresentation of the facts.

Yet misrepresentation need not always be undertaken in execution of a vicious campaign of malignment. It can also come about in the process of overemphasizing or underemphasizing some things at the expense of others, or leaving out some things altogether, depending on the relevance of such details to the matter under discussion, especially where the primary goal is to establish one's own thesis against any others thereby rejected, possibly with a lack of attention to detail or fair play, and consequently perhaps even with a certain degree of unplanned yet convenient distortion of the facts. Such distortion need not be grounded either in ignorance or in malevolence. And Aristotle need not be insulted as his testimony is rejected.

Two stock reservations turn up routinely whenever scholars of ancient philosophy find themselves facing Aristotle as the only source, or as the main source, regarding a point of contention in Plato. The first is the difficulty of ascertaining whether Aristotle is talking specifically about Plato himself or more generally about Platonists, the latter of which may or may not include Plato, depending on whether the context is sufficiently clear to identify the parties intended. The second is the alleged tendency of Aristotle either to misunderstand and therefore to misinterpret Plato (as he does with more than a few others) or to misinform us for some other reason and in some other way (also in line with what he does with others), typically in the process of demonstrating that Plato is wrong on something Aristotle thinks himself right.

Given the enormous potential for learning about Plato from Aristotle, that is, for learning more about Plato than we can learn through the dialogues alone, as against the serious reservations concerning the reliability of Aristotle, we are at an impasse of sorts. We have two contradictory presumptions, one favoring and the other opposing Aristotle, both based on apparently reasonable generalizations. It will not do to declare the position a stalemate and to proceed to ignore the matter. Nor will it do to follow Aristotle blindly just because he was there. And it certainly will not do to reject his testimony on specific matters on the basis of generalizations about how he got things wrong when he talked about the views of others. There can be no substitute for a direct appraisal of the accuracy and consistency of Aristotle's testimony relevant to the matter on hand. Exposing specific problems in that regard is the aim of the next section.

The three points of testimony under consideration in this chapter are, to repeat, Plato's development of metaphysical principles more fundamental than the Forms, his reduction of Forms to numbers, and his recognition of mathematicals as intermediates between Forms and sensible phenomena. The most prominent of these, judging by the scholarly attention over the centuries, as well as the philosophical implications for proper interpretation, is the primacy of the one and the-great-and-the-small as metaphysical first principles. Aristotle's testimony on the foundational position and function of the twin principles is not only broadly consistent with Plato's dialogues, especially with developments generally agreed to belong to his mature thought, but also evidently corroborated by third parties whose testimonies are now lost to us (see Thesleff 1999, 93 [= 2009, 475]). Yet the other two items of testimony jointly mathematizing Plato's world are suspect, perhaps not in every detail, but certainly in essentials. And it is those two items, especially the one directly concerning intermediates, that are at the forefront here.

The minimally acceptable criteria for reliability in testimonial evidence are accuracy and consistency. We can reasonably expect Aristotle to enlighten us without contradicting either Plato or himself. The best way to determine whether that is what we get from him is to concentrate on a piece of testimony that affords some possibility of verification in the Platonic corpus, while monitoring the internal consistency of the same bit of testimony throughout the Aristotelian corpus. Given that neither the equivalence of Forms and numbers nor the existence of intermediates can be tested directly in any of Plato's works, we need to follow the next most relevant thread of evidence in the dialogues: the Forms. The reduction of Forms to numbers may or may not (depending on the interpretation) be consistent with the restriction of intermediates to mathematicals, but either possibility is at odds with Plato's tendency to recognize a Form for just about anything. The latter makes for a perfect test case.

7.4. Discrepancies and Contradictions

Was Aristotle really a bad historian of philosophy? The question may be too broad for a meaningful answer. It invites sweeping generalizations, which could conceivably go either way, without bringing any clarity to the matter. Restricting the scope of consideration in some way, for example, by focusing strictly on Aristotle's testimony on Plato, would put us in a good position to investigate whether we are getting reliable information specifically in that context. And the relevant context indeed shows that what Aristotle says about Plato tends to contradict what Plato says, as well as undermining what Aristotle says about Plato elsewhere.

To cite just one example, if we were to go by what Aristotle says about Plato's approach to Forms, we would have to believe both that Plato restricted Forms to numbers (*Metaphysics* 991b9–10, 1073a17–22) and that Plato restricted Forms to natural kinds (*Metaphysics* 1070a18–19), as Aristotle testifies with apparently no regard for internal consistency, while Plato himself embraces a wide range of Forms with no such conditions, qualifications, or limitations: "As you know, we customarily hypothesize a single form in connection with each of the many things to which we apply the same name" (*Republic* 596a).

The discrepancy between text and testimony runs deep. Even if we were to resolve the mutually inconsistent restrictions in Aristotle's testimony in favor of one restriction or the other, we would find that both the restriction to numbers and the restriction to natural kinds is inconsistent with the actual allowance for a Form for everything with a common name (*Republic* 596a), which would seem, at least on the face of it, to include not just mathematical objects and natural kinds, somehow both the only things that can have a Form in Aristotle's testimony, but also artifacts and whatever else may be grouped together in a sensible way.

For example, the contradiction between Plato's position and Aristotle's testimony disappears if Plato's generalization is interpreted either as a playful rumination, or as a loose description of how Forms work, or as a dialectical exploration of abstraction and concept formation, never seriously adopted as a formal principle. None of these alternatives, however, has anything to recommend it against the credibility of the original passage (*Republic* 596a), which is not itself undermined by anything more specific than the widely acknowledged and broadly applicable difficulty of establishing anything Plato says in the dialogues as a conviction or doctrine firmly held by Plato himself.[31] There is otherwise nothing particularly wrong, nor even merely counterintuitive, about the general rule of a Form for every identifiable group of things. We cannot reasonably ignore it, or reject it, just to make Aristotle come out right.[32]

As a matter of fact, Plato is not just serious about allowing a broad and inclusive range for Forms but also quite persistent and successful in maintaining such a range without any restrictions or reservations, especially without arbitrary ones. If the unrestricted range specified in the *Republic* were just a passing fancy, conjured up in a brainstorm never to be revisited, Plato would not have described it as a customary hypothesis: "we customarily hypothesize a single form in connection with each of the many things to which we apply the same name" (*Republic* 596a).[33] Nor would he have returned to it elsewhere as a perpetual claim: "our perpetual claim that there exists an intelligible Form for each thing" (*Timaeus* 51c). Nor would he have described its recognition and comprehension as

---

31. The central question is whether Plato's characters express Plato's views. There is no clear answer. Obviously, not all characters do, for some of them contradict each other, and some of them sound outright unreasonable. But then who, if anyone, speaks for Plato? Diogenes Laërtius (3.52) does not hesitate to name names: Socrates, Timaeus, the Athenian Stranger, and the Eleatic Stranger. Likewise without hesitation, but in this case without names, Thesleff (1993a, 259–266; 1999, 6 [= 2009, 392]; 2000, 53–66) argues that the drama itself, rather than any particular character, speaks for Plato. An assortment of other perspectives can be found in a collection of essays edited by Press (2000) in examination of this question.

32. Moreover, the only contradiction resolved in that case would be the one between Plato's liberal formulation of the range of Forms and Aristotle's tendency to restrict that range. We would still be left with the contradiction between Aristotle's testimony that Plato limits Forms to numbers (*Metaphysics* 991b9–10, 1073a17–22) and Aristotle's testimony that Plato limits Forms to natural kinds (*Metaphysics* 1070a18–19).

33. The *Republic* itself contains at least one clear precedent for this generalization, making it reasonable for Plato to say that we "customarily" hypothesize in this manner (*Republic* 596a): "And beauty itself and good itself and all the things that we thereby set down as many, reversing ourselves, we set down according to a single form of each, believing that there is but one, and call it 'the being' of each" (*Republic* 507b).

a special gift: "Only a very gifted man can come to know that for each thing there is some kind, a being itself by itself" (*Parmenides* 135a–b).

The last of the supporting quotations in the preceding paragraph is from the *Parmenides*, a dialogue that may be tempting in some respects to introduce in opposition to, rather than in validation of, the principle of a Form for each multitude of things with a group identity. The temptation would be to point out that Plato portrays the Socrates of the *Parmenides* as accepting Forms for some things (justice, beauty, goodness at 130b), rejecting Forms for other things (hair, mud, dirt at 130c–d), and being torn about still others (man, fire, water at 130c). Yet this is no exception. It is no exception because the Socrates of the *Parmenides* is no philosopher.[34] He is just a bright young man with a promising future and a long way to go to get there (130e).

The same Socrates, in the same work, expresses serious reservations about his own inclinations to accept Forms only for some things and not for others (130d). It is almost as if he were deliberately bringing up clear examples together with confusing examples to emphasize just how counterintuitive it is to accept Forms only for some things rather than for all things (130d), thereby creating a dramatic opportunity for Plato to assert the comprehensive relevance of Forms. This reading finds credence in the feedback the young Socrates gets from the elderly Parmenides, who tells him that his confusion is due to inexperience, adding that Socrates will surely be able to see the folly of excluding Forms on a whim once he receives the dialectical training required to turn him into a proper philosopher (130e, 135c–d).

Comprehension through the requisite training requires not just a gift in learning, as indicated in the passage quoted above and repeated below (*Parmenides* 135a–b), but also a gift in teaching, as the same passage continues:

> Only a very gifted man can come to know that for each thing there is some kind, a being itself by itself; but only a prodigy

---

34. Note also that, even if we were to adopt the convictions of the young Socrates without question or reflection, perhaps failing to recognize the dramatic hesitation anchored to his lack of experience, the Forms he affirms with confidence (justice, beauty, goodness at *Parmenides* 130b) are restricted neither to numbers (cf. *Metaphysics* 991b9–10, 1073a17–22) nor to natural kinds (cf. *Metaphysics* 1070a18–19), which again contradicts Aristotle's attribution of those restrictions to Plato.

more remarkable still will discover that and be able to teach someone else who has sifted all these difficulties thoroughly and critically for himself. (Plato: *Parmenides* 135a–b; Gill and Ryan translation)[35]

The importance of the passage is in identifying the difficulties troubling Socrates as philosophical problems to be solved toward a proper grasp of reality through the Forms, where restricting the population of Forms prior to achieving such an understanding is sure to impede the understanding. The greater the problem, the more important the solution. The utter confusion of the young Socrates, otherwise portrayed as an experienced philosopher in any other dialogue where he is present at all, is a dramatic endorsement of the role of dialectical training in philosophical enlightenment. Firmly positioning restrictive tendencies as weaknesses to be overcome through training, the *Parmenides* thus reinforces the broad correspondence indicated elsewhere (*Republic* 596a; *Timaeus* 51c) between Forms and particulars. The danger, in fact, is not in making a liberal allowance for the range of Forms but in doing just the opposite, failing to make that allowance:

"Yet on the other hand, Socrates," said Parmenides, "if someone, having an eye on all the difficulties we have just brought up and others of the same sort, won't allow that there are forms for things and won't mark off a form for each one, he won't have anywhere to turn his thought, since he doesn't allow that for each thing there is a character that is always the same. In this way he will destroy the power of dialectic entirely. But I think you are only too well aware of that." (Plato: *Parmenides* 135b–c; Gill and Ryan translation)

Plato's reluctance to restrict the population of Forms, and especially his refusal to impose arbitrary restrictions, is evident not just in the general rule of a Form for every multitude, or strictly speaking, for every nameable multitude, as explicated through comparably worded principles in various dialogues (*Republic* 596a; *Parmenides* 130d–e, 135a–d; *Timaeus*

---

35. Socrates immediately and enthusiastically expresses full agreement, thus removing any suspicions of a conflict between his position and that of Parmenides: " 'I agree with you, Parmenides,' Socrates said. 'That's very much what I think too' " (*Parmenides* 135b).

51c), but also in itemized lists provided in illustration of all such principles. The most explicitly informative version, the general rule of the *Republic* (596a), where nameability is invoked in support of classifiability, is initially elucidated through a reference to the Form of bed and the Form of table as examples (596b, 597c–d), followed by a long list of items illustrating the full range of Forms in question:

> Wait a minute, and you'll have even more reason to say that, for this same craftsman is able to make, not only all kinds of furniture, but all plants that grow from the earth, all animals (including himself), the earth itself, the heavens, the gods, all the things in the heavens and in Hades beneath the earth. (Plato: *Republic* 596c; Grube translation)

The itemized list of the *Republic* has its counterpart in the *Phaedo* where we find enthusiastic agreement on a comparably unrestricted range of Forms:

> SOCRATES: What about the following, Simmias? Do we say that there is such a thing as the Just itself, or not?
>
> SIMMIAS: We do say so, by Zeus.
>
> SOCRATES: And the Beautiful, and the Good?
>
> SIMMIAS: Of course.
>
> SOCRATES: And have you ever seen any of these things with your eyes?
>
> SIMMIAS: In no way.
>
> SOCRATES: Or have you ever grasped them with any of your bodily senses? I am speaking of all things such as Bigness, Health, Strength and, in a word, the reality of all other things, that which each of them essentially is. (Plato: *Phaedo* 65d; Grube translation; speaker names added)

The list in the *Phaedo* may not be as long or as tidy as the one in the *Republic*, but the corresponding range is just as broad, and unmistakably so, as indicated by the presence of entries as diverse as justice, largeness, and health. The manifest diversity is further strengthened by an open-ended extension of the specified coverage to absolutely everything without qualification: "I am speaking of all things . . . all other things" (*Phaedo* 65d). The unrestricted extensibility predicated of the list is confirmed a little later through a few more items rounded out and bound together by the same appeal to everything or, more specifically, to everything in itself, as it is in itself:

> Therefore, if we had this knowledge, we knew before birth and immediately after not only the Equal, but the Greater and the Smaller and all such things, for our present argument is no more about the Equal than about the Beautiful itself, the Good itself, the Just, the Pious and, as I say, about all those things which we mark with the seal of "what it is," both when we are putting questions and answering them. So we must have acquired knowledge of them all before we were born. (Plato: *Phaedo* 75c–d; Grube translation)

The same liberal coverage of Forms as things in themselves may be found in the great myth of the *Phaedrus* (246e–249d), where a cosmic pilgrimage, undertaken by gods and mortals alike, just to see the Forms, includes noetic insight into justice, temperance, and knowledge, as representative examples of "all the things that are as they are" (*Phaedrus* 247–e):

> On the way around it [= the soul] has a view of Justice as it is; it has a view of Self-control; it has a view of Knowledge—not the knowledge that is close to change, that becomes different as it knows the different things which we consider real down here. No, it is the knowledge of what really is what it is. And when the soul has seen all the things that are as they are and feasted on them, it sinks back inside heaven and goes home. (Plato: *Phaedrus* 247d–e; Nehamas and Woodruff translation)

The three items explicitly listed here, namely justice, temperance (self-control), and knowledge, are quickly followed by a more detailed analysis of a fourth, in a striking account of the experience of souls with beauty (*Phaedrus* 249d–250e), which turns out to be the one Form among all that makes itself felt the most strongly in our phenomenal experience. The examination of beauty further enhances the diversity of the Forms specified by name, but here, too, what leaves no room for doubt is the extra effort to indicate that these are merely representative examples of an unrestricted range.

The liberal coverage in all three lists (*Republic* 596b–c, 597c–d; *Phaedo* 65d, 75c–d; *Phaedrus* 247d–e, 249d–250e) is further corroborated by the broadly inclusive range of Forms in the *Seventh Letter* (342d):

> The same thing is true of straight-lined as well as of circular figures; of color; of the good, the beautiful, the just; of body in general, whether artificial or natural; of fire, water, and all the elements; of all living beings and qualities of souls; of all actions and affections. (Plato: *Seventh Letter* 342d; Morrow translation)

On the other hand, Plato's procedural rule of thumb (*Republic* 596a; *Parmenides* 130d–e, 135a–d; *Timaeus* 51c) is not meant to serve as a nomological principle to be consulted and applied without exception in connection with the range of Forms. It is neither sufficiently specific in formulation nor therefore adequately informative in isolation. It is a generalization from the natural order of things, as opposed to an organizational principle assigning a Form to anything of which there could conceivably be more than one, or even to everything of which there actually is more than one.

The liberal allowance may indeed read like anything goes, provided that the Form contemplated has a name, or can be given one, which would then seem to support the existence of a Form for just about anything, so long as it is part of a multitude with features that are common and peculiar to it in distinction from all other things. We know for a fact, however, that Plato imposes conceptual restrictions on the range of Forms. The reason why he still ends up with a liberal allowance is that his restrictions are not geared toward arbitrarily excluding certain kinds of things, while arbitrarily including other kinds, as in denying a Form of owl but accepting the Form of eagle, or denying a Form of bird but accepting the Form of fish, or denying Forms of inorganic substances but accepting those of living creatures, or denying Forms of types but accepting those of properties. His restrictions, rather, are geared toward weeding out arbitrary classifications, regardless of the kind of thing under consideration.

The prime example of his classification exceptions and restrictions is his explicit rejection of Forms for people who are not Greek and numbers that are not ten thousand (*Statesman* 262d–e), which confirms that the existence of a multitude, with or without a name in common parlance, is not conclusive evidence of the existence of a Form, given that "barbarian" (*barbaron*), meaning not-Greek, is indeed a name but has no Form as its referent, and that not-ten-thousand, denoting all the numbers other than ten thousand, has neither a name, at least not a natural or conventional one, nor a Form corresponding to it. The justification for the restriction comes from a distinction between parts and types, where not all parts are types even though all types are parts (*Statesman* 263a–b). A part of something is not necessarily a type, kind, or class of its own, but every type, kind, or class is naturally a part of something greater and more general. The distinction is thus between part and whole, as against genus and species, though Plato himself does not use the latter two terms together to mark the distinction through juxtaposition, for which we must turn to Aristotle and Speusippus.

This explanation is a reflection of Plato's conception of classification, constituting the impetus behind his approach to definition, as a process of "division" (*diairesis*) at natural joints, complemented by a correlative process of "collection" (*synagōgē*). Introduced in the *Phaedrus* (265d–e, 266b–c; cf. 249b–c, 273d–e, 277b), and developed further in the *Sophist* (253d–e, 259e), *Statesman* (262b–263b, 287c), and *Philebus* (16c–e), possibly including some early hints in the *Gorgias* (464b–466a), as well as a warning against excessive and inappropriate use in the *Hippias Major* (301b), the "method of division and collection" (or "collection and division") emerges as an alternative, though possibly a complementary one, to the "method of hypothesis" familiar from the *Phaedo* (100b, 102a–b), *Republic* (510b, 511a–c, 531c–539d), and *Parmenides* (135d–136a). Plato presents the two dimensions of the process as follows:

> SOCRATES: The first consists in seeing together things that are scattered about everywhere and collecting them into one kind, so that by defining each thing we can make clear the subject of any instruction we wish to give. Just so with our discussion of love: Whether its definition was or was not correct, at

least it allowed the speech to proceed clearly and consistently with itself.

PHAEDRUS: And what is the other thing you are talking about, Socrates?

SOCRATES: This, in turn, is to be able to cut up each kind according to its species along its natural joints, and to try not to splinter any part, as a bad butcher might do. (Plato: *Phaedrus* 265d–e; Nehamas and Woodruff translation)

The transition in the *Phaedrus* to division and collection as the primary focus of dialectical activity becomes official as it is formalized through the enthusiastic endorsement of Socrates, prefiguring various implementations in the *Sophist*, *Statesman*, and *Philebus*:

SOCRATES: Well, Phaedrus, I am myself a lover of these divisions and collections, so that I may be able to think and to speak; and if I believe that someone else is capable of discerning a single thing that is also by nature capable of encompassing many, I follow "straight behind, in his tracks, as if he were a god." God knows whether this is the right name for those who can do this correctly or not, but so far I have always called them "dialecticians." (Plato: *Phaedrus* 266b–c; Nehamas and Woodruff translation)

Although the method of division and collection is technically a binary process, the emphasis is predominantly on division. The inherent duality is more prominent in the *Phaedrus* (cf. 265d–e) than elsewhere. Indeed, the presentation and promotion of dialectic as a systematic inquiry into the organizational structure of Forms as an ontological collective, including any interaction between them (*Sophist* 253b–254b), as manifested in the "communion of kinds," or "combination of genera" (*koinōnia tōn genōn* at *Sophist* 253d–e), facilitating the "interweaving of Forms" (*sumplokē tōn eidōn* at *Sophist* 259e), marks the culmination of a methodological evolution beginning with the *Phaedrus*, where dialectic, and thereby the purpose and conduct of philosophy, is transformed into a reciprocal process of division and collection, leaving behind the standard hypothetical inquiry of, say, the *Phaedo*, where the methodological guidelines laid out at 99d–e are followed by a logical implementation at 100c–105c, thus anchoring the final proof of the immortality of the soul to the hypothesis that the Forms exist. Yet the *Sophist* and the *Statesman*, where the new process is illustrated ad nauseam, differ from the *Phaedrus* in privileging division over collection, nearly to the exclusion of the latter, which is largely ignored (cf. *Sophist* 253d), if not altogether abandoned (especially in the *Statesman*, despite the reference at 285a–b), whereby the singular focus of dialectic eventually becomes division according to kinds, famously satirized in a fragment of Epicrates (fr. 11 [II 287–288 Kock]).

These methodological developments shed light on how to read the general rule of the *Republic* (596a) regarding the range of Forms. Even on the most liberal, permissive, or inclusive interpretation, the apparent absence of limitations and restrictions in the generalization there cannot reasonably be read as a formal endorsement of all conceivable Forms. There has to be some rhyme or reason to the structure of discernible collections worthy of a name, and therefore of a Form (*Republic* 596a), given the methodological requirement of division at the natural joints (*Phaedrus* 265d–e), so that we may arrive at types, kinds, or classes, as opposed to indiscriminate multitudes constituting incoherent or insignificant parts of wholes, otherwise amenable to more meaningful analysis and classification (*Statesman* 262b–263b).[36] Aristotle is at pains to supply the relevant rhyme and reason, introducing ostensibly Platonic restrictions that are somehow conspicuously absent from the dialogues, as in the mutually inconsistent restrictions to numbers and to natural kinds, but he thereby contradicts

---

36. One might conceivably object that the requirement of division at natural joints does not necessarily preclude the possibility of Forms that are not thus divided but instead simply excludes such Forms from the process of division and collection, which is a dialectical operation in the service of philosophical inquiry in general, so the objection would continue, as opposed to a confirmation mechanism for the existence or reality of individual Forms. This would be to object that the process of division and collection proceeds with Forms that already qualify as Forms rather than making that qualification contingent upon the outcome of the corresponding divisions and collections. While this interpretation does not directly contradict anything in the texts, it misses both the point and the significance of division at natural joints, which is a foundational epistemological and metaphysical requirement essential for proper insight into reality and therefore supremely relevant to the existence and essence of Forms.

himself in the process, while at the same time repeatedly restricting the range of Forms beyond all indications and tendencies in the dialogues.

Plato nowhere even appears to be restricting the range of Forms to numbers or natural kinds. He is indeed after what is natural, but only in the sense of what is rational. Natural in this sense is opposed to unnatural rather than to artificial. Plato's "division at natural joints" is about resisting arbitrary divisions, and consequently avoiding haphazard classifications, whether or not the process and the results are confined to the realm of nature.[37] The injunction, therefore, is not against postulating Forms for things that are not part of the natural world but against making too much of multitudes of things that lack distinctive characteristics making them similar to each other yet different from everything else in a meaningful way. Aristotle mistakes this for a restriction to natural kinds: "And so Plato was not far wrong when he said that there are as many forms as there are kinds of natural things (if there are forms at all)" (*Metaphysics* 1070a18–19).[38] Aristotle's praise for Plato here is commonly taken as confirmation of Plato's rejection of Forms for artifacts, hence not just as a recognition of Forms for natural kinds but also as a restriction of Forms to natural kinds.

Alexander of Aphrodisias elsewhere construes Aristotle as testifying to a rejection of Forms for artifacts by Platonists in general, where Plato would seem to be included, though the evidence is not conclusive, at least because the reference is not explicit:

---

37. Plato's conception of what qualifies as natural is liberal enough to include not just physical artifacts but also any type of intellectual creation, including legislation and artwork, among other things: "The legislator should defend the claim of law itself and of art to be natural, or no less real than nature, since they are products of mind in accordance with sound reasoning" (*Laws* 890d).

38. Aristotle is not alone in giving a naturalistic interpretation of Plato's Forms. The sense of nature or naturalness, however, is not distinctive enough in the testimonies of third parties to shed light on the disagreement between Plato and Aristotle. Diogenes Laërtius, for example, speaks of a "world of natural objects": "As already stated, [Plato] assumes the Ideas to be causes and principles whereby the world of natural objects is what it is" (Diogenes Laërtius 3.77). Proclus, for his part, reports Xenocrates as describing the Forms as Plato's causal agents in conformity with nature: "For this reason [Plato] ascended to these as first principles and made the whole of creation depend on them, in accord with what Xenocrates says, who defines the Ideas as the paradigmatic cause of whatever is composed continually in accordance with nature" (Proclus: *In Platonis Parmenides* 888.18–19 Cousin [= Xenocrates fr. 30 Heinze]).

And the last argument, in addition to the fact that it does not prove that there are Ideas, will also be seen to establish Ideas of things for which the Platonists do not wish there to be Ideas. For if, because medicine is not a science of this health but simply of health, there is such a thing as health-itself, there will also be [something of this sort] in the case of each of the arts. For [an art] does not deal with the particular thing nor the 'this,' but simply with that which is its object, as carpentry simply with bench, not with this bench, and simply with bed, not this bed; in similar fashion both sculpture, and painting, and building, and each of the other arts is related to the things subject to it. Therefore, there will also be an Idea for each of the objects of the arts, the very thing the Platonists do not wish. (Alexander of Aphrodisias: *In Aristotelis Metaphysica Commentaria* 79.21–80.6, in reference to *Metaphysics* 990b11, translator's own bracketed interpolations)

Richard Bluck (1947) warns that a restrictive reading of the testimonial dimension of Aristotle's commendation is not the only possible interpretation, nor even the only reasonable one (see chapter 5, section 5.2, of the present volume for further discussion).[39] It is possible, after all, to praise Plato for recognizing Forms for natural kinds, regardless of whether Plato accepted or rejected Forms for anything else, including, but not limited to, artifacts. Bluck himself prefers this alternative, thereby absolving Aristotle of any misunderstanding or misrepresentation. His appeal is more to the logic than to the evidence, as the evidence is already contained in the corresponding statement, which Bluck recommends reading without a logically illicit jump from the recognition of Forms for natural kinds to the restriction of Forms to natural kinds (Bluck 1947). Aristotle could arguably be applauding Plato's acknowledgment of Forms for natural kinds, without intending any implication or indication of what Plato may have said or thought about Forms for anything else.

---

39. Bluck's warning (1947) constitutes a dissenting opinion against the scholarly consensus. The standard interpretation takes Aristotle to be saddling Plato with a naturalistic reduction in the strict sense of nature, and thereby with a decided position against the possibility of Forms for artifacts. Discussions of the proper interpretation, together with the associated problems, include Cherniss (1944, 235–260, especially 243–244), Fine (1993, 81–88), Robin (1908, 173–181), and Ross (1951, 171–175).

Since Bluck is only pursuing and promoting a plausible alternative, without denying that the restrictive reading he opposes is both reasonable in itself and consistent with the relevant passage, his analysis is valid, but only insofar as the passage in question is pruned exactly as quoted above: "And so Plato was not far wrong when he said that there are as many forms as there are kinds of natural things (if there are forms at all)" (*Metaphysics* 1070a18–19). Aristotle actually goes on, however, to introduce some exceptions that narrow the focus down to the restrictive sense of nature and naturalness. Here is the passage in full: "And so Plato was not far wrong when he said that there are as many forms as there are kinds of natural things (if there are forms at all),—though not of such things as fire, flesh, head; for all these are matter, and the last matter is the matter of that which is in the fullest sense substance" (*Metaphysics* 1070a18–22).[40] The rejection of Forms for such things as fire, flesh, and head seems to be in recognition of their potential presence, in some way, in various different natural kinds. Fire could conceivably be present in anything that is hot, with all such things having their own Form, while flesh and head may be found in all sorts of life forms, each of which would presumably have its own Form.[41] But identifying the precise reason or motivation for Aristotle's exemptions is not as important as recognizing the consequent reduction to a restrictive sense of naturalism, with fire, flesh, and head all being found in nature.

Although it is not immediately clear whether the exclusion of fire, flesh, and head applies to Aristotle's praise or to Plato's position, that distinction is not relevant in this case, given that either scenario leaves us with the same sense of nature, the restrictive sense excluding artifacts.

---

40. The original is as follows: *Dio dē ou kakōs Platōn ephē hoti eidē estin hoposa physei, eiper estin eidē alla toutōn hoion pyr sarx kephalē: hapanta gar hylē esti, kai tēs malist' ousias hē teleutaia. Ta men oun kinounta aitia hōs progegenēmena onta, ta d' hōs ho logos hama* (*Metaphysics* 1070a18–22).

41. If what is bothering Aristotle here, and motivating him to exclude such things as fire, flesh, and head (*Metaphysics* 1070a19), is indeed the implied compresence of Forms in sensible phenomena, or the participation of Forms in one another, or perhaps both at once, he is grossly underestimating Plato's interest in the "communion of kinds" (*Sophist* 253d–e) and the "interweaving of Forms" (*Sophist* 259e). Note also that a Form of fire is explicitly validated in the *Timaeus*, where the question is put in no uncertain terms: "Is there such a thing as a Fire *by itself*?" (*Timaeus* 51b). The short answer is yes. The long answer, also affirmative, is best read in the original where it immediately follows the question. Both answers are confirmed in the *Seventh Letter* (342d), where fire is likewise acknowledged to have a Form.

Aristotle could be saying one of two things: (1) Plato was not far wrong when he said that there are as many Forms as there are kinds of natural things, for which observation he is to be commended, but he was certainly wrong to include among them such things as fire, flesh, and head. (2) Plato was not far wrong when he said that there are as many Forms as there are kinds of natural things, quite astutely excluding from their ranks such things as fire, flesh, and head, for which exception he is to be further commended. While these are competing interpretations, the mutual contrast between natural things and such things as fire, flesh, and head suggests that a naturalistic sense of natural things in general is to be modified by an amendment introducing exceptions within the same naturalistic interpretation. Nature and naturalness are taken on either reading in a narrower sense denoting the natural world rather than in a broader sense pointing to the rational world.

If this were not a matter of elaborating on the blanket assignment of Forms to "natural things" by laying out the exceptions required to demonstrate what kinds of natural things do and what kinds do not have Forms, all of them still firmly located in the realm of nature, a token artificial object certainly could and probably would have been included among the three items invoked for the contrast between natural things and such things as fire, flesh, and head. For example, having already invoked artifacts, specifically in mentioning houses, in the sentence (*Metaphysics* 1070a13–18) immediately preceding the one just quoted (*Metaphysics* 1070a18–22), Aristotle could have helpfully employed the example of windows or doors, either of which would have stood in the same relation to houses as flesh and heads presumably do to animals.[42]

---

42. The relevant passage runs as follows: "Now in some cases the 'this' does not exist apart from the composite substance, e.g. the form of house does not so exist, unless the art of building exists apart (nor is there generation and destruction of these forms, but it is in another way that the house apart from its matter, and health, and all things of art, exist and do not exist); but if it does it is only in the case of natural objects" (*Metaphysics* 1070a13–18). Note that Aristotle's reference to houses is in the context of his own objection to transcendent Forms rather than in the context of any testimony regarding whether Plato countenanced a Form for houses. Hence, the reference does not support or contradict any inclination on Aristotle's part to hold Plato to a restrictive sense of the natural world as excluding artifacts. As discussed further in the main text, however, Aristotle does bring up houses, together with rings, in exactly that way elsewhere (*Metaphysics* 991b3–8, 1080a3–10), where they do point to a smaller population of Forms than Bluck sees Aristotle attesting to in Plato.

Instead, he moves straight from houses, of which he later presents Plato as denying transcendent Forms (*Metaphysics* 991b3-8, 1080a3-10), to natural things, whose Forms he praises Plato for recognizing, with the exceptions just mentioned, which collectively suggest that the praise is for natural things in a naturalistic sense, which then indicates further approval for the rejection of artifacts. There would have been little reason for Aristotle to praise Plato for acknowledging the existence of Forms for natural things if Aristotle believed that Plato was inclined to assign a Form to anything that could be named, including not just artifacts but whatever attracted his attention.

Yet Bluck's point is too important to dismiss without refutation. It is not so much that Bluck himself is standing on firm ground as it is that too much is hanging in the balance. If Bluck is right, so might be Aristotle. And in all fairness, the ambiguity in references to nature or naturalness need not, in the absence of conclusive evidence to the contrary, be resolved in a way that makes Aristotle miss the point in Plato. The two philosophers could possibly both be invoking nature in the same sense. This would be true, as Bluck obviously recognizes, if and only if Aristotle were invoking nature or naturalness in some sense of normalcy within the bounds of reason, particularly as employed in pattern recognition, for Plato is clearly not pursuing or promoting nature or naturalness in any other sense in his various discussions of division and collection. Hence, again in the absence of further evidence, the advocate of Aristotle could consistently deny that Aristotle is saying anything different in his commendation of Plato for restricting Forms to natural things than Plato is saying about carving nature at the joints.

The problem, however, is that the qualification concerning the evidence does not hold: Further evidence is not absent. We know, if nothing else, that Aristotle elsewhere cites houses and rings, hence artifacts, as examples of things that Plato does not consider to have Forms (*Metaphysics* 991b3-8, 1080a3-10), which then points to a strictly naturalistic as opposed to broadly diairetical interpretation of the passage applauding Plato's restriction of Forms to "natural things" (*Metaphysics* 1070a18-19).

Although the rejection of Forms for houses and rings, and thereby of Forms for artifacts in general, is not attributed specifically to Plato, at least not by name, the corresponding passages (*Metaphysics* 991b3-8, 1080a3-10), repeated almost word for word in parts, make it difficult to deny that Plato is included in the target group. The first passage is in the first book of the *Metaphysics*:

In the *Phaedo* the case is stated in this way—that the Forms are causes both of being and of becoming; yet when the Forms exist, still the things that share in them do not come into being, unless there is some efficient cause; and many other things come into being (e.g. a house or a ring), of which we say there are no Forms. Clearly, therefore, even the other things can both be and come into being owing to such causes as produce the things just mentioned. (Aristotle: *Metaphysics* 991b3–8; Ross translation)

The second passage, nearly identical with the first, is in the penultimate book of the *Metaphysics*:

In the *Phaedo* it is stated in this way—that the Forms are causes both of being and of becoming. Yet though the Forms exist, still things do not come into being, unless there is something to move them; and many other things come into being (e.g. a house or a ring), of which they say there are no Forms. Clearly therefore even the things of which they say there are Ideas can both be and come into being owing to such causes as produce the things just mentioned, and not owing to the Forms. (Aristotle: *Metaphysics* 1080a3–10; Ross translation)

The most salient difference is the first-person plural narrative of the first passage, as against the third-person plural narrative of the second, which shows Aristotle speaking both as a member and as a critic of the Academy in the first passage, and only as a critic of it in the second. The reference to the *Phaedo* in both places serves as an unmistakable anchor to Plato, making it highly unlikely that either the "we" in the first passage or the "they" in the second passage excludes Plato.

Of course, the mutual relevance and mutual resolution of these references makes only Bluck wrong, not Aristotle. Aristotle's allusions to Plato's rejection of Forms for houses and rings (*Metaphysics* 991b3–8, 1080a3–10) are entirely consistent with Aristotle's praise for Plato's commitment to Forms for "natural things" (*Metaphysics* 1070a18–19), the allusions thereby confirming that the praise is not just for recognizing Forms for natural kinds but for restricting Forms to natural kinds. Where Aristotle gets into trouble is in the discrepancy between the joint testimony indicated by the allusions and the praise, which together reveal a naturalistic view of Forms, and his own testimony elsewhere, contradicting the naturalistic interpretation with a mathematical interpretation.

But where does Aristotle get the notion of an opposition by Plato to the Forms of artifacts? The testimony is inconsistent not just with Plato's various formulations of a general principle proposing an unrestricted range of Forms (*Republic* 596a; *Parmenides* 130d–e, 135a–d; *Timaeus* 51c), which should ipso facto include the Forms of artifacts, but also with Plato's specific references to various different artifact Forms. The most obvious examples of artifact Forms in Plato are those of the bed and the table in the *Republic* (596b, 597c–d), and of the shuttle and the awl in the *Cratylus* (389a–d), all of which are assigned their own Forms. These particular items are, in each case, merely token examples of a wholesale admission of artifacts in general, explicitly mentioning, among other things, all furniture in the *Republic* (596c) and all tools in the *Cratylus* (389c–d). It is also significant that manufactured things are placed in the same segment of the divided line as living things (*Republic* 510a), suggesting a comparable ontological status, where the assignment of a Form for one can reasonably be expected to be extended, on principle alone, to the other.

Plato's placement of artifacts (*to skeuaston holon genos* at *Republic* 510a) in the second segment of the line does not include artistic creations of any kind. Those belong in the lowest segment, together with images (shadows and reflections), though Plato does not explicitly say so in constructing the analogic model. Probing the inherent difference, Léon Robin distinguishes between "imitations de l'Art" and "produits de l'Art" (1908, 178), largely in reflection of principles of classification and ontological gradation employed by Plato himself, invariably rejecting Forms for artifacts originating in the *imitative arts*, while accepting them for artifacts contributed by the *productive arts*. Robin's distinction captures the hierarchy Plato describes as stretching from the thing itself-by-itself, to its phenomenal manifestation, to its reproduction in art. In illustration of that hierarchy, the iconic bed of the *Republic* has a Form, as it is made by the carpenter in instantiation of the ideal bed, while the painting of the bed does not have a Form, as it is made by the painter in imitation of the physical bed (596b–598e). The difference between the two cases exemplifies Plato's assessment of art as twice removed from truth and reality (*Republic* 597e, 599d; cf. 595a; note exceptions at 607a–d; see the differentiation in accordance with merit at *Laws* 817a–e). The count is sometimes (erroneously) taken to make art thrice removed from truth and reality, simply because it is in the third position, starting with the original in the first position, but that still makes it only twice "removed" from the original, unless one insists that the original is (once) removed from itself.

Even with artistic creations excluded from consideration, however, there are plenty of compelling signs of Plato's commitment to Forms for artifacts. The sweeping endorsement of all furniture in the *Republic* (596c) and all tools in the *Cratylus* (389c–d) is complemented by a general account of the craftsman as working with an eye on the Form of whatever he happens to be making, as indicated in the *Timaeus* (28a6–b1) and the *Laws* (965b7–c8). To these may be added the broadly inclusive range of Forms embraced in the *Seventh Letter*, which naturally includes the Forms of artifacts, explicitly so in the reference to "body in general, whether artificial or natural" (342d).

Plato's acknowledgment of Forms for artifacts appears, in fact, to be such common knowledge in philosophical circles, not just within the Academy but also outside it, that word of this position even makes its way into anecdotal accounts, quite telling, whether true or false. When Diogenes of Sinope, for example, protests that he can see the cups and tables but not the cupness or tableness, Plato replies, so the story goes, that Diogenes has the eyes required to see the cups and tables but lacks the reason required to grasp the cupness or tableness, thus remaining blind to the conceptual apparatus binding them together in meaningful distinction from everything else (Diogenes Laërtius 6.53). The relevant question is not whether this exchange really ever took place, but whether it is indicative of the convictions of the person inspiring the story. The scattered references throughout the Platonic corpus, as exemplified in the preceding paragraph, though obviously not exhaustively so, demonstrate that the story is eminently believable.

The same story can be found in Simplicius, among others, with Antisthenes replacing Diogenes of Sinope as the antagonist, and horses replacing cups and tables as the vehicle of illustration (Simplicius: *In Aristotelis Categorias Commentarium* 208.28–32). The version with Antisthenes is covered in chapter 4 (section 4.2) of the present volume.[43] Either story could be true, and both might be false. Antisthenes and Diogenes of Sinope were both contemporaries of Plato. Antisthenes was born several

---

43. The Antisthenes version of the story, traditionally cited through Simplicius (*In Aristotelis Categorias Commentarium* 208.28–32), is corroborated by Ammonius, David, Elias, and Tzetzes. All the relevant sources, together with copious documentation and accompanying commentary, can be found in Prince (2015, 428–445).

decades before Diogenes of Sinope, though their lifespans also overlap for several decades. Plato was almost exactly in the middle. More important than the veracity of the stories, however, is the perfect fit between them in illustration of Plato's acceptance of Forms both for artifacts, in opposition to Diogenes of Sinope (as related by Diogenes Laërtius), and for natural kinds, in opposition to Antisthenes (as related by Simplicius). Evidently, Plato's recognition of both types of Forms was common knowledge, so much so as to inspire both stories, with the creation of the second one (whichever came second) being especially telling in that regard, since no one would have bothered to duplicate the original story if the second version were not also grounded in the well-known convictions of the master.

Aristotle's failure to acknowledge the underlying truth, as indicated by his denial of artifact Forms in Plato, may well be why Plato goes out of his way to invite a comparison between Socrates and Aristotle as the youngest characters in the *Parmenides*. We know that their presence together at any age, let alone as a couple of youngsters, makes it impossible that one of these characters should be the historical Socrates while the other is the historical Aristotle. And Plato lets us know straightaway that the young Aristotle in the dialogue is the Aristotle who later becomes a member of the Thirty (*Parmenides* 127d). Yet there can be no doubt that the presence of a dramatic Aristotle has critical implications for the position of the philosopher Aristotle on the topics under discussion.[44] Having already established that Socrates, thoroughly lacking in experience, is in need of extensive training in dialectic before he can develop the kind and degree of insight into truth and reality that is characteristic of true philosophers

---

44. Thesleff, for one, confirms the association: "And I would regard it as almost certain that the character of Aristoteles in the *Parmenides*, besides being a 'Charmides redivivus' (127d2), also represents Plato's famous pupil. . . . I can see no point in introducing the long-since forgotten 5th century politician Aristoteles, other than the desire to refer to the philosopher" (Thesleff 1982, 158–159 [= 2009, 306], cf. n. 464 for a list of scholars in agreement and in opposition). Thirty-five years later, he identifies the "pivotal point of the dialogue" to be the designation of Aristotle as the formal interlocutor of Parmenides (Thesleff 2017, 204), reasserting his confidence in that association in a footnote: "Mentioned at 127d2. I find it clear (though many doubt it) that this is again a Platonic play with names. In fact the criticism of Plato's theory of Forms which we find in some of the Aristotelian πραγματεῖαι corresponds very closely with what Parmenides has said in his above questioning of 'young Socrates.' And it is tempting to think that the Academy at this time had about 30 'members'" (Thesleff 2017, 204, n. 69).

(*Parmenides* 130e, 135c–d), Plato places Aristotle on an even lower level of sophistication, further removed from wisdom, in identifying him as the youngest character in the dramatis personae (*Parmenides* 137b–c). The second part of the dialogue unfolds in the form of a dialectical exercise with Aristotle assisting Parmenides as his designated interlocutor, a position traditionally belonging to the youngest person in the audience (as with Glaucon in the *Republic*).

What is most remarkable here about Plato's emphasis on Aristotle's lack of experience, and thereby on his lack of insight and wisdom, is his deliberate association of all the philosophical shortcomings of the young Socrates with the even younger Aristotle, through a dramatic transference where the cumulative dialectical training of the character Aristotle is reduced to his exposure to the faulty ideas of the character Socrates. The alleged errors the young Socrates makes in the central dramatic setting in discussion with Parmenides are identified as the same ones he kept making "the other day" in a conversation with Aristotle:

> "Socrates, that's because you are trying to mark off something beautiful, and just, and good, and each one of the forms, too soon," [Parmenides] said, "before you have been properly trained. I noticed that the other day too, as I listened to you conversing with Aristotle here." (Plato: *Parmenides* 135c–d; Gill and Ryan translation)

The message seems to be that Plato considers the historical Aristotle's various objections and disagreements concerning the range of Forms, among other relevant issues (including the vicious regress of the Third Man), to be grounded in a lack of experience and understanding, not unlike the same Aristotle's apparent unawareness of Plato's methodological requirements for proper classification (*Phaedrus* 249b–c, 265d–e, 266b–c, 273d–e, 277b; *Sophist* 253d–e, 259e; *Statesman* 262b–263b, 287c; *Philebus* 16c–e).

Curiously, Aristotle's testimony regarding Plato's position on the Forms of artifacts contradicts not just Plato's position as revealed in the dialogues but also Aristotle's own testimony elsewhere. While presenting Plato as limiting Forms to natural kinds (*Metaphysics* 1070a18–19), which implies the rejection of Forms for artifacts, which are nevertheless rejected explicitly and specifically, for good measure, through the rejection of Forms for houses and rings (*Metaphysics* 991b3–8, 1080a3–10), Aristotle also, and rather inexplicably, presents Plato as acknowledging a Form for tables:

Yet what happens is the contrary; the theory is not a reasonable one. For they make many things out of the matter, and the form generates only once, but what we observe is that one table is made from one matter, while the man who applies the form, though he is one, makes many tables. (Aristotle: *Metaphysics* 988a1–5; Ross translation)

Aristotle's reference here to tables comes in the process of explaining why he does not find the "theory" of transcendent Forms reasonable. While the reason he gives is not that the proponents of the theory acknowledge a Form of table, the reference nevertheless suggests that its proponents do indeed acknowledge a Form of table, since that is the example Aristotle chooses in ventilating what he finds wrong with the theory. The testimony is consistent with various references in the Platonic corpus to the Forms of artifacts, including a reference specifically to a Form of table (*Republic* 596b), as well as the aforementioned anecdotal evidence in Diogenes Laërtius (6.53) concerning an exchange between Plato and Diogenes of Sinope on the matter of Forms for cups and tables. The immediate and extensive evidentiary fit makes it all the more difficult to understand why Aristotle does not just follow this path instead of contradicting himself, to say nothing of his contradiction of all the primary and secondary evidence, with the additional testimony of a restriction to natural kinds, accompanied by a rejection of Forms for houses and rings.

The curiosity reaches a peak where Aristotle, contradicting all the restrictions he introduces elsewhere, which remain mutually inconsistent as they are anyway, testifies instead that Plato embraced a full range of Forms, just as Plato himself repeatedly indicates throughout the canonical corpus:

For to each set of substances there answers a Form which has the same name and exists apart from the substances, and so also in the case of all other groups in which there is one character common to many things, whether the things are in this changeable world or are eternal. (Aristotle: *Metaphysics* 990b6–8; cf. 990a33–991a8, 1079a7–b3; Ross translation)

The range Aristotle allows here confirms the ontological perspective Plato openly and persistently promotes in dialogues as far apart in theme, methodology, and relative date of composition (so far as we can tell) as the *Republic* (596a), the *Parmenides* (130d–e, 135a–d), and the *Timaeus*

(51c).⁴⁵ Although Aristotle's reference does not specify Plato by name, instead loosely invoking "those who posit the Ideas as causes," this allusion to anonymous advocates comes shortly after an explicit reference to Plato in the last sentence of *Metaphysics* A8, which would then seem to place Plato among those intended by the looser and more general reference following it in the first paragraph of *Metaphysics* A9. There is no good reason to think that the reference would exclude Plato, given that Plato does in fact "posit the Ideas as causes" and that the central message is consistent with what we know of Plato from his own works as well as from external testimony and commentary.

Contradicting Plato is not Aristotle's only problem. Even if we had nothing besides Aristotle's testimony for insight into Plato's philosophy, we would still have to explain the discrepancy between the mathematical (*Metaphysics* 991b9–10, 1073a17–22), naturalistic (*Metaphysics* 1070a18–19), and unrestricted (*Metaphysics* 990b6–8) versions of his testimony regarding the range of Forms. Had Plato restricted the range of Forms to numbers, he could not reasonably have extended the range to natural kinds, and had

---

45. The range Aristotle seems to acknowledge here for Forms (*Metaphysics* 990b6–8) may or may not be the same as the population indicated in the Platonic corpus (*Republic* 596a; *Parmenides* 130d–e, 135a–d; *Timaeus* 51c). They are difficult to compare. One reason for hesitation is that Aristotle seems to anchor the range to substances, as opposed to just any group of things that admits of natural classification and correlative nomenclature, the latter of which is the only condition Plato brings up in the corresponding references. While Aristotle does go on to include "all other groups in which there is one character common to many things" (*Metaphysics* 990b6–8), that just makes it all the more curious why he would want to single out substances, which would normally be included in such a comprehensive reference to "groups in which there is one character common to many things." Given a restriction to substances, if there is such a restriction, the liberal range Aristotle acknowledges may not be as liberal as its counterpart in Plato, though Plato's own restriction to division at natural joints (*Phaedrus* 265d–e) is liable to minimize any difference in that regard (cf. *Phaedrus* 249b–c, 266b–c, 273d–e, 277b; *Sophist* 253d–e, 259e; *Statesman* 262b–263b, 287c; *Philebus* 16c–e). Note also that Aristotle describes Plato as holding Forms, intermediates, and sensible phenomena alike to be substances (*Metaphysics* 1028b19–21), which then makes it unclear whether Aristotle's indexation of Plato's range of Forms to substances in the passage above makes any difference, since Plato reportedly regards all Forms as substances anyway. Commentary is inexhaustible on Aristotle's conception of substance, articulated at one point as "that which is primarily and *is* simply (not is something)" (*Metaphysics* 1028a30). Gerson (1984) may be consulted for an example that is relevant to the question on hand.

he restricted the range in either way, he could not reasonably have cast it without restriction, unless he kept changing his mind to embrace wildly contradictory positions, each of which he might then have defended so strenuously for so long that they all got reported at least by Aristotle. Even the mathematical interpretation itself, the most prominent one in Aristotle, is not entirely consistent in itself, as the Forms are restricted to numbers, yet there are also Forms for geometrical figures, both in the Platonic corpus and in Aristotelian testimony.[46]

Moreover, whether it is just numbers, or just the objects of mathematics, or just natural kinds, or even more broadly, all the objects of mathematics, plus all natural kinds, plus all artifacts, the corresponding range in Aristotle fails to include the most obviously favored Forms in Plato, the ones that even the gods adore: justice and temperance and knowledge and the like (*Phaedrus* 247d; cf. 246e–249d for the pilgrimage by gods and mortals alike to see these Forms). In other words, even if Aristotle had never contradicted himself in his testimony on Plato, and even if we were to allow Aristotle the closest match between his testimony and the Platonic corpus, which intersect most favorably in the most liberal allowance of Aristotle for the range of Forms, Aristotle would still be guilty of leaving out the Forms dearest to Plato, at least in his specification of restrictions that are already defective for other reasons.

7.5. Implications for Reliability

The problems taken up in the preceding section revolve around a single theme constituting just one example of how things can go wrong in trying to learn about Plato from Aristotle. Space does not permit the enumeration and discussion of all the discrepancies between Aristotle's testimony and Plato's philosophy, or between Aristotle's testimony and Aristotle's

---

46. Specific references are hardly necessary to establish Aristotle's perspective on Plato as welcoming Forms for geometrical figures (though see, for example, *Metaphysics* 1090b1, 1090b24–30). His entire testimony on mathematicals as intermediates is proof of that (*Metaphysics* 987b14–18, 1028b19–21). The objects of mathematics, including geometrical figures as well as numbers, cannot possibly be intermediates, unless there are corresponding Forms for all mathematicals, hence for geometrical figures as well as numbers, to serve as anchors for intermediation at the eidetic end of the ontological spectrum.

testimony. What they all have in common is an explanation, whatever it may be, that is almost always impossible to falsify. Aristotle leaves nothing out and gets nothing wrong. No matter the problem, there is a solution. There is even a pattern to all the explanations so that we may conveniently collect them under a single decision procedure designed to uphold the testimony of Aristotle:

(1) Apparent contradictions between what Aristotle seems to be saying about Plato in one place and what he seems to be saying about Plato in another may well be the result of our confusing Aristotle's references to Plato with his references to Platonists other than Plato, or possibly even of our confusing Aristotle's references to some Platonists other than Plato with his references to other Platonists other than Plato, where Plato does not even enter into the picture as far as Aristotle is concerned.

(2) Even where there is no doubt that Aristotle is talking about Plato, apparent contradictions between what Aristotle says about Plato in one place and what he says about Plato in another could conceivably be a reflection of either (a) the difference between ideas that Plato shared directly and orally with Aristotle and words that Plato saw fit, for whatever reason, to put into the mouth of one of his characters in one of his dialogues or (b) the difference between ideas that Plato shared directly and orally with Aristotle at one time and ideas that Plato shared directly and orally with Aristotle at another, regardless of whether what Plato said at either time ever made it into any of the dialogues in the Platonic corpus.[47]

(3) Even where there is no doubt that Aristotle is talking about Plato, and even on the assumption that Aristotle was never exposed to mutually contradictory statements

---

47. Although the examples in the second step may seem to build up to the matter of apparent contradictions in the Platonic corpus itself, only to leave them out at the last minute, differences between what Plato wrote in one place and what he wrote in another are not relevant in this context, as we would presumably not try to pin such contradictions on Aristotle.

by Plato, be it in oral communication or through written work, any remaining contradiction between what Aristotle says about Plato in one place and what he says about Plato in another can be resolved as the effective equivalence of the apparently contradictory things that are said, either through the reduction of one thing to the other as an alternative expression of basically the same thing, presumably in reference to a common or more general truth, or through the subsumption of one thing under the other as an implication or corollary.

These three considerations are sufficient, at least in combination, but often severally as well, to resolve any apparent problems with Aristotle's testimony on Plato. Let us briefly reconsider in this light the most memorable discrepancies in what Aristotle says about Plato's conception of Forms: (1) Plato limited Forms to numbers (*Metaphysics* 991b9–10, 1073a17–22). (2) Plato limited Forms to natural kinds (*Metaphysics* 1070a18–19). (3) Plato accepted Forms for some artifacts but rejected them for others, acknowledging a Form for tables (*Metaphysics* 988a1–5), for instance, but denying any for houses or rings (*Metaphysics* 991b3–8, 1080a3–10). (4) Plato allowed Forms for any multitude of things with a common name (*Metaphysics* 990b6–8), though possibly limiting them to substances.

Even where the first two steps of the decision procedure above are inapplicable, or applicable yet insufficient to remove all the inconsistencies, any discrepancy between Aristotle's testimony that Plato restricted Forms to numbers, on the one hand, and either his further testimony or direct textual evidence that Plato accepted this or that Form in apparent contradiction of a restriction to numbers, on the other hand (as in a contradiction through the acknowledgment of Forms for all types, or for all properties, or for both, thus including not just horses and cups and tables, and indeed houses and rings, but also justice and beauty and knowledge), can be explained through the assumption of a radical reductionism making a mathematical model of the world the central element in Plato's metaphysical paradigm of reality. This would be to explain the world through numbers, without denying the horses and cups and tables we encounter in our phenomenal experience, and without forsaking the values shaping our response to our environment and our relationship with others. It would not be contradictory to restrict Forms to numbers, while speaking also of Forms for horses, houses, and justice, for example, if all of the latter were somehow reducible to numbers.

Hardly any objection to Aristotle's testimony on Plato can survive the explanatory power of the decision procedure outlined above. While such infallibility is always reassuring, it is also the single most suspicious thing about Aristotelian testimony. And even if infallibility and unfalsifiability were not suspicious in themselves, the corresponding explanations would not add up to a compelling case for trusting Aristotle at all times, in all circumstances, especially not in the absence of the slightest hint of confirmation by Plato, and certainly not in the presence of a clear contradiction by Plato. That is precisely why the matter has still not been put to rest, though opposition to Aristotle, or rather resistance to taking Aristotle's word for everything he says about Plato, is not as strong as it used to be.

Obviously, not everything Aristotle says about Plato is false. Most of it seems to be true. But the relevant truths of Aristotle are typically buried under apparent contradictions and often dependent upon supporting interpretations. While it is conceivable that any given discrepancy has an explanation where Aristotle is the only party that is not at fault—either because we have misunderstood the corresponding references or because Plato himself has changed his position or because an implicit condition removes the discrepancy—that still leaves us with testimony that is unreliable unless it is first put through an interpretive filter especially designed to weed out such discrepancies. The point is not that Aristotle got Plato wrong, though he sometimes actually did, but that Aristotle left us with testimony that is not conducive to getting Plato right, even if Aristotle himself got Plato right. Testimony that is misleading, or difficult to interpret, through no fault of Aristotle, is still testimony that is misleading or difficult to interpret.

With reference to the matter under discussion, it is admittedly conceivable, though not at all convincing, that Plato would have fully embraced the mathematical metaphysics indicated, consequently adopting all the ideas attributed to him by Aristotle, including the fundamental metaphysical principles prior both in importance and in causal relevance to the Forms, the reduction of Forms to numbers, and the existence of intermediates between Forms and sensible phenomena. Yet aside from any and all specific discrepancies between what Aristotle says and what Plato says, and between what Aristotle says in one place and what he says in another, a strong motivation for skepticism is the difficulty of explaining why any of that should be missing from the Platonic corpus, making it nearly impossible to explain why all of it is missing from the Platonic corpus.

Assuming that we are in possession of everything that Plato ever wrote, for which the evidence is compelling, and given that the subject matter here is too important to have slipped Plato's mind while composing the dialogues, there are only a few possibilities left: either (1) the unwritten doctrines were late developments in Plato's thought that he never got a chance to incorporate into his written work, or (2) they were esoteric teachings intended for a close circle of associates and disciples sworn to secrecy, or (3) they were philosophical insights, difficult to communicate in writing and best grasped through proper dialectical training, thus making them unsuitable for publication, or (4) they were not so much secret or difficult lessons as they were the sole examples of Plato's philosophical convictions, the dialogues themselves having been intended, not as doctrinal disquisitions, but as training material, at most with protreptic and propaedeutic functions.

The first of these possibilities is entirely at odds with what we know of Plato's life and career, namely that he was active and productive through the end of his days, so much so that his final and longest work, the *Laws*, is said to have been found inscribed in wax tablets, barely finished and yet to be transcribed, at the time of his death (Diogenes Laërtius 3.37). It follows, then, that if he was still working on the *Laws* right before he died, he could not have come up with any part of the unwritten doctrines after he finished the *Laws* and before he died. On the other hand, if he had come up with the unwritten doctrines before he started the *Laws*, or while he was working on the *Laws*, there would have been at least hints of these doctrines in the *Laws* (given that the scenario under consideration is that the unwritten doctrines were unwritten for a lack of time and not for a lack of will), or failing that, he would have either delegated the production of the *Laws* to students or abandoned that project altogether in favor of the unwritten doctrines (given their status as his considered opinion on what is real and what is important).[48] What this means is not

---

48. If his role in the production of the *Laws* was a largely supervisory one, with associates and students undertaking the actual work, as Nails and Thesleff (2003), for example, maintain (see also Thesleff 1967, 151-154 [= 2009, 125-127]; 1982, 186-187, 202-203 [= 2009, 333-334, 348-349]; 2017, 210), Plato should have been relatively free to work on the more important matters constituting the unwritten doctrines.

that the unwritten doctrines could not possibly have been a late development but that their being a late development does not explain why they remained unwritten.

The other three possibilities on the list are even less convincing. The second possibility, invoking sectarian esotericism with sacrosanct doctrines, contradicts the very existence of testimony by Aristotle, who as a student of Plato, would not have been, or at least should not have been, even tempted to reveal any inside information the master considered secret or sacred. The third possibility is the least tenable, for it contradicts the existence and essence of the entire Platonic corpus, which is brimming with philosophical insights, all of which, under this scenario, should have been reserved, no less than the unwritten doctrines, for dialectical training, instead of being published or otherwise circulated in written form.[49] The fourth possibility, like the third, contradicts the nature and contents of the Platonic corpus, which manifests itself, at least in parts, as a serious presentation and promotion of philosophical perspectives rather than a dispassionate examination of philosophical problems through a survey of the strengths and weaknesses of potential and proposed solutions.

Even if we accept one of these explanations, or an altogether different one, all designed to validate our faith in Aristotle's testimony on Plato, a nagging question remains: With Aristotle saying so much about Plato that does not seem familiar, even if all of it is, in fact, accurate, why did he not bother to point out, both to inform those who did not know any better and to remind those who did, (1) that Plato's views evolved so dramatically as to make his philosophical outlook at the end of his life radically different from what it was at the beginning of his career, or (2) that Plato regarded his dialogues as a vehicle for doing philosophy, and thereby as an invitation to philosophy, as opposed to an outlet for promulgating

---

The possibility alone makes it unlikely that any part of these doctrines should have remained unwritten for a lack of time, given that the time freed up through secretarial participation would have been the equivalent of however long it took for the completion of Plato's latest and longest work.

49. The alternative that the unwritten doctrines were kept out of the dialogues either because they were too difficult to articulate in words or because they were too difficult for anyone to understand, as opposed to their being merely better appreciated if pursued through dialectical training, is not very convincing either, since it contradicts the evidence of Plato's writings that are already difficult to follow, the hypothetical portion of the *Parmenides* being a good example.

philosophical doctrines, or (3) that Plato's adoption of the dialogue form was his way of capturing with the written word the pedagogical advantages of the spoken word, or (4) whatever it is that is supposed to cancel out discrepancies and contradictions in what Aristotle says about Plato?

The question, of course, is rhetorical. It is supposed to emphasize the apparent unreliability of Aristotle's testimony on Plato. With crucial aspects of Plato's philosophy crammed into a few pages of Aristotle, yet unverifiable in the dozens of dialogues constituting the Platonic corpus, one indeed wonders why Aristotle never once bothered to comment, even in passing, on why Plato kept so much of his deepest thoughts out of the dialogues or, if it was not a deliberate decision, why so much of it happened to be left out anyway. Why would Aristotle keep reporting what Plato said yet did not write, without ever acknowledging how different the two were, let alone explaining why that was so? Actually, that may be a bit of an exaggeration, even for a rhetorical question, as there is some acknowledgment, though only of the existence of a difference, and not of the reasons for it, nor of the extent of it. The closest that Aristotle comes to addressing the matter at all is in the second chapter of the fourth book of his *Physics*:

> This is why Plato in the *Timaeus* says that matter and space are the same; for the 'participant' and space are identical. (It is true, indeed, that the account he gives there of the 'participant' is different from what he says in his so-called unwritten teaching. Nevertheless, he did identify place and space.) I mention Plato because, while all hold place to be something, he alone tried to say *what* it is. (Aristotle: *Physics* 209b11–16; Hardie and Gaye translation)

The fact that Aristotle acknowledges the difference in this case enhances the relevance of the rhetorical question. One wonders why, if this single difference, on this one occasion, is worth noting, the grand chasm between the unwritten doctrines and the Platonic corpus is still not worth explaining.

One answer that comes to mind is that both the chasm and its explanation may have been common knowledge for the immediate audiences of both Plato and Aristotle.[50] That could arguably have obviated any need,

---

50. The common knowledge in question may have been something as simple as the reservations regarding writing, as adumbrated in the *Phaedrus* (275c–277a), the *Second*

at least in antiquity, to dwell on either the difference or the reasons for it, even if the explanation is now lost to us, leaving our present insight at the mercy of an inference to the best explanation. But that contradicts the actual efforts of Aristotle to go out of his way to note the difference in the case of the *Timaeus*. If a doctrinal discrepancy specific to a single dialogue is noteworthy, then so must be everything else collectively driving a wedge between the Platonic corpus and Aristotelian testimony.

Aristotle simply says too much about Plato that we do not get from Plato himself. And all of it is important. That is because Aristotle's testimony presumably represents the most current and significant ideas of Plato. What this amounts to is that Plato's deepest thoughts and most profound contributions, since they are supposedly not in the Platonic corpus, would have been lost forever had it not been for Aristotle's testimony. Given the huge gap between the works of Plato and the testimony of Aristotle, either we owe Aristotle a great debt or he owes us a serious apology. There is no doubt, of course, that we owe Aristotle a great debt for his contributions to philosophy. Any hesitation is restricted to his contributions as an unwitting historian of philosophy, particularly when it comes to the philosophy of Plato.

The most striking and important aspect of Aristotle's testimony on Plato is the shift in emphasis from Forms to more fundamental metaphysical principles, namely the one and the-great-and-the-small, as discussed earlier (see section 7.2.2). That shift comes with a correlative transition from the polarized metaphysics of Forms versus sensible phenomena to a gradation of reality between Forms and sensible phenomena, primarily in accommodation of mathematicals as intermediate ontological entities or constructs. And those differences are accompanied by a reduction of Forms to numbers, that is to say, the restriction of the range of Forms to the Forms of numbers. None of that can be corroborated in the dialogues, while some of it is, at least in appearance, contradicted by the dialogues. Should we, then, accept it all because it comes from Aristotle, reject it all because it is difficult to verify, or ignore it all because it is neither entirely acceptable nor quite expendable?

Letter (314a–c), and the *Seventh Letter* (341c–342a), but whatever it was must have been both compelling and widely known, at least in scholarly circles, for we have a hard time now drawing any conclusions regarding the matter from bits and pieces of hints and suggestions in this sparse selection of works, one dialogue and two letters, not all of which we are even able to verify as authentic.

The question is a little deceptive. It puts everything in the same basket. Anyone convinced that the separate issues are already in the same basket may answer the question exactly as formulated. But a better approach is to address the separate issues separately. It is not difficult, for example, to accept Plato's later thought as culminating in a mathematical metaphysics, with the one as the formal principle, interacting with the-great-and-the-small as the material principle, in mutual fulfillment of their foundational position in the constitution of the universe. There is also nothing particularly counterintuitive about the existence of intermediate ontological entities between Forms and sensible phenomena, but the restriction of such entities to the objects of mathematics introduces a provision that completely ignores the broader ontological platform that is otherwise freely, persistently, and successfully explored throughout the Platonic corpus. In the same vein, the reduction of Forms to numbers is inconsistent both with the Platonic corpus and with parts of Aristotle's own testimony. That being so, the central focus of the unwritten doctrines, the part pertaining to metaphysical first principles, seems to be the only part that is not riddled with specific and serious problems with either the accuracy or the consistency of the corresponding testimony.

Although this does not show that the portion of the testimony under consideration here is false, it does show that its truth is not clear or certain, and its acceptance not compelling. It is not enough that it comes from Aristotle. We need better reasons for its acceptance, just as we need valid reasons for its rejection. As Aristotle said of Plato: "Plato is dear to us, but the truth, dearer still."[51] This haunting expression of the essence of dialectical inquiry should serve as a reminder of how dear Aristotle can be to us.

---

51. This is a legendary quotation found everywhere but originating nowhere. The closest we get to verification is a loosely relevant passage in the *Nicomachean Ethics*: "We had perhaps better consider the universal good and discuss thoroughly what is meant by it, although such an inquiry is made an uphill one by the fact that the Forms have been introduced by friends of our own. Yet it would perhaps be thought to be better, indeed to be our duty, for the sake of maintaining the truth even to destroy what touches us closely, especially as we are philosophers; for, while both are dear, piety requires us to honour truth above our friends" (*Nicomachean Ethics* 1096a11–16).

7.6. Plato through Plato

The various discrepancies and contradictions in Aristotle's testimony engender suspicion and hesitation. They make him difficult to trust as a guide to Plato. While every last one of such discrepancies and contradictions may have a logically acceptable explanation, as at least some scholars invoking Aristotle in this context seem prepared to argue, the end result is still too much explanation and not enough evidence. The apparent lack of clarity and plausibility is amplified all the more for anyone inclined to reject the Aristotelian evidence anyway. That predisposition, in turn, is supported by the traditional interpretation of Plato's metaphysics in terms of a dualism of Forms versus sensible phenomena, where there is no room for anything in between or in addition.

Aristotle has to be very convincing indeed to get anyone to accept intermediates against such a deep-seated inclination to polarize the world into Forms and sensible phenomena. The various problems in his testimony, whether they are merely apparent or indubitably real, keep him from being as convincing as required, perhaps not for everyone, but definitely for a sufficient number of dissenters to keep the debate alive. Yet rejecting intermediates just because Plato's world could conceivably be divided fully and evenly between Forms and sensible phenomena, even though Plato himself never identifies the division as either exhaustive or symmetrical (thus leaving room for a debate over Formless things as well as empty Forms), is no better than accepting intermediates, and doing so exclusively in mathematics, just because Aristotle says Plato made a special allowance for them in mathematics while refusing to acknowledge them elsewhere, even though Plato himself never makes or supports such a distinction in any of his works.[52] Having already examined the case against intermediates despite Aristotle, the remainder of the chapter makes a case for intermediates despite Aristotle.

What makes this a matter of supporting intermediates despite Aristotle, and not with Aristotle, is partly that Aristotle reports a restriction to mathematics and mathematicals, and partly that intermediates of any kind

---

52. See Alican (2012, 103–104) and chapter 5 of the present volume for a discussion of the relationship between Forms and sensible phenomena in terms of whether they are mutually exclusive and jointly exhaustive (of the world), with particular attention devoted to the possibility of Formless things (section 5.3) and empty Forms (section 5.4). See section 7.4 of this chapter for a discussion of the range of Forms.

make such a natural fit with Plato's philosophical outlook that we do not even need Aristotle's input to find a place for them in Plato. It may well be true that Plato accepted intermediates in mathematics, presumably as witnessed by associates and students exposed to his unwritten doctrines, and further true that he never engaged in oral discussion of intermediates outside the context of mathematics, but the reasons and motivations Aristotle adduces for Plato's postulation of intermediates do not appear in any way to require a restriction to mathematics and mathematicals, nor therefore to preclude generalizability across all relationships between Forms and sensible phenomena at all levels of reality. The restriction of intermediates to mathematics is neither a logical implication, nor a methodological requirement, nor a natural corollary of the postulation of intermediates in mathematics. It is additional information. It stands alone as an independent provision that Aristotle himself regards as an inconsistency (*Metaphysics* 997b12–32, 1059b2–9; cf. 991a6–8).[53]

We would thus be doing Plato a favor, perhaps doing Aristotle one as well, to demonstrate the possibility of intermediates across the board. The best way to do that is to abandon the dualism of worlds traditionally attributed to Plato, which we should readily abandon for its own flaws anyway. The dualism of worlds is grounded, with a leap of faith rather than compelling evidence, in the dualism of Forms versus sensible phenomena, with the former separated from yet manifested in the latter, coinciding with a correlative distinction between intelligibility and perceptibility. The dualism of Forms versus sensible phenomena is a fact, at least a textual one, whereas the dualism of worlds is an interpretation. When the otherwise innocuous dualism of Forms and sensible phenomena is taken to require a hard separation of mutually exclusive and jointly exhaustive constituents, it naturally becomes inimical to intermediates of any kind, mathematical or otherwise.

Of course, on a strict enough interpretation, or application, any dualism posits two and only two realities, thereby precluding the very

---

53. This is not to say that Aristotle would have endorsed Plato's intermediates had Plato not restricted them to mathematicals. He probably would not have. He very likely would have found even more things to oppose, extending to all other intermediates what he already opposes in mathematicals. What we are trying to determine here, however, is not whether Plato is right, according to Aristotle, but what Plato said, according to Aristotle. And what he said is supposedly something to the effect that intermediates are limited to mathematicals, or that intermediation is unique to mathematics, or both (*Metaphysics* 997b12–32, 1059b2–9, cf. 991a6–8).

possibility of a third. The problem in this particular case, however, is not a logical or metaphysical one that can be traced to firm principles in the Platonic corpus. It is more of an interpretive barrier, whereby the traditional emphasis on the complementary relationship between Forms and sensible phenomena, even without Plato explicitly ruling out any other parts or aspects of reality to reduce the world to a binary bundle of Forms and sensible phenomena, is taken to be a complete model as the default interpretation, thus leaving little motivation to contemplate how the rest of Plato's world might work. It leaves no details to be filled out or worked out. And it thus leaves no apparent room for intermediates.

Yet a dualism of such strict proportions is neither required nor supported nor even indicated in the Platonic corpus. There is indeed a dualism of Forms versus sensible phenomena, but only as complementary aspects and constituents of a single reality best explained through the interaction of Forms and sensible phenomena, and not as the sole ingredients of the world thereby explained. Given any interaction between Forms and sensible phenomena, intermediates become not just possible but also plausible, if not outright indispensable, since Forms and sensible phenomena would otherwise have to remain separate. This, then, is not so much a dualism as it is a unitary pluralism with a gradation of reality both between and beyond Forms and sensible phenomena, between them because their interaction requires intermediation and holds an inexhaustible potential for it, beyond them because they are not the only things in the world.

Plato's world, to elaborate on just the metaphysics, is a cosmic matrix of formal and material objects best understood in reference to two main levels of reality: an upper level hosting intelligible Forms, and a lower level hosting sensible phenomena, with countless subdivisions in between. Although the Forms are in the upper level, and sensible phenomena in the lower, they are not necessarily at the very top and the very bottom of their levels. Nor do they exhaust their levels, for they would then jointly exhaust the world itself, leaving nothing else for our consideration. Nor do the levels represent a division right down the middle so that each one corresponds to precisely one half of all there is. Nor is the division necessarily uneven. There are, in fact, hardly any firm features save for the gradation of reality, where the Forms reside in the upper level and sensible phenomena in the lower level, with a microcosm of ontological stratification effecting their separation while at the same time establishing their connection and facilitating their interaction.

The Forms, to be more specific, come in three varieties, all subsumed under the good (the Form of the good) at the very top. Sensible phenomena, in turn, occupy the lower level, though sitting above the less substantial aspects or constituents of reality at the very bottom, as in the images of *eikasia* in the simile of the divided line (*Republic* 509d–511e). As for the variation in Forms, that is a further reflection of the fluid gradation of reality in Plato, where not even the Forms themselves, as we are accustomed to speaking of them, are all exactly the same kind of ontological entity or construct. They are instead a heterogeneous group of universal concepts with objective reality, all discovered, or invented, depending on the perspective, through the various thought experiments Plato conducted in abstraction and concept formation, with all sorts of different problems in mind. They all have a solid claim to an existence outside the mind, with permanent positions in the upper level of reality, but they are not all the same kind of thing:

- Ideal Forms: These are noetic realities representing all that is intrinsically valuable in the world, including moral, aesthetic, and religious values, as in justice, beauty, and piety, as well as things that are not actual values but are nevertheless valuable in and of themselves, as in knowledge, health, and life itself.

- Conceptual Forms: These are reified universals corresponding to Plato's various experiments with abstraction and concept formation without a value orientation, thus covering most of what we commonly think of now as types (e.g., horses, cups, tables) and properties (e.g., redness, roundness, equality).

- Relational Forms: These are complementary metaphysical categories conceived as correlative universal relations constituting a structural blueprint of cosmic reality in the form of paired contrasts, best exemplified by the "greatest kinds" (*megista genē*) of the *Sophist* (254d–e): rest versus motion, same versus other.

There is no proof in the strictest sense of the term that this unitary yet graded reality accommodating a trinitarian classification of Forms in the upper level, complemented by a commensurate range of sensible phenomena in the lower level, with infinite possibilities in between, is the correct interpretation of Plato, just as there is no proof in the strictest sense of the term that an exclusive dualism of Forms versus sensible phenomena, whether as constituting two separate worlds or as jointly exhausting the essence and ingredients of the one and only world, is the correct interpretation of Plato.[54] Nor does the unitary pluralism espoused here in the form of a gradation of reality constitute proof, or come with proof, that Plato actually embraced intermediates. It merely provides an interpretive framework that is at once plausible in itself, consistent with the evidence, and open to intermediates of all kinds in the world of Plato.

The aim here is not to refute the traditional model but to present a reasonable alternative demonstrating that intermediates need not be rejected just because the limelight in Plato is on the reciprocal ontological layers pressing upon them on either side, namely the Forms and sensible phenomena, which are then overinterpreted as precluding anything in between. Plato's system, if he had one, could conceivably be consistent with a gradation of reality, even without Plato explicitly defending or emphatically illustrating the concomitant cosmological intermediation in his metaphysical writings. Rejecting intermediates because the focus is on Forms and sensible phenomena is like denying the brush because the painting is oil on canvas.

The sense in which hard proof is unavailable, or rather irrelevant, is that determining the best model in this context is not a matter of deductive reasoning or textual discovery. Plato was forever engaged in thought experiments to reconcile his phenomenal experience of "the world as it appears" with his best insight into "the world as it is." The Forms are at the center of all such efforts, but they are only as clear, as substantial, and as definitive as the particular problems they are meant to address, in the particular way, or ways, in which they are invoked in any given dialogue. Some problems require emphasis on some features, while other problems bring out other features, with yet other features possibly not even making it into the dialogues in the absence of a relevant occasion for discussion. This is only natural given that the dialogues themselves are not a complete catalog of Plato's philosophical convictions.

---

54. The paradigm of a unitary pluralism with a trinitarian classification of Forms is initially explicated in the introduction, fully articulated in chapter 2, and further developed in subsequent chapters. The sketch in the present chapter is deliberately brief to focus more on implications for intermediates than on methodological and structural details, the latter of which can be found in abundance in the references just mentioned. The brevity here is not intended to shift the burden of proof elsewhere but to get on with the application where there is no proof anyway, at least not in the strictest sense of the term, as already indicated above in the main text.

Consider an analogy from physics. The vibration of strings commonly thought to underlie observable reality, manifested variously as waves and particles, is comparable to the ontological stratification underlying the dualism of Forms versus sensible phenomena. We are accustomed to thinking of Plato's world through the received view of a complementary relationship between Forms and sensible phenomena. But what if there is something beyond that? Modern physics tells us that waves and particles are correlative observational perspectives on the frequency distribution of vibrations, where neither the waves nor the particles need be considered ultimate, nor both in conjunction be considered exhaustive of universal reality. Much in the same way, the relationship between Forms and sensible phenomena is closer to a heuristic device for interpreting Plato's world than to a comprehensive breakdown of its organizational structure. The inherent ontological stratification amenable to representative modeling through Forms and sensible phenomena ultimately exhibits a much finer gradation of reality than a strict dualism would seem to indicate.

Theoretical construction and reconstruction, of course, go only so far toward persuasion. Some practical demonstration is required even with a frank denial of the possibility of proof in the strictest sense. As it turns out, what is possible and available by way of demonstration is quite persuasive and may indeed prove sufficient as well as necessary. Despite the absence of proof as such, the possibility of intermediates in a gradation of reality has at least one thing to recommend it: Whatever proof it is susceptible of is on a methodological par with whatever makes mathematical intermediates plausible as reported by Aristotle. The methodological equivalence of their justification is confirmed by questions concerning their utility: What exactly do they do? Why would Plato need them? How does he use them?

The answer with respect to mathematics, as already covered in the expository and critical discussion dedicated to mathematicals (see sections 7.2.4 and 7.4), is that it is impossible to do mathematics with Forms. This is because Forms cannot be added or subtracted, multiplied or divided, and so on, even if they are the Forms of numbers. As a matter of fact, the Forms of numbers do not work any better in that role than any other Forms might. For example, the Form of two plus the Form of three results in nothing more meaningful than the Form of horse divided by the Form of table. Likewise, geometrical figures can be taken apart, put back together, combined with one another, and so on, while the Forms of geometrical figures cannot be manipulated in that way at all. The Form of square, for instance, does not split into two separate Forms of triangles when intersected by the Form of diagonal extending from the

Form of one corner to the Form of the opposite corner. Both arithmetic and geometry require repeatable and combinable elements for standard operations.[55] Hence, the need for mathematical intermediates, "differing from sensible things in being eternal and unchangeable, from Forms in that there are many alike, while the Form itself is in each case unique" (Aristotle: *Metaphysics* 987b16–18).

There is no good reason why the practical problem preventing the direct utilization of Forms in mathematics should not be a general problem preventing the direct utilization of Forms in any other aspect of reality, thereby precluding their unmediated operational relevance to and interaction with any other part of the world. Just as mathematical intermediates are required to compensate for the impossibility of doing mathematics with Forms, so too may nonmathematical intermediates be required to compensate for the impossibility of processing sense data with nothing but Forms, which are supposed to be separate from the very data requiring interpretation and comprehension. What makes mathematical intermediates indispensable in mathematics is not their nature as mathematicals but their function as intermediates. That is why a restriction of intermediates to mathematicals is entirely counterintuitive. The raison d'être of intermediates is universal, much like the utility of intermediation.

To take just one example, the Form of beauty may make things beautiful but not variably so. In other words, even if all things are beautiful in reference to beauty itself, which makes the Form of beauty the causal explanation for anything's being beautiful, that same Form of beauty is insufficient to explain why one thing might be more beautiful than another, or why any beautiful thing can become more beautiful or less beautiful over time, perhaps even eventually ceasing to be beautiful altogether. Just as Forms are not addable, divisible, and so on, they are also not variable or destructible. The explanation for such variability must rest in intermediates facilitating and regulating the interaction between Forms and sensible phenomena.

---

55. Annas (1975) concludes, as discussed earlier (section 7.2.4), that the most reasonable reading of Aristotle's testimony concerning intermediates in Plato is that Aristotle took Plato to have invented mathematical intermediates because it is impossible to do mathematics with Forms. Wedberg (1955) likewise argues that it is not possible to do arithmetic with Forms, especially not as they are presented in the *Republic* and *Philebus*, among other works, where it is clear that Forms do not work like numbers, at least because they are neither repeatable nor combinable whereas numbers are (as in 2 + 2 = 4).

It may be objected that the variability in question can be readily explained through sensible phenomena alone with no need for intermediates or intermediation. The explanation would presumably be that some things, more than others, embody, reflect, or resemble the relevant Form, thus introducing variability without requiring intermediates in the process. But that is not an adequate explanation. It is neither relevant nor meaningful. The variability of sensible phenomena in the instantiation of any given Form is precisely what is to be explained, which then remains unexplained if the explanation offered is that sensible phenomena exhibit variability in their instantiation of the corresponding Form, which is to restate, without explanation, the phenomenon still requiring explanation. That is to say nothing better than that Forms and sensible phenomena interact in mysterious ways. Intermediates break the circle and present a linear alternative, even if there is still something of a mystery left in the explanation, this time in regard to precisely how intermediates themselves work.

This appeal to common sense is not the only recourse we have in the absence of proof in the strictest sense. There are also specific examples indicative of intermediates in the Platonic corpus. Plato's gradation of reality, including hints of his experimentation with intermediation processes, is always just below the surface of his never-ending exploration of the nature of reality and the structure of the cosmos. The alternative of unitary pluralism with ontological stratification is, at the very least, buried no deeper in any dialogue than is the dualism of worlds traditionally attributed to Plato. Some dialogues are not only consistent with a gradation of reality but also demonstrative of it. Others point to various intermediates without explicitly and simultaneously developing a gradation of reality as a contextual substratum. One place where elements of both come together in a telling demonstration of intermediates and intermediation is the *Phaedo*.

The prime candidates for intermediates are the *Phaedo*'s causal intermediaries, invoked repeatedly to explain the world at large, including everything in it, as the manifestation of Forms through sensible phenomena. These causal intermediaries come up in the methodological groundwork (96a–105a) for the final argument for the immortality of the soul (105b–107a), where the soul emerges as the most memorable candidate for an ontological intermediate in the whole of the Platonic corpus, accounting as it does for the presence of life in the body.[56] Attesting to

---

56. See Alican (2012, 446–450) for a critical analysis of the final argument of the *Phaedo* for the immortality of the soul (cf. 431–446 for a detailed discussion of causal intermediation in the methodological groundwork for the final argument).

their importance is the dramatic announcement of a "second sailing" (*deuteros plous* at 99c–d), a nautical metaphor artfully complementing the opening reference to the naval mission to Delos led by Theseus (58a–c) and marking a turning point in the dialogue's treatment of causal explanation.

The reference to a "second sailing" is an idiomatic expression denoting the natural recourse sailors had to rowing when sailing was precluded by failing winds (see Ross 1951, 27). The sense is, therefore, of a slower alternative, and obviously also of a more difficult one, though not necessarily of an inferior one (unless being faster and easier is all there is to being superior), despite a tendency by commentators to describe the dramatic turn as a transition to a second-best dialectical strategy. Burnet (1911, 108, n. 99c9), for one, considers Plato's usage to be not just metaphorical but also ironical.

However that may be, the naval leitmotif of the *Phaedo*, firmly established with the opening reference to the traditional mission to Delos (58a–c), and further enhanced through a "second sailing" (99c–d), is hard to miss. The references clearly constitute an extended nautical metaphor, but the symbolism is not easy to interpret. Perhaps the dramatic Socrates is the legendary Theseus and death is the mythical Minotaur. That combination would make life on earth the labyrinth, with the Forms serving as the golden thread showing the way out. The path thus traced, however, would not be a way out of death as the separation of soul from body, which is inevitable, but a way out of life on earth, departure from which is not to be feared, especially not by the philosopher.

This interpretation has the additional advantage of making sense of the misology interlude at the dramatic center of the dialogue (*Phaedo* 89b–91c). We must never turn our backs on logos, we are told, arguably because that is our only source of access to the golden thread of the Forms. Plato may then be taken as Ariadne, providing the thread, though the role of Daedalus is also open to him, albeit not very consistently with the rest of the symbolism just imagined. Note also that the thought of Socrates as Theseus, while supremely appealing upon initial consideration, is inconsistent with some of the facts of the mission, as Theseus is accompanied by fourteen people, while Socrates on his last day on earth is accompanied by fifteen associates identified by name (59b–c), plus his wife Xanthippe (escorted away by Crito's people at 60a–b), and yet others confirmed to be present though not identified by name.[57]

---

57. Three associates are explicitly identified as absent: Aristippus of Cyrene, Cleombrotus of Ambracia, and most notably, Plato himself (*Phaedo* 59b–c).

An alternative interpretation is to anchor the nautical metaphor to the ancient puzzle associated with, and known as, the Ship of Theseus. While there is no definitive solution to the puzzle itself, the symbolism could be read as the message that life goes on even if nothing else does, with the soul surviving endless reincarnations through countless bodies, just as the naval mission goes on even if the perpetually recycled ship is never the same as it ever was. We cannot be sure whether the puzzle dates back to the time of Plato. Plutarch dates it as far back as Demetrius Phalereus (*Vita Thesei* 23.1), who was born just a few years before Plato died. This suggests that Plutarch would have named Plato as well, or perhaps even instead, had he believed that Plato was familiar with the puzzle, but it does not show that Plato did not know about the puzzle, just that Plutarch did not know whether Plato did. Plato himself was certainly no stranger to identity problems, as demonstrated at least by the dialectical reasoning conducted in the second part of the *Parmenides* and by various references to paradoxes of flux in Heraclitus (*Cratylus* 401d–402c; *Republic* 498a–b; *Symposium* 187a; *Theaetetus* 152e, 160d), whose views he is said to have studied with Cratylus (Aristotle: *Metaphysics* 987a29–b1; cf. 1010a10–14).

Yet even if the nautical metaphor(s) of the *Phaedo*, including the second sailing, remain open to interpretation, the underlying attempt to attract and redirect the attention of the audience is plain to see. The dramatic turn introduced by the second sailing comes with a methodological transition from teleological explanation anchored to final causes to hypothetical explanation anchored to formal causes. The transition is the culmination and resolution of an intellectual autobiography by the dramatic Socrates (very likely representing the intellectual autobiography of Plato himself), whose pursuit of an adequate account of causal explanation begins in his youth with a mechanistic approach dealing with physical causes (96a–97b), followed by a period of infatuation with the teleological explanation promised in the emphasis of Anaxagoras on mind yet never successfully delivered in application (97b–99d), and leading finally to the method of hypothesis where the Forms come into play.[58] It is during

---

58. While this is a fair summary of the relevant parts of the *Phaedo*, there is, perhaps somewhat surprisingly, a remarkable lack of consensus on the proper interpretation of the nature and implications of a "second sailing" (*Phaedo* 99c–d) in this context. The bulk of the disagreement is on what exactly the intended second sailing might be (see Rose 1966; Preus and Ferguson 1969), though some of it is instead on what the implicit first sailing might have been, that is, on what the second sailing is supposed to be second to (see Ross 1982).

this transition that we are confronted with various entities or constructs competing for our attention as candidates for ontological intermediates in the form of causal intermediaries, chief among them, the soul.

The soul (*psuchē*, literally "life" or "spirit") is a central topic of discussion in Plato, who brings it up in various different contexts, with vastly different conceptions, including apparently incompatible ones, and a series of proofs, or arguments, for its immortality.[59] The main concern in the matter on hand, namely in the most salient implications of causal intermediation, is the ontological status of the soul, specifically of the soul of the *Phaedo* in the final argument for personal immortality (105b–107a). Although it is clear that the soul of the *Phaedo* is a causal intermediary, it is not clear whether it is therefore ontologically different both from Forms and from sensible phenomena, the alternative being that it might be a Form that facilitates intermediation, counting as an immanent Form when it is joined with a body and as a transcendent one when it is not.

Both the ontological status of the soul[60] and the possibility of immanent Forms[61] are a matter of ongoing scholarly debate. My own position,

---

59. See Alican (2012) for Plato's various conceptions of the soul throughout his writings (478–489) and for the corresponding proofs he offers for the immortality of the soul (446–450, 457–477).

60. The literature on Plato's conception(s) of the soul is too vast to cover in a footnote. What is important here is his treatment of it in the final argument of the *Phaedo* (96a–107a, especially 105b–107a) for the immortality of the soul. While not everything can be covered even within this limited scope, a short list must surely include critical editions and translations of the *Phaedo* that can be consulted for insight into various aspects of the dialogue through a combination of overviews, commentaries, and notes. Sources that work particularly well in that capacity include the Greek editions by Archer-Hind (1883), Burnet (1911), and Geddes (1863), and the English translations by Bluck (1955), Gallop (1975), and Hackforth (1955). These can be combined profitably with relevant monographs on the *Phaedo*, including those by Bostock (1986a), Burger (1984), Dorter (1982), and White (1989). Any attempt to determine the ontological status of the soul in the final argument of the *Phaedo* will also benefit from essays devoted specifically to that question, including those by Bostock (1986b), Frede (1978), Keyt (1963), Prince (2011), and Schiller (1967). A broader exploration of Plato's conception(s) of the soul can be accommodated through the anthologies by Barney, Brennan, and Brittain (2012) and Wagner (2001), each bringing together a variety of approaches to the subject.

61. Problems with the immanence of Forms typically arise in connection with the transcendence of Forms. The central question is how they can be immanent if they are transcendent, or to put it in Aristotelian terms, how they can be in something if they are separate. Some scholars treat transcendence and immanence as correlative

stated briefly, is that the soul of the *Phaedo* is a causal intermediary in the sense of an ontological intermediate rather than in that of an immanent Form, hence an intermediate constituting a separate ontological category between Forms and sensible phenomena. I further believe that there are no such things as immanent Forms, particularly if their existence is conceived as requiring an additional ontological category besides Forms, intermediates, and sensible phenomena, or alternatively, but to the same effect, as requiring a division of the ontological category already reserved for Forms, into two separate categories, one for transcendent Forms, another for immanent Forms.[62]

Some elaboration may be in order in connection with both the ontological status of the soul and the possibility of immanent Forms. To be perfectly clear about my understanding of Plato's conception of the soul, I do not mean to deny that there is a Form of soul in the *Phaedo*, or in the Platonic corpus, or in Plato's philosophical outlook in general. I mean to deny only that the soul in the final argument of the *Phaedo* (105b–107a) is the Form of soul. It is not. It is an ontological intermedi-

---

problems deserving equal attention and a joint resolution: Devereux (1994), Perl (1999), Rist (1964). Others focus primarily on transcendence, though in appreciation of its obvious correlation with immanence in terms of the problematic possibility of their mutual consistency: Fine (1984), Lewis (1979), Mabbott (1926), Morrison (1985a), Spellman (1995), Vlastos (1987). Yet others do the opposite, focusing primarily on immanence, while discussing implications for transcendence: Dancy (1991, 9–23, 53–56), Fine (1986), Matthen (1984). Arguably the most thorough approach is by Fine, whose contributions on separation (1984) and immanence (1986) have become classics in the literature. Morrison's (1985b) critique of Fine, Fine's (1985) reply to Morrison, and Morrison's (1985c) reply to Fine's reply further clarify the issues. See Wood (2017) for a more recent treatment with an exclusive focus on the *Philebus*.

62. Demos (1948) defends the opposite view with well-chosen references from the relevant texts: "In short, forms are divisible into two groups: forms which are transcendent, 'invisible,' abstract, and forms which are immanent, visible and concrete. Thus the *Republic* refers to the visible forms (ὁρώμενα εἴδη, 510d). The distinction is made even more explicitly in the *Parmenides* (130d) where Plato contrasts likeness as such (αὐτῃ) and the likeness which we possess. But the best source for my point is the *Phaedo* (102d–3b) which gives us the following pairs: largeness itself (αὐτὸ τὸ μέγεθος) and largeness in us (ἐν ἡμῖν), smallness itself and smallness in us. Again in the *Phaedo*, Plato distinguishes opposites (or forms) into those which are in nature (ἐν τῇ φύσει) and those which are in us, the latter being characterized as immanent (ἐνόντα). Recollection is of the transcendent forms, and what stimulates such recollection is presumably the perception of immanent forms" (Demos 1948, 456).

ate functioning as a causal intermediary. The soul of the final argument makes life possible as a metaphysical process in the same way that the numbers and figures in Aristotle's testimony make mathematics possible as an operational procedure.

There is a Form of soul, to be sure, but it is entirely irrelevant to the final argument of the *Phaedo*, and it is therefore never brought up there at all. The reason that the Form of soul is irrelevant in this context is that the emphasis on the soul in the final argument is specifically on the soul's intermediation in bringing life, which it does through its participation in the Form of life. The fact that the soul also happens to participate in the Form of soul, which is what makes any soul a soul, is extraneous information that would add nothing to the argument. The only thing that matters in context is the soul's participation in the Form of life. We nevertheless know that there is a Form of soul, simply because there are no intermediates without a corresponding Form.[63] If the soul is an intermediate, then there must be a Form of soul. It is there in the background, just not relevant to the argument, and hence not operative in the proof.

As for any tension between transcendence and immanence, the thrust of my reasoning for denying immanent Forms, particularly in a literal sense, is as follows:[64] If Forms are transcendent, which the ones in Plato are clearly meant to be, they cannot also be immanent, except in an entirely metaphorical sense describing their instantiation in our phenomenal experience. Privileging transcendence over immanence is an acceptable way of reading Plato so long as it is not taken as an excuse to exaggerate transcendence beyond what it is while reducing immanence to

---

63. The question of the correspondence between Forms and ontological intermediates can be settled with certainty, unlike the question of the correspondence between Forms and sensible phenomena. This is because intermediates are invoked precisely to establish representation, enable instantiation, and facilitate causality where there are, in fact, Forms and sensible phenomena to be connected through logical, ontological, and epistemological processes relevant to our phenomenal experience. The correspondence between Forms and sensible phenomena (chapter 5), on the other hand, may conceivably be disrupted at either end through the possibility of Formless things (section 5.3) or that of empty Forms (section 5.4).

64. See chapter 3 (section 3.4) for a general appraisal of the interpretive tension between transcendence and immanence in Plato's Forms, and chapter 5 (section 5.4) for a specific analysis of ontological independence in the context of the transcendence of Forms, including any implications for the simultaneous possibility of immanence.

an impossibility. Transcendence itself is not an absolute separation in the sense of a limiting condition severing Forms from sensible phenomena with the finality of discrete worlds. It is instead a mark of ontological independence wherein Forms do not depend either for their existence or for their essence on sensible phenomena. Immanence, in turn, is nothing other than instantiation, which is not so much about the Forms themselves as it is about our efforts and ability to make sense of them, hence not so much an ontological phenomenon as an epistemological one. The tallness in Simmias (*Phaedo* 102b–d), for example, is not the Form of tallness, which cannot be in Simmias in the relevant sense, because it is not anywhere at all in the relevant sense, just like all other Forms, which are nowhere in particular, save for a metaphorical presence in heaven (*Republic* 509d), and even "outside" or "beyond" heaven (*Phaedrus* 247c).

The example of the soul as an ontological intermediate may, at first glance, be found disanalogous to the case of numbers and figures as mathematical intermediates. One reason for suspicion may be that the soul is responsible for the presence of life in the body, and thereby ostensibly for something other than itself, whereas mathematicals are evidently responsible only for themselves, so to speak, with arithmetical numbers representing ideal numbers and geometrical figures representing ideal figures. But the distinction is not as telling as it may seem. The soul of the *Phaedo* in the final argument (105b–107a) for immortality has an existential and essential bond with life itself, whereby the soul and life become metaphysically inseparable while remaining numerically distinct. The existence and essence of the soul in our phenomenal experience, at least as far as Plato is concerned, is nothing other than the instantiation of life in the body.

What Plato is at pains to demonstrate is that the connection between soul (*psuchē*) and life (*zōē*) is ontologically necessary and metaphysically interminable, which is why the existence of the body is irrelevant to the immortality of the soul. The instantiation of life in any particular body supervenes upon a universal reality, which remains just as real upon the end of the instantiation of life in that particular body, because it is the sole reason for that instantiation in the first place. The soul as the unitary consciousness responsible for mental activity, as we commonly understand the concept, is admittedly different from life itself, not just numerically but also ontologically. Yet the two are much closer in Plato, where "life" is not just a reasonable rendition but a literal translation of both *psuchē* and *zōē*.

Upon closer examination, then, the methodological position and dialectical function of the soul of the *Phaedo*, particularly in the final argument (105b–107a), is not a far cry from how Aristotle describes the arithmetical numbers he positions between the Forms of numbers and the sensible phenomena that instantiate them, or from the geometrical figures he positions between the Forms of figures and the sensible phenomena that instantiate them. The soul can no more cease to be alive, come what may, than the number three can cease to be odd, come what may. That is the nature and strength of their connection, soul with life (105c–e), three with oddness (104a–e). There are still differences, of course, between the soul and mathematicals, given that the soul is an active causal principle, whereas numbers and figures are passive intermediates. But that only shows that intermediation is not a uniform phenomenon or process, instead exhibiting both active and passive iterations, the former through causal intermediaries, the latter through catalytic intermediaries. In any event, a closer correlation with mathematical intermediates must surely be admitted where we encounter the tallness in Simmias (102b–d), already mentioned above.

The analogy between the soul as an ontological intermediate and numbers and figures as mathematical intermediates is actually much closer than it may seem in the face of the apparent difference between intermediation in connection with the defining Form (as in mathematical numbers facilitating the instantiation of ideal numbers) and intermediation in connection with the enabling Form (as in the soul facilitating the instantiation of life). Note that the explanation given in the *Phaedo* for the oddness of a number of sensible things is not oddness itself but unity (105c), which brings oddness, hence something other than its own Form, just as the soul, in bringing life to a body, brings a Form other than its own. Any mathematical number, although the full generalization is not articulated in the text, will therefore bring oddness or evenness, in addition to its ideal number, to the sensible phenomena it affects. The explicit generalization for odd numbers (105c) is obviously warranted even though the closest we come to a specific example in the text is the connection between the number three and oddness (104a–e). Strictly speaking, the case of the number three is not one of the four examples adduced specifically as intermediate agents responsible for bringing Forms other than their own to sensible phenomena (105c) but one of the earlier examples illustrating the military metaphor of advancing and retreating opposites (102b–105b). Yet it is clear that it would work perfectly well in either capacity.

A closer look at the examples just mentioned may help. The proof in the final argument of the *Phaedo* rests on Plato's illustration of a "safe and sophisticated" approach (105b–c) to causal explanation, specifically through causal intermediaries, as against the "safe yet unsophisticated" approach already examined as the direct attribution of all causality to the relevant Forms. This is the difference between attributing the hotness of a sensible object to heat itself and attributing it instead to the fire that brings the heat. Fire indeed becomes the first of a series of examples illustrating the safe and sophisticated approach to causality, thereby introducing an assortment of candidates for ontological intermediaries serving as causal intermediaries (105c): (1) fire as a causal intermediary responsible for the instantiation of heat in sensible phenomena; (2) fever as a causal intermediary responsible for the instantiation of sickness in living beings; (3) unity as a causal intermediary responsible for the instantiation of oddness in mathematical numbers; (4) soul as a causal intermediary responsible for the instantiation of life in biological organisms.

But why take these causal intermediaries, including countless others like them (for they are explicitly said to be representative examples), specifically as ontological intermediaries and not as Forms or as sensible phenomena? The answer must be formulated from a negative perspective, given that Plato nowhere says anything like: "These causal intermediaries are ontological intermediaries, much like the mathematical intermediates I have been telling Aristotle about." The negative formulation runs something like this: None of the four causal intermediaries is either identified outright as a Form (*eidos* or *idea*) or couched expressly in Platonic language typical of Forms (*auto kath' hauto*) or distinguished by implication as a Form through previously established assumptions and relationships. As for the possibility of their being intended as sensible phenomena, the four examples as a group appear to be chosen specifically and carefully with sufficient diversity to avoid their being confused with sensible phenomena.[65]

---

65. Another aspect of the diversity of the causal intermediaries introduced through the final argument of the *Phaedo* for the immortality of the soul (105b–107a) is an implicit indifference between necessary and sufficient causes. Fire and fever both seem to be sufficient causes, while unity and soul both seem to be necessary as well as sufficient causes (105c).

Had fire been the only example, it might have perhaps been mistaken for sensible fire, but the variety established through the selection presented leaves little room for doubt that the examples are neither concrete things nor Forms. It may conceivably be objected that the fire in question could still be sensible fire even if all three of the other examples are ontological intermediates analogous to mathematical intermediates. But it is unlikely that Plato would have included one example among many that runs counter to the illustration intended through the rest. The examples seem to be chosen specifically to ensure that ontological intermediates in general are not mistaken for sensible phenomena, in which case it would be disingenuous to insist that one of them does not work, especially since giving that one up would still leave the other three, to say nothing of the countless others implied by extension: "and so with other things" (*Phaedo* 105c).

While mine is not the standard view on the matter, there does not seem to be anything approximating a consensus in the literature. Scholars disagree sharply over the ontological status of the soul, where interpretations range all the way from a Form to a personal essence, both finding advocates in different parts of the final argument of the *Phaedo* (96a–107a, including the groundwork, but especially 105b–107a, as the decisive development). A case in point is Reginald Hackforth (1955), who protests "what may be called a change in Plato's conception of the logical status of the soul," which he claims is "most clearly apparent from 106e5-7," where "[Plato] treats it no longer as a form or immanent character, but as a subject which contains or possesses a form, an immaterial subject on a level, save for its immateriality, with snow which contains the form 'cold' and excludes the form 'hot'" (1955, 165). He identifies this move as a transition from "soul as form to soul as possessor of form" (Hackforth 1955, 165).

Confirming the purportedly illicit move detected by Hackforth, David Keyt (1963) goes even further to charge Plato with a couple of logical fallacies in the same context: "the passage [*Phaedo* 102a–107b] contains two fallacies: first, the fallacy of equivocation; and, secondly, a form of the fallacy of composition" (1963, 167). The equivocation in question is not on *psuchē*, but on *athanaton*, which Keyt (1963, 170) accuses Plato of construing first as "alive" (105e2-3) and then as "immortal" (106e1). The version of the fallacy of composition Keyt has in mind is the logical error committed "whenever one infers that one concept is an instance of a second because the first concept is subordinate to the second" (1963, 167). He accuses Plato of doing this in treating the "soul as if it were an immanent form" (Keyt 1963, 169) and consequently inferring its immortality and indestructability from its subordination to the immanent Form of immortality (*to athanaton*) and the immanent Form of indestructability (*to anōlethron*) (1963, 171).

Objecting to both Hackforth and Keyt, Jerome Schiller argues that Plato "never treats the soul as an immanent form in the course of the argument" (1967, 50). David Gallop likewise denies that the soul is a Form, instead finding it "preferable to take the whole of the present passage [*Phaedo* 105c9–d12] as referring to a particular soul, or soul-stuff" (1975, 214). Dorothea Frede agrees with Gallop that the soul is not a Form but disagrees with his reading of the preliminary examples setting up the final argument for immortality (1978, especially 35). References can be multiplied indefinitely but not to the point of either validating or overturning my position on the intermediate status of the soul in the final argument of the *Phaedo*.

My strongest ally here is Plato himself, who seems to confirm my interpretation, earlier in the same dialogue, where he says almost outright that the soul is an ontological intermediate: "the soul is most like the divine, deathless, intelligible, uniform, indissoluble, always the same as itself, whereas the body is most like that which is human, mortal, multiform, unintelligible, soluble and never consistently the same" (*Phaedo* 80a). The passage serves as Socrates's recapitulation of the premises of the analogic argument for the immortality of the soul, the third of the four proofs in the *Phaedo*, also known as the affinity argument (78b–80b for the logical core, 80c–84b for the supporting imagery).[66] The conclusion of the argument is that the soul is not the kind of thing that will just dissipate in the wind upon separation from the body, given that it is a simple and partless entity not subject to dispersal or decomposition, and further that it is an immaterial entity not vulnerable to the elements, and in short that it is a special entity more like the Forms than like sensible phenomena.

The argument does not constitute conclusive proof that the soul is immortal, because the premises claim only an affinity and not an identity between the soul, on the one hand, and the Forms and the gods, on the other. The reasoning is otherwise accepted in context. The objection of the audience is not that the soul is not like the Forms and the gods but that

---

66. See Alican (2012, 418–424) and chapter 4 (section 4.3) of the present volume for a critical examination of the analogic argument of the *Phaedo* (78b–80b logical core, 80c–84b supporting imagery).

we cannot assume immortality for it on the basis of a nebulous likeness, which may or may not include immortality. The possibility of an affinity too weak to guarantee immortality is not the only complication in the argument. An even greater threat is the possibility of an affinity too strong to establish immortality, making the soul just like the Forms, rather than vaguely similar to them. The danger there is that the soul would then not even be alive, let alone immortal, given that the Forms themselves are not alive. Yet nobody in the dramatic audience brings this up as a potential problem. They focus instead on the possibility of a weak affinity that does not guarantee immortality in the sense of indestructibility, which is why the dialogue then moves on to the fourth and final argument, after an exchange of objections and replies, including an interlude with misology: the hatred of rational thought and dialectical inquiry (both logical and scientific).

The possibility of a weak affinity, however, does not undermine the possibility of the soul as an intermediate. On the contrary, the weaker the affinity, the greater the indication that the soul is not a Form. Even though the analogic argument fails to establish the immortality of the soul, it seems at least to establish the intermediate ontological status of the soul. And this lends further support to my understanding of the soul of the final argument as an ontological intermediate, together with the parallel examples of fire, fever, and unity (*Phaedo* 105c).

The reason that I have pursued the final argument rather than the analogic argument in illustration of the soul as an example of ontological intermediates is that the final argument assigns intermediation a central role in instantiation, whereas the analogic argument is largely silent on intermediation, which remains incidental to the main considerations and developments there. This is because the final argument works with causal intermediaries directly responsible for the phenomenal instantiation of Forms, whereas the analogic argument merely invokes an affinity that suggests an intermediate status with no apparent bearing upon instantiation. Something's being intermediate between one thing and another is not evidence of its instantiating either thing in the other, which is how mathematicals work in Aristotle's testimony, and which is therefore how ontological intermediates must be shown to work to match and expand Aristotle's example. The reason that I have invoked the analogic argument at all is that the intermediate ontological status of the soul in the final argument is not universally recognized, which then makes any additional evidence relevant and helpful if not conclusive.

We may never be quite sure what Plato thought of the soul, but we can be reasonably confident that he made room for ontological intermediates on a par, conceptually, methodologically, and metaphysically, with the mathematical intermediates in Aristotle's testimony, and furthermore that much of what he says about the soul is consistent with that correlation. While the soul is not the only example of causal intermediaries that are ontological intermediates, no others are likely to generate agreement where the soul fails to do so. This is not necessarily because the soul is the best example, but because there are no indisputable examples in the text. That is precisely the situation we have with mathematical intermediates, which Aristotle insists are at the center of Plato's philosophical orientation. There is no reason why ontological intermediates should not be an integral part of Plato's philosophical outlook, save for Aristotle's testimony indicating a restriction of intermediates to mathematicals (*Metaphysics* 997b12–32, 1059b2–9).

Possibly the greatest evidence for ontological intermediates in the philosophy of Plato is the striking visual aid he offers at the center of his greatest work: the divided line of the *Republic* (509d–511e). Recall that the line is divided, not once, but three times, thus producing two main sections and four subsections. Had his sole intention been to distinguish Forms from sensible phenomena, postulating nothing between or beyond the two, the dramatic Socrates could have moved on after the first cut, leaving the line with only two sections. This may not prove that one of the subsections is reserved for intermediates, but it does confirm that there is room in Plato's world for more than just Forms and sensible phenomena. No matter what the four subsections represent severally, they point collectively to a rich and deep gradation of reality capable of accommodating a variety of intermediates, both ontological and mathematical.

As a matter of fact, both the ontological category of intermediates and the metaphysical process of intermediation are fluid enough to include more than the intermediates required and responsible for facilitating the instantiation of one thing in another, or what is the same, of one thing by another. My aim in pursuing the soul of the final argument of the *Phaedo* as an example of ontological intermediates was to approximate mathematical intermediates with a specific example that captures both the ontological category and the metaphysical process. But intermediation in Plato is open to further possibilities. Some intermediates, for example, may serve as bridges between one level of reality and another without necessarily intermediating a specific event or process.

The various dimensions of metaphysical intermediation in Plato are brought out rather well by Daryl McGowan Tress (1999, 139; cf. 144, 156–160), who identifies seven distinct examples of intermediates in the *Timaeus* alone: demiurge, soul (*psuchē*), receptacle, mathematicals, marrow (*muelos*), love (*eros*), and lust (*epithumia*). Her intermediates are spread out through four areas, with the demiurge and soul serving as intermediates between being and becoming, the receptacle and mathematicals as intermediates between reason and necessity, marrow as an intermediate between body and soul, and love and lust as intermediates between male and female (Tress 1999, 145–146). These are not intermediates in the same sense that numbers and figures are mathematical intermediates, or fire, fever, unity, and soul are ontological intermediates. But that is perfectly acceptable and quite welcome. Indeed, intermediates are not limited to a single function, purpose, or mode of existence. The possibility of intermediates is the possibility of a proliferation of metaphysical categories and/or divisions through ontological stratification in a gradation of reality. And there seems to be ample room for that in Plato even if the evidence is not conclusive.

7.7. Conclusion

The purpose of this chapter has been to present an interpretive model that fully accommodates intermediates in Plato, not just those identified by Aristotle, but any and all manner of others. While Aristotle tells us that there are mathematical intermediates in Plato (*Metaphysics* 987b14–18, 1028b19–21), adding incidentally that there are no others (*Metaphysics* 997b12–32, 1059b2–9), discrepancies and contradictions throughout his testimony provide grounds for suspicion. That makes it reasonable to doubt both whether there really are mathematical intermediates in Plato, as Aristotle informs us, and whether there really are no other intermediates in Plato, as Aristotle assures us.

On the other hand, the availability of carefully constructed explanations for the discrepancies and contradictions in Aristotle's testimony, as illustrated above through a representative decision procedure (section 7.5), arguably makes it reasonable to continue to believe whatever he says about Plato, particularly what he says Plato said, if not what he says Plato meant. As we turn to the Platonic corpus to decide which way to go with Aristotle's testimony, that is, to decide whether to accept or to reject his testimony based on the evidence in Plato, the last thing we need is a stock reading of Plato, prejudicing the matter either in favor of Aristotle's testimony or against it. Yet that is indeed the prospect awaiting anyone indoctrinated through the received view of Plato.

The traditional approach to the philosophical orientation of Plato, particularly to his metaphysics, revolves around a fundamental distinction between Forms and sensible phenomena. The distinction itself is apposite to the context but only as a demonstration of the fundamental constituents of reality and not as a complete map of its structure and contents. Nevertheless, this traditional model is popular enough that it stands as a natural impetus for scholarly resistance to intermediates in Plato. The possibility of intermediates is ruled out by the assumption of a two-world ontology of metaphysical dualism as manifested in a static contrast between Forms and sensible phenomena. The alternative model presented and promoted here replaces the strict dualism of the traditional model with a gradation of reality in a single world that has plenty of room for intermediates.

Despite corroborating intermediates, which is partly consistent with Aristotle's testimony, the model is not a defense of Aristotle but an explanation of Plato. It is not a defense of Aristotle, because the unitary pluralism it is built on is nothing like what Aristotle says Plato said. Be that as it may, the only interpretive mistake more grievous than ignoring Aristotle's testimony on Plato is embracing it without critical reflection. What Aristotelian testimony has going for it is a direct link with Plato, but there is something to be said for consistency as well, both the internal kind and the external kind. While anything Aristotle says about Plato has the apparent advantage of coming practically straight from Plato, the model in this chapter has the normally trivial but here significant advantage of consistency, both within itself and with the canonical corpus.

The received view of Plato has one too many worlds and not enough variety in either one. The alternative proposed here imposes strict limits on the number of worlds, reducing it to just the one we all live in, while lifting all limits and limitations on the variegation in its population, thereby opening it up to the reality of things beyond our phenomenal experience. The model constitutes monism as opposed to dualism from the perspective of how many different worlds Plato countenances, while representing pluralism as opposed to dualism from the perspective of how many different kinds of things he recognizes. The combination amounts to a unitary pluralism where a single world hosts and exhibits all the ingredients and relationships required to explain the whole of reality. In the final analysis, then, Plato's world accommodates both mathematical intermediates and ontological intermediates as part of its overarching allowance for unlimited ontological stratification in a liberal gradation of reality.

Works Cited

Adam, James. 1902. *The Republic of Plato*. Two volumes. Greek text, edited with critical notes, commentary, and appendices. Cambridge: Cambridge University Press. Preceded by a text-only edition, without commentary, released through the same publisher in 1897. Second edition, with an introduction by D. A. Rees, issued by the same publisher in 1963.

Ademollo, Francesco. 2013. "Plato's Conception of the Forms: Some Remarks." In *Universals in Ancient Philosophy*, edited by Riccardo Chiaradonna and Gabriele Galluzzo, 41–85. Seminari e Convegni 33. Pisa: Edizioni della Normale.

Alexander of Aphrodisias. 1891. *In Aristotelis Metaphysica Commentaria*. Greek text with Latin critical apparatus, available in vol. 1 of *Commentaria in Aristotelem Graeca* (= CAG), the standard edition of ancient Greek commentaries on Aristotle. Berlin: Georg Reimer (De Gruyter). Translated into English by various hands as *Alexander of Aphrodisias: On Aristotle Metaphysics*, in four volumes in *Ancient Commentators on Aristotle* (= ACA), a series produced at King's College London, under the general editorship of Richard Sorabji, with Michael Griffin as coeditor. London: Gerald Duckworth (Bloomsbury). Ithaca: Cornell University Press, 1989–1994.

Alican, Necip Fikri. 2012. *Rethinking Plato: A Cartesian Quest for the Real Plato*. Amsterdam: Editions Rodopi (Brill).

Alican, Necip Fikri. 2014. "Rethought Forms: How Do They Work?" *Arctos: Acta Philologica Fennica* 48: 25–55.

Alican, Necip Fikri. 2015. "A Horse Is a Horse, of Course, of Course, but What about Horseness?" In *Second Sailing: Alternative Perspectives on Plato*, edited by Debra Nails and Harold Tarrant in collaboration with Mika Kajava and Eero Salmenkivi, 307–324. Commentationes Humanarum Litterarum 132. Helsinki: Societas Scientiarum Fennica.

Alican, Necip Fikri. 2017a. "Ontological Symmetry in Plato: Formless Things and Empty Forms." *Analysis and Metaphysics* 16: 7–51.

Alican, Necip Fikri. 2017b. "The Good, the Bad, and the Ugly: Does Plato Make Room for Negative Forms in His Ontology?" *Cosmos and History: The Journal of Natural and Social Philosophy* 13, no. 3: 154–191.

Alican, Necip Fikri. 2018. "Who Mourns for Adonais? Or, Where Have All the Gods Gone?" *Analysis and Metaphysics* 17: 38–94.

Alican, Necip Fikri, and Holger Thesleff. 2013. "Rethinking Plato's Forms." *Arctos: Acta Philologica Fennica* 47: 11–47.

Allen, Reginald Edgar. 1959. "Anamnesis in Plato's *Meno* and *Phaedo*." *Review of Metaphysics* 13, no. 1 (September): 165–174.

Allen, Reginald Edgar. 1960. "Participation and Predication in Plato's Middle Dialogues." *Philosophical Review* 69, no. 2 (April): 147–164. Reprinted as chapter 4 of *Studies in Plato's Metaphysics*, edited by Reginald Edgar Allen, 43–60. London: Routledge and Kegan Paul, 1965.

Allen, Reginald Edgar, ed. 1965. *Studies in Plato's Metaphysics*. International Library of Philosophy and Scientific Method. London: Routledge and Kegan Paul.

Allen, Reginald Edgar. 1970. *Plato's 'Euthyphro' and the Earlier Theory of Forms*. London: Routledge and Kegan Paul.

Allen, Reginald Edgar. 1997. *Plato's Parmenides*. Revised edition. English translation with commentary. New Haven: Yale University Press.

Annas, Julia Elizabeth. 1975. "On the 'Intermediates.'" *Archiv für Geschichte der Philosophie* 57, no. 2: 146–166.

Annas, Julia Elizabeth, ed. 1976. *Aristotle's Metaphysics: Books M and N*. English translation with introduction and notes. Clarendon Aristotle Series. Oxford: Clarendon Press.

Annas, Julia Elizabeth. 1981. *An Introduction to Plato's Republic*. Oxford: Oxford University Press.

Annas, Julia Elizabeth. 2003. *Plato: A Very Short Introduction*. Oxford: Oxford University Press.

Archer-Hind, Richard Dacre. 1883. *The Phaedo of Plato*. Greek text with introduction, notes, and appendices. London: Macmillan. Second edition, 1894.

Aristotle. 1831–1870. *Aristotelis Opera*. Five volumes. Greek text of the complete works of Aristotle, prepared by the Prussian Academy of Sciences, under the general editorship of Immanuel Bekker. Berlin: Georg Reimer (De Gruyter).

Aristotle. 1984. *The Complete Works of Aristotle: The Revised Oxford Translation*. Two volumes. Edited by Jonathan Barnes. Princeton: Princeton University Press.

Aristoxenus. 1902. *Elementa Harmonica (The Harmonics of Aristoxenus)*. Greek text with English translation. Edited and translated into English by Henry Stewart Macran, with introduction and critical apparatus. Oxford: Clarendon Press.

Armstrong, David Malet. 1978. *Nominalism and Realism*. Vol. 1 of his *Universals and Scientific Realism*. Two volumes. Cambridge: Cambridge University Press.

Armstrong, David Malet. 1989. *Universals: An Opinionated Introduction*. Boulder: Westview Press.

Asclepius. 1888. *In Aristotelis Metaphysicorum Libros A–Z Commentaria*. Greek text with Latin critical apparatus, available in vol. 6 of *Commentaria in Aristotelem Graeca* (= CAG), the standard edition of ancient Greek commentaries on Aristotle. Berlin: Georg Reimer (De Gruyter).

Baldry, Harold Caparne. 1934. "Plato's Technical Terms." *Classical Quarterly* 31, no. 3/4 (July–October): 141–150.

Baltes, Matthias. 1997. "Is the Idea of the Good in Plato's *Republic* beyond Being?" In *Studies in Plato and the Platonic Tradition: Essays Presented to John Whittaker*, edited by Mark Joyal, 1–23. London: Ashgate.

Barford, Robert. 1978. "The Context of the Third Man Argument in Plato's *Parmenides*." *Journal of the History of Philosophy* 16, no. 1 (January): 1–11.

Barney, Rachel, Tad Brennan, and Charles Brittain, eds. 2012. *Plato and the Divided Self*. Cambridge: Cambridge University Press.

Benson, Hugh H., ed. 2006. *A Companion to Plato*. Oxford: Blackwell.

Bestor, Thomas W. 1978. "Common Properties and Eponymy in Plato." *Philosophical Quarterly* 28, no. 112 (July): 189–207.

Blackson, Thomas A. 1995. *Inquiry, Forms, and Substances: A Study in Plato's Metaphysics and Epistemology*. Dordrecht: Kluwer Academic (Springer).

Block, Irving. 1964. "Plato, Parmenides, Ryle and Exemplification." *Mind*, n.s., 73, no. 291 (July): 417–422.

Bluck, Richard Stanley Harold. 1947. "Aristotle, Plato, and Ideas of *Artefacta*." *Classical Review* 61, no. 3 (December): 75–76.

Bluck, Richard Stanley Harold. 1955. *Plato's Phaedo*. English translation with introduction, notes, and appendices. London: Routledge and Kegan Paul.

Bostock, David. 1986a. *Plato's Phaedo*. Oxford: Oxford University Press.

Bostock, David. 1986b. "The Soul and Immortality." Chapter 2 of his *Plato's Phaedo*, 21–41. Oxford: Oxford University Press. Revised and reprinted as chapter 18 of *Plato 2: Ethics, Politics, Religion, and the Soul*, edited by Gail Judith Fine, 404–424. Oxford: Oxford University Press, 1999. Revised and reprinted as chapter 10 of *Essays on Plato's Psychology*, edited by Ellen Wagner, 241–262. Lanham: Lexington Books, 2001.

Brandwood, Leonard. 1976. *A Word Index to Plato*. Leeds: Maney and Son.

Brandwood, Leonard. 1990. *The Chronology of Plato's Dialogues*. Cambridge: Cambridge University Press. Revision of his doctoral dissertation presented and accepted as *The Dating of Plato's Works by the Stylistic Method: A Historical and Critical Survey*. London: University of London Press, 1958.

Brentlinger, John A. 1972. "Incomplete Predicates and the Two-World Theory of the *Phaedo*." *Phronesis* 17, no. 1: 61–79.

Brisson, Luc. 2012. "Why Is the *Timaeus* Called an *Eikôs Muthos* and an *Eikôs Logos*?" Chapter 18 of *Plato and Myth: Studies on the Use and Status of Platonic Myths*, edited by Catherine Collobert, Pierre Destrée, and Francisco J. Gonzalez, 369–391. Leiden: Brill.

Broadie, Sarah. 2004. "Plato's Intelligible World." *Aristotelian Society* (Supplementary Volume) 78, no. 1 (July): 65–79.

Broadie, Sarah. 2007. "Why No Platonistic Ideas of Artefacts?" Chapter 12 of *Maieusis: Essays in Ancient Philosophy in Honour of Myles Burnyeat*, edited by Dominic Scott, 232–253. Oxford: Oxford University Press.

Brown, Lesley. 2012. "Negation and Not-Being: Dark Matter in the *Sophist*." Chapter 11 of *Presocratics and Plato: A Festschrift at Delphi in Honor of Charles Kahn*, edited by Richard Patterson, Vassilis Karasmanis, and Arnold Hermann, 233–254. Papers presented at the Festschrift Symposium in Honor of Charles Kahn, organized by the Hyele Institute for Comparative Studies, European Cultural Center of Delphi, 3–7 June 2009. Las Vegas: Parmenides.

Burger, Ronna. 1984. *The Phaedo: A Platonic Labyrinth*. New Haven: Yale University Press.

Burnet, John. 1911. *Plato's Phaedo*. Greek text with introduction and notes. Oxford: Clarendon Press.

Burnet, John. 1914. *Greek Philosophy: Thales to Plato*. London: Macmillan. Originally published as *Greek Philosophy: Part I: Thales to Plato*, with the part designation dropped from the title after the author's death, coinciding with the fourth printing in 1928.

Burnyeat, Myles Fredric. 1992. "Utopia and Fantasy: The Practicability of Plato's Ideally Just City." Chapter 13 of *Psychoanalysis, Mind and Art: Perspectives on Richard Wollheim*, edited by James Hopkins and Anthony Savile, 297–308. Oxford: Blackwell.

Burnyeat, Myles Fredric. 2000. "Plato on Why Mathematics Is Good for the Soul." *Proceedings of the British Academy* 103: 1–81.

Burnyeat, Myles Fredric. 2005. "*Eikōs Muthos*." *Rhizai* 2, no. 2: 143–165. Reprinted in *Plato's Myths*, edited by Catalin Partenie, 167–186. Cambridge: Cambridge University Press, 2009.

Butler, Travis. 2007. "On Today's Two-Worlds Interpretation: Knowledge and True Belief in Plato." *Southern Journal of Philosophy* 45, no. 1 (Spring): 31–56.

Campbell, Lewis. 1867. *The Sophistes and Politicus of Plato, with a Revised Text and English Notes*. Oxford: Clarendon Press.

Campbell, Lewis. 1896. "On the Place of the *Parmenides* in the Chronological Order of the Platonic Dialogues." *Classical Review* 10, no. 3 (April): 129–136.

Cherniss, Harold Fredrik. 1935. *Aristotle's Criticism of Presocratic Philosophy*. Baltimore: Johns Hopkins Press.

Cherniss, Harold Fredrik. 1944. *Aristotle's Criticism of Plato and the Academy*. Baltimore: Johns Hopkins Press.

Cherniss, Harold Fredrik. 1945. *The Riddle of the Early Academy*. Berkeley: University of California Press.

Cherniss, Harold Fredrik. 1954. "The Sources of Evil According to Plato" (Read: 13 November 1953). *Proceedings of the American Philosophical Society* 98, no. 1 (15 February 1954): 23–30.

Cherniss, Harold Fredrik. 1957. "The Relation of the *Timaeus* to Plato's Later Dialogues." *American Journal of Philology* 78, no. 3 (Whole No. 311): 225–266.
Chilcott, Catherine Mary. 1923. "The Platonic Theory of Evil." *Classical Quarterly* 17, no. 1 (January): 27–31.
Cleary, John J. 1988. *Aristotle on the Many Senses of Priority*. Carbondale: Southern Illinois University Press.
Clegg, Jerry S. 1973. "Self-Predication and Linguistic Reference in Plato's Theory of the Forms." *Phronesis* 18, no. 1: 26–43.
Collobert, Catherine. 2002. "Aristotle's Review of the Presocratics: Is Aristotle Finally a Historian of Philosophy?" *Journal of the History of Philosophy* 40, no. 3 (July): 281–295.
Cooper, John Madison. 1997. Introduction (July 1996) to *Plato: Complete Works*, edited by John Madison Cooper, vii–xxvi. Indianapolis: Hackett.
Corkum, Phil. 2008. "Aristotle on Ontological Dependence." *Phronesis* 53, no. 1: 65–92.
Cornford, Francis MacDonald. 1937. *Plato's Cosmology: The Timaeus of Plato*. English translation with commentary. London: Kegan Paul, Trench, Trübner.
Cornford, Francis MacDonald. 1939. *Plato and Parmenides: Parmenides' Way of Truth and Plato's Parmenides Translated with an Introduction and a Running Commentary by Francis MacDonald Cornford*. London: Kegan Paul, Trench, Trübner.
Cresswell, Maxwell John. 1975. "Participation in Plato's *Parmenides*." *Southern Journal of Philosophy* 13, no. 2 (Summer): 163–171.
Crombie, Ian MacHattie. 1963. *An Examination of Plato's Doctrines: II. Plato on Knowledge and Reality*. London: Routledge and Kegan Paul.
Dancy, Russell M. 1991. *Two Studies in the Early Academy*. Albany: State University of New York Press.
Dancy, Russell M. 2004. *Plato's Introduction of Forms*. Cambridge: Cambridge University Press.
de Vogel, Cornelia Johanna. 1986. *Rethinking Plato and Platonism*. Mnemosyne: Bibliotheca Classica Batava. Supplementum 92. Leiden: Brill.
Demos, Raphael. 1939. *The Philosophy of Plato*. New York: Charles Scribner's Sons.
Demos, Raphael. 1948. "Note on Plato's Theory of Ideas." *Philosophy and Phenomenological Research* 8, no. 3 (March): 456–460.
Denyer, Nicholas. 1983. "Plato's Theory of Stuffs." *Philosophy* 58, no. 225 (July): 315–327.
Denyer, Nicholas. 2007. "The *Phaedo*'s Final Argument." Chapter 5 of *Maieusis: Essays in Ancient Philosophy in Honour of Myles Burnyeat*, edited by Dominic Scott, 87–96. Oxford: Oxford University Press.
des Places, Édouard. 1964. *Lexique de la Langue Philosophique et Religieuse de Platon*. Two Books. Vol. 14 of *Platon: Oeuvres Complètes*. Fourteen volumes. Collection des Universités de France (= Collection Budé) Série Grecque.

Publiée sous le patronage de l'Association Guillaume Budé. Paris: Société d'Édition Les Belles Lettres.

Descartes, René. 1641. *Meditations*. Originally published in Latin as *Meditationes de Prima Philosophia, in qua Dei Existentia et Animæ Immortalitas Demonstratur*. Paris: Michael Soly, 1641. Translated into French by Louis-Charles d'Albert de Luynes (Duke of Loynes) as *Méditations Métaphysiques*. Paris: Jean Camusat and Pierre le Petit, 1647. Numerous English editions available, typically with the title *Meditations on First Philosophy*, often bundled together with Descartes's *Discourse on Method* (1637), sometimes as part of a larger collection. The standard collection in English is *The Philosophical Writings of Descartes*. Three volumes. Translated by John Cottingham, Robert Stoothoff, Dugald Murdoch, and Anthony Kenny. Cambridge: Cambridge University Press, 1984-1991. The translation of the *Meditations* is the first item (3-49) in the second volume (1984).

Devereux, Daniel T. 1977. "Pauline Predications in Plato." *Apeiron* 11, no. 1 (June): 1-4.

Devereux, Daniel T. 1994. "Separation and Immanence in Plato's Theory of Forms." *Oxford Studies in Ancient Philosophy* 12: 63-90.

Diogenes Laërtius. *Lives of Eminent Philosophers*. Various editions: (1) Cambridge (Greek): *Lives of Eminent Philosophers*. Edited by Tiziano Dorandi. Cambridge Classical Texts and Commentaries 50. Cambridge: Cambridge University Press, 2013. (2) Teubner (Greek): *Vitae Philosophorum*. Three volumes. First two volumes edited by Miroslav Marcovich (1999), third volume, reserved for indexes, edited by Hans Gärtner (2002). Bibliotheca Scriptorum Graecorum et Romanorum Teubneriana. Munich: K. G. Saur (De Gruyter). (3) Loeb (Greek and English): *Lives of Eminent Philosophers*. Two volumes. Greek text with parallel English translation by Robert Drew Hicks. Loeb Classical Library. Cambridge: Harvard University Press, 1925. Reprinted with an introduction by Herbert Strainge Long, 1972. This is still the standard English edition, though no longer the definitive critical edition.

Dittenberger, Wilhelm. 1881. "Sprachliche Kriterien für die Chronologie der Platonischen Dialoge." *Hermes* 16, no. 3: 321-345.

Dorter, Kenneth. 1982. *Plato's Phaedo: An Interpretation*. Toronto: University of Toronto Press.

Dorter, Kenneth. 1994. *Form and Good in Plato's Eleatic Dialogues: The Parmenides, Theaetetus, Sophist, and Statesman*. Berkeley: University of California Press.

Durrant, Michael. 1975. "*Parmenides* 127e-130e." *Philosophical Papers* 4, no. 2: 105-115.

Durrant, Michael. 1979. "Plato, The 'Third Man' and the Nature of the Forms." *Southern Journal of Philosophy* 17, no. 3 (Fall): 287-304.

Else, Gerald Frank. 1936. "The Terminology of the Ideas." *Harvard Studies in Classical Philology* 47: 17-55.

Erler, Michael. 2007. *Platon*. Edited by Hellmut Flashar. Vol. 2.2 of *Grundriss der Geschichte der Philosophie: Die Philosophie der Antike*. Basel: Schwabe Verlag.

Ferber, Rafael. 1984. *Platos Idee des Guten*. Sankt Augustin: Academia Verlag Richarz. Second, revised and expanded edition, 1989. Third edition, 2015.

Ferber, Rafael. 2017/2018. "Le Bien de Platon et le Problème de la Transcendance du Principe: Encore une Fois l'ἐπέκεινα τῆς οὐσίας de Platon." χώρα (*Chôra*): *Revue d'Études Anciennes et Médiévales* 15–16: 31–43.

Ferber, Rafael, and Gregor Damschen. 2015. "Is the Idea of the Good beyond Being? Plato's *epekeina tēs ousias* Revisited (*Republic* 6, 509b8–10)." In *Second Sailing: Alternative Perspectives on Plato*, edited by Debra Nails and Harold Tarrant in collaboration with Mika Kajava and Eero Salmenkivi, 197–203. Commentationes Humanarum Litterarum 132. Helsinki: Societas Scientiarum Fennica.

Ferguson, Alexander Stewart. 1921. "On a Supposed Instance of Dualism in Plato." *Philosophical Review* 30, no. 3 (May): 221–237.

Field, Guy Cromwell. 1930. *Plato and His Contemporaries: A Study in Fourth-Century Life and Thought*. London: Methuen. Second edition, 1948.

Findlay, John Niemeyer. 1974. *Plato: The Written and Unwritten Doctrines*. London: Routledge and Kegan Paul.

Findlay, John Niemeyer. 1978a. "The Myths of Plato." *Dionysius* 113: 19–34.

Findlay, John Niemeyer. 1978b. *Plato and Platonism: An Introduction*. New York: Times Books.

Findlay, John Niemeyer. 1983. "Plato's Unwritten Dialectic of the One and the Great and Small." *Society for Ancient Greek Philosophy Newsletter* 113: 1–18.

Fine, Gail Judith. 1978. "Knowledge and Belief in *Republic* V." *Archiv für Geschichte der Philosophie* 60, no. 2: 121–139. Reprinted as chapter 3 of Fine's *Plato on Knowledge and Forms: Selected Essays*, 66–84. Oxford: Clarendon Press, 2003.

Fine, Gail Judith. 1980. "The One over Many." *Philosophical Review* 89, no. 2 (April): 197–240.

Fine, Gail Judith. 1984. "Separation." *Oxford Studies in Ancient Philosophy* 2: 31–87. Reprinted as chapter 11 of Fine's *Plato on Knowledge and Forms: Selected Essays*, 252–300. Oxford: Clarendon Press, 2003.

Fine, Gail Judith. 1985. "Separation: A Reply to Morrison." *Oxford Studies in Ancient Philosophy* 3: 159–165.

Fine, Gail Judith. 1986. "Immanence." *Oxford Studies in Ancient Philosophy* 4: 71–97. Reprinted as chapter 12 of Fine's *Plato on Knowledge and Forms: Selected Essays*, 301–325. Oxford: Clarendon Press, 2003.

Fine, Gail Judith. 1988. "The Object of Thought Argument: Forms and Thoughts." *Apeiron* 21, no. 3 (September): 105–145. Revised and reprinted as chapter 9 of Fine's *On Ideas: Aristotle's Criticism of Plato's Theory of Forms*, 120–141. Oxford: Oxford University Press, 1993.

Fine, Gail Judith. 1990. "Knowledge and Belief in *Republic* V–VII." Chapter 5 of *Epistemology*, edited by Stephen Everson, 85–115. Companions to Ancient Thought 1. Cambridge: Cambridge University Press. Reprinted as chapter 4 of Fine's *Plato on Knowledge and Forms: Selected Essays*, 85–116. Oxford: Clarendon Press, 2003.

Fine, Gail Judith. 1993. *On Ideas: Aristotle's Criticism of Plato's Theory of Forms*. Oxford: Oxford University Press.

Fine, Gail Judith, ed. 1999. *Plato*. Vol. 1: *Metaphysics and Epistemology*. Vol. 2: *Ethics, Politics, Religion, and the Soul*. Oxford: Oxford University Press. All references here are to the first volume.

Fine, Gail Judith. 2003. *Plato on Knowledge and Forms: Selected Essays*. Oxford: Clarendon Press.

Frances, Bryan. 1996. "Plato's Response to the Third Man Argument in the Paradoxical Exercise of the *Parmenides*." *Ancient Philosophy* 16, no. 1 (Spring): 47–64.

Franklin, Lee. 2013. "Commentary on Nails." *Proceedings of the Boston Area Colloquium in Ancient Philosophy* 28: 102–109, 110–112.

Frede, Dorothea. 1978. "The Final Proof of the Immortality of the Soul in Plato's *Phaedo* 102a–107a." *Phronesis* 23, no. 1: 27–41.

Frede, Dorothea. 1999. "Plato on What the Body's Eye Tells the Mind's Eye." *Proceedings of the Aristotelian Society*, n.s., 99: 191–209.

Frede, Dorothea. 2012. "Forms, Functions, and Structure in Plato." Chapter 17 of *Presocratics and Plato: A Festschrift at Delphi in Honor of Charles Kahn*, edited by Richard Patterson, Vassilis Karasmanis, and Arnold Hermann, 367–390. Papers presented at the Festschrift Symposium in Honor of Charles Kahn, organized by the Hyele Institute for Comparative Studies, European Cultural Center of Delphi, 3–7 June 2009. Las Vegas: Parmenides.

Gaiser, Konrad. 1960. "Platons Ungeschriebene Lehre und der Platonismus des Aristoteles." Postdoctoral thesis, Eberhard Karls Universität Tübingen. Revised and published as *Platons Ungeschriebene Lehre: Studien zur Systematischen und Geschichtlichen Begründung der Wissenschaften in der Platonischen Schule*. Stuttgart: E. Klett, 1963. Second (revised and enlarged) edition released by the same publisher in 1968. An appendix bringing together sources on the "unwritten doctrine" is of particular interest: "Testimonia Platonica. Quellentexte zur Schule und Mündlichen Lehre Platons."

Gaiser, Konrad. 1980. "Plato's Enigmatic Lecture 'On the Good.'" *Phronesis* 25, no. 1: 5–37.

Gallop, David. 1975. *Plato: Phaedo*. English translation with critical notes. Oxford: Clarendon Press.

Geach, Peter Thomas. 1956. "The Third Man Again." *Philosophical Review* 65, no. 1 (January): 72–82.

Geddes, William Duguid. 1863. *The Phaedo of Plato*. Greek text with introduction and notes. London: Williams and Norgate.

Gerson, Lloyd P. 1981. "Dialectic and Forms in Part One of Plato's *Parmenides*." *Apeiron* 15, no. 1 (June): 19–28.
Gerson, Lloyd P. 1984. "Artifacts, Substances, and Essences." *Apeiron* 18, no. 1 (June): 50–58.
Gerson, Lloyd P. 1990. *God and Greek Philosophy: Studies in the Early History of Natural Theology*. London: Routledge.
Gerson, Lloyd P. 1999a. "The Concept in Platonism." Chapter 4 of *Traditions of Platonism: Essays in Honour of John Dillon*, edited by John J. Cleary, 65–80. Aldershot: Ashgate.
Gerson, Lloyd P. 1999b. "The Recollection Argument Revisited." In *Recognition, Remembrance, and Reality: New Essays on Plato's Epistemology and Metaphysics*, edited by Mark L. McPherran. Kelowna: Academic Printing and Publishing. *Apeiron* 32, no. 4 (December): 1–15.
Gerson, Lloyd P. 2002. "Plato's Development and the Development of the Theory of Forms." Chapter 2 of *Plato's Forms: Varieties of Interpretation*, edited by William A. Welton, 85–109. Lanham: Lexington Books.
Gerson, Lloyd P. 2004a. "Plato on Identity, Sameness, and Difference." *Review of Metaphysics* 58, no. 2 (December): 306–332.
Gerson, Lloyd P. 2004b. "Platonism and the Invention of the Problem of Universals." *Archiv für Geschichte der Philosophie* 86, no. 3 (September): 233–256.
Gerson, Lloyd P. 2014. "Harold Cherniss and the Study of Plato Today." *Journal of the History of Philosophy* 52, no. 3 (July): 397–409.
Gerson, Lloyd P. 2015. "Ideas of Good?" In *Second Sailing: Alternative Perspectives on Plato*, edited by Debra Nails and Harold Tarrant in collaboration with Mika Kajava and Eero Salmenkivi, 225–242. Commentationes Humanarum Litterarum 132. Helsinki: Societas Scientiarum Fennica.
Giannantoni, Gabriele, ed. 1990. *Socratis et Socraticorum Reliquiae* (= SSR). Four volumes. Collection of *Sōkratikoi logoi*, excluding Plato and Xenophon. Greek original with Latin translation and Italian commentary. Naples: Bibliopolis.
Goldstein, Laurence, and Paul Mannick. 1978. "The Form of the Third Man Argument." *Apeiron* 12, no. 2 (December): 6–13.
Gonzalez, Francisco J. 1996. "Propositions or Objects? A Critique of Gail Fine on Knowledge and Belief in *Republic* V." *Phronesis* 41, no. 3: 245–275.
Gonzalez, Francisco J. 2002. "Plato's Dialectic of Forms." Chapter 1 of *Plato's Forms: Varieties of Interpretation*, edited by William A. Welton, 31–83. Lanham: Rowman and Littlefield.
Grabowski, Francis A., III. 2008. *Plato, Metaphysics and the Forms*. London: Continuum.
Grube, George Maximilian Anthony. 1935. *Plato's Thought*. London: Methuen. Reprinted with additional material by Donald J. Zeyl (new introduction, bibliographic essay, and bibliography). Indianapolis: Hackett, 1980.
Guthrie, William Keith Chambers. 1957. "Aristotle as a Historian of Philosophy: Some Preliminaries." *Journal of Hellenic Studies* 77, no. 1 (November): 35–41.

Guthrie, William Keith Chambers. 1975. *A History of Greek Philosophy*. Vol. 4: *Plato: The Man and His Dialogues: Earlier Period*. Cambridge: Cambridge University Press.

Guthrie, William Keith Chambers. 1978. *A History of Greek Philosophy*. Vol. 5: *The Later Plato and the Academy*. Cambridge: Cambridge University Press.

Hackforth, Reginald. 1955. *Plato's Phaedo*. English translation with introduction and commentary. Cambridge: Cambridge University Press.

Hackforth, Reginald. 1959. "Plato's Cosmogony (*Timaeus* 27 D ff.)." *Classical Quarterly*, n.s., 9, no. 1 (May): 17–22.

Halfwassen, Jens. 2014. "The Metaphysics of the One." Chapter 12 of *The Routledge Handbook of Neoplatonism*, edited by Pauliina Remes and Svetla Slaveva-Griffin, 182–199. London: Routledge.

Hankins, James. 1990. *Plato in the Italian Renaissance*. Two volumes (continuous pagination). Leiden: Brill.

Harte, Verity. 2002. *Plato on Parts and Wholes: The Metaphysics of Structure*. Oxford: Oxford University Press.

Harte, Verity. 2007. "Language in the Cave." Chapter 10 of *Maieusis: Essays in Ancient Philosophy in Honour of Myles Burnyeat*, edited by Dominic Scott, 195–215. Oxford: Oxford University Press.

Harte, Verity. 2019. "Plato's Metaphysics." Chapter 19 of *The Oxford Handbook of Plato*, second edition, edited by Gail Judith Fine, 455–480. Oxford: Oxford University Press. Originally published in 2008 as chapter 8 of the first edition of the same volume (191–216).

Hathaway, Ronald F. 1971. "The Second 'Third Man.'" In *Patterns in Plato's Thought: Papers Arising Out of the 1971 West Coast Greek Philosophy Conference*, edited by Julius Matthew Emil Moravcsik, 78–100. Dordrecht: D. Reidel (Springer).

Heinaman, Robert. 1989. "Self-Predication in Plato's Middle Dialogues." *Phronesis* 34, no. 1: 56–79.

Helmig, Christoph. 2004. "What Is the Systematic Place of Abstraction and Concept Formation in Plato's Philosophy? Ancient and Modern Readings of *Phaedrus* 249b-c." In *Platonic Ideas and Concept Formation in Ancient and Medieval Thought*, edited by Gerd Van Riel and Caroline Macé with the assistance of Leen Van Campe, 83–97. Ancient and Medieval Philosophy. De Wulf-Mansion Centre. Series 1. Vol. 32. Leuven: Leuven University Press.

Helmig, Christoph. 2007. "Plato's Arguments against Conceptualism: *Parmenides* 132b3–c11 Reconsidered." *Elenchos* 28, no. 2: 303–336.

Helmig, Christoph. 2012. *Forms and Concepts: Concept Formation in the Platonic Tradition*. Vol. 5 of *Commentaria in Aristotelem Graeca et Byzantina*. Berlin: De Gruyter.

Herrmann, Fritz-Gregor. 2007a. "The Idea of the Good and the Other Forms in Plato's *Republic*." Chapter 10 of *Pursuing the Good: Ethics and Metaphysics in Plato's Republic*, edited by Douglas Cairns, Fritz-Gregor Herrmann, and Terry Penner, 202–230. Edinburgh: Edinburgh University Press.

Herrmann, Fritz-Gregor. 2007b. *Words & Ideas: The Roots of Plato's Philosophy*. Swansea: Classical Press of Wales.

Hetherington, Stephen, and Nicholas D. Smith, eds. 2019. *What the Ancients Offer to Contemporary Epistemology*. London: Routledge.

Hintikka, Jaakko. 1984. "Are There Nonexistent Objects? Why Not? But Where Are They?" *Synthese* 60, no. 3 (September): 451–458.

Hoffleit, Herbert B. 1937. "An Un-Platonic Theory of Evil in Plato." *American Journal of Philology* 58, no. 1 (Whole No. 229): 45–58.

Howlett, Sophia. 2016. *Marsilio Ficino and His World*. New York: Palgrave Macmillan.

Hubert, Kurt. 1914. "Leben und Unterricht in der Akademie." *Sokrates: Zeitschrift für das Gymnasialwesen*, n.s., 2 (May): 256–263.

Huxley, George. 1972. "On Aristotle's Historical Methods." *Greek, Roman and Byzantine Studies* 13, no. 2: 157–169.

Hyland, Drew A. 2002. "Against a Platonic 'Theory' of Forms." Chapter 10 of *Plato's Forms: Varieties of Interpretation*, edited by William A. Welton, 257–272. Lanham: Rowman and Littlefield.

Irwin, Terence, ed. 1995. *Plato's Metaphysics and Epistemology*. New York: Garland.

Jackson, Henry. 1882. "On Plato's *Republic* VI 509 D sqq." *Journal of Philology* 10, no. 19: 132–150.

Jackson, Henry. 1882–1886. "Plato's Later Theory of Ideas." *Journal of Philology* (*JP*). London: Macmillan. Cambridge: Deighton, Bell. A series of articles with their own subtitles under the same title ("Plato's Later Theory of Ideas"): (1) "The *Philebus* and Aristotle's *Metaphysics* I 6," *JP* 10, no. 20 (1882): 253–298. (2) "The *Parmenides*," *JP* 11, no. 22 (1882): 287–331. (3) "The *Timaeus*," *JP* 13, no. 25 (1885): 1–40. (4) "The *Theaetetus*," *JP* 13, no. 26 (1885): 242–272. (5) "The *Sophist*," *JP* 14, no. 28 (1885): 173–230. (6) "The *Politicus*," *JP* 15, no. 30 (1886): 280–305.

Kahn, Charles H. 1996. *Plato and the Socratic Dialogue: The Philosophical Use of a Literary Form*. Cambridge: Cambridge University Press.

Kahn, Charles H. 2002. "On Platonic Chronology." Chapter 4 of *New Perspectives on Plato: Modern and Ancient*, edited by Julia Elizabeth Annas and Christopher J. Rowe, 99–127. Cambridge: Harvard University Press. Originates in a contribution to a colloquium held in August 1999 at the Center for Hellenic Studies, Trustees for Harvard University.

Kant, Immanuel. 1781/1787. *Kritik der reinen Vernunft* (= KrV). Riga: Johann Friedrich Hartknoch. Volumes 3 (both editions together) and 4 (first edition alone) of *Kants gesammelte Schriften* (29 volumes), edited by the Königlich Preussischen Akademie der Wissenschaften. Berlin: Georg Reimer (De Gruyter), 1900 et seq. Numerous English translations (*Critique of Pure Reason*), including those by Norman Kemp Smith (London: Macmillan, 1929), Werner Schrutka Pluhar (Indianapolis: Hackett, 1996), and Paul Guyer and Allen W. Wood (Cambridge: Cambridge University Press, 1998).

Katz, Emily. 2013. "Aristotle's Critique of Platonist Mathematical Objects: Two Test Cases from *Metaphysics* M2." *Apeiron* 46, no. 1 (January): 26–47.

Katz, Emily. 2014. "An Absurd Accumulation: *Metaphysics* M.2, 1076b11–36." *Phronesis* 59, no. 4: 343–368.

Keyt, David. 1963. "The Fallacies in *Phaedo* 102a–107b." *Phronesis* 8, no. 1/2: 167–172.

Klibansky, Raymond, 1981. *The Continuity of the Platonic Tradition during the Middle Ages, Together with Plato's Parmenides in the Middle Ages and the Renaissance*. Munich: Kraus. Brings together a previously published book (with a new preface and four supplementary chapters) and a previously published essay (with a new introductory preface) by the same author. The book (*The Continuity of the Platonic Tradition during the Middle Ages: Outlines of a Corpus Platonicum Medii Aevi*) was originally published in London: Warburg Institute, 1939. The essay ("Plato's *Parmenides* in the Middle Ages and the Renaissance: A Chapter in the History of Platonic Studies") was originally published in *Mediaeval and Renaissance Studies* 1, no. 2 (1943): 281–330.

Kouremenos, Theokritos. 2015. *The Unity of Mathematics in Plato's Republic*. Stuttgart: Franz Steiner Verlag.

Kouremenos, Theokritos. 2018. *Plato's Forms, Mathematics and Astronomy*. Berlin: De Gruyter.

Krämer, Hans Joachim. 1957. "Arete bei Platon und Aristoteles: Zum Wesen und zur Geschichte der Platonischen Ontologie." Doctoral dissertation, Eberhard Karls Universität Tübingen. Revised and published as part of *Abhandlungen der Heidelberger Akademie der Wissenschaften. Philosophisch-Historische Klasse*. Heidelberg: Carl Winter, 1959. Second ("new") edition published in Amsterdam: Schippers, 1967.

Krämer, Hans Joachim. 1964. "Retraktationen zum Problem des Esoterischen Platon." *Museum Helveticum* 21: 137–167.

Krämer, Hans Joachim. 1990. *Plato and the Foundations of Metaphysics: A Work on the Theory of the Principles and Unwritten Doctrines of Plato with a Collection of the Fundamental Documents*. Edited and translated by John R. Catan from the third edition (1989) of the Italian translation of the unpublished original in German. Albany: State University of New York Press. Originally published in Italian as *Platone e i Fondamenti della Metafisica. Saggio sulla Teoria dei Principi e sulle Dottrine non Scritte di Platone*. Translated by Giovanni Reale from the unpublished original in German. Milan: Vito a Pensiero, 1982. Subsequent editions: 1987, 1989, 1993, 1994, 2001.

Kraut, Richard, ed. 1992. *The Cambridge Companion to Plato*. Cambridge: Cambridge University Press.

Lafrance, Yvon. 1984. "Sur une Lecture Analytique des Arguments Concernant le Non-être (*Sophiste*, 237b10–239a12)." *Revue de Philosophie Ancienne* 2, no. 2: 41–76.

Larsen, Peter D. 2018. "Are There Forms of Sensible Qualities in Plato?" *Journal of the American Philosophical Association* 4, no. 2 (Summer): 225–242.
Ledger, Gerard R. 1989. *Re-counting Plato: A Computer Analysis of Plato's Style.* Oxford: Clarendon Press.
Lee, Edward N. 1971. "The Second 'Third Man': An Interpretation." In *Patterns in Plato's Thought: Papers Arising Out of the 1971 West Coast Greek Philosophy Conference*, edited by Julius Matthew Emil Moravcsik, 101–122. Dordrecht: D. Reidel (Springer).
Lee, Edward N. 1972. "Plato on Negation and Not-Being in the *Sophist*." *Philosophical Review* 81, no. 3 (July): 267–304.
Lehrer, Keith. 2011. *Art, Self and Knowledge.* New York: Oxford University Press.
Lehrer, Keith. 2019. *Exemplars of Truth.* New York: Oxford University Press.
Lewis, Frank A. 1976. "Plato on 'Not.'" *California Studies in Classical Antiquity* 9: 89–115.
Lewis, Frank A. 1979. "Parmenides on Separation and the Knowability of the Forms: Plato *Parmenides* 133a ff." *Philosophical Studies* 35, no. 2 (February): 105–127.
Lloyd, Geoffrey Ernest Richard. 1962. "Right and Left in Greek Philosophy." *Journal of Hellenic Studies* 82: 56–66.
Lloyd, Geoffrey Ernest Richard. 1964. "The Hot and the Cold, the Dry and the Wet in Greek Philosophy." *Journal of Hellenic Studies* 84: 92–106.
Lloyd, Geoffrey Ernest Richard. 1966. *Polarity and Analogy: Two Types of Argumentation in Early Greek Thought.* Cambridge: Cambridge University Press.
Lohr, Charles H. 2002. "The Ancient Philosophical Legacy and Its Transmission to the Middle Ages." Chapter 1 of *A Companion to Philosophy in the Middle Ages*, edited by Jorge J. E. Gracia and Timothy B. Noone, 15–22. Oxford: Blackwell.
Lovejoy, Arthur Oncken. 1936. *The Great Chain of Being: A Study of the History of an Idea.* The William James lectures delivered by the author at Harvard University, 1933. Cambridge: Harvard University Press.
Lowry, James M. P. 1980. "Aristotle and Modern Historical Criticism." *Laval Théologique et Philosophique* 36, no. 1: 17–27.
Lutoslawski, Wincenty. 1897. *The Origin and Growth of Plato's Logic, with an Account of Plato's Style and of the Chronology of His Writings, by Wincenty Lutoslawski.* London: Longmans, Green.
Mabbott, John David. 1926. "Aristotle and the Χωρισμός of Plato." *Classical Quarterly* 20, no. 2 (April): 72–79.
Malcolm, John. 1981. "Semantics and Self-Predication in Plato." *Phronesis* 26, no. 3: 286–294.
Malcolm, John. 1991. *Plato on the Self-Predication of Forms: Early and Middle Dialogues.* Oxford: Oxford University Press.
Mates, Benson. 1979. "Identity and Predication in Plato." *Phronesis* 24, no. 3: 211–229.

Matthen, Mohan. 1984. "Forms and Participants in Plato's *Phaedo*." *Noûs* 18, no. 2 (May): 281–297.

Matthews, Gareth B., and S. Marc Cohen. 1968. "The One and the Many." *Review of Metaphysics* 21, no. 4 (June): 630–655.

Maula, Erkka. 1967. "On Plato and Plenitude." *Ajatus* 29: 12–50.

McCabe, Mary Margaret Anne. 1994. *Plato's Individuals*. Princeton: Princeton University Press.

McKeon, Richard. 1940. "Plato and Aristotle as Historians: A Study of Method in the History of Ideas." *Ethics* 51, no. 1 (October): 66–101.

Meinwald, Constance C. 1991. *Plato's Parmenides*. Oxford: Oxford University Press.

Meinwald, Constance C. 1992. "Good-bye to the Third Man." Chapter 12 of *The Cambridge Companion to Plato*, edited by Richard Kraut, 365–396. Cambridge: Cambridge University Press.

Mignucci, Mario. 1990. "Plato's 'Third Man' Arguments in the *Parmenides*." *Archiv für Geschichte der Philosophie* 72, no. 2: 143–181.

Mohr, Richard D. 1978. "Plato's Final Thoughts on Evil: *Laws* X, 899–905." *Mind*, n.s., 87, no. 348 (October): 572–575.

Mohr, Richard D. 1980. "The Sources of Evil Problem and the ἀρχή κινήσεως Doctrine in Plato." *Apeiron* 14, no. 1 (June): 41–56.

Mohr, Richard D. 2010. "Plato's Cosmic Manual: Introduction, Reader's Guide, and Acknowledgments." Introductory essay in *One Book, The Whole Universe: Plato's Timaeus Today*, edited by Richard D. Mohr and Barbara M. Sattler, 1–26. Las Vegas: Parmenides.

Moravcsik, Julius Matthew Emil. 1963. "The 'Third Man' Argument and Plato's Theory of Forms." *Phronesis* 8, no. 1: 50–62.

Morris, T. F. 1985. "How Can One Form Be in Many Things?" *Apeiron* 19, no. 2 (March): 53–56.

Morrison, Donald Ray. 1985a. "Χωριστός in Aristotle." *Harvard Studies in Classical Philology* 89 (1985): 89–105.

Morrison, Donald Ray. 1985b. "Separation in Aristotle's Metaphysics." *Oxford Studies in Ancient Philosophy* 3: 125–157.

Morrison, Donald Ray. 1985c. "Separation: A Reply to Fine." *Oxford Studies in Ancient Philosophy* 3: 167–173.

Nails, Debra. 1993. "Problems with Vlastos's Platonic Developmentalism." *Ancient Philosophy* 13, no. 2 (Fall): 273–291.

Nails, Debra. 1994. "Plato's 'Middle' Cluster." *Phoenix* 48, no. 1 (Spring): 62–67.

Nails, Debra. 1995. *Agora, Academy, and the Conduct of Philosophy*. Dordrecht: Kluwer Academic (Springer).

Nails, Debra. 2002. *The People of Plato: A Prosopography of Plato and Other Socratics*. Indianapolis: Hackett.

Nails, Debra. 2013. "Two Dogmas of Platonism." *Proceedings of the Boston Area Colloquium in Ancient Philosophy* 28: 77–101, 110–112.

Nails, Debra, and Holger Thesleff. 2003. "Early Academic Editing: Plato's *Laws*." In *Plato's Laws: From Theory into Practice*, edited by Samuel Scolnicov and Luc Brisson, 14–29. Proceedings of the 6th Symposium Platonicum: Selected Papers. Vol. 15 of International Plato Studies. Sankt Augustin: Academia Verlag.

Nehamas, Alexander. 1973. "Predication and Forms of Opposites in the *Phaedo*." *Review of Metaphysics* 26, no. 3 (March): 461–491.

Nehamas, Alexander. 1975. "Plato on the Imperfection of the Sensible World." *American Philosophical Quarterly* 12, no. 2 (April): 105–117.

Nehamas, Alexander. 1979. "Self-Predication and Plato's Theory Forms." *American Philosophical Quarterly* 16, no. 2 (April): 93–103.

Nehamas, Alexander. 1982. "Participation and Predication in Plato's Later Thought." *Review of Metaphysics* 36, no. 2 (December): 343–374.

Nerlich, Graham Charles. 1960. "Regress Arguments in Plato." *Mind*, n.s., 69, no. 273 (January): 88–90.

O'Brien, Denis. 2013. "A Form That 'Is' of What 'Is Not': Existential *Einai* in Plato's *Sophist*." Chapter 12 of *The Platonic Art of Philosophy*, edited by George Boys-Stones, Dimitri El Murr, and Christopher Gill, 221–248. Cambridge: Cambridge University Press.

Otto, K. Darcy. 2017. "Resemblance and the Regress." 50, no. 1 *Apeiron* (January): 81–101.

Owen, Gwilym Ellis Lane. 1953. "The Place of the *Timaeus* in Plato's Dialogues." *Classical Quarterly*, n.s., 3, no. 1/2 (January–April): 79–95.

Parsons, Terence. 1982. "Are There Nonexistent Objects?" *American Philosophical Quarterly* 19, no. 4 (October): 365–371.

Patterson, Richard. 1985a. *Image and Reality in Plato's Metaphysics*. Indianapolis: Hackett.

Patterson, Richard. 1985b. "On the Eternality of Platonic Forms." *Archiv für Geschichte der Philosophie* 67, no. 1: 27–46.

Pelletier, Francis Jeffry. 1990. *Parmenides, Plato, and the Semantics of Not-Being*. Chicago: University of Chicago Press.

Pelletier, Francis Jeffry, and Edward N. Zalta. 2000. "How to Say Goodbye to the Third Man." *Noûs* 34, no. 2 (June): 165–202.

Penner, Terry. 1987. *The Ascent from Nominalism: Some Existence Arguments in Plato's Middle Dialogues*. Dordrecht: D. Reidel (Springer).

Penner, Terry. 2006. "The Forms and the Sciences in Socrates and Plato." Chapter 12 of *A Companion to Plato*, edited by Hugh H. Benson, 165–183. Oxford: Blackwell.

Perl, Eric D. 1997. "Sense-Perception and Intellect in Plato." *Revue de Philosophie Ancienne* 15, no. 1: 15–34.

Perl, Eric D. 1999. "The Presence of the Paradigm: Immanence and Transcendence in Plato's Theory of Forms." *Review of Metaphysics* 53, no. 2 (December): 339–362.

Philoponus. 1887–1888. *In Aristotelis Physica Commentaria*. Greek text with Latin critical apparatus, available in vols. 16 and 17 of *Commentaria in Aristotelem Graeca* (= CAG), the standard edition of ancient Greek commentaries on Aristotle. Berlin: Georg Reimer (De Gruyter). Translated into English by various hands as *Philoponus: On Aristotle Physics*, in eleven volumes (including *On Aristotle on the Void*) in *Ancient Commentators on Aristotle* (= ACA), a series produced at King's College London, under the general editorship of Richard Sorabji, with Michael Griffin as coeditor. London: Gerald Duckworth (Bloomsbury). Ithaca: Cornell University Press, 1991–present.

Plato. 1900–1907. *Platonis Opera*. Five volumes. Critical texts with introductions and notes. Edited by John Burnet. Oxford Classical Texts. Oxford: Oxford University Press. Reprinted 1967–1968. New edition under way since 1995.

Plato. 1920–1956. *Oeuvres Complètes*. Fourteen volumes. Greek texts with running French translations by various hands. Collection des Universités de France (= Collection Budé) Série Grecque. Publiée sous le patronage de l'Association Guillaume Budé. Paris: Société d'Édition Les Belles Lettres.

Plato. 1997. *Complete Works*. English translations by various hands. Edited, with an introduction and notes, by John Madison Cooper. Indianapolis: Hackett.

Plutarch. 1914–1926. *Bioi Parallèloi*. Greek text with parallel English translation by Bernadotte Perrin available as *Plutarch: Lives* in eleven volumes in the Loeb Classical Library. Cambridge: Harvard University Press.

Plutarch. 1976. *Quaestiones Platonicae*. Greek text with parallel English translation by Harold Fredrik Cherniss available as a section of *Platonic Essays*, the first part of the thirteenth of fifteen volumes dedicated to Plutarch's *Moralia* in the Loeb Classical Library (LCL 427: Plutarch, *Moralia*, Vol. 13: Part 1: *Platonic Essays*). Cambridge: Harvard University Press.

Press, Gerald Alan, ed. 1993. *Plato's Dialogues: New Studies and Interpretations*. Lanham: Rowman and Littlefield.

Press, Gerald Alan, ed. 2000. *Who Speaks for Plato? Studies in Platonic Anonymity*. Lanham: Rowman and Littlefield.

Press, Gerald Alan. 2007. *Plato: A Guide for the Perplexed*. London: Continuum.

Press, Gerald Alan, ed. 2012. *The Continuum Companion to Plato*. London: Continuum.

Preus, Mary, and John Ferguson. 1969. "A Clue to the *Deuteros Plous*." *Arethusa* 2, no. 1 (Spring): 104–107.

Prince, Brian D. 2011. "The Form of Soul in the *Phaedo*." *Plato: The Electronic Journal of the International Plato Society* 11: 1–34.

Prince, Susan. 2015. *Antisthenes of Athens: Text, Translations, and Commentary*. Ann Arbor: University of Michigan Press.

Prior, William J. 1980. "Plato's Analysis of Being and Not-Being in the *Sophist*." *Southern Journal of Philosophy* 18, no. 2 (Summer): 199–211.

Prior, William J. 1983. "*Timaeus* 48e–52d and the Third Man Argument." *Canadian Journal of Philosophy* 13 (Special Issue: *New Essays on Plato*), Supplementary Vol. 9, Supplement 1: 123–147.

Prior, William J. 1985. *Unity and Development in Plato's Metaphysics*. London: Croom Helm.

Proclus. *In Platonis Parmenides*. Various editions. The standard critical edition, replacing several earlier ones, is *Procli in Platonis Parmenidem Commentaria*. Edited by Carlos G. Steel and Leen van Campe. Three volumes. Oxford: Oxford University Press, 2007–2009. An English translation, by Glenn R. Morrow and John M. Dillon, of an earlier edition (Victor Cousin's second edition, dated 1864) is available as *Proclus' Commentary on Plato's Parmenides*. Princeton: Princeton University Press, 1987.

Quine, Willard Van Orman. 1986. "Reply to Hilary Putnam." In *The Philosophy of W. V. Quine*, edited by Lewis Edwin Hahn and Paul Arthur Schilpp, 427–431. The Library of Living Philosophers 18. La Salle: Open Court.

Rankin, Kenneth W. 1969. "The Duplicity of Plato's Third Man." *Mind*, n.s., 78, no. 310 (April): 178–197.

Rankin, Kenneth W. 1970. "Is the Third Man Argument an Inconsistent Triad?" *Philosophical Quarterly* 20, no. 81 (October): 378–380.

Reale, Giovanni. 1975–1980. *Storia della Filosofia Antica*. Five volumes. Milan: Vita e Pensiero. Numerous editions. Reorganized in four volumes for an English edition translated by John R. Catan and published as *A History of Ancient Philosophy*. Vol. 1 (1987): *From the Origins to Socrates*, translated from the fourth Italian edition. Vol. 2 (1990): *Plato and Aristotle*, translated from the fifth Italian edition. Vol. 3 (1985): *The Systems of the Hellenistic Age*, translated from the third Italian edition. Vol. 4 (1990): *The Schools of the Imperial Age*, translated from the fifth Italian edition. Albany: State University of New York Press, 1985–1990.

Reale, Giovanni. 1984. *Per una Nuova Interpretazione di Platone: Rilettura Della Metafisica dei Grandi Dialoghi alla Luce Delle "Dottrine Non Scritte."* Milan: Vita e Pensiero. Numerous editions. Translated into English, from the tenth Italian edition, by John R. Catan and Richard Davies: *Toward a New Interpretation of Plato: A Rereading of the Metaphysics of the Great Dialogues in the Light of the Unwritten Doctrines*. Washington, DC: Catholic University of America Press, 1997.

Reale, Giovanni. 1990. *A History of Ancient Philosophy: Plato and Aristotle*. Second of four volumes of *A History of Ancient Philosophy* (1985–1990), edited and translated, by John R. Catan, from the Italian original. SUNY Series in Philosophy. Albany: State University of New York Press.

Reeve, C. D. C. (Charles David Chanel). 2006. *Philosopher-Kings: The Argument of Plato's Republic*. Indianapolis: Hackett. Reprint of the original published in Princeton: Princeton University Press, 1988.

Reynolds, Leighton Durham, and Nigel Guy Wilson. 1968. *Scribes and Scholars: Guide to the Transmission of Greek and Latin Literature*. Subsequent editions: 1974, 1991, 2013.
Rickless, Samuel Charles. 2007. *Plato's Forms in Transition: A Reading of the Parmenides*. Cambridge: Cambridge University Press.
Rist, John Michael. 1964. "The Immanence and Transcendence of the Platonic Form." *Philologus* 108, no. 1/2 (December): 217–232.
Rist, John Michael. 1967. "Knowledge and Value in Plato." *Phoenix* 21, no. 4 (Winter): 283–295.
Ritter, Constantin. 1910. *Neue Untersuchungen über Platon*. Munich: Oskar Beck.
Ritter, Constantin. 1931. *Die Kerngedanken der Platonischen Philosophie*. Munich: E. Reinhardt. Translated into English by Adam Alles as *The Essence of Plato's Philosophy*. London: George Allen and Unwin, 1933.
Robin, Léon. 1908. *La Théorie Platonicienne des Idées et des Nombres d'après Aristote: Étude Historique et Critique*. Paris: Librairies Félix Alcan et Guillaumin Réunies.
Robinson, Richard. 1942. "Plato's *Parmenides*." Published in two parts: Part 1: *Classical Philology* 37, no. 1 (January): 51–76. Part 2: *Classical Philology* 37, no. 2 (April): 159–186.
Robjant, David. 2012. "The Earthy Realism of Plato's Metaphysics, or: What Shall We Do with Iris Murdoch?" *Philosophical Investigations* 35, no. 1 (January): 43–67.
Rohr, Michael David. 1978. "Empty Forms in Plato." *Archiv für Geschichte der Philosophie* 60, no. 3: 268–283. Shortened version of an essay written earlier but published later in *Reforging the Great Chain of Being: Studies of the History of Modal Theories*, edited by Simo Knuuttila, 19–56. Synthese Historical Library 20. Dordrecht: D. Reidel (Springer), 1981.
Rose, Lynn E. 1966. "The *Deuteros Plous* in Plato's *Phaedo*." *Monist* (*Philosophy of Plato*) 50, no. 3 (July): 464–473.
Ross, Donald L. 1982. "The *Deuteros Plous*, Simmias' Speech, and Socrates' Answer to Cebes in Plato's 'Phaedo.'" *Hermes* 110, no. 1: 19–25.
Ross, William David. 1951. *Plato's Theory of Ideas*. Oxford: Clarendon Press. Second edition, 1953.
Rowe, Christopher J. 2005. "What Difference Do Forms Make for Platonic Epistemology?" Chapter 10 of *Virtue, Norms, and Objectivity: Issues in Ancient and Modern Ethics*, edited by Christopher Gill, 215–232. Oxford: Clarendon Press.
Russell, Bertrand Arthur William. 1911–1912. "On the Relation of Universals and Particulars." *Proceedings of the Aristotelian Society*, n.s., 12: 1–24.
Russell, Bertrand Arthur William. 1912. *The Problems of Philosophy*. London: Williams and Norgate.
Russell, Bertrand Arthur William. 1945/1946. *A History of Western Philosophy, and Its Connection with Political and Social Circumstances from the Earliest*

Times to the Present Day. New York: Simon and Schuster, 1945. London: George Allen and Unwin, 1946.

Ryle, Gilbert. 1939. "Plato's *Parmenides*." Published in two parts. Part 1: *Mind*, n.s., 48, no. 190 (April): 129–151. Part 2: *Mind*, n.s., 48, no. 191 (July): 302–325. Reprinted as chapter 6 of *Studies in Plato's Metaphysics*, together with an afterword dated 1963 and prepared for the book, edited by Reginald Edgar Allen, 97–147 and 145–147. London: Routledge and Kegan Paul, 1965.

Sayre, Kenneth M. 1983. *Plato's Late Ontology: A Riddle Resolved*. Princeton: Princeton University Press.

Sayre, Kenneth M. 1993. "Why Plato Never Had a Theory of Forms." *Proceedings of the Boston Area Colloquium in Ancient Philosophy* 9: 167–199.

Sayre, Kenneth M. 1996. *Parmenides' Lesson: Translation and Explication of Plato's Parmenides*. Notre Dame: University of Notre Dame Press.

Sayre, Kenneth M. 2002. "Do Forms Have a Role in Plato's *Philebus*?" Chapter 6 of *Plato's Forms: Varieties of Interpretation*, edited by William A. Welton, 169–191. Lanham: Rowman and Littlefield.

Scaltsas, Theodore. 1989. "The Logic of the Dilemma of Participation and of the Third Man Argument." *Apeiron* 22, no. 4 (December): 67–90.

Scaltsas, Theodore. 1992. "A Necessary Falsehood in the Third Man Argument." *Phronesis* 37, no. 2: 216–232.

Schiller, Jerome Paul. 1967. "*Phaedo* 104–105: Is the Soul a Form?" *Phronesis* 12, no. 1: 50–58.

Schipper, Edith Watson. 1965. *Forms in Plato's Later Dialogues*. The Hague: Martinus Nijhoff.

Schleiermacher, Friedrich Daniel Ernst. 1804–1828. *Platons Werke*. Three volumes. Translated from the Greek into German, with extensive critical commentary, by Friedrich Daniel Ernst Schleiermacher. Berlin: Realschulbuchhandlung and Georg Reimer. Vol. 1, part 1 (1804): *Phaedrus*; *Lysis*; *Protagoras*; *Laches*. Vol. 1, part 2 (1805): *Charmides*; *Euthyphro*; *Parmenides*; *Apology*; *Crito*; *Ion*; *Hippias Minor*; *Hipparchus*; *Minos*; *Alcibiades 2*. Vol. 2, part 1 (1805): *Gorgias*; *Theaetetus*; *Meno*; *Euthydemus*. Vol. 2, part 2 (1807): *Cratylus*; *Sophist*; *Statesman*; *Symposium*. Vol. 2, part 3 (1809): *Phaedo*; *Philebus*; *Theages*; *Erastae*; *Alcibiades 1*; *Menexenus*; *Hippias Major*; *Clitophon*. Vol. 3, part 1 (1828): *Republic*. A second edition of the collection appeared in 1817, before the third volume, thus covering only the first two volumes. The reason that the collection is broken down into three volumes and six parts, as opposed to the simpler structure of six volumes with no further divisions, is that the superstructure of three volumes follows Schleiermacher's division of Plato's works into three groups, while the substructure of parts reflects choices in time management in the production schedule of the translation project. The output is not limited to the authentic works of Plato, as evidenced at least by the inclusion of the *Erastae*, which Schleiermacher deemed patently spurious but translated nonetheless. His death in 1834 precluded the completion of the effort, missing the *Timaeus*, *Critias*, *Laws*, and *Epinomis*, which would have collectively rounded out the third volume. Two centuries later, the contribution remains authoritative, still valued for the translations as well as the commentary, with the introductions to the dialogues attracting international readership. The introductions were translated into English by William Dobson as *Schleiermacher's Introductions to the Dialogues of Plato*. Cambridge: J. and J. J. Deighton, 1836.

Schleiermacher, Friedrich Daniel Ernst. 1836. *Schleiermacher's Introductions to the Dialogues of Plato*. Translated by William Dobson. Cambridge: J. and J. J. Deighton. English translations of Schleiermacher's introductions to his own translations of Plato's dialogues from the Greek into German, with the collection originally appearing in three volumes as *Platons Werke*. Berlin: Realschulbuchhandlung and Georg Reimer, 1804–1828.

Schumacher, Lydia. 2010. "Rethinking Recollection and Plato's Theory of Forms." *Lyceum* 11, no. 2 (Spring): 1–19.

Schweizer, Paul. 1994. "Self-Predication and the Third Man." *Erkenntnis* 40, no. 1 (January): 21–42.

Scolnicov, Samuel. 2003. *Plato's Parmenides*. Translation with introduction and commentary. Berkeley: University of California Press.

Sedley, David Neil. 2007a. *Creationism and Its Critics in Antiquity*. Berkeley: University of California Press.

Sedley, David Neil. 2007b. "Equal Sticks and Stones." Chapter 4 of *Maieusis: Essays in Ancient Philosophy in Honour of Myles Burnyeat*, edited by Dominic Scott, 67–86. Oxford: Oxford University Press.

Sedley, David Neil. 2013. "Plato and the One-over-Many Principle." In *Universals in Ancient Philosophy*, edited by Riccardo Chiaradonna and Gabriele Galluzzo, 113–137. Seminari e Convegni 33. Pisa: Edizioni della Normale.

Sedley, David Neil. 2016. "An Introduction to Plato's Theory of Forms." *Royal Institute of Philosophy Supplement* (Supplement to *Philosophy*) 78, no. 1 (July): 3–22.

Sellars, Wilfrid Stalker. 1955. "Vlastos and 'The Third Man.'" *Philosophical Review* 64, no. 3 (July): 405–437.

Sharma, Ravi. 2005. "What Is Aristotle's 'Third Man' Argument against the Forms?" *Oxford Studies in Ancient Philosophy* 28 (Summer): 123–160.

Sharma, Ravi. 2006. "On *Republic* 596a." *Apeiron* 39, no. 1 (March): 27–32.

Sharma, Ravi. 2007. "The Anatomy of an Illusion: On Plato's Purported Commitment to Self-Predication." *Apeiron* 40, no. 2 (June): 159–198.

Sharvy, Richard. 1986. "Plato's Causal Logic and the Third Man Argument." *Noûs* 20, no. 4 (December): 507–530.

Shields, Christopher, ed. 2003. *The Blackwell Guide to Ancient Philosophy*. Oxford: Blackwell.

Shorey, Paul. 1884/1982. *De Platonis Idearum Doctrina atque Mentis Humanae Notionibus Commentatio*. Munich: Theodor Ackermann, 1884. English translation by R. S. W. Hawtrey, published with a preface by Rosamond Kent Sprague, as "A Dissertation on Plato's Theory of Forms and on the Concepts of the Human Mind," *Ancient Philosophy* 2, no. 1 (Spring 1982): 1–59.

Shorey, Paul. 1903. *The Unity of Plato's Thought*. Decennial Publications of the University of Chicago (First Series, vol. 6): *Investigations Representing the Departments: Greek; Latin; Comparative Philology; Classical Archeology*, 129–214. Chicago: University of Chicago Press. Numerous reprints as a standalone book available through the original publisher as well as through others. The original comes with a dual pagination scheme: Each entry is paginated in itself at the top outside margin, while the volume as a whole is paginated at the bottom center. Any page numbers given here are for the internal pagination of the entry by Shorey.

Shorey, Paul. 1927. "Ideas and Numbers Again." *Classical Philology* 22, no. 2 (April): 213–218.

Shorey, Paul. 1933. *What Plato Said*. Chicago: University of Chicago Press.

Silverman, Allan Jay. 1990. "Self-Predication and Synonymy." *Ancient Philosophy* 10, no. 2 (Fall): 193–202.

Silverman, Allan Jay. 2002. *The Dialectic of Essence: A Study of Plato's Metaphysics*. Princeton: Princeton University Press.

Simplicius of Cilicia. 1882–1895. *In Aristotelis Physica Commentaria*. Greek text with Latin critical apparatus, available in vols. 9 and 10 of *Commentaria in Aristotelem Graeca* (= CAG), the standard edition of ancient Greek commentaries on Aristotle. Berlin: Georg Reimer (De Gruyter). Translated into English by various hands as *Simplicius: On Aristotle Physics*, in twelve volumes in *Ancient Commentators on Aristotle* (= ACA), a series produced at King's College London, under the general editorship of Richard Sorabji, with Michael Griffin as coeditor. London: Gerald Duckworth (Bloomsbury). Ithaca: Cornell University Press, 1989–present.

Simplicius of Cilicia. 1907. *In Aristotelis Categorias Commentarium*. Greek text with Latin critical apparatus, available in vol. 8 of *Commentaria in Aristotelem Graeca* (= CAG), the standard edition of ancient Greek commentaries on Aristotle. Berlin: Georg Reimer (De Gruyter). Translated into English by various hands as *Simplicius: On Aristotle Categories*, in four volumes in *Ancient Commentators on Aristotle* (= ACA), a series produced at King's College London, under the general editorship of Richard Sorabji, with Michael Griffin as coeditor. London: Gerald Duckworth (Bloomsbury). Ithaca: Cornell University Press, 2000–2003.

Smith, John Alexander. 1917. "General Relative Clauses in Greek." *Classical Review* 31, no. 3/4 (May–June): 69–71.

Smith, Nicholas D. 1980. "The Various Equals at Plato's *Phaedo* 74b–c." *Journal of the History of Philosophy* 18, no. 1 (January): 1–7.

Smith, Nicholas D. 2000. "Plato on Knowledge as a Power." *Journal of the History of Philosophy* 38, no. 2 (April): 145–168.

Smith, Nicholas D. 2012. "Plato on the Power of Ignorance." In *Virtue and Happiness: Essays in Honour of Julia Annas*, edited by Rachana Kamtekar, 51–73. *Oxford Studies in Ancient Philosophy* (Special Issue). Oxford: Oxford University Press.

Smith, Nicholas D. 2019. *Summoning Knowledge in Plato's Republic*. Oxford: Clarendon Press.

Soccio, Douglas J. 2015. *Archetypes of Wisdom: An Introduction to Philosophy*. Ninth edition. Boston: Cengage Learning.

Spellman, Lynne. 2002. "The Separation of Platonic Forms." Chapter 1 of her *Substance and Separation in Aristotle*, 5–20. Cambridge: Cambridge University Press.

Stevenson, John Graham. 1974. "Aristotle as Historian of Philosophy." *Journal of Hellenic Studies* 94 (November): 138–143.

Stewart, John Alexander. 1909. *Plato's Doctrine of Ideas*. Oxford: Clarendon Press.

Stone, Sophia Alexandra. 2014. "The Role of ἀριθμός in Plato's *Phaedo*." *Southwest Philosophy Review* 30, no. 1 (January): 137–149.

Stone, Sophia Alexandra. 2015. "Soul as an Intermediate Object in Plato's *Phaedo*." Presentation: "Société d'Etudes Platoniciennes Workshop." Paris: Université Paris Ouest Nanterre La Défense, 25–26 June 2015.

Stone, Sophia Alexandra. 2018. "Μονάς and ψυχή in the *Phaedo*." *Plato Journal* 18: 55–69. Revised version of a paper delivered at a conference organized by the author herself in collaboration with Nicholas Baima: "Τὰ Μεταξύ— Knowing Where to Draw the Line: Intermediates and Dianoia in Plato." Jupiter, Florida, Harriet L. Wilkes Honors College, Florida Atlantic University, 9–10 March 2018.

Syrianus. 1902. *In Aristotelis Metaphysica Commentaria* (Books 3–4, 13–14). Greek text with Latin critical apparatus, available in vol. 6 of *Commentaria in Aristotelem Graeca* (= CAG), the standard edition of ancient Greek commentaries on Aristotle. Berlin: Georg Reimer (De Gruyter). Translated into English by John Dillon and Dominic O'Meara as *Syrianus: On Aristotle Metaphysics*, in two volumes in *Ancient Commentators on Aristotle* (= ACA), a series produced at King's College London, under the general editorship of Richard Sorabji, with Michael Griffin as coeditor. Books 3–4: 2008. Books 13–14: 2006. London: Gerald Duckworth (Bloomsbury). Ithaca: Cornell University Press.

Szlezák, Thomas Alexander. 1985–2004. *Platon und die Schriftlichkeit der Philosophie*. Two volumes. Vol. 1 (1985): *Interpretationen zu den Frühen und*

Mittleren Dialogen. Vol. 2 (2004): *Das Bild des Dialektikers in Platons Spaten Dialogen*. Berlin: De Gruyter.
Szlezák, Thomas Alexander. 1993a. *Platon Lesen*. Stuttgart: Frommann-Holzboog. Translated into English by Graham Zanker as *Reading Plato*. London: Routledge, 1999.
Szlezák, Thomas Alexander. 1993b. "Zur Üblichen Abneigung gegen die *Agrapha Dogmata*." *Méthexis: International Journal for Ancient Philosophy* 6, no. 1 (March): 155–174. Translated into English by Luis Guzman and Morgan Meis as "On the Standard Aversion to the *Agrapha Dogmata*." *Graduate Faculty Philosophy Journal* (New School for Social Research) 22, no. 2 (July 2001): 147–163.
Szlezák, Thomas Alexander. 1998. "Notes sur le Débat Autour de la Philosophie Orale de Platon." *Les Études Philosophiques* 1: 69–90. (Numbering of volumes discontinued starting with issues corresponding to 1968–1969.)
Szlezák, Thomas Alexander, and Tanya Staehler. 2014. "Plato's Unwritten Doctrines: A Discussion." *Journal of Ancient Philosophy* 8, no. 2: 160–166.
Tarrant, Harold. 2000. *Plato's First Interpreters*. Ithaca: Cornell University Press.
Taylor, Alfred Edward. 1908. *Plato*. London: Archibald Constable. Reprinted as *The Mind of Plato*, 1922.
Taylor, Alfred Edward. 1911. *Varia Socratica: First Series*. First of two planned volumes that were never completed. St. Andrews University Publications, No. 9. Oxford: James Parker.
Taylor, Alfred Edward. 1915–1916. "Parmenides, Zeno, and Socrates." *Proceedings of the Aristotelian Society*, n.s., 16: 234–289. Reprinted as chapter 2 of his *Philosophical Studies*, 28–90. London: Macmillan, 1934.
Taylor, Alfred Edward. 1926a. *Plato: The Man and His Work*. London: Methuen. Numerous editions, four in the author's lifetime, six in total. Second edition, 1927. Third edition, 1929. Fourth edition, 1937. Fifth edition, 1948. Sixth edition, 1949.
Taylor, Alfred Edward. 1926b–1927. "Forms and Numbers: A Study in Platonic Metaphysics." Part 1: *Mind*, n.s., 35, no. 140 (October 1926): 419–440. Part 2: *Mind*, n.s., 36, no. 141 (January 1927): 12–33. Reprinted as chapter 3 of his *Philosophical Studies*, 91–150. London: Macmillan, 1934.
Taylor, Alfred Edward. 1928. *A Commentary on Plato's Timaeus*. Oxford: Clarendon Press.
Taylor, Alfred Edward. 1963. *Platonism and Its Influence*. New York: Cooper Square.
Teloh, Henry. 1981. *The Development of Plato's Metaphysics*. University Park: Pennsylvania State University Press.
Thesleff, Holger. 1967. *Studies in the Styles of Plato*. Helsinki: Societas Scientiarum Fennica. Reprinted in his *Platonic Patterns*, 1–142. Las Vegas: Parmenides, 2009.

Thesleff, Holger. 1982. *Studies in Platonic Chronology*. Helsinki: Societas Scientiarum Fennica. Reprinted in his *Platonic Patterns*, 143–382. Las Vegas: Parmenides, 2009.

Thesleff, Holger. 1989. "Platonic Chronology." *Phronesis* 34, no. 1/3: 1–26.

Thesleff, Holger. 1993a. "In Search of Dialogue." Chapter 15 of *Plato's Dialogues: New Studies and Interpretations*, edited by Gerald Alan Press, 259–266. Lanham: Rowman and Littlefield.

Thesleff, Holger. 1993b. "Looking for Clues: An Interpretation of Some Literary Aspects of Plato's 'Two-Level Model.'" Chapter 2 of *Plato's Dialogues: New Studies and Interpretations*, edited by Gerald Alan Press, 17–45. Lanham: Rowman and Littlefield.

Thesleff, Holger. 1999. *Studies in Plato's Two-Level Model*. Helsinki: Societas Scientiarum Fennica. Reprinted in his *Platonic Patterns*, 383–506. Las Vegas: Parmenides, 2009.

Thesleff, Holger. 2000. "The Philosopher Conducting Dialectic." Chapter 4 of *Who Speaks for Plato? Studies in Platonic Anonymity*, edited by Gerald Alan Press, 53–66. Lanham: Rowman and Littlefield.

Thesleff, Holger. 2002. "Plato and His Public." In *Noctes Atticae: 34 Articles on Graeco-Roman Antiquity and Its Nachleben. Studies Presented to Jørgen Mejer on His Sixtieth Birthday, March 18, 2002*, edited by Bettina Amden, Pernille Flensted-Jensen, Thomas Heine Nielsen, Adam Schwartz, and Christian Gorm Tortzen, 289–301. Copenhagen: Museum Tusculanum Press, University of Copenhagen. Reprinted in his *Platonic Patterns*, 541–550. Las Vegas: Parmenides, 2009.

Thesleff, Holger. 2009. *Platonic Patterns: A Collection of Studies by Holger Thesleff*. Las Vegas: Parmenides. A selection of Thesleff's previously published contributions to Plato scholarship, three books and four articles, reprinted here with the original pagination indicated in the margins. Books: *Studies in the Styles of Plato* (1967); *Studies in Platonic Chronology* (1982); *Studies in Plato's Two-Level Model* (1999). Articles: "Theaitetos and Theodoros" (1990); "The Early Version of Plato's *Republic*" (1997); "Plato and His Public" (2002); "A Symptomatic Text Corruption: Plato, *Gorgias* 448a5" (2003).

Thesleff, Holger. 2017. "Pivotal Play and Irony in Platonic Dialogues." *Arctos: Acta Philologica Fennica* 51: 179–220.

Thesleff, Holger, and Kalevi Loimaranta. 1981. "Applying Cluster Analysis to the Platonic Question." *Actes du Congrès International Informatique et Sciences Humaine*, 861–868. Laboratoire d'Analyse Statistique des Languages Anciennes. Liège: Université de Liège.

Thomas, Christine J. 2008. "Speaking of Something: Plato's *Sophist* and Plato's Beard." *Canadian Journal of Philosophy* 38, no. 4 (December): 631–667.

Thorp, John. 1984. "Forms, Concepts and *To Mē On* [τὸ μὴ ὄν]." *Revue de Philosophie Ancienne* 2, no. 2: 77–92.
Tress, Daryl McGowan. 1999. "Relations and Intermediates in Plato's *Timaeus*." Chapter 6 of *Plato and Platonism*, edited by Johannes M. Van Ophuijsen, 135–162. Washington, DC: Catholic University of America Press.
Vlastos, Gregory. 1939. "The Disorderly Motion in the *Timaios*." *Classical Quarterly* 33, no. 2 (April): 71–83. Reprinted as chapter 18 of *Studies in Plato's Metaphysics*, together with a follow-up titled "Creation in the *Timaeus*: Is It a Fiction?," edited by Reginald Edgar Allen, 379–399 and 401–419. London: Routledge and Kegan Paul, 1965.
Vlastos, Gregory. 1954. "The Third Man Argument in the *Parmenides*." *Philosophical Review* 63, no. 3 (July): 319–349. Reprinted with an addendum as chapter 12 of *Studies in Plato's Metaphysics*, edited by Reginald Edgar Allen, 231–263 and 261–263. London: Routledge and Kegan Paul, 1965. Also reprinted as chapter 12a of Vlastos's *Socrates, Plato, and Their Tradition*, the second volume of his *Studies in Greek Philosophy*, edited by Daniel W. Graham, 166–190. Princeton: Princeton University Press, 1995.
Vlastos, Gregory. 1955. "Addenda to the Third Man Argument: A Reply to Professor Sellars." *Philosophical Review* 64, no. 3 (July): 438–448. Reprinted as chapter 12c of the author's *Socrates, Plato, and Their Tradition*, the second volume of his *Studies in Greek Philosophy*, edited by Daniel W. Graham, 194–203. Princeton: Princeton University Press, 1995.
Vlastos, Gregory. 1956. "Postscript to the Third Man: A Reply to Mr. Geach." *Philosophical Review* 65, no. 1 (January): 83–94. Reprinted as chapter 12d of the author's *Socrates, Plato, and Their Tradition*, the second volume of his *Studies in Greek Philosophy*, edited by Daniel W. Graham, 204–214. Princeton: Princeton University Press, 1995.
Vlastos, Gregory. 1963. "*Arete bei Platon und Aristoteles. Zum Wesen und zur Geschichte der Platonischen Ontologie* by Hans Joachim Krämer." *Gnomon: Kritische Zeitschrift für die gesamte Klassische Altertumswissenschaft* 35, no. 7 (November): 641–655.
Vlastos, Gregory. 1965a. "Addendum to the Third Man Argument in the *Parmenides*." Addendum to Vlastos 1954, drafted in 1963 and published in 1965, as part of chapter 12 of *Studies in Plato's Metaphysics*, edited by Reginald Edgar Allen, 261–263. London: Routledge and Kegan Paul. Reprinted as chapter 12b of Vlastos's *Socrates, Plato, and Their Tradition*, the second volume of his *Studies in Greek Philosophy*, edited by Daniel W. Graham, 191–193. Princeton: Princeton University Press, 1995.
Vlastos, Gregory. 1965b. "Creation in the *Timaeus*: Is It a Fiction?" In *Studies in Plato's Metaphysics*, edited by Reginald Edgar Allen, 401–419. London: Routledge and Kegan Paul.

Vlastos, Gregory. 1965c. "Degrees of Reality in Plato." In *New Essays on Plato and Aristotle*, edited by Renford Bambrough, 1–19. London: Routledge and Kegan Paul. Reprinted as chapter 3 of his *Platonic Studies*, 58–75. Princeton: Princeton University Press, 1973.

Vlastos, Gregory. 1965d–1966. "A Metaphysical Paradox." *Proceedings and Addresses of the American Philosophical Association* 39: 5–19. Reprinted as chapter 2 of his *Platonic Studies*, 43–57. Princeton: Princeton University Press, 1973.

Vlastos, Gregory. 1969a. "Plato's 'Third Man' Argument (*Parm.* 132a1–b2): Text and Logic." *Philosophical Quarterly* 19, no. 77 (October): 289–301. Reprinted with revisions and appendixes as chapter 14 of his *Platonic Studies*, 342–365. Princeton: Princeton University Press, 1973.

Vlastos, Gregory. 1969b. "Reasons and Causes in the *Phaedo*." *Philosophical Review* 78, no. 3 (July): 291–325. Reprinted as chapter 4 of his *Platonic Studies*, 76–110. Princeton: Princeton University Press, 1973.

Vlastos, Gregory. 1969c. " 'Self-Predication' in Plato's Later Period." *Philosophical Review* 78, no. 1 (January): 74–78.

Vlastos, Gregory, ed. 1971. *Plato: A Collection of Critical Essays*. Vol. 1: *Metaphysics and Epistemology*. Vol. 2: *Ethics, Politics, and Philosophy of Art and Religion*. Garden City: Anchor Books. All references here are to the first volume.

Vlastos, Gregory. 1973. *Platonic Studies*. Princeton: Princeton University Press.

Vlastos, Gregory. 1974. "A Note on 'Pauline Predications' in Plato." *Phronesis* 19, no. 2: 95–101.

Vlastos, Gregory. 1981. "On a Proposed Redefinition of 'Self-Predication' in Plato." *Phronesis* 26, no. 1: 76–79.

Vlastos, Gregory. 1987. " 'Separation' in Plato." *Oxford Studies in Ancient Philosophy* 5: 187–196.

Vlastos, Gregory. 1991. *Socrates: Ironist and Moral Philosopher*. Cambridge: Cambridge University Press.

Vlastos, Gregory. 1994. *Socratic Studies*. Cambridge: Cambridge University Press.

Vlastos, Gregory. 1995. *Socrates, Plato, and Their Tradition*. Second of two volumes constituting the author's *Studies in Greek Philosophy*, a collection of his previously published articles, edited by Daniel W. Graham. Princeton: Princeton University Press.

von Arnim, Hans Friedrich August. 1896. *De Platonis Dialogis Quaestiones Chronologicae*. Vorlesungsverzeichnis der Universität Rostock für das Wintersemester. Rostock: Typis Academicis Adlerianis.

von Arnim, Hans Friedrich August. 1912. "Sprachliche Forschungen zur Chronologie der Platonischen Dialoge." *Sitzungsberichte der Kaiserlichen Akademie der Wissenschaften in Wien: Philosophisch-Historischen Klasse* 169, no. 1: 1–210.

Wagner, Ellen, ed. 2001. *Essays on Plato's Psychology*. Lanham: Lexington Books.

Warner, D. H. J. 1965. "Form and Concept." *Journal of the History of Philosophy* 3, no. 2 (October): 159–166.

Watson, Richard Allan ("Red"). 1995. *Representational Ideas: From Plato to Patricia Churchland*. Dordrecht: Kluwer Academic (Springer).
Wedberg, Anders Erik Otto. 1955. *Plato's Philosophy of Mathematics*. Stockholm: Almqvist and Wiksell.
Welton, William A., ed. 2002. *Plato's Forms: Varieties of Interpretation*. Lanham: Rowman and Littlefield.
White, David A. 1989. *Myth and Metaphysics in Plato's Phaedo*. Selinsgrove: Susquehanna University Press. London: Associated University Presses.
White, F. C. 1976. "Particulars in *Phaedo* 95e-107a." *Canadian Journal of Philosophy* 6 (Special Issue: *New Essays on Plato and the Pre-Socratics*) Supplementary Vol. 2, Supplement 1: 129-147.
White, F. C. 1977. "Plato's Middle Dialogues and the Independence of Particulars." *Philosophical Quarterly* 27, no. 108 (July): 193-213.
White, F. C. 1978a. "On Essences in the *Cratylus*." *Southern Journal of Philosophy* 16, no. 3 (Fall): 259-274.
White, F. C. 1978b. "The *Phaedo* and *Republic* V on Essences." *Journal of Hellenic Studies* 98 (November): 142-156.
White, F. C. 1981. *Plato's Theory of Particulars*. New York: Arno Press.
White, F. C. 1982. "Problems of Particulars in Plato's Later Dialogues." *Apeiron* 16, no. 1 (June): 53-62.
White, F. C. 1988. "Plato's Essentialism: A Reply." *Australasian Journal of Philosophy* 66, no. 3 (September): 403-413.
Whittaker, John. 1968. "The 'Eternity' of the Platonic Forms." *Phronesis* 13, no. 2: 131-144.
Williams, Bernard Arthur Owen. 2006. "Plato: The Invention of Philosophy." Chapter 10 of his *The Sense of the Past: Essays in the History of Philosophy*, edited, with an introduction, by Myles Fredric Burnyeat, 148-186. Princeton: Princeton University Press. Originally published as a book of the same name, appearing as vol. 23 of the Great Philosophers Series. London: Phoenix, 1998.
Wilson, Nigel Guy. 1996. *Scholars of Byzantium*. Second ("revised") edition. London: Gerald Duckworth (Bloomsbury). Originally published in 1983.
Wood, James L. 2009. "Is There an *Archê Kakou* in Plato?" *Review of Metaphysics* 63, no. 2 (December): 349-384.
Wood, James L. 2017. "The Unorthodox Theory of Forms in Plato's *Philebus*." *Journal of Ancient Philosophy* 11, no. 2: 45-81.
Yang, Moon-Heum. 1999. "The 'Square Itself' and 'Diagonal Itself' in *Republic* 510d." *Ancient Philosophy* 19, no. 1 (Spring): 31-35.
Zeller, Eduard Gottlob. 1839. *Platonische Studien*. Tübingen: C. F. Osiander.
Zeller, Eduard Gottlob. 1844-1852. *Die Philosophie der Griechen: Eine Untersuchung über Charakter, Gang und Hauptmomente ihrer Entwicklung*. Three volumes. Tübingen: Ludwig Friedrich Fues. Subsequent editions bear a

slightly different title: *Die Philosophie der Griechen in ihrer Geschichtlichen Entwicklung*. Numerous editions. The edition and volume most frequently consulted in the present context, for example, as referenced by Adam (1902 [vol. 2], 161), Ross (1951, 79, n. 3, 173, n. 3), and Shorey (1884/1982, 33, n. 2), is the second volume of the fourth edition (1874). English translations have been pursued piecemeal as separate projects, determined largely by the production schedule of the original: *A History of Greek Philosophy from the Earliest Period to the Time of Socrates*, translated by Sarah Frances Alleyne (1881). *Socrates and the Socratic Schools*, translated by Oswald J. Reichel (1868, 1877, 1885). *Plato and the Older Academy*, translated by Sarah Frances Alleyne and Alfred Goodwin (1876, 1888 ["new edition"], both based on the second section of the second part of the second volume in its third edition [1875], according to the preface in the translation). *Aristotle and the Earlier Peripatetics*, translated by Benjamin Francis Conn Costelloe and John Henry Muirhead (1897). *A History of Eclecticism in Greek Philosophy*, translated by Sarah Frances Alleyne (1883).

Zeller, Eduard Gottlob. 1876. *Plato and the Older Academy*. English translation of "Plato und die ältere Akademie," a portion of the author's three-volume *Die Philosophie der Griechen*, corresponding to the second section of the second part of the second volume in its third edition (1875), the correspondence being identified as such in the preface to the translation (1876). Translated by Sarah Frances Alleyne and Alfred Goodwin. London: Longmans, Green. The full set in German was originally published in Tübingen: Ludwig Friedrich Fues, 1844–1852.

Zeller, Eduard Gottlob. 1883. *Grundriss der Geschichte der Griechischen Philosophie*. Leipzig: Fue's Verlag (R. Reisland). Abbreviated version of his *Die Philosophie der Griechen* (1844–1852).

Zuckert, Catherine H. 2009. *Plato's Philosophers: The Coherence of the Dialogues*. Chicago: University of Chicago Press.

Index

Adam, James, 176, 291n24
Ademollo, Francesco, 42n13, 70, 74n2, 183n24, 196n, 197n48
Alexander of Aphrodisias, 1, 60–61, 206–208, 275, 284n19, 295n, 314–315
Alican, Necip Fikri, 52n, 65, 73n, 74n2, 77n4, 78n6, 82n15, 100n50, 108, 113–114, 133n26, 145n, 147nn3–4, 156n10, 158n, 169n1, 170n3, 172n8, 203n57, 207n59, 225n, 226n, 228n, 230n6, 246n16, 250n22, 255n28, 256nn30–31, 290n22, 291n23, 335n, 342n, 345n59, 352n
Allen, Reginald Edgar, 28, 54n23, 61n, 68, 71, 74n2, 132nn24–25, 140n37, 141n40, 174n9, 174n11, 197n50
Annas, Julia Elizabeth, 52n, 78n6, 119n, 175, 281nn17–18, 289–290, 341n
Antisthenes, 94, 150–151, 163, 321–322
Archer-Hind, Richard Dacre, 345n60
Aristotle, 1, 13–14, 17–19, 23, 32, 40–43, 60–61, 66, 80–84, 89n28, 104–105, 119, 126n, 134n29, 138n31, 141, 154, 165n22, 171–178, 192–196, 200n, 204–206, 230n6, 263, 265–357
  Aristotle as historian, 293–334
  Aristotle on Plato, 265–334, 355–357
  discrepancies and contradictions in Aristotle's testimony, 304–334
  Plato's Forms as numbers, 280–284
  Plato's fundamental principles, 14, 104–105, 111, 126n, 272–280, 292, 301–303, 333–334
  Plato's lecture on the good, 82n15, 230n6, 295–300
  Plato's mathematicals as intermediates, 284–292
  Plato's unwritten doctrines, 14, 104–105, 126n, 272–292, 299–301, 330–336
Aristoxenus, 230n6, 295–297
Armstrong, David Malet, 19–30, 62n26, 63n29, 199–200, 213
Asclepius, 257, 281n17, 295n

Baldry, Harold Caparne, 42n13, 183n24
Baltes, Matthias, 230n5
Barford, Robert, 61n
Barney, Rachel, 162n, 345n60

Benson, Hugh H., 189n33
Bestor, Thomas W., 61n
Blackson, Thomas A., 68, 74n2
Block, Irving, 61n
Bluck, Richard Stanley Harold, 176–177, 315–319, 345n60
Bostock, David, 162n, 345n60
Brandwood, Leonard, 66n
Brennan, Tad, 162n, 345n60
Brentlinger, John A., 118n7, 147n2
Brisson, Luc, 210n65
Brittain, Charles, 162n, 345n60
Broadie, Sarah, 90n30, 118n7, 147n2, 171n6, 178n15, 208n
Brown, Lesley, 227n
Burger, Ronna, 345n60
Burnet, John, 274, 296, 343, 345n60
Burnyeat, Myles Fredric, 210n65, 216n68, 263
Butler, Joseph (Bishop), 48
Butler, Travis, 78n7, 118n8, 147n2

Campbell, Lewis, 66n
Cherniss, Harold Fredrik, 61n, 68, 82n15, 140n36, 171n6, 175n, 227n, 230n6, 274, 292–299, 315n
Chilcott, Catherine Mary, 227n
Cleary, John J., 194n43
Clegg, Jerry S., 61n
Cohen, S. Marc, 175n
Collobert, Catherine, 293
Conceptual Forms, 3–4, 9, 73–75, 84–91, 93–99, 110–111, 115–117, 123–128, 134n28, 135–137, 142, 163–164, 172, 183–188, 218–220, 251–254, 268, 338. *See also* Forms
Cooper, John Madison, 79n9
Corkum, Phil, 194n43, 195n46
Cornford, Francis MacDonald, 61n, 129, 209n65

counting numbers, 84n, 128n, 204n, 267, 273–277, 282–283, 291n24, 341, 348–350, 355. *See also* numbers
Cresswell, Maxwell John, 61n
Crombie, Ian MacHattie, 35, 40, 171n6, 277

Damschen, Gregor, 230n5
Dancy, Russell M., 68, 74n2, 89n28, 172n7, 346n61
de Vogel, Cornelia Johanna, 80, 118, 268n
Demos, Raphael, 129, 346n62
Denyer, Nicholas, 38–40, 100n50, 154, 164
des Places, Édouard, 97nn41–42
Descartes, René, 201
deuteros plous (second sailing), 100, 343–344
Devereux, Daniel T., 61n, 63n28, 79n8, 79n11, 131–132, 134n29, 172n7, 346n61
Diogenes Laërtius, 66, 94n37, 150n, 180n20, 297, 305n31, 314n38, 321–324, 330
Diogenes of Sinope, 150n, 321–324
Dittenberger, Wilhelm, 66n
Dorter, Kenneth, 68, 345n60
Durrant, Michael, 61n

eidetic numbers (formal numbers = ideal numbers), 84n, 105, 128n, 204n, 273–277, 280–284, 290–291, 303–306, 313–314, 325–329, 333–334, 340–341, 347–350. *See also* numbers
Else, Gerald Frank, 42n13, 183n24
Erler, Michael, 74n2, 77n5, 93, 100n50

Ferber, Rafael, 82n15, 230nn5–6, 295n

Ferguson, Alexander Stewart, 72, 118n7, 147n2
Ferguson, John, 344n
Field, Guy Cromwell, 296
Findlay, John Niemeyer, 72, 274, 292n
Fine, Gail Judith, 32, 49n, 50n, 61n, 69–71, 74n2, 79n8, 79n11, 118n8, 130–131, 134n29, 147n2, 171n6, 172n7, 175n, 177–178, 182, 186n28, 192–197, 206–211, 315n, 346n61
first principles (metaphysical first principles), 14, 104–105, 111, 126n, 272–280, 292, 301–303, 333–334
  great-and-the-small (indefinite dyad), the, 14, 104–105, 111, 126n, 272–280, 292, 301–303, 333–334
  one, the, 14, 104–105, 111, 126n, 272–280, 292, 301–303, 333–334
Form of the good, 18n4, 76, 81–82, 85–86, 102–103, 104n, 109, 111, 141n38, 186, 225–246, 258–259, 261–263, 268, 295–300, 337
formal numbers (eidetic numbers = ideal numbers), 84n, 105, 128n, 204n, 273–277, 280–284, 290–291, 303–306, 313–314, 325–329, 333–334, 340–341, 347–350. See also numbers
Forms
  classification, 3–4, 7–10, 73–77, 82–86, 109–112, 123–143, 163–167, 172, 183–188, 218–223, 251–254, 268, 337–338
    Conceptual Forms, 3–4, 9, 73–75, 84–91, 93–99, 110–111, 115–117, 123–128, 134n28, 135–137, 142, 163–164, 172, 183–188, 218–220, 251–254, 268, 338
    Ideal Forms, 3–4, 9–10, 73–75, 84–93, 110–111, 115–117, 123–129, 134n28, 135–137, 142, 163–164, 172, 183–188, 193, 218–223, 226, 244n14, 251–254, 268, 338
    Relational Forms, 3–4, 9, 73–75, 84–91, 99–104, 110–111, 115–117, 123–128, 134n28, 136–137, 142, 163–164, 172, 183–188, 218–219, 251–252, 268, 338
  conceptualization and formalization, 93–98
  continuum of abstraction, 135–142
  Form of the good, 18n4, 76, 81–82, 85–86, 102–103, 104n, 109, 111, 141n38, 186, 225–246, 258–259, 261–263, 268, 295–300, 337
  Forms of numbers, 84n, 105, 128n, 204n, 273–277, 280–284, 290–291, 303–306, 313–314, 325–329, 333–334, 340–341, 347–350 (see also numbers)
  negative Forms, 6, 8, 12–13, 77, 92–93, 98–99, 102, 106–109, 111, 117n4, 165n21, 225–263
    acceptance, 236–245
    rejection, 246–254
  ontological ascent, 10, 94, 110, 117, 126, 136, 141–142, 164–165, 185–187, 252
  ontological eminence, 96, 117, 125–126, 135–137, 164n19, 186, 251
  ontological stratification, 2, 5, 10, 75–80, 96, 112, 116, 118–123, 130n21, 135–142, 147, 186, 250, 269, 335–357

Forms *(continued)*
  terminology, 14, 31–32, 38–42, 53, 64–65, 79n10, 82, 86–91, 97, 105n55, 106–107, 129, 183n24
  transcendence vs. immanence, 17–34, 49, 77–82, 98, 118–123, 128–135, 166n25, 192–197, 345–348
Frances, Bryan, 61n
Franklin, Lee, 236n9
Frede, Dorothea, 70, 72, 74n2, 162n, 345n60, 352
fundamental principles (metaphysical first principles), 14, 104–105, 111, 126n, 272–280, 292, 301–303, 333–334
  great-and-the-small (indefinite dyad), the, 14, 104–105, 111, 126n, 272–280, 292, 301–303, 333–334
  one, the, 14, 104–105, 111, 126n, 272–280, 292, 301–303, 333–334

Gaiser, Konrad, 21n, 82n15, 230n6, 274, 295–300
Gallop, David, 162n, 345n60, 352
Geach, Peter Thomas, 61n
Geddes, William Duguid, 345n60
geometrical figures, 84n, 86, 128n, 203–204, 274–276, 326, 340–341, 348–349, 355. *See also* mathematicals
Gerson, Lloyd P., 37, 42n14, 46–47, 50–51, 61n, 74n2, 137n31, 140n35, 155, 230–231, 275n, 292n, 325n
Giannantoni, Gabriele, 150n
Gill, Mary Louise, 307, 323
Goldstein, Laurence, 61n
Gonzalez, Francisco J., 52n, 70, 74n2, 78n6, 118n8, 119n, 132n24, 147n2

good
  Plato's Form of the good, 18n4, 76, 81–82, 85–86, 102–103, 104n, 109, 111, 141n38, 186, 225–246, 258–259, 261–263, 268, 295–300, 337
  Plato's lecture on the good, 82n15, 230n6, 295–300
Grabowski, Francis A., III, 31, 35, 69
great-and-the-small (indefinite dyad), the, 14, 104–105, 111, 126n, 272–280, 292, 301–303, 333–334
Grube, George Maximilian Anthony, 91n32, 308–309
Guthrie, William Keith Chambers, 77n5, 97n42, 227n, 293
Guyer, Paul, 171n4

Hackforth, Reginald, 209n65, 345n60, 351–352
Halfwassen, Jens, 230n5
Hankins, James, 271n5, 271n7
Harte, Verity, 50–51, 60n, 70, 74n2, 99n46, 175
Hathaway, Ronald F., 61n
Heinaman, Robert, 61n
Helmig, Christoph, 42nn14–15, 69, 137n31, 138n32, 140, 174n11
Herrmann, Fritz-Gregor, 42n13, 227n
Hintikka, Jaakko, 205
Hoffleit, Herbert B., 227n
Howlett, Sophia, 271nn6–7
Hubert, Kurt, 296
Huxley, George, 293
Hyland, Drew A., 52n, 78n6, 119n

Ideal Forms, 3–4, 9–10, 73–75, 84–93, 110–111, 115–117, 123–129, 134n28, 135–137, 142, 163–164, 172, 183–188, 193, 218–223, 226, 244n14, 251–254, 268, 338. *See also* Forms

ideal numbers (eidetic numbers = formal numbers), 84n, 105, 128n, 204n, 273–277, 280–284, 290–291, 303–306, 313–314, 325–329, 333–334, 340–341, 347–350. See also numbers
Ideas. See Forms
immanence, 32, 49, 79–80, 98, 120, 128–135, 166n25, 172n7, 192–197, 345–348, 351–352. See also Forms, transcendence vs. immanence
immortality of the soul, 99–100, 107–109, 125n17, 149n, 156–162, 191, 207n59, 255–256, 290, 313, 342–354
   analogic (affinity) argument of *Phaedo*, 108, 125n17, 149n, 156–162, 207n59, 256n30, 352–353
   causal (final) argument of *Phaedo*, 100, 108, 159, 191, 207n59, 256n31, 290, 313, 342, 345–354
   patterns of destruction argument of *Republic*, 99, 255
indefinite dyad (great-and-the-small), the, 14, 104–105, 111, 126n, 272–280, 292, 301–303, 333–334
intermediates, 3, 8, 13, 84n, 125, 128n, 204n, 265–357
   mathematical intermediates, 13, 84n, 86, 128n, 203–204, 267–269, 272–277, 284–292, 303–304, 326–357
   ontological intermediates, 335–357
Irwin, Terence, 71

Jackson, Henry, 74n2, 189n33

Kahn, Charles H., 66n, 70, 132n25
Kant, Immanuel, 170–171
Katz, Emily, 287n
Kemp Smith, Norman, 171n4

Keyt, David, 162n, 345n60, 351–352
Klibansky, Raymond, 270n4–271n7
Kouremenos, Theokritos, 69, 273n
Krämer, Hans Joachim, 21n, 274
Kraut, Richard, 189n33

Lafrance, Yvon, 140n36
Larsen, Peter D., 40n
lecture on the good, 82n15, 230n6, 295–300. See also good
Ledger, Gerard R., 66n, 107n
Lee, Edward N., 61n, 227n
Lewis, Frank A., 227n, 346n61
Lloyd, Geoffrey Ernest Richard, 119
Lohr, Charles H., 271n4, 271n6
Loimaranta, Kalevi, 66n
Lovejoy, Arthur Oncken, 171n6
Lowry, James M. P., 293
Lutoslawski, Wincenty, 66n

Mabbott, John David, 346n61
Malcolm, John, 61n, 69, 74n2
Mannick, Paul, 61n
Mates, Benson, 61n
mathematical numbers (counting numbers), 84n, 128n, 204n, 267, 273–277, 282–283, 291n24, 341, 348–350, 355. See also numbers
mathematicals, 13, 84n, 86, 128n, 203–204, 267–269, 272–277, 284–292, 303–304, 326–357
   geometrical figures, 84n, 86, 128n, 203–204, 274–276, 326, 340–341, 348–349, 355
   mathematical numbers (counting numbers), 84n, 128n, 204n, 267, 273–277, 282–283, 291n24, 341, 348–350, 355 (*see also* numbers)
Matthen, Mohan, 172n7, 346n61
Matthews, Gareth B., 175n
Maula, Erkka, 171n6, 201, 214, 216

McCabe, Mary Margaret Anne, 31, 35, 41, 48, 50–51, 69, 74n2, 83n17, 117n5, 196n
McKeon, Richard, 293
Meinwald, Constance C., 61n, 74n2
metaphysical dualism, 1–14, 15–72, 73–80, 111–112, 118–119, 145, 165–166, 174n9, 250, 265–270, 273, 335–342, 355–357
metaphysical eminence, 96, 117, 125–126, 135–137, 164n19, 186, 251
metaphysical first principles, 14, 104–105, 111, 126n, 272–280, 292, 301–303, 333–334
   great-and-the-small (indefinite dyad), the, 14, 104–105, 111, 126n, 272–280, 292, 301–303, 333–334
   one, the, 14, 104–105, 111, 126n, 272–280, 292, 301–303, 333–334
metaphysical monism, 1–14, 76, 184–185, 249n20, 255, 268, 356.
   See also unitary pluralism
Mignucci, Mario, 61n
Mohr, Richard D., 128, 227n
Moravcsik, Julius Matthew Emil, 61n
Morris, T. F., 63n28
Morrison, Donald Ray, 172n7, 194n43, 346n61
Morrow, Glenn R., 310

Nails, Debra, 6, 12, 18n4, 66n, 72, 74n2, 77n4, 78n7, 79n10, 80n12, 104n, 105n56, 118n7, 134n29, 145n, 147n2, 174n9, 189n35, 193n41, 225, 228, 232, 235–245, 254–263, 330n
   negative Forms, 236–245 (*see also* negative Forms)
negative Forms, 6, 8, 12–13, 77, 92–93, 98–99, 102, 106–109, 111, 117n4, 165n21, 225–263
   acceptance, 236–245

   rejection, 246–254
   See also Forms
Nehamas, Alexander, 61n, 118n7, 147n2, 171n6, 309, 312
Nerlich, Graham Charles, 61n
numbers
   ideal numbers (eidetic numbers = formal numbers), 84n, 105, 128n, 204n, 273–277, 280–284, 290–291, 303–306, 313–314, 325–329, 333–334, 340–341, 347–350
   mathematical numbers (counting numbers), 84n, 128n, 204n, 267, 273–277, 282–283, 291n24, 341, 348–350, 355

O'Brien, Denis, 227n
one, the, 14, 104–105, 111, 126n, 272–280, 292, 301–303, 333–334
ontological ascent, 10, 94, 110, 117, 126, 136, 141–142, 164–165, 185–187, 252
ontological eminence, 96, 117, 125–126, 135–137, 164n19, 186, 251
ontological stratification, 2, 5, 10, 75–80, 96, 112, 116, 118–123, 130n21, 135–142, 147, 186, 250, 269, 335–357
opposition, 2–9, 31, 98–99, 101, 107–108, 119–123, 134n28, 147, 164, 185, 226, 237, 251, 253, 267–269, 278
Otto, K. Darcy, 61n
Owen, Gwilym Ellis Lane, 61n

Parsons, Terence, 205
Patterson, Richard, 69–70, 74n2, 171n6, 176n, 180–181, 209n64
Pelletier, Francis Jeffry, 61n, 74n2
Penner, Terry, 69, 154, 164
Perl, Eric D., 72, 130n20, 131n23, 172n7, 181, 196n, 197n50, 346n61

Philoponus, 279, 295n
Plato
  Plato's Form of the good, 18n4, 76,
    81–82, 85–86, 102–103, 104n,
    109, 111, 141n38, 186, 225–246,
    258–259, 261–263, 268, 295–300,
    337
  Plato's Forms
    Conceptual Forms, 3–4, 9,
      73–75, 84–91, 93–99, 110–111,
      115–117, 123–128, 134n28,
      135–137, 142, 163–164, 172,
      183–188, 218–220, 251–254,
      268, 338
    Ideal Forms, 3–4, 9–10, 73–75,
      84–93, 110–111, 115–117,
      123–129, 134n28, 135–137,
      142, 163–164, 172, 183–188,
      193, 218–223, 226, 244n14,
      251–254, 268, 338
    Relational Forms, 3–4, 9, 73–75,
      84–91, 99–104, 110–111,
      115–117, 123–128, 134n28,
      136–137, 142, 163–164, 172,
      183–188, 218–219, 251–252,
      268, 338
    See also Forms
  Plato's fundamental principles
    (metaphysical first principles),
    14, 104–105, 111, 126n, 272–280,
    292, 301–303, 333–334
    great-and-the-small (indefinite
      dyad), the, 14, 104–105, 111,
      126n, 272–280, 292, 301–303,
      333–334
    one, the, 14, 104–105, 111,
      126n, 272–280, 292, 301–303,
      333–334
  Plato's Ideas (*see* Forms)
  Plato's lecture on the good, 82n15,
    230n6, 295–300
  Plato's metaphysical dualism, 1–14,
    15–72, 73–80, 111–112, 118–119,
    145, 165–166, 174n9, 250,
    265–270, 273, 335–342, 355–357
  Plato's metaphysical monism, 1–14,
    76, 184–185, 249n20, 255, 268,
    356 (*see also* unitary pluralism)
  Plato's thought experiments, 14,
    29, 45, 48–52, 75–77, 80–87, 95,
    105, 110–111, 115–116, 131–132,
    153, 163, 166, 187–188, 192n39,
    216, 219n, 250–251, 254, 263,
    338–339, 342
  Plato's two-level model, 1–14, 73–112,
    113–134, 146–147, 155–157,
    164–166, 174n9, 183, 186–187,
    218–219, 244n13, 249–250, 253–
    255, 258, 268–269, 323, 336–338,
    354 (*see also* unitary pluralism)
  Plato's unitary pluralism, 1–14, 15,
    27, 72, 73–75, 111–112, 120,
    185–186, 218–219, 249–250, 255,
    268–270, 337–339, 342, 356–357
  Plato's unwritten doctrines, 14,
    104–105, 126n, 272–292,
    299–301, 330–336
Pluhar, Werner Schrutka, 171n4
Plutarch, 278, 344
Porphyry, 295n
Press, Gerald Alan, 44, 75n, 79n9,
  80nn12–13, 91n32, 122n13,
  180n20, 189n35, 305n31
Preus, Mary, 344n
Prince, Brian D., 162n, 345n60
Prince, Susan, 150n, 321n
principles (metaphysical first
  principles), 14, 104–105, 111,
  126n, 272–280, 292, 301–303,
  333–334
  great-and-the-small (indefinite
    dyad), the, 14, 104–105, 111,
    126n, 272–280, 292, 301–303,
    333–334
  one, the, 14, 104–105, 111, 126n,
    272–280, 292, 301–303, 333–334

Prior, William J., 61n, 63n28, 69, 196n, 227n
Proclus, 231, 314n38

Quine, Willard Van Orman, 235n7

Rankin, Kenneth W., 61n
Reale, Giovanni, 105n55, 274
Reeve, C. D. C. (Charles David Chanel), 227n
Relational Forms, 3-4, 9, 73-75, 84-91, 99-104, 110-111, 115-117, 123-128, 134n28, 136-137, 142, 163-164, 172, 183-188, 218-219, 251-252, 268, 338. *See also* Forms
Reynolds, Leighton Durham, 271n5, 271n7
Rickless, Samuel Charles, 69, 74n2, 174n10, 182, 189n33
Rist, John Michael, 172n7, 227n, 346n61
Ritter, Constantin, 66n
Robin, Léon, 315n, 320
Robinson, Richard, 61n
Robjant, David, 72, 118n7, 147n2
Rohr, Michael David, 171n6, 199n
Rose, Lynn E., 344n
Ross, Donald L., 344n
Ross, William David, 61n, 69, 74n2, 82n15, 88n24, 92n, 97n42, 171n6, 227n, 230n6, 274, 277, 279-281, 285, 288, 295n, 315n, 319, 324, 343
Rowe, Christopher J., 74n2, 78n7, 118n8, 147n2
Russell, Bertrand Arthur William, 17-30, 74n3-75n3, 153
Ryan, Paul, 307, 323
Ryle, Gilbert, 61n

Sayre, Kenneth M., 52n, 69, 74n2, 78n6, 91n32, 119n, 189n33
Scaltsas, Theodore, 61n

Schiller, Jerome Paul, 162n, 345n60, 352
Schipper, Edith Watson, 69, 74n2, 189n33
Schleiermacher, Friedrich Daniel Ernst, 274
Schumacher, Lydia, 42n14, 137n31, 140, 174n11
Schweizer, Paul, 61n
Scolnicov, Samuel, 74n2
second sailing (*deuteros plous*), 100, 343-344
Sedley, David Neil, 21-30, 55, 62-63, 70, 74n2, 100n49, 171n6, 175n, 210n65, 227n
Sellars, Wilfrid Stalker, 61n
Sharma, Ravi, 61n, 176, 284n19
Sharvy, Richard, 61n
Shields, Christopher, 189n33
Shorey, Paul, 69, 274, 285-286, 291-293
Silverman, Allan Jay, 61n, 70, 74n2, 91n32, 182, 196n
Simplicius of Cilicia, 150n, 295n, 321-322
Smith, John Alexander, 176
Smith, Nicholas D., 25n8, 72, 78n7, 118n8, 147n2, 174n9, 190
Soccio, Douglas J., 91n32
soul
  immortality of the soul, 99-100, 107-109, 125n17, 149n, 156-162, 191, 207n59, 255-256, 290, 313, 342-354
  analogic (affinity) argument of *Phaedo*, 108, 125n17, 149n, 156-162, 207n59, 256n30, 352-353
  causal (final) argument of *Phaedo*, 100, 108, 159, 191, 207n59, 256n31, 290, 313, 342, 345-354
  patterns of destruction argument of *Republic*, 99, 255

Spellman, Lynne, 346n61
Staehler, Tanya, 21n, 274
Stevenson, John Graham, 293
Stewart, John Alexander, 70, 74n2, 189n33
Stone, Sophia Alexandra, 290n23–291n23
Syrianus, 279
Szlezák, Thomas Alexander, 21n, 272n8, 274

Tarrant, Harold, 6, 93n35, 145n
Taylor, Alfred Edward, 42n13, 61n, 62n27, 170–171, 183n24, 209n65, 274, 296
Teloh, Henry, 74n2
Thesleff, Holger, 6, 9, 11, 12, 29, 43–44, 48, 66n, 70, 73–112, 113–143, 145–147, 157, 163–167, 172n8, 174n9, 180n20, 183n24, 184n26, 186n27, 186n29, 226, 228, 230n6, 235–236, 244n13, 246–254, 258–259, 261–262, 268n, 275, 295n, 298–299, 303, 305n31, 322n, 330n
  Plato's classification of Forms, 3–4, 7–10, 73–77, 82–86, 109–112, 123–143, 163–167, 172, 183–188, 218–223, 251–254, 268, 337–338
  Plato's two-level model, 1–14, 73–112, 113–143, 146–147, 155–157, 164–166, 174n9, 183, 186–187, 218–219, 244n13, 249–250, 253–255, 258, 268–269, 323, 336–338, 354 (*see also* unitary pluralism)
  thought experiments, 14, 29, 45, 48–52, 75–77, 80–87, 95, 105, 110–111, 115–116, 131–132, 153, 163, 166, 187–188, 192n39, 216, 219n, 250–251, 254, 263, 338–339, 342
Thomas, Christine J., 207n60

Thorp, John, 42n14, 137n31, 140n35
transcendence, 3–4, 15–36, 43–49, 77–84, 87, 91, 98, 102, 111, 118–136, 164n19, 166n25, 172n7, 177, 185, 192–197, 209n63, 251, 317–318, 324, 345–348. See *also* Forms, transcendence vs. immanence
Tredennick, Hugh, 281n17
Tress, Daryl McGowan, 355
two-level model, 1–14, 73–112, 113–134, 146–147, 155–157, 164–166, 174n9, 183, 186–187, 218–219, 244n13, 249–250, 253–255, 258, 268–269, 323, 336–338, 354. See *also* unitary pluralism

unitary pluralism, 1–14, 15, 27, 72, 73–75, 111–112, 120, 185–186, 218–219, 249–250, 255, 268–270, 337–339, 342, 356–357
unwritten doctrines, 14, 104–105, 126n, 272–292, 299–301, 330–336
  Plato's Forms as numbers, 280–284
  Plato's fundamental principles (metaphysical first principles), 14, 104–105, 111, 126n, 272–280, 292, 301–303, 333–334
  great-and-the-small (indefinite dyad), the, 14, 104–105, 111, 126n, 272–280, 292, 301–303, 333–334
  one, the, 14, 104–105, 111, 126n, 272–280, 292, 301–303, 333–334
  Plato's mathematicals as intermediates, 284–292

Vlastos, Gregory, 61–65, 71, 74n2, 92, 171n6, 172n7, 189n35, 201, 209n65, 214, 216, 227n, 274, 284n19, 346n61
von Arnim, Hans Friedrich August, 66n

Wagner, Ellen, 162n, 345n60
Warner, D. H. J., 42n14, 137n31, 140n35
Watson, Richard Allan (Red), 36–40
Wedberg, Anders Erik Otto, 341n
Welton, William A., 70–71, 74n2–75n3, 154, 164
White, David A., 345n60
White, F. C., 33n
Whitehead, Alfred North, 142n43
Whittaker, John, 209n64
Williams, Bernard Arthur Owen, 52n, 78n6, 119n

Wilson, Nigel Guy, 271n5, 271n7
Wood, Allen W., 171n4
Wood, James L., 227n, 346n61
Woodruff, Paul, 309, 312

Yang, Moon-Heum, 204n

Zalta, Edward N., 61n
Zeller, Eduard Gottlob, 274, 281n17, 291n24
Zuckert, Catherine H., 189n35, 190n36

www.ingramcontent.com/pod-product-compliance
Lightning Source LLC
Chambersburg PA
CBHW020257240426
43673CB00039B/629